THE CLASS CEILING

Why it Pays to be Privileged

Sam Friedman and Daniel Laurison

First published in Great Britain in 2019 by

Policy Press
University of Bristol
1-9 Old Park Hill
Bristol
BS2 8BB
UK
t: +44 (0)117 954 5940
pp-info@bristol.ac.uk
www.policypress.co.uk

North America office:
Policy Press
c/o The University of Chicago Press
1427 East 60th Street
Chicago, IL 60637, USA
t: +1 773 702 7700
f: +1 773 702 9756
sales@press.uchicago.edu
www.press.uchicago.edu

British Library Cataloguing in Publication Data
A catalogue record for this book is available from the British Library.

Library of Congress Cataloging-in-Publication Data
A catalog record for this book has been requested.

ISBN 978-1-4473-3606-8 hardcover
ISBN 978-1-4473-3608-2 ePub
ISBN 978-1-4473-3609-9 Mobi
ISBN 978-1-4473-3607-5 ePdf

Cover design by Lyn Davies
Front cover image: Martin Parr, Cartier Polo. G.B England. Ascot. 1998, Magnum Photos.

Printed and bound in Great Britain by TJ International, Padstow
Policy Press uses environmentally responsible print partners

For our daughters, Cora, Skye, Ingrid and Freja

Contents

List of figures and tables

Figures

Tables

Acknowledgements

Although there are only two names on the front of this book, a number of people have made important contributions to the wider project that the book emerges from. First and foremost, we would like to record our debt to our Research Assistant, Ian McDonald, who carried out the majority of the fieldwork at Coopers, our architecture case study firm. Ian recruited the firm, conducted the fieldwork and analysed the data in just six months. The insight this research generated has proven invaluable to the project. Ian was also a crucial source of general intellectual support, feeding into the writing and editing of large portions of the book, even when not being paid to do so.

We would also like to thank other important collaborators, including Dave O'Brien who carried out a large number of our interviews with actors, and Kenton Lewis who conducted several interviews at Turner Clarke. These individuals helped not only in the collection of data but have been pivotal in the formation and development of many of the key ideas and arguments expressed in this book.

Bringing together our fieldwork and quantitative analyses to actually write this book has been a long, sometimes torturous, frequently revelatory, and overall thoroughly all-consuming process. In doing so we have been very lucky to be able to call upon the support of many academic colleagues. We would particularly like to thank Mike Savage, who has provided outstanding mentorship and invaluable feedback throughout, including much-needed encouragement when the project was in its infancy. Jouni Kuha, Mike Hout, Lindsey Macmillan and Aaron Reeves have, at various times, provided essential guidance for our quantitative analysis and, similarly, our case study fieldwork would not have been possible without the help of Oona King, Scarlett Brown, Pascale Waltho and Ade Rawcliffe.

We are also indebted to a number of colleagues – academic and non-academic – who generously provided comments, and invaluable insights, on earlier drafts of the book, including Annette Lareau, Pascale Waltho, Nik Miller, Scarlett Brown, Maren Toft, Lucinda Platt, Derron Wallace, Sarah Wilie-LeBreton, Sherelle Ferguson, Carolyn Chernoff, Tim Burke, Joy Charlton, Peter Harvey, Peter Catron, Campbell Glennie and David Karen. We also want to thank the anonymous reviewers at the *American Sociological Review* who pushed us to really develop the conceptual contribution we could make.

In the process of developing the book, we also benefited immensely from insightful and challenging questions and conversations with a range of audiences who heard us talk about the project. There are too many to mention, but John Goldthorpe, Richard Breen, Judy Wajcman, Tom DiPrete, Florencia Torche, Juan Pablo Pardo-Guerra, John Hills, Steven Machin, Dawn Dow, and Geoff Payne all provided feedback, or pushed us to think further, in ways that stuck with us through the project.

This kind of mixed-methods research is a time and resource-intensive endeavour, and simply would not have been possible without the generous support of Sam's ESRC Future Research Leaders grant. Staff at the UK Data Service at the University of Essex were also very patient in helping us to figure out the best way to work with the Labour Force Survey data. And staff at our own institutions – Louisa Lawrence at LSE, and Rose Maio at Swarthmore, in particular – were instrumental in helping us manage the logistical and administrative work. We are also extremely grateful to the team at Policy Press who have helped guide us towards publication. Particular thanks here goes to Alison Shaw for giving us the opportunity to make the book a reality, Rebecca Tomlinson for her patience and support, Jess Mitchell for her keen editorial eye and Sharon Mah at Soapbox Design for beautifully visualising key pieces of our data.

We would also like to recognise our research participants, and especially those individuals in our case study organisations who helped us gain and navigate institutional access. This research would have been impossible without their enduring enthusiasm, insight, generosity and candid honesty.

Acknowledgements

Finally, we would like to pay particular thanks to our respective families. Sam's parents, Andy and Pat, both provided insightful thoughts on an earlier draft of the book, as did his partner, Louise – in heroic snatches between feeding a newborn. Daniel's partner Hannah was (and is) a force for good in the world, offering thoughts and encouragement for this book while also raising our two amazing kids *and* taking on the daunting task of organising resistance to Trump's policies in Pennsylvania.

Note on language usage

This book is about the UK, and we use British English spelling, grammar, and vocabulary throughout. Where there is a big difference between US and UK usage, or we think something might be unclear to Americans, we have explained in the endnotes.

One topic where the two countries differ substantially is in the language used to refer collectively to members of racial and ethnic minority groups. There is no perfect language for groups that are categorised the way they are because of both countries' histories of colonialism and racism, and there is some disagreement within these groups about which words and phrases are best in the face of oppressive histories. After consulting with scholars, friends and Twitter in both countries, we most often write 'racial and ethnic minorities' (although it would be even more accurate to talk about 'minoritised' or 'racialised' people). In the UK, people most often talk about ethnicity, whereas in the US they would say race; we often use 'racial-ethnic' to emphasise the overlap between these two terms. The standard approach in the UK is to use the abbreviation BME, for Black and Minority Ethnic, so we use this as well; we also occasionally use 'people of colour', which is common in the US but may be unfamiliar to those in the UK. Similarly, we use phrases like 'women and racial-ethnic minorities' when we mean 'women of all racial-ethnic groups and racial-ethnic minorities of all genders'. Throughout, we follow contemporary scholars of race and ethnicity (e.g. Kehal, n.d.), critical race theory (Crenshaw, 1988; Harris, 1991) and their predecessors (e.g. DuBois, 1971), and capitalise 'Black' and other minoritised racial-ethnic group names, while using the lower case for 'white'.

Fundamentally, this is a book about class. But there is also widespread disagreement – even among scholars who study class! – about what different class terms should mean (we explore these debates in detail in Chapter Ten). In this book we focus on people whose class destinations are in 'elite' higher professional, managerial or cultural occupations. And when we talk about class origins, we use three broad class categories based on the UK government's National Statistics Socio-economic Classification (NS-SEC). The people we say are from 'professional and managerial', 'upper middle-class' or 'privileged' backgrounds all had at least one parent whose job was in the top two classes of the NS-SEC; those we refer to as from 'intermediate' or 'lower-middle-class' origins had a parent who was self-employed or doing a clerical, technical, or lower-supervisory job; finally, we use 'working-class' backgrounds to describe people whose parents did routine or semi-routine jobs, or were long-term unemployed.

Introduction

Mark[1] has one of the most coveted jobs in television. As Head of Current Affairs at 6TV,[2] he has commissioned some of the UK's most high-profile and critically acclaimed programmes. He controls a budget extending to the tens of millions. And every day a steady stream of independent television producers arrive at his desk desperate to land a pitch. He is, for many, the ultimate gatekeeper.

At just 39 Mark is young to wield such power. Certainly he's enjoyed a swift ascension. After making his name as a programme maker, Mark initially became a commissioner at a rival broadcaster before being headhunted by 6TV some five years ago. A string of hits later and Mark is now one of the biggest players at the channel.

Of course we know all of this before we interview him; it is detailed in multiple, glowing journalistic profiles hailing his creative talents. Yet when we meet Mark, on the top floor of 6TV's futuristic aluminium and glass-clad headquarters, and invite him to narrate his career in his own words, a very different account emerges. It's not that Mark disavows his success; he is clearly very proud of what he has achieved. But what is striking is his candid honesty; his career trajectory, he tells us, particularly its rapid speed and relative smoothness, has been contingent on "starting the race" with a series of profound advantages.

He starts from the beginning. Mark is from a privileged background. His father was a successful scientist and he was educated at one of London's top private schools, before going on to Oxford. This privilege, he tells us, was pivotal in facilitating his entry into television. Specifically, he explains, while at university he went to New York – subsidised by his parents – to research his undergraduate dissertation.[3] While there he landed free accommodation with a contact his father had made at his school. "So, because my dad had met someone at the side of the rugby pitch, I ended up in this empty flat in New York", he recalls, shaking his head and smiling. The contact then promptly introduced him to a friend in television:

> And so I went out with Ross the cameraman and met this director who was making a BBC series. She said "What are you doing?" I was like, "I'm at Oxford." And she was like, "Ooh, Oxford." And then when I came out of university I wrote to her and said, "Any chance of work experience?" So I went in and she walked me around and said to her colleagues, "This is Mark, he's very bright, just graduated from Oxford." And from then on I was just sort of in, it was kind of an informal deal, and after a few weeks they said, "You seem alright, stick around, here's a three-month contract." And another. And another.

From here, as the journalistic profiles attest, Mark's ascent has been rapid. But again, he tells a less romantic story of career progression than his profilers. Of course, he acknowledges that he has a lot of "objective merits" – prestigious educational credentials, a strong work ethic, certain skills (an "eye for narrative", for example, or a knack for "idea generation"). But the most crucial thing, he tells us, was that these talents were given a platform – a "chance to develop" and an "opportunity to shine". Much of this was to do with the help of others. There was the family money at the start, a safety net that "tided [him] over" when he was jockeying around for a permanent contract. But even more significant, he says, were the senior colleagues who fast-tracked him, facilitating jobs or advocating on his behalf at key moments. He tells us: "It's interesting, I mean I could almost give you my whole trajectory in sponsors, because it's sort of, it's quite medieval in television. You serve apprenticeships and you have a patron."

Finding sponsors was partly about being astute, being "strategic politically." In Mark's case this meant "attaching myself to people who I thought were good and trying to be their left-hand man." But at the same time being able to make these kinds of connections was contingent on a broader ability to "sort of fit in with the telly tribe." This means superficial things like dress, he says, pointing to his pristine-white and expensive-looking sneakers: "I don't know why I wear these, I suppose it's a uniform isn't it? Like a businessman wears a suit."

But it's also about being able to "connect" with colleagues, often in informal settings. He recalls a big break in his mid-20s: "I remember the bloke sat opposite me was on secondment making a documentary about Isaac Hayes[4] and I said 'Oh, I love Isaac Hayes.' So we had a big long chat, went to the pub, talked about music for about three hours, [and] at the end he said, 'Actually, I need a researcher for a film I am making.'" They went on to spend several years working together.

Questions of 'fit' became even more powerful, Mark says, as he entered the upper echelons of television commissioning. Vital here, he notes, was a sense of how to perform in the kind of collaborative and creative decision-making settings common to television. And again here Mark makes an explicit link between what he calls the "rules of the game" and the specificities of his class background: "Let me give you an example," he says, recalling a period after being promoted to the senior production team on a news programme:

> So every day we had this morning meeting where we decided what stories to do and everyone pitches for what should be the running order and what our angle should be. And it was instantly recognisable to me, exactly like the common rooms I encountered at Oxford, and at school. The rules were – it's good to be right, but it's better to be funny! And there's a certain kind of *Private Eye*,[5] *Have I Got News For You*,[6] cerebral humour. So making a good pun, that was great, or dropping a clever reference.

Significantly, Mark did not seem particularly embarrassed or threatened by these admissions. Neither did his narrative smack of calculated modesty or performative middle-class guilt. Instead he had been "thinking about our interview," he tells us, for some time before we met. The topic had prompted him to retrace his career trajectory but also to think, for the first time, about how it connected to his background. The resulting conversation, especially within the secure confines of an anonymous interview, seemed almost cathartic for him. As he summed up: "It is not like I think I am rubbish, I mean I've seen lots of peers with greater networks and privilege screw up because they just weren't good enough. But at the same time it is mad to sort of pretend there's not been an incredibly strong following wind throughout my career."

This idea of a 'following wind', or a gust of privilege, gets to the heart of what this book is about. Mark is just one of 175 people we interviewed for this project,[7] across a variety of elite occupations, and from a range of different class backgrounds. In some ways Mark represented a typical case. We met many from similarly advantaged backgrounds who had reached the top of their professions. Yet in other ways, Mark was very unusual. Most we spoke to told very different stories of success, particularly those from privileged backgrounds. Career progression, according to the majority of these interviewees, had always rested most decisively on 'merit'.[8]

This is not particularly surprising. Western cultures have long lionised the idea of 'meritocratic' achievement. As Max Weber famously argued as early as 1915,

> The fortunate man is seldom satisfied with the fact of being fortunate. Beyond this, he needs to know that he has a right to his good fortune. He wants to be convinced that he "deserves" it, and above all, that he deserves it in comparison with others … good fortune thus wants to be legitimate fortune.[9]

Yet in this book we challenge the belief that success in elite occupations is simply a matter of 'legitimate fortune'. Instead, we demonstrate that not only are those who earn the most, and who get to the top, disproportionately drawn from privileged backgrounds, but their success cannot be explained by 'merit' alone. Instead we uncover a number of hidden mechanisms that propel them forward, and ahead of those from less advantaged backgrounds. And it is here, in understanding the nature of these following winds, that Mark's story proves particularly illuminating. Mark was legitimately meritorious in all the ways we conventionally think about 'merit' – he had achieved highly in the education system, he had worked hard, and he had amassed a wealth of valuable experience. Yet, as he explained, Mark had also been given a particular *platform* to demonstrate his 'merits', and a platform where his package of 'merits', and the way he had presented them, was readily recognised by senior figures. This ability to *land* 'merit', and how it is connected to a person's background, is central to this book. Indeed, the themes that flanked Mark's trajectory – the Bank of Mum and Dad, informal sponsorship, the luxury of fitting in – were echoed throughout our interviews. And as we argue in the chapters that follow, each play a critical role in erecting, and maintaining, the UK's class ceiling.

In this introductory chapter we sketch out the main arguments put forward in this book. But before we do so, it is important to provide both the political and sociological context for our enquiry – where do the questions that underpin this project come from, and why do they matter? We should say from the outset that we do not attempt to summarise whole swathes of academic literature here. Of course we are strongly invested in scholarly debates surrounding class and social mobility, and for this reason we include a more academic discussion, and justification, of our 'class ceiling' approach in Chapter Ten. Yet fundamentally we intend this to be an accessible book, and therefore this Introduction aims to provide a readable and provocative lead-in to our enquiry.

The (premature) death of class

In the 1980s and 1990s, numerous politicians and academics lined up to proclaim 'the end of class'. As a marker of inherited social division, class was seen to have no place in the contemporary world. In the UK, successive prime ministers embraced a vision of a new classless society built on meritocracy[10] and characterised by limitless, 'perfect' social mobility.[11] As Tony Blair famously proclaimed in 1999, 'The class war is over. But the struggle for true equality has only just begun.'[12]

This notion was hardly original to politicians. Many academic commentators were equally convinced that the age of social class was over. As influential German sociologist, Ulrich Beck, famously asserted, class was now a 'zombie category'.[13] Instead, he and others like Anthony Giddens[14] and Zygmunt Bauman[15] heralded the rise of a new post-modern world order based on 'individualisation'. Central to this was the contention that widespread social change had released us from 'historically prescribed social forms and commitments' such as class, and instead catapulted us into a more individually orientated era where we 'must produce, stage, and cobble together' our own biographies.[16]

One of the key assumptions fuelling the 'end of class' narrative[17] was that we were living through a transformative age of social mobility. It was certainly true that, in many high-income countries, a dynamic and expanding post-Second World War economy had ushered in strong rates of economic growth, the widespread expansion of state education and steady improvements in the living standards of many.[18] Flowing from this, there was also a steep increase in the number of those from working-class backgrounds who experienced upward mobility into management and the professions. In the UK this was due in large part to changes in the occupational structure, particularly the decline of industry and manufacturing and the large-scale expansion of the professional and managerial sector. From the 1920s to the 1990s, for example, the percentage of the total workforce doing professional and managerial work more than doubled, from under 15% to 37%.[19] In this way, there was now significantly more 'room at the top', and many from working-class backgrounds, often via a grammar school education,[20] rose to fill these new positions.

One of the misconceptions about this period, however, is that Britain became more socially open. The pioneering work of sociologist John Goldthorpe definitively busted this myth. He showed that while there was certainly an increase in the absolute number of people enjoying upward mobility, the *relative* chances, or odds, of someone born into a working-class family making it into the professions (ahead of someone from a privileged background) remained consistently low throughout the 20th century.[21] Nonetheless, the shifts in absolute mobility were very important to people's *perception* of openness.[22] Many saw or knew others who had experienced upward mobility, and this fed a sense that the old mechanisms of class reproduction were gradually unravelling.

This post-war expansion of 'room at the top' also coincided with a period of decreasing, and historically low, income inequality: the share of income going to the top 1% of earners declined from upwards of 15% before the war to as low as 6% in 1980.[23] The rich, of course, remained far richer than everyone else, but not by nearly as much as they had been.

But, slowly, both the increases in absolute mobility and income equality fizzled. The finance-led and service-based economy championed by Thatcher's Conservative government in the 1980s, allied to the globalisation of trade, produced what now appears as highly volatile economic growth. Much of the apparent success was premised on the one-off rewards made possible by deregulation and the selling of public assets rather than through the sustained productivity growth that secured the longer-term gains of the post-war decades. Meanwhile, those at the bottom of the social hierarchy were most likely to be at the sharp end of cuts in public spending.[24] In these conditions inequality – particularly at the top end of the income distribution – has mushroomed, climbing, by many measures, towards levels not seen since the 1930s.[25]

The political discourse, unsurprisingly, has come full circle. There is now a growing consensus that class divisions are hardening,[26] and a widespread concern that the contemporary dynamics of inequality, especially post-Brexit, are taking severe turns that demand urgent political intervention.[27]

Social mobility and the politics of inequality

Amid rising inequality, and the growing public unrest it has generated, social mobility has emerged as the key rhetorical tool through which politicians are staging their response. In the latest iteration, as expressed by Theresa May in her maiden speech as Prime Minister, Britain must become '*the* great meritocracy'; this is the primary means to addressing society's 'burning injustices'.[28]

This impassioned sloganeering is partially rooted in concerns that Britain is becoming less and less open. Certainly, the post-war expansion of 'room at the top' has slowed.[29] And rates of absolute upward social mobility have begun to decline. There is even some evidence that relative rates have decreased.[30]

But the reality is that there have not been big changes in overall rates of mobility, however measured. So why is the rhetoric of social mobility so frequently deployed in discussions about inequality? Well, a big part of the reason is that the topic of social mobility speaks directly to the larger principle of *fairness*. If some people are more likely than others to get the most highly prized jobs, regardless of whether they are the most able or work the hardest, most people would agree that this is unfair.[31] Moreover, jobs at the top of the class distribution almost always pay better – so the question of who has access to those jobs is also a question of economic inequality, of how fair the distribution of earnings is.

Accordingly, for a long time the dominant political view held that economic inequality is not necessarily a problem as long as there is equality of opportunity. From this perspective, if those from different backgrounds have fair *access* to the most desirable jobs and the highest incomes, any inequality in *outcome* that follows is acceptable, and possibly even desirable (as higher rewards should motivate the most capable to seek the most prized jobs[32]). Social mobility, through this lens, is therefore a key means of justifying inequality, imbuing inequality with what Goldthorpe has called 'meritocratic legitimacy'.[33]

But there are signs that this consensus is shifting. Landmark texts on inequality, such as those by Richard Wilkinson and Kate Pickett,[34] Thomas Piketty[35] and Danny Dorling,[36] as well as hard-hitting reports by high-profile organisations like the International Monetary Fund (IMF)[37] and the World Bank,[38] have convinced many that vast income inequalities are actually a more pressing dimension of fairness. There are also many politicians – mainly on the left but also some on the right – who are increasingly making the argument that however justly people access jobs, there is no reason for one person to be earning millions while others scrape by on ten thousand or less.[39] Nonetheless, these politicians also support increasing social mobility, and see it as an important metric of societal openness. They tend to be especially concerned with the intergenerational transfer of privilege, and the question of how to keep the well-off from passing on so many advantages to their children.[40]

Fair access to the top

It is perhaps not surprising, considering the common ground between these two ideological orientations, that the most politically potent dimension of social mobility tends to be social closure[41] at the top, and specifically within elite occupations. This is an issue all politicians can get behind, at least rhetorically, it seems. Particularly influential in bringing this issue to the public attention has been the former Labour minister Alan Milburn. Milburn experienced profound upward mobility himself, from a council estate[42] in Durham to front-bench Cabinet politics. Yet the obstacles he faced during his own upward journey, particularly in the select arena of politics, convinced Milburn that working towards equitable access to the professions represented the lynchpin in improving social mobility.[43] In 2009 he authored the damning *Unleashing Aspiration* report to the Panel on Fair Access to the Professions, which became known as the Milburn Report. In it he argued emphatically that certain professions such as media, law and medicine remained a 'closed shop' and were not doing enough to 'open themselves up to a wider pool of talent'.[44] As Chair of the Social Mobility Commission (SMC), he continued to apply political pressure in this area until, in late 2017, he quit in protest at the government's unwillingness to take action.

Yet while Milburn and the SMC have consistently kept the issue of elitism on the political agenda, the reality is that they have always been limited by the evidence base at their disposal. We actually have remarkably limited insight, for example, into how socially open different elite occupations truly are.[45]

This wasn't always the case. In the middle of the 20th century there was a very lively sociological tradition of interrogating the social make-up of elites.[46] Yet from the 1980s onwards this 'sociology of elite recruitment' was eclipsed by researchers more interested in looking at broader patterns of social mobility throughout the class structure. This approach, first championed by Goldthorpe but now adopted as standard by mobility researchers around the globe, proceeds by aggregating individual occupations into 'big' social classes.[47] From here, researchers can then match people's class origin (in terms of their parent's occupation) with their class destination (in terms of their own occupation) and measure the movement or mobility in between. This is, of course, an essential platform for analysis. It has allowed researchers to address central questions of both change, in terms of whether social mobility in a given country is increasing or decreasing,[48] and cross-national comparisons, in terms of how mobility varies among different countries.[49]

Yet this has also left rather glaring gaps in our knowledge. In particular, we know little about how open or closed different elite professions are, and therefore precisely *where* in the labour market elite reproduction is taking place.

In this book we seek to redress this balance. In particular, we capitalise on new and game-changing data on social mobility released via Britain's largest employment survey, the Labour Force Survey (LFS).[50] Specifically, we pool LFS data from July 2013 to July 2016 – giving us access to over 18,000 people working in elite jobs. This furnishes us with an unprecedented opportunity to shine a light on the openness of the upper echelons of British society.

Origins and destinations in contemporary Britain

To set the scene for our analysis, it is first important to explain the basic architecture of social mobility in Britain. Amid the maelstrom of political sloganeering and technocratic debate about mobility rates, this basic empirical picture is often overlooked; how many people actually work in Britain's elite occupations, and what are their class origins?

Figure 0.1 demonstrates that the link between people's origins and destinations remains doggedly persistent in contemporary Britain. On the left it shows three different class origins, based on the occupation of the main breadwinner in a person's household when they were growing up.[51] At the top are people from upper-middle-class backgrounds whose parents were professionals or managers. Below them are those from lower-middle-class backgrounds, whose parents did intermediate jobs such as secretary, office manager or police officer. And below them people from working-class backgrounds, whose parents did routine and semi-routine jobs such as cleaner, lorry driver, labourer, or who had no earnings.

On the right side of Figure 0.1 are four class destinations. These are the same as the origin groups, except that we split professionals and managers into two groups; we distinguish 'lower'[52] professional and managerial occupations such as nursing, teaching and social work from 'elite occupations'. We define elite occupations as the 'higher professional and managerial occupations' that make up the top class of the UK government's National Statistics Socio-Economic Classification (NS-SEC).[53] These include traditionally prestigious professional jobs like accountant, academic or architect. We then also add a number of cultural and creative occupations, such as journalists and those working in film and television, the performing arts and advertising. These jobs may not be as well remunerated as many of the top professions, but they are arguably as (if not more) competitive, desirable and influential.[54] We should say that we don't regard these elite occupations as somehow equivalent to a 'governing elite' or a 'power elite' in the sense others[55] have used the term. Instead, we see elite occupations as distinct in terms of their *relational* level of prestige, autonomy and earnings. For example, people in our elite occupations earn, on average, £45,000 a year (roughly US$60,000), while people in working-class occupations have average annual earnings of around £15,000 (or about US$20,000). Moreover, in terms of broader issues of power and influence, these elite occupations are significant in the sense that they normally constitute the main 'reservoir or recruiting market'[56] from which governing or power elites are drawn.[57]

The flows from left to right in Figure 0.1 represent the people from each class origin who move into each class destination, and the thickness of each line shows the proportion who take each possible path.

We can see that the thickest lines – the most common paths – denote people staying in roughly the same class position as they started in. In Britain about half of those who get elite jobs

Figure 0.1: Flows from origins to destinations in the UK

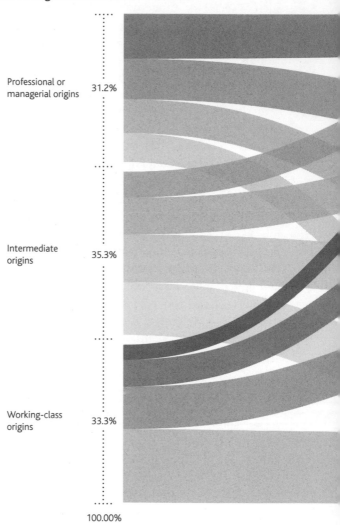

see colour version in plate section

Professional or
managerial origins   31.2%

Intermediate
origins   35.3%

Working-class
origins   33.3%

100.00%

are from upper-middle-class backgrounds, although only about a third of all Brits come from these backgrounds. People from working-class origins do sometimes make it into elite jobs, but it is rare; only about 10% of people from working-class backgrounds (3.3% of people overall) traverse the steepest upward

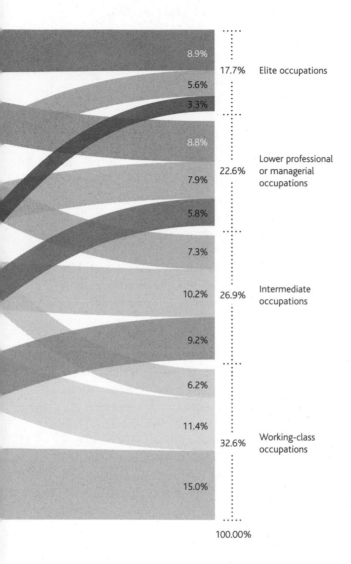

8.9%

17.7% Elite occupations

5.6%

3.3%

8.8%

22.6% Lower professional
or managerial
7.9%   occupations

5.8%

7.3%

10.2% 26.9% Intermediate
occupations

9.2%

6.2%

11.4%

32.6% Working-class
occupations

15.0%

100.00%

see colour version in plate section

mobility path. Put another way, people from upper–middle–class origins have about 6.5 times the chance of landing an elite job compared to people from working–class backgrounds.[58] Origins, in other words, remain strongly associated with destinations in contemporary Britain.[59]

Bourdieu and the long shadow of class origin

To make sense of these patterns of mobility, we need to understand what class origin means and how it matters. So far we have adopted a fairly limited definition of class origin, which looks at what someone's main breadwinning parent did for a living, and then places this occupation in a classification of socio-economic classes. In this book we use this kind of measure for largely *pragmatic* reasons. We think occupation is probably the best approximation we have for class origin, the single piece of information that on its own tells us the most about the probable socio-economic conditions that characterised a person's upbringing. Yet, for us, occupation is only that, a *proxy* for class.

Our own approach to class, and especially class origin, is strongly influenced by the work of French sociologist Pierre Bourdieu. While we devote a full discussion to his work and its influence on our approach in Chapter Ten, these ideas can also be fairly simply distilled.

At root a Bourdieusian lens insists that our class background is defined by our parents' stocks of three primary forms of capital:[60] economic capital (wealth and income), cultural capital (educational credentials and the possession of legitimate knowledge, skills and tastes) and social capital (valuable social connections and friendships). These not only structure the overarching conditions of our childhoods, but we also tend to inherit them. This process is straightforward in terms of economic and social capital: upper-middle-class parents are able to directly pass on to their children both financial assets and valuable social contacts, both of which go on to confer advantage in fairly self-evident ways.

The inheritance of cultural capital is more complex. The material affluence of the educated upper-middle classes, Bourdieu argued, affords them a certain distance from economic necessity that is then strongly reflected in the way they socialise their children. In particular, they inculcate a certain 'habitus' – a set of *dispositions* that organise how their children understand and relate to the world around them. Some of these dispositions are embodied; they manifest through specific modes of bodily *comportment* such as accent, inflection, gesture and posture, as well as styles of dress, etiquette and manners.[61] But perhaps most significant is the way in which privileged parents imprint in early childhood a propensity for what Bourdieu called 'symbolic mastery'. This includes a certain mode of using language, including an elaborate vocabulary and 'correct' grammar, a general familiarity with abstraction and theoretical ideas, and also a particular detached, knowing aesthetic orientation to culture and taste.

For Bourdieu the significance of this aesthetic disposition, as well as other aspects of symbolic mastery and embodiment associated with a privileged upbringing, is that they tend to be *(mis)recognised* as legitimate in social life. They constitute only one – fairly arbitrary, in Bourdieu's view – way of knowing the world. Yet nonetheless, in most developed societies they are consistently assigned high value, functioning as widely recognised signals of cultural distinction. Moreover, this is especially significant in reproducing class privilege because the inheritance of cultural capital is more veiled than the transmission of social and economic capital. For instance, it is possible, at least in theory, to trace the genesis of a person's economic assets or their social connections. In contrast, it is much harder to detect the intergenerational transfer of cultural capital, and therefore we tend to (mis)read it in everyday life as a signal of a person's 'natural' sophistication (that they have an 'an eye for fashion' or a 'sophisticated palate', for example), or even their innate intelligence.[62] In other words, simply by expressing their tastes or opinions, the privileged are able to cash in their embodied cultural capital in multiple settings.

These ideas are, of course, somewhat abstract and theoretical. However, there is now a rich body of empirical research that has investigated more precisely how the transmission of cultural capital actually plays out in everyday life. One of the most influential examples comes from the US sociologist Annette Lareau, who looked at the ways cultural capital is inculcated in the family.[63] She studied the home lives of 9- and 10-year-olds from different class backgrounds, and found large and consequential class differences in parenting styles. The upper-middle-class parents (those with professional jobs and university degrees) approached raising their children as a project in 'concerted cultivation' – providing extensive support with homework, carefully curating complements of extra-curricular activities and engaging their children consistently in conversation and discussion, all of which acted to cultivate their capacity for symbolic mastery.

Working-class and poor parents, on the other hand, practised what Lareau calls 'the accomplishment of natural growth'. These parents were just as committed to ensuring that their children grew into healthy, secure adults. But they approached their roles differently. Their children got to spend much more time making their own entertainment, inventing games with neighbourhood children, or watching television. This was partly a result of the economic constraints parents faced. But it was also about different views about child-rearing and the world at large; where upper-middle-class parents believed it was important to manage every moment of their children's time and advocate on their behalf, working-class parents had a greater belief in children's independence, and a greater deference to institutions such as schools.

Lareau is careful to emphasise, and we agree, that neither of these approaches is intrinsically better or worse, and that there are advantages and disadvantages to *both* approaches from the perspective of child development. Nonetheless, because upper-middle-class people tend to be in charge of schools, most workplaces, and many other institutions, there are enduring advantages to being raised middle class. For example, Lareau's working-class children had very different experiences with school than their middle-class counterparts; they saw school as primarily an interaction with authority, where the goal was to avoid getting into trouble, and were less likely to find success and satisfaction there. When they finished high school, they were less likely to go to university, and when they entered the workforce, generally found less desirable jobs.

Of course, parenting styles differ across national contexts and they also change over time. But broadly speaking, Lareau's observations about class difference have been consistently echoed in other contexts, including the UK.[64] In particular, subsequent work has reiterated Lareau's core observation: upper-middle-class families tend to familiarise their children with dispositions that function as cultural capital, and this provides them with concrete advantages at primary school,[65] secondary school[66] and university.[67] Others have also shown how this cultural capital, especially when expressed through particular tastes and aesthetic styles, has a more everyday currency as a signal of cultural distinction.[68]

The effects of class origin, this research on cultural capital suggests, are pervasive and long-lasting. And class origin shapes who you are in ways that a simple change in circumstances – having more money, a university education or a better job than your parents – will not necessarily erase. This is not to say that people do not learn and change over their lives, and adapt to new situations – of course we do.[69] But this work suggests our early years leave a deep, and classed, imprint. As Annette Kuhn, a British film critic, famously argued, 'class is something beneath your clothes, under your skin, in your reflexes, your psyche, at the very core of your being'.[70]

Lessons from the glass ceiling

A wealth of research suggests, then, that class origin casts a long shadow over people's lives. Yet this work stops short of interrogating precisely *how* it matters in the arena we focus on in this book: careers in elite occupations. Still, drawing on two rich and allied research traditions can provide important clues.

The first is based on the experiences of members of racial–ethnic minority groups and white women in the elite labour market. Here the metaphor of glass, and particularly the glass *ceiling*, has been usefully deployed to highlight the invisible yet durable barriers that these groups face in achieving the same rewards as white men in the same positions.[71] A range of mechanisms is at play here, from direct discrimination (in terms of sexism and racism) to the subtler and more insidious effects of stereotyping, microaggressions, tokenism and homophily (the tendency among decision-makers to favour those who are, in various ways, like themselves).[72] This work has also highlighted how these groups tend to be shut out of what is colloquially called the 'old boys' network', the informal social connections that help people find out about job opportunities and navigate promotions.[73]

The key point that emerges from this glass-ceiling literature is that what we conventionally understand as 'merit' is not the only, or maybe even the main, determinant of career success. Study upon study has shown that even when women and racial-ethnic minorities are just as capable, talented and hard-working as white men in every way these attributes can be measured, they are still less likely to get on. This has obvious implications for our study. We know that those from working-class backgrounds have also been historically excluded from elite occupations[74] (albeit for different reasons), so to what extent might the mechanisms driving the glass ceiling also apply to class origin?

But connecting insights about the glass ceiling to the topic of class is not just about drawing parallels. After all, class, gender, race (and many other aspects of social division) do not operate as separate and mutually exclusive axes of inequality. Instead, they almost always build on each other and work together. This, of course, is the key insight introduced by the concept of *intersectionality*.[75] In the context of social mobility an intersectional lens is key. For example, there is compelling evidence that the *experience* of upward social mobility is distinct, and often particularly difficult, for women, and for members of racial-ethnic minority groups. As Steph Lawler has explained, no female equivalent exists of the heroic tale of 'the working-class boy made good', and instead 'women's desires for, and envy of, respectability and material goods' have long been portrayed as markers of pretence and triviality.[76] A number of leading female academics, including Beverley Skeggs, bell hooks, Diane Reay, Kalwant Bhopal, and Lynsey Hanley, have also underlined the specificity of women's and ethnic minorities' mobility experiences via vivid accounts of their own complex and uneasy upward trajectories.[77] While rich and varied, what unites these accounts is the enduring sense of dislocation felt by these women, a feeling that they do not fully 'fit' in the social spaces of past or present.[78] As Skeggs notes, while she feels like a 'fraud' among academic colleagues, her working-class family cannot provide refuge. Instead, in this context, she is a disappointment, someone who 'got above herself', who reneged on her duty to family and particularly the traditional female role she was expected to play within it.[79, 80]

This work underlines the centrality of intersectionality in understanding the *lived experience* of social mobility, and therefore the importance of exploring possible intersections between gender, race and ethnicity, and class movement within Britain's elite occupations.

From getting 'in' to getting 'on'

The other reason to expect working-class people may face challenges *within* elite occupations is that we know that they face acute barriers 'getting in' in the first place. Two scholars have been formational in elucidating these issues of access. In the US, Lauren Rivera has shown that every step of the recruitment and hiring process at elite professional service firms works to favour the already-privileged. First, top firms eliminate nearly every applicant who did not attend an elite college or university. They then put applicants through a series of 'informal' recruitment activities, such as cocktail parties and mixers, that are generally uncomfortable and unfamiliar to those from working-class backgrounds. Finally, when formal interviews happen, selectors often eschew formal criteria and evaluate candidates more on how *at ease* they seem, whether they build rapport in the interview, and whether they share common interests. Rivera describes this process as 'cultural matching'.[81]

In a UK context, Louise Ashley has found similar dynamics among elite firms operating in law, accountancy and banking – particularly those situated in the City (of London). In particular, she highlights how recruiters routinely misrecognise as 'talent' classed performances of 'cultural display'. For example, recruiters seek a 'polished' appearance, strong debating skills and a confident manner; traits, she argues, that can be closely traced back to an upper-middle-class upbringing.[82]

While these studies are illuminating, their analysis starts and finishes with the issue of occupational admission. In many ways this is understandable. Nearly all sociologists and politicians tend to conceptualise social mobility as an issue of who 'gets in'.[83]

Yet there is a danger of reducing social mobility to this one-dimensional issue of access; it assumes that social mobility finishes at the point of occupational entry. But, as we have already explained, a wealth of evidence suggests that class origins are 'sticky', and that strongly inherited (yet hidden) resources such as cultural capital may continue to have very long-lasting impacts on people's career trajectories. In this way, it is worth returning to Figure 0.1. While this shows that 10% of those from working-class backgrounds secure admission into Britain's elite occupations, it cannot tell us whether these people go on to achieve the same levels of success as those from more privileged backgrounds.

Investigating this issue represents the real driving force behind this book – social mobility not just into but *within* elite occupations, from 'getting *in*' to 'getting *on*'. Specifically, we ask three linked questions. First, do the upwardly mobile attain the same levels of earnings or seniority as those from privileged backgrounds? Second, if not, does a 'class ceiling' persist even when we compare otherwise similar people from different class backgrounds? And third, if a class ceiling does exist, what are the dynamics that drive it?

Layout of this book

Why it pays to be privileged

Our book has a logical form and is best read in sequence. In tackling the central questions posed above, we begin by drawing on the empirical advances provided by the new LFS data. This allows us first, in Chapter One, to move beyond the highly aggregated parameters of standard social mobility research and instead mine down to focus on Britain's elite occupations. These occupations, we find, are dominated by those from privileged backgrounds. Inequalities in educational attainment are partly implicated in this skew, we show, but they only go so far in explaining patterns of access. Strikingly, we demonstrate that even when people from working-class backgrounds attend top universities, and even when they receive the highest degree grades, they are *still* less likely than those from privileged origins (with the same credentials) to be found in top jobs. This effect is further exacerbated for certain racial–ethnic groups. Bangladeshi people from working-class backgrounds, for example, are only half as likely as working-class white people to make it into top jobs, despite attending university at much higher rates.

We also show significant variation across elite fields. Management is generally more open than the professions, and there are also striking differences *between* professions. Those from upper-middle-class backgrounds, for example, are 12 times more likely to become doctors than those from working-class backgrounds, whereas they are only twice as likely to become engineers.

In Chapter Two we shift our focus from access to progression. Here we demonstrate that there is a significant and previously undetected 'class pay gap' at play in Britain's elite occupations. Specifically, those from working-class backgrounds earn on average 16% less in elite occupations than colleagues from privileged backgrounds. This is exacerbated for women, people with disabilities and certain racial–ethnic groups from working-class backgrounds, who all face a clear double disadvantage. We also demonstrate that the class pay gap is concentrated in certain elite fields: finance, law, medicine, accountancy and acting all stand out.

The question this raises, of course, is *why* – a question we begin to unravel in Chapter Three. Here we use the rich array of information in our dataset to unpick what might be driving the class pay gap. This demonstrates, first, that demographic differences between people from different class backgrounds definitively do *not* explain differences in pay. In fact, the pay gap is actually significantly higher when we compare people from different backgrounds who are the same in terms of age, gender and ethnicity. We also find that many conventional indicators of 'merit' go little way in explaining the pay gap. We find no evidence, for example, that the upwardly mobile work fewer hours, have less training or have less experience than their privileged colleagues.

One marker of 'merit' is important, however – educational attainment. Those from working-class backgrounds are less likely to have degrees and less likely to have attended prestigious universities, both of which are associated with higher earnings. Yet, tellingly, even when the upwardly mobile do achieve the highest credentials, including Oxbridge degrees and/or first class[84] grades, they are not able to convert them into the same earnings premium as the privileged.

We also uncover three other important mechanisms. The privileged are more likely to work in London, in large firms and in certain elite occupations such as medicine, law and finance. Crucially, all of these factors are associated with higher pay. Yet these 'sorting' mechanisms are neither innocent nor 'meritocratic', we argue. For example, the ability to forge a career in London is often contingent on leveraging the Bank of Mum and Dad, while lucrative professions and large firms have both been shown to tilt unfairly towards the privileged in graduate recruitment.[85]

Chapter Three culminates by calculating the cumulative effects of all of these explanatory mechanisms. Importantly, even when we control for these and a whole host of further factors, a substantial class pay gap remains.

Investigating a class ceiling

Next we push *further* to understand the drivers of the pay gap. We argue that this demands moving beyond survey data and towards an understanding of the lived experience inside Britain's elite occupations. In the second part of the book we therefore turn to four in-depth case studies. Here we go behind the closed doors of elite firms and interview people working across different elite occupations. In Chapter Four we introduce these (anonymised) case studies: a national television broadcaster, 6TV; a large multinational accounting firm, Turner Clarke; an architecture practice, Coopers; and an examination of the field of self-employed actors. In each case we combined analysis of survey data with informal observations and an extensive programme of 175 in-depth interviews (30–50 per case).[86] These interviews allowed us to move beyond one-dimensional occupational measures of class origin and properly register the Bourdieusian capitals that participants carried with them into occupations, as well as the impact these inherited resources had on their subsequent career trajectories.[87] We elaborate on the contours of this research design in our Methodological appendix, as well as other important issues such as how we measured class and social mobility, how and why we selected our case studies, and our own positionality as researchers (white men – one of us transgender, one cisgender – from different class backgrounds and countries).

Chapter Four goes on to provide a detailed profile of each case study. This demonstrates that the issue at stake is not just a class pay gap but, in many cases, a *class ceiling*. At 6TV and Turner Clarke, in particular, those from working-class backgrounds tend to sort into less prestigious specialisms and rarely reach the top of the organisational hierarchy.

'It's all about confidence': The fallacy of invidualised explanations

To understand this class ceiling, we began our qualitative analysis by reflecting on what interviewees themselves thought might be the key drivers.[88] While we expected a wide array of theories, people's initial responses were strikingly similar. Most paused, visibly grappled with the question, and then landed on a single word: confidence. Of course the term was deployed in different ways, and with varying degrees of approval or disapproval. But the underlying sentiment, irrespective of class background, was remarkably consistent. Those from privileged backgrounds, we were told over and over again, are simply more confident; they possess a distinct sense of self-efficacy or certainty about their ability to progress, and this is then decisive in helping them get ahead.

At one level this is an important finding. It reveals something significant about how people observe and make sense of class difference. It is also, to some extent, supported by academic literature – particularly in psychology.[89] Here many studies have found a relationship between class background and self-confidence, self-esteem and what is sometimes termed 'locus of control' (the extent to which an individual feels they have control over what happens in their life).

But digging a little deeper, it soon became clear that the explanatory power of confidence was limited in quite fundamental ways. As people explained more about what they meant by confidence and how it manifested, and we compared this to what they had already told us about their careers earlier in interviews, it became clear that confidence was too broad and simplistic as an explanatory mechanism. In particular, we noticed, it very often operated as a holding term, a vessel through which a myriad of other, often quite distinct, processes were folded into. In Chapters Five to Nine we introduce each of these mechanisms.

The (hidden) drivers of the class ceiling

Interviewees most frequently talked about confidence in the context of who is willing to take risks in their career. Yet delving into these narratives revealed that this was less about individual inclination and more about the resources at a person's disposal. Specifically, these were often stories about people who did or did not have access to economic capital, usually provided by parents, that allowed them to take risks, or to feel that they could if they wished. In Chapter Five we explore this issue in depth, explaining the profound occupational advantages afforded to those who can draw on the Bank of Mum and Dad. Those with this kind of financial cushion, we show, are insulated from much of the uncertainty associated with forging an elite career, both in terms of negotiating the cost of living in settings like London – where many of the best opportunities are clustered – but also more psychologically in terms of feeling like they can spend more time on networking, or take more uncertain or short-term roles, all of which may have long-term pay-offs. This was particularly evident in cultural industries like television and acting where employment is often very precarious and getting to the top is often contingent on negotiating many years of short-term contracts. In contrast, we found that people who lacked family money described the day-to-day reality of making a living in these occupations as a kind of economic chaos – or, as actor Ray aptly put it, "like skydiving without a parachute."

Another context in which confidence was mentioned was in terms of consciously pushing forward in one's career, actively seeking promotions or negotiating pay rises. The privileged were often cast here as being more willing to demand that their efforts receive the rewards they deserve. We did find some evidence for this – interviewees from privileged backgrounds *had* made these type of requests more frequently. However, these individuals rarely made such decisions in isolation. Indeed, our interviews revealed that decisions to push for promotion or pay rises almost always resulted from the advice of others, particularly senior advocates. In Chapter Six we explore the importance of such channels of sponsorship, where senior staff take junior staff under their wing and, often operating beneath formal processes, are able to fast-track their careers. Yet while this is largely presented as an innocent process of talent spotting, we found that sponsor relationships were rarely established on the basis of work performance. Instead they are almost always forged, in the first instance at least, on cultural affinity, on sharing humour, interests and tastes. And as those currently occupying senior positions are themselves overwhelmingly from upper-middle-class backgrounds, these homophilic bonds tend to advantage the already-privileged.

The other main way that confidence was seen to drive the class pay gap was through its emboldening capacities in key work settings like meetings, presentations and interviews. Here there was a sense that those from privileged backgrounds are simply more able to assert their voice or opinion. But, again, our analysis revealed confidence to be a somewhat misleading explanation. For example, many of the upwardly mobile interviewees who told us they lacked confidence in such settings talked of other environments where they were very much at ease, such as with family or in certain leisure settings. In other words, it wasn't necessarily that these people lacked confidence per se, but that they lacked confidence *in the workplace*. Or, to put this another way, certain social environments inhibited their confidence while emboldening others. It is therefore not so much confidence that is the explanatory mechanism here but, as we explain in Chapters Seven and Eight, the behavioural and cultural codes that dictate people's sense of fit within elite workplaces. In Chapter Seven we compare the field-specific codes that underpin notions of fit, from corporate polish at Turner Clarke to studied informality at 6TV. While these codes may look different, they function in much the same way, we argue, setting shared norms and expectations – around dress, accent, taste and etiquette – that are then routinely *misrecognised* as markers of 'objective' skill, talent and ability. We develop this further in Chapter Eight, explaining that an even narrower notion of fit tends to circulate in executive cultures – where a command of legitimate culture is often a prerequisite for navigating gladiatorial executive environments, or where a particular type of person is considered most 'suitable' to represent organisations in public or with clients.

Most importantly, we see a clear pattern in terms of *who* tends to 'fit'. Across Chapters Seven and Eight we demonstrate that it is the privileged who are most comfortable adopting, mastering and playing with dominant behavioural codes, who feel most able to 'bring their whole self to work' and, more generally, give the impression that such codes are 'naturally' embodied. We argue that this is rooted in the way that the collective understanding of many elite occupations is an image *of* the privileged, allowing them to appear intrinsically more suitable – particularly when they reach the upper echelons.

In contrast, in Chapter Nine, we explore how it feels not to fit, and how this often mutes the aspirations of the upwardly mobile. Yet rather than interpreting such dented ambitions in terms of a deficit in intrinsic confidence, we argue that it is often an entirely logical response to the anticipation of the very real barriers that lie ahead. In this way, we are particularly attentive here to what mobility means for the people who experience it, and understand the decisions of many to stop pushing upward as an act of 'self-elimination'.

The mechanisms explored in Chapters Five through Nine are, in our view, often obscured by discussions that attribute the successes of the privileged to intrinsic self-confidence. This is because most regard confidence as an inherent personality trait, an individualised competency that some simply have more or less of. Accordingly, many policy-makers prescribe solutions (to the problem of low social mobility) that are similarly individualised. They argue that what we need, based on this kind of explanation of class and other pay gaps, is simply to build the confidence, character and aspirations of those from disadvantaged backgrounds, to 'top them up' with the 'qualities' they 'lack' via individual coaching, training or 'better' parenting.[90]

Yet our analysis points towards the need for a very different approach. Certainly, confidence is what people notice most readily when they observe differences in elite workplaces among those from different backgrounds. But delving further, as we do in this book, reveals that this confidence is fundamentally situational – it is a smokescreen that is often shaped by how people experience their workplace, whether they feel they belong, whether they feel supported and how this acts to fundamentally embolden some and inhibit others. Drawing on these insights, we close this book by outlining 10 practical steps that organisations can take to tackle the class ceiling.

Fundamentally, this book demonstrates that class-origin differences in career success are *not* about the character deficiencies of those from working-class backgrounds. And neither are they adequately explained by 'natural' differences in 'merit'. In fact, as we show in the chapters that follow, much of what is routinely categorised as 'merit' in elite occupations is actually impossible to separate from the 'following wind' of privilege.

ONE

Getting in

Social mobility has become one of the central political issues of our times; certainly across the Western world, it has emerged as the rhetorical weapon of choice for a generation of political leaders.[1] Impassioned speeches abound. "The American Dream is dead," Donald Trump declared throughout his 2016 presidential campaign, "But I will bring it back."[2] In France, Emmanuel Macron has made similar promises.[3] It is in the UK, however, that mobility is most explicitly centre-stage. As Theresa May proclaimed in her maiden speech as Prime Minister: "We won't entrench the advantages of the fortunate few; we will do everything we can to help anybody, whatever your background, to go as far as your talents will take you."[4]

The bellwether for how nations are doing on social mobility, as we explained in the Introduction, is very often access to the top – who gets into elite occupations and how this relates to their class background. This is perhaps partly due to the limited slice of society that politicians tend to see in their everyday lives. But it also reflects the way in which elite careers are routinely held up by politicians as what we should all be striving towards – occupational destinations that offer high incomes, high status and considerable decision-making power.[5] Such political narratives are fairly obviously undermined, however, if such highly prized arenas are seen as inaccessible, or rigged in favour of the privileged.

But there has long been a perception that many high-status occupations in the UK, such as law, medicine and journalism, are exactly that: professions that have traditionally been, and remain today, stubbornly elitist. As Alan Milburn wrote before resigning in protest as Chair of the UK Social Mobility Commission

(SMC), 'the most pressing policy priority facing the country is opening up the top of British society.' Britain, he argued, 'remains – at heart – elitist.'[6]

Yet despite the impassioned political rhetoric surrounding 'fair access', the truth is that our actual understanding of this issue has long lagged behind. This is because the surveys traditionally used to look at social mobility have at most a few thousand respondents. That is more than enough for capturing the overall relationship between origins and destinations in terms of 'big social classes'. But to understand more fine-grained patterns of mobility – who becomes a doctor, an accountant or a CEO – and how these differ from one another – requires much bigger data.

Fortunately, in 2014 Britain's largest employment survey, the Labour Force Survey (LFS), introduced, for the first time, questions about class origin. The key question here was about the job of the main income-earning parent when a subject was 14. (In Figure 1.1 we show how we used this to identify three

Figure 1.1: How we measure social mobility into elite occupations

see colour version in plate section

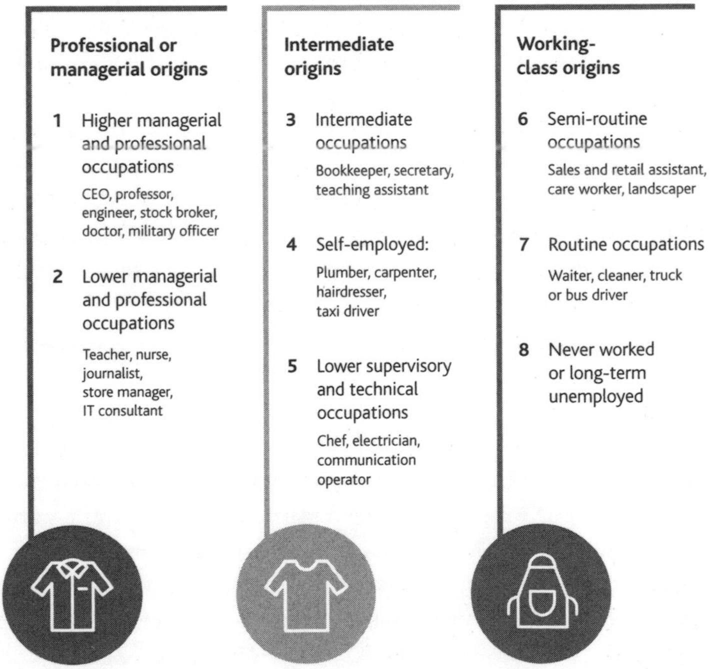

Professional or managerial origins	Intermediate origins	Working-class origins
1 Higher managerial and professional occupations CEO, professor, engineer, stock broker, doctor, military officer	3 Intermediate occupations Bookkeeper, secretary, teaching assistant	6 Semi-routine occupations Sales and retail assistant, care worker, landscaper
2 Lower managerial and professional occupations Teacher, nurse, journalist, store manager, IT consultant	4 Self-employed: Plumber, carpenter, hairdresser, taxi driver	7 Routine occupations Waiter, cleaner, truck or bus driver
	5 Lower supervisory and technical occupations Chef, electrician, communication operator	8 Never worked or long-term unemployed

broad class origin groups.) We immediately jumped on this new data and began work. In this chapter, we bring together three years of analysis. Specifically, we pool LFS data from July 2013 to July 2016, giving us access to a nationally representative sample of nearly 108,000 individuals[7] and over 18,000 people in top jobs. This furnishes us with an unprecedented level of detail.

We begin by analysing the openness of top jobs as a whole, and across 19 specific elite occupations. We next look at whether inequalities by class can be explained by patterns of educational attainment, and then examine the relationships between class and other axes of privilege and disadvantage, including race and ethnicity, gender and disability status.

The reproduction of privilege

In the UK, those who start out ahead are the ones most likely to succeed. As we showed in the Introduction, the biggest stream of people moving into elite occupations are those from upper-middle-class backgrounds.

Figure 1.2 reiterates that about *half* the people in top jobs had parents who did similarly high-status work, while less than 20% come from working-class backgrounds. In other words, the privileged are disproportionately getting into the most desirable, high-powered, glamorous and influential occupations, and those from the working class are too often left – or kept – out.

Figure 1.2: The privileged dominate the UK's elite occupations

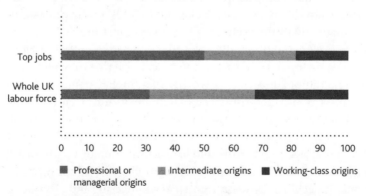

Note: Percentage of people from each class origin in the whole UK labour force, and in our top jobs.
Source: LFS

This general pattern is well established.[8] And the UK is certainly not unique. In nearly all high-income countries it is possible to discern a similar link between origins and destinations.[9] While these cross-national patterns vary to some extent, a fairly basic point holds; there is considerably more class reproduction than should be the case if everyone truly had an equal chance to succeed. What is less well known, however, is the extent to which rates of social mobility vary across *different* elite occupations. Next we therefore zoom in to compare these different areas.

Access across elite occupations

Figure 1.3 shows the class origins of those working in 19 different top professions or elite jobs.[10] Occupations with the largest portion of people from privileged origins are at the top, and the most class-diverse or 'open' areas are at the bottom. Looking across these professional fields, a few important things emerge. First, there is substantial, meaningful variety. While these occupations are routinely grouped together as a coherent whole, a 'big social class', there are clearly real limitations with this lens. It hides the fact that there is tremendous diversity in the exclusiveness of different high-status occupations.

It is possible to detect some telling patterns in these access figures. First, we can see an important distinction between management and the professions. While those in senior management positions in both the private and public sector (who together make up just over a quarter of those in top jobs) are from relatively diverse class backgrounds, most of the professions are markedly more exclusive. This may reflect the fact that the professions have historically enjoyed much higher status in British society, owing in large part to the perception that they recruited more 'cultured' individuals worthy of a 'higher standing'.[11] Yet Figure 1.3 also demonstrates that there is also a clear divide within the professions between the traditional and the technical. For example, the traditional – or 'gentlemanly'[12] – professions of medicine, law, architecture and journalism contain a particularly high concentration of people from privileged backgrounds. In contrast, technical professions such as engineering and IT contain

Figure 1.3: Some elite occupations are a lot more closed than others

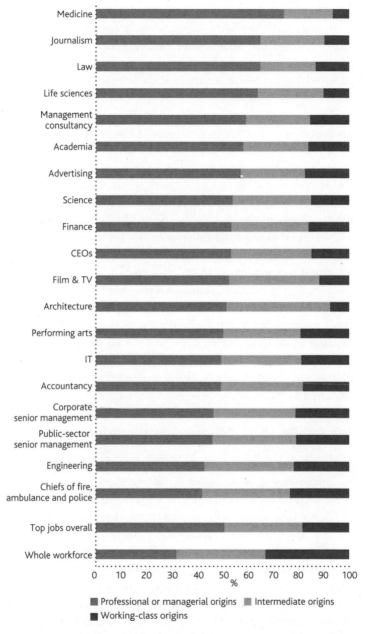

see colour version in plate section

■ Professional or managerial origins ■ Intermediate origins
■ Working-class origins

Note: Percentage of people in each elite occupation (as well as top jobs overall, and the whole workforce) who are from each class origin group.
Source: LFS

a higher than average (among these top jobs) percentage of the upwardly socially mobile.

These patterns are also reflected in what are called 'odds ratios' – the relative chances, in this case, of being in each of our top jobs depending on different class origins. An odds ratio of 1 would mean that people from working-class backgrounds have an equal chance of being in top jobs when compared with people from privileged origins. Instead, overall, people from upper-middle-class backgrounds are 3.6 times more likely to be in one of our top jobs (vs anywhere else in the class distribution) when compared to working-class-origin people.[13] But again, there is wide variation in the odds ratios for different top jobs, especially between traditional and technical areas. Privileged-origin people are about 12 times more likely to be doctors as those from working-class backgrounds, for example, and 7.5 times more likely as to be found in architecture, while they are only about twice as likely to be engineers.

However, it is worth pointing out that *none* of our fields have the representation of working-class-origin people we might expect or hope for in a society where recruitment to top jobs was truly open to all. Even the most 'open' fields in terms of working-class representation, such as public-sector management, still have about 30% fewer working-class-origin people than the workforce as a whole.

It's a family affair: Micro-class reproduction

Some of the exclusivity in these fields is due to what sociologists call 'micro-class reproduction',[14] the tendency of children to follow directly in their parents' occupational footsteps. Figure 1.4 shows that those with a parent in their same field, the 'micro-stable', are over-represented in every elite occupation, except for management consulting. But medicine, law, and film and television really stand out. People with parents who are doctors are a somewhat staggering 24 times more likely to be doctors than those whose parents did any other type of work. Similarly, the children of lawyers are 17 times more likely to go into law and the children of those in film and television are 12 times more likely to make it into these fields. The reasons for

Figure 1.4: The children of doctors become doctors (a lot!)

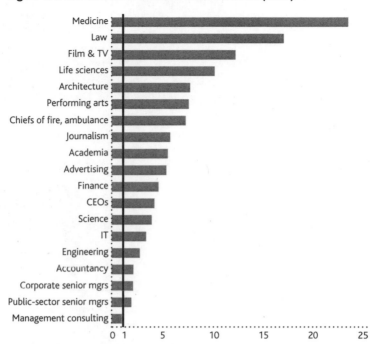

Note: Odds ratios for being in a given occupation (as opposed to any other), for people whose parents were in each occupation as compared with people whose parents were not in that occupation.
Source: LFS

this very specific form of reproduction are complex. But most research in this area tends to emphasise the ability of parents to pass on specific forms of knowledge and guidance about what is valued in their own profession (the 'rules of the game', as several interviewees in this book called it), as well as providing valuable professional contacts and even directly leveraging opportunities (through organising internships or entry-level jobs, for example) that then give their children a particular advantage.[15]

Explaining class reproduction: The role of education

How might we explain this profound demographic skew in access to top jobs? Well, one explanation favoured by many is that these inequalities can be explained by patterns of educational attainment. It is well established that those from

Figure 1.5: Class matters for who gets a degree

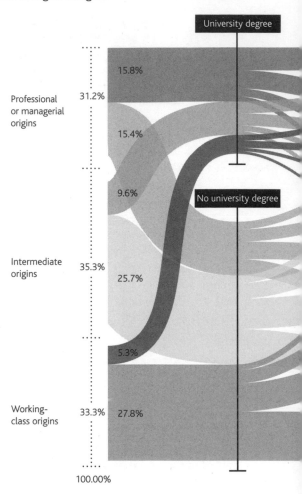

see colour version in plate section

University degree

15.8%

Professional
or managerial   31.2%
origins

15.4%

9.6%

No university degree

Intermediate   35.3%
origins

25.7%

5.3%

Working-   33.3%   27.8%
class origins

100.00%

working–class backgrounds perform less well in the education
system. The reasons for this are complex and have been explored
extensively elsewhere.[16] The important point for our purposes
is that, as educational credentials are key to accessing many elite
occupations, these inequalities in attainment may be important
in explaining unequal outcomes at the top of the labour market.
After all, access to many elite occupations, such as medicine,

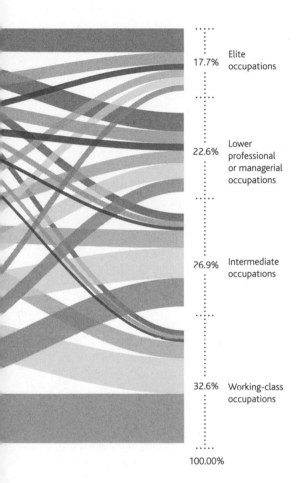

17.7%   Elite
        occupations

22.6%   Lower
        professional
        or managerial
        occupations

26.9%   Intermediate
        occupations

32.6%   Working-class
        occupations

100.00%

see colour version in plate section

law and architecture, is contingent on obtaining high levels of educational attainment.

Education is indeed an essential way that class advantages and disadvantages are reproduced. Figure 1.5, for example, shows that class still matters a great deal for whether or not one gets an undergraduate degree. While half of people from professional and managerial backgrounds have an undergraduate degree or more, less than 30% of those from intermediate origins, and only about one in every eight people from working-class origins, have first degrees. And as mentioned, because degrees are required or at least helpful for many top jobs, this strong association between class and education *is* part of the reason people tend to stay in in the same class position as their parents.

Yet this is only part of the story. At every level of education, those from professional and managerial backgrounds are still more likely to be found in top jobs than those from working-class backgrounds. Privileged-origin people without a degree are more than twice as likely to reach a top job than working-class people without a degree. Further, only 27% of working-class-origin people *with* a degree go into one of our top jobs, but 39% of similarly-educated professional-origin people do.

You might legitimately ask here, but isn't it more about *which* universities people attend? And the grades they get there? Perhaps those from privileged backgrounds simply go to more prestigious universities and do better when they get there. These are certainly important considerations.[17]

But again, this more 'meritocratic' story only takes us so far. Figure 1.6 is telling here. It shows that even when working-class-origin people attend top universities, and even when they receive the highest degree grades, they are *still* less likely than those from privileged origins (who do similarly well) to be found in top jobs. More specifically, within every degree class, at both highly prestigious and other kinds of universities, there is still a class gradient in who gets top jobs. For example, while nearly two-thirds (64%) of privileged-origin respondents who achieved first class degrees from Russell Group[18] universities progress to a top job, less than half (45%) of those from working-class origins with the exact same achievements do so. Put another way, this is even more striking. Figure 1.6 shows that among those who went to Russell Group universities, those from privileged backgrounds who only got a lower second class degree are still more likely to enter a top occupation than those from working-class backgrounds who come out of university with a first.

Even the most strident believers in Britain's meritocracy must surely balk at these findings. While they show that education does play an important role in explaining inequalities of access,

Figure 1.6: Even when working-class students outperform the privileged, they are less likely to get top jobs

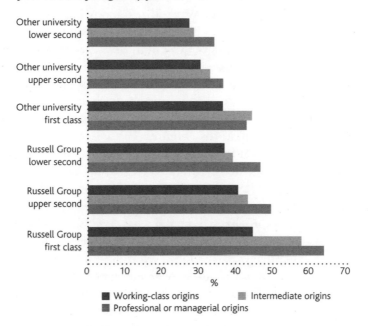

see colour version in plate section

Note: Percentage of people from each combination of university type, degree class and class origin who make it into our set of elite occupations.
Source: LFS

it certainly does not wash away the effects of class background. So despite the hopes and convictions of generations of politicians and policy-makers, educational attainment is not the 'great equaliser' in contemporary Britain.

Exclusions beyond class

Class is not the only mechanism through which people may be excluded from top jobs, of course. Traditionally, top jobs in the UK were the reserve of not just the privileged but a particular white, heterosexual, able-bodied, privileged man, often embodied in the figure of the 'gentleman'.[19] It is possible to see the residue of this in our results. Taking all our fields together, women, many groups of ethnic minorities and people with disabilities[20] are all significantly under-represented in top jobs. People with disabilities are nearly half (47%) as likely to be found in top jobs as in our population as whole, and women are 30% under-represented. While Black and Minority Ethnic (BME)[21] groups[22] are just as likely to be found in top jobs as in the whole workforce, grouping all non-white people together hides important variation – Black, Bangladeshi and Pakistani people, for example, are about 40% under-represented[23] in top jobs, and therefore we focus on those groups here.

Again, however, these inequalities vary significantly across different elite occupations. Figures 1.7 and 1.8 show the percentages of people in each of our top fields who are Black, Pakistani or Bangladeshi, members of other racial-ethnic minority groups (Figure 1.7) and women (Figure 1.8).[24]

Significantly, openness to people from working-class origins does not always go hand in hand with inclusion of other disadvantaged groups. While medicine and other life sciences (dentistry, pharmacy, psychology, veterinary) are among the most closed in class terms, these fields are markedly more open to women and to Black, Pakistani and Bangladeshi people than most other top occupations. Conversely, the top layers of the police, fire and ambulance services, and engineering, are all unusually open in terms of class, yet disproportionately white and male – especially engineering, where fewer than one in ten are women. Some fields, however, are exclusive all around – CEOs and film and television are on the low end of representation for working-class-origin people, and among the least diverse in terms of minority ethnic groups and women; remarkably, there is not a single Black, Pakistani or Bangladeshi person among the 216 CEOs in our dataset.[25]

Class, race and gender intersections

The results in Figures 1.7 and 1.8 are striking. But in many ways they represent a misleading, even unhelpful, portrait of workplace 'diversity'. This is because none of the inequalities associated with these demographic characteristics operate in isolation. For example, it may be that racial-ethnic inequalities in access to top jobs are partly driven by the fact that members of disadvantaged racial-ethnic groups are also more likely to

Figure 1.7: Many racial-ethnic groups are under-represented in many top fields

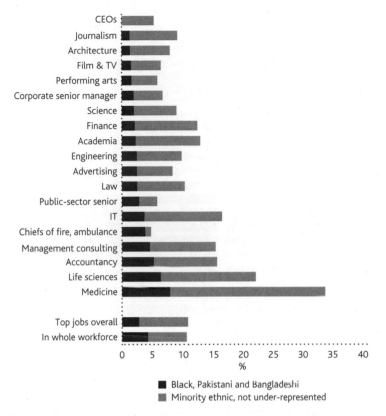

see colour version in plate section

Legend:
- ■ Black, Pakistani and Bangladeshi
- ■ Minority ethnic, not under-represented

Note: Percentage of people in each elite occupation who are members of under-represented racial-ethnic groups (Black, Pakistani or Bangladeshi) or other racialised groups that are not under-represented in UK elite occupations (people who are categorised as Chinese, other Asian, Indian, Mixed or Multiple races, or other racial groups).
Source: LFS

be from working-class backgrounds, and together this creates intersecting barriers or exclusions.[26]

Here we examine these intersections between class origin and other axes of inequality. Although women are as likely to be found across class-origin groups,[27] a person's racial-ethnic group and disability status has a more significant relationship with their class origin. The relationship with disability is rather straightforward – working-class-origin people are more likely to report having any kind of disability than privileged-origin

Figure 1.8: Women are also under-represented in most top jobs

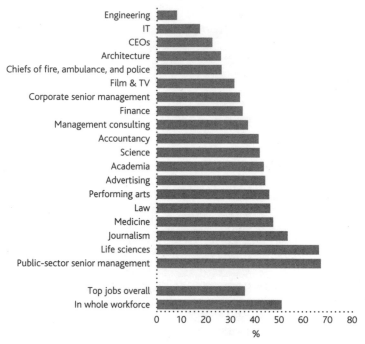

see colour version in plate section

Note: Percentage of people in each elite occupation who are women.
Source: LFS

people (18% vs 10% in the population as a whole; 9% vs 6% in the top jobs).

The picture is more complicated for ethnicity. People from Indian, Chinese, and Mixed, Multiple or Other racial–ethnic backgrounds are more likely to have had parents in professional or managerial occupations than white people in the UK, while Black, Pakistani and Bangladeshi people are far *less* likely than white people to have come from privileged origins. This makes it hard to tell how much the under–representation of these groups in top jobs is about race and ethnicity, class background or their combination.

Figure 1.9 gives the percentage of people from each combination of class and racial–ethnic background in top jobs. We can see a few important patterns here. First, within every ethnic group, people from privileged backgrounds are the

Figure 1.9: The privileged are more likely to get into top jobs in every racial-ethnic group

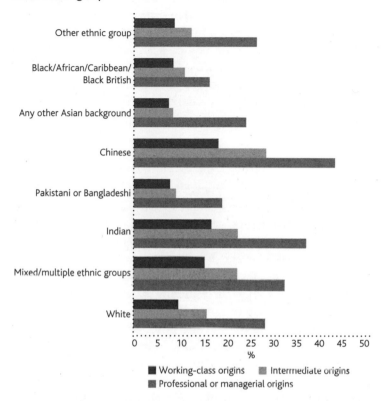

see colour version in plate section

Legend:
■ Working-class origins ■ Intermediate origins
■ Professional or managerial origins

Note: Percentage of people from each combination of racial-ethnic group and class origin who work in our elite occupations.
Source: LFS

most likely to be in top jobs, and people from working-class backgrounds are the least likely to make it into top jobs.

However, it is also possible to see the ways class and racial-ethnic disadvantage overlap and intersect. On the one hand, Indian and Chinese people from professional backgrounds are actually more likely than white British people from the same background to be found in top jobs (this is largely because they are more likely to have attended university than their white British peers from similar backgrounds; see the Methodological appendix, Figure A.3). In contrast, Black, Pakistani and Bangladeshi British people are less likely than white British people from the same class background to land in top jobs – while 10% of working-class white British people attain high-status jobs, only 5% of working-class Bangladeshi people do (despite attending university at much higher rates than white people).

Taken together we can see that class barriers exist across racial and ethnic groups, but operate differently for different groups. Black, Pakistani and Bangladeshi people in the UK are under-represented in top jobs even when we compare them to those from similar class origins and/or with similar levels of education.

From access to progression

In this chapter we have shown the extent of the skew in the make-up of Britain's top occupations. Specifically, our results demonstrate that people from working-class backgrounds, women, Black, Pakistani and Bangladeshi people, and those with disabilities are all substantially under-represented. Or, to put it another way, these jobs remain the bastion of the privileged.

Yet there is a danger of reducing social mobility to this one-dimensional issue of access. In particular it assumes that a person's trajectory finishes at the point of occupational entry. But the reality is that while many working-class people may secure admission into elite occupations, they do not necessarily go on to achieve the same levels of success as those from more privileged backgrounds. In the next chapter we therefore shift our focus from access to progression. Specifically, and drawing on the 'glass ceiling' concept so fruitfully developed by feminist scholars, we examine whether there is also a 'class ceiling' at play in the UK.

TWO

Getting on

The publication of the BBC annual report is normally a fairly sedate affair. A 200-page document covering all areas of the Corporation's governance and accounts, it's fair to say that it doesn't exactly make waves. But in 2017 things were very different. Dedicated to publishing the names of all staff earning over £150,000, the report uncovered for the first time a striking glass ceiling at 'The Beeb'. Specifically it showed that over two-thirds of high-earners were men, as well as all seven of the highest paid BBC executives. It also detailed stark gender pay gaps between stars of similar experience, fame and stature. Sports presenters Gary Lineker and Claire Balding provide an arresting example. Both are longstanding and much-loved BBC personalities, yet in 2017 Balding earned only one-tenth of Lineker's £1.75m salary.[1]

In the days following the report, countless prominent figures – both inside and outside the organisation – lined up to denounce a normalised culture of gender discrimination at the BBC.[2] The embattled BBC Director-General, Tony Hall, took swift action, authorising an immediate audit of staff pay,[3] promising to end the gender pay gap by 2020 and later agreeing to reduce the salaries of six highly paid male presenters.[4]

This scandal is significant for several reasons. First and foremost, it reveals the sheer scale of gender inequality at the upper echelons of British society. At the same time, however, it also shows the significant progress that has been made in elevating the gender pay gap to the top of the public agenda. After decades of campaigning and countless high-profile studies, pay gaps by gender (and, to a lesser extent, ethnicity) are now finally being meaningfully and pragmatically addressed. The response from Tony Hall, while not going as far as many wished, clearly reflected this shift. While in the past senior leaders may have tried to contest, or at least deflect, a scandal like this, Hall's response was fairly unequivocal – the BBC had a serious problem, he admitted, and action must be taken.

The BBC annual report was also significant in the context of this book. It detailed, for the first time, data on the class backgrounds of BBC staff. Yet curiously, this was almost entirely ignored by the media. Only one journalist, Sky's Lewis Goodall, picked up on the omission. Forty-five per cent of the BBC's top earners were privately educated, he calculated, compared to 7% in the UK as a whole.[5] This disparity showed that the BBC was actually less representative in terms of class than gender *or* ethnicity.

Our point here is not to somehow pitch these different types of disadvantage against one another. This is both counterproductive and belies the intersectional and overlapping nature of demographic pay gaps. But at the same time, this example illustrates a stark difference in the *relative scrutiny* placed on these different kinds of inequality. The gender pay gap now rightly reaches the very top of the news agenda. Yet when it comes to social class, there is a clear lack of parity. Political and policy attention, as we explored in the previous chapter, remains fixated on the issue of access. The implicit assumption here is that once we ensure a more diverse intake of people into elite occupations, the stratifying effect of class will evaporate. As far as we know, however, there is no evidence that supports this assertion. Indeed, as the BBC example illustrates, although people from working-class backgrounds may secure admission into prestigious fields, they do not necessarily enter with the same resources as individuals from more privileged backgrounds, and therefore may not necessarily achieve the same levels of success. In this chapter, we interrogate this question systematically for the first time.[6]

The class pay gap

In Chapter One we demonstrated that there is wide variation in the social openness of different high-status jobs. Here we extend this to look at how people from different class origins fare once *within* elite occupations. To understand this, we look at people's earnings. Earnings are clearly an important marker of success in their own right. They also often indicate other forms of success, such as how high someone has reached within their organisation, the status and prestige of the company they work for, and the value their employer places on them.

Our results are striking. They show that even when those from disadvantaged backgrounds 'get in', they struggle to 'get on'. More specifically, Figure 2.1 demonstrates that those in elite occupations from working-class origins earn on average £6,400 less a year than their colleagues from privileged backgrounds. There is, in other words, a significant 'class pay gap' in the contemporary UK; those from upper-middle-class origins earn 16% more than those from working-class backgrounds, even in the same set of jobs.[7]

These gaps are even larger if we look at class origin in more detail. Those from the most disadvantaged backgrounds, where neither parent was earning any income, earn on average over £10,000 less a year (in elite jobs) than those whose parents worked in higher managerial and professional jobs like medicine, law and engineering.[8] These pay gaps, we argue, point to a worrying and previously undetected form of class inequality within Britain's elite occupations.

We should say here that this is not just a problem in the UK. Working with colleagues in France and Australia, we have recently conducted follow-up comparative work looking at top occupations in both of these countries.[9] This has revealed that although the UK has the largest class pay gap, the same effect is also found in both France and Australia. In France, for example, the average earnings of those in top jobs from privileged backgrounds is almost 5,000 Euros or 14% higher than those from working-class backgrounds. In Australia the gap is much smaller, around 8%, but still statistically significant. Others' analyses have indicated similar patterns in the US, Sweden and Norway.[10]

Figure 2.1: The class pay gap

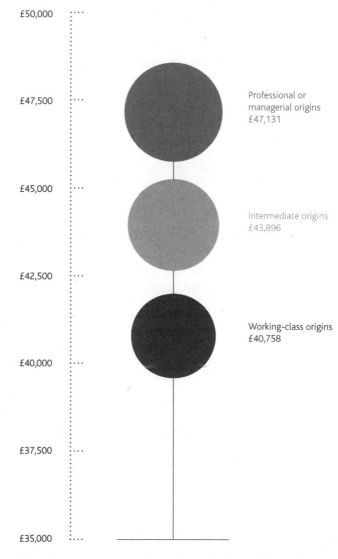

Note: Estimated average annual earnings for people in top jobs from each class-origin group.
Source: LFS

The scale of the class pay gap

One way to grasp the significance of this class pay gap is to compare it to other labour market inequalities. Figure 2.2 underlines that the class pay gap – at its most extreme, at least – is as large as or larger than the gender and racial-ethnic pay gaps. Men earn over £10,000 more than women on average in our elite occupations, and there are also significant pay gaps for certain ethnic groups such as Pakistani and Black British people.[11] People with disabilities in top jobs also earn about £4,000 less per year on average than non-disabled people.

We note that this is not to somehow suggest that class inequality is any more pressing than these other forms of inequality. Instead,

Figure 2.2: The gender, ethnicity and disability pay gaps in elite occupations

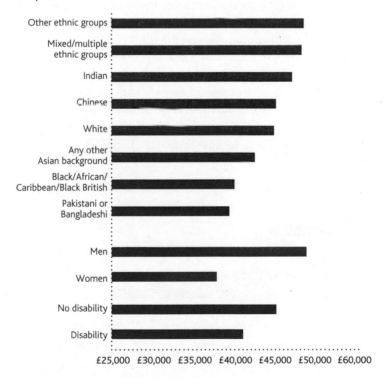

Note: Estimated average annual earnings for people in our top jobs, by racial-ethnic group, gender and disability status.
Source: LFS

the utility of placing the class pay gap in this comparative context is that it illustrates quite what a major gap currently exists in our understanding of workplace 'diversity', particularly considering the political attention and organisational resources devoted to tackling these other types of disadvantages.

Double jeopardy

Comparing the class pay gap to gender and racial-ethnic pay gaps, however, implies that these factors work in isolation from each other. Instead, as we explained in Chapter One, women and men, and people of all racial and ethnic groups, come from different class backgrounds. Individuals, in this way, are the sum of multiple, complex social characteristics that together constitute intersecting features of their identities. The important question, then, is how do *intersecting* forms of disadvantage or advantage play out in top jobs?

First, we look at gender. Figure 2.3 shows us that, overall, not only do women earn less than men, but *working-class women are at a double disadvantage* – they earn on average £7,500 less per year than privileged-origin women, who in turn earn £11,500 less than privileged-origin men. This means that the pay gap between the most advantaged men and the least advantaged women works out to a somewhat staggering 60%.

Figure 2.3: Socially mobile women face a double disadvantage in earnings

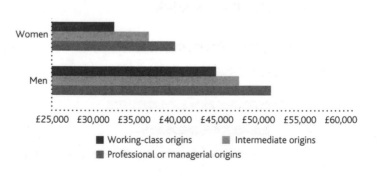

Note: Average estimated annual earnings for men and women from each class origin.
Source: LFS

What is particularly striking about this pay gap is that it is about £2,000 a year higher[12] than if we just added the class and gender pay gap together. This suggests that the penalties associated with being from a working-class background *and* being a woman are not just additive but can also be multiplicative.[13] In other words, disadvantages can *interact* to the detriment of people at certain demographic 'intersections'. This chimes strongly with an extensive body of qualitative research that has explored the ways in which upward mobility is often particularly difficult for women.[14] Not only does this work emphasise how women from working-class backgrounds are particularly marked as 'other' in British culture,[15] but as Steph Lawler has pointed out, their upward mobility often carries a particular jeopardy as the desire to 'escape' the working class, and assume a 'respectable' middle-class status and identity, has long been cast as an especially feminine envy – and accordingly pathologised as a signal of pretentiousness.[16]

Of course this does not mean that women from working-class backgrounds never earn as much as privileged-origin men, or that class and gender in and of themselves determine earnings. But it does imply a strong possibility that there are forms of discrimination or disadvantage that make it particularly hard for women from working-class backgrounds to progress in elite occupations.

We also see double disadvantages for individuals with a disability and for people from racial-ethnic minority groups who have experienced social mobility.[17] Focusing on ethnicity in Figure 2.4, a few things are worth pulling out. First, there are class pay gaps *within* each of our racial-ethnic groups. In fact, for those from working-class Chinese, Pakistani and Bangladeshi and Mixed/multiple backgrounds, the class pay gap within their ethnic group is actually much larger than that experienced by white people. Second, many people appear to be penalised both for their ethnicity and class background. Black British individuals from working-class backgrounds, for example, earn on average about £6,000 less than Black British colleagues from privileged backgrounds, and over £11,000 less than privileged-origin white people.[18]

Figure 2.4: Many socially mobile racial-ethnic minorities also face a double disadvantage

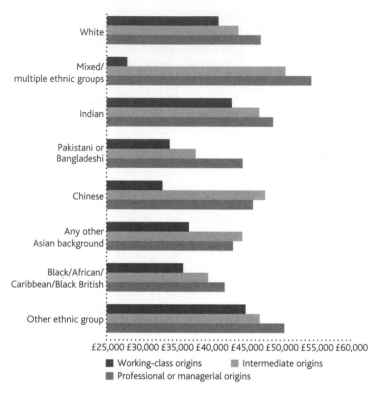

see colour version in plate section

Note: Average estimated annual earnings for each class-origin and racial-ethnic group.
Source: LFS

Many people, of course, are members of multiple disadvantaged groups, and we also find forms of *triple* disadvantage in elite occupations, particularly among working–class women of colour. Black British working-class women, for example, have average earnings in top jobs that are £20,000 less per year than those of privileged-origin white men.

Locating the class pay gap

We saw in the last chapter that *access* to elite occupations works very differently depending on one's field. Figure 2.5 reveals that there are similarly telling variations in the magnitude of the

Figure 2.5: The class pay gap is biggest in law, medicine and finance

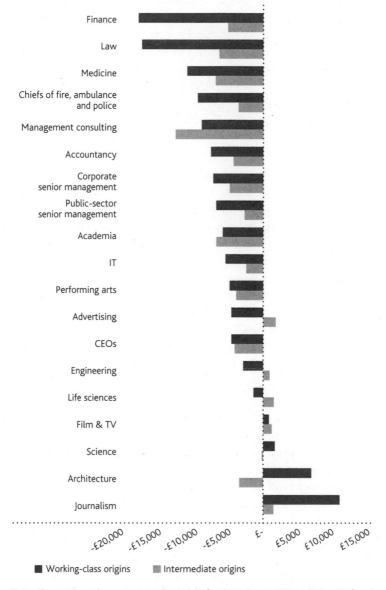

see colour version in plate section

■ Working-class origins ■ Intermediate origins

Note: Class pay gaps between upwardly mobile (working-class or intermediate origin) and professional-managerial-origin people in each of our 19 elite occupational groups. Average earnings differences are statistically significant at p<0.05 for one or both upwardly mobile groups in finance, law, medicine, chiefs of fire, ambulance and police, management consulting, accountancy, corporate senior management, public sector senior management, and IT.
Source: LFS

class pay gap. The biggest gaps are found in two areas. First, we can see that the traditional high-status professions of law and medicine are not only highly socially exclusive but also appear to tilt in favour of the privileged when it comes to progression. This is perhaps most concerning in medicine, where one might expect that the standardisation of training and pay across the National Health Service (NHS) would militate against this kind of earnings inequality.

Figure 2.5 also indicates that there are huge pay gaps in the elite business sector. In finance, for example, those from privileged backgrounds earn on average a massive £17,500 a year more than colleagues from working-class backgrounds.

Yet it is also worth noting that there are some top occupations where there is no sign of a class pay gap.[19] Engineering, for example, is both relatively open in terms of access *and* progression.

The differences outlined in Figure 2.5 also provide some context for the four occupations – accountancy, architecture, acting and television – that we choose to focus on in this book. While we discuss our motivations for selecting these case studies in more detail in both Chapter Four and the Methodological appendix, it is worth noting here that our choices were strongly informed by a basic desire to understand the patterns in Figure 2.5, that is, why class origin appears to matter more in some elite occupations than others. We can see that the class pay gap is very high in accountancy. We also see significant pay gaps in some performing arts occupations. While the numbers in any given portion of the performing arts are too small in the LFS to be broken down further, analysing the average household incomes of the large sample of actors (another of our case study occupations) contained within the BBC Great British Class Survey, a large web survey which ran from 2011 to 2013, reveals a huge class pay gap. Actors from professional or managerial backgrounds enjoy average annual (household) incomes between £7,000 and £21,000 higher than other actors.[20]

Yet the patterns in our other case studies are quite different. Architecture, for example, is exclusive in terms of access, but once 'in', the socially mobile do not appear to have problems progressing. Similarly, film and television, often portrayed as an exclusive arena, actually has a negligible class pay gap (at a national level at least).

We have demonstrated that across the UK's elite occupations those from working-class backgrounds experience a powerful class pay gap. Yet this presents a more pressing question – why? How might we explain the fact that even when working-class-origin people gain access to top jobs they are paid less than those from privileged origins? Is this a simple matter of class discrimination, or are there 'meritocratic' differences between people from different backgrounds that provide more legitimate reasons for their differences in pay? It is towards this black box of explanation that our enquiry now turns.

THREE

Untangling the class pay gap

'Does this control for IQ?' This was the question libertarian commentator Toby Young tweeted to us when the Social Mobility Commission (SMC) published the first part of our class pay gap research in 2017. It was a fairly predictable response. Young has written extensively about the relationship between cognitive ability and life outcomes, and has never disguised his view that IQ is both higher among the socially advantaged and tends to be passed between generations.[1] Reading between the lines, Young's tweet betrayed a certain scepticism about our findings so far. Yes, there may be a class pay gap, but this is probably driven by entirely legitimate differences in intelligence, he appeared to suggest. Young is not necessarily alone in this view.[2] The US political scientist Charles Murray has long made similar arguments about the association between IQ and race,[3] and more recently authored *Coming apart*, which blames the travails of the white working class in the US on their purported lower cognitive abilities. Back in the UK, former Foreign Secretary Boris Johnson has also drawn on these arguments, arguing that economic inequality is the 'inevitable' by-product of 'human beings who are already very far from equal in raw ability, if not spiritual worth'.[4]

These views may seem a little extreme. Certainly, empirical research connecting social mobility, intelligence and genetics is highly disputed.[5] But we start this chapter with such provocations to make a broader point. While the class pay gap uncovered in Chapter Two is striking, it is important not to jump to the conclusion that it is driven entirely by class prejudice and discrimination. In fact, many readers probably spent the last chapter generating their own explanations for the class pay gap; maybe working-class people are simply younger on average than those from privileged backgrounds and therefore less far along in their careers? Or perhaps the privileged have higher rates of educational attainment and are earning more based on superior credentials? Maybe they just work harder, or perform better at work?

This chapter offers a direct dialogue with such sceptical readers. While we may not be able to measure something like IQ – or indeed wish to[6] – it is not unreasonable to ask whether the class pay gap could be explained by other differences in what we often consider to be 'merit', such as educational attainment, job experience, level of training, or job performance. These are plausible mechanisms that deserve careful scrutiny. Similarly, however, there may also be less innocent or legitimate drivers of the class pay gap: perhaps people from privileged backgrounds are better able to relocate to take up lucrative job opportunities, or enjoy advantages in accessing the most prestigious types of occupations or the best-paying firms?

In this chapter we begin the task of untangling these potential drivers. Employing statistical techniques called regression analysis and decomposition,[7] we adjust or 'control' for four sets of factors. First, we examine the influence of demographic differences in ethnicity, gender, age, disability status and national origin. Second, we look at the effects of educational attainment. Third, we group together a number of other drivers that might be considered 'meritocratic': the amount of hours worked, and level of experience and training. Finally, we move away from 'merit' to examine the more troubling ways that class origin may shape important career decisions such as where in the country to work, in what sort of occupation and in what sort of firm.

This chapter will show how some differences between those from privileged origins and those from intermediate and working-class origins 'explain' some of the class-origin pay gap we saw in the last chapter. That is, when we take those differences, and their effects on pay, into account, the class-origin pay gap that is left is smaller. Crucially, however, even after taking into account every plausible measure available in the Labour Force Survey (LFS), there is still a substantial gap in earnings by class background.

Aren't the privileged just older, whiter and more male?

The first set of differences we look at are demographic. As mentioned before, one fairly innocent explanation for the class pay gap may be that the privileged are simply older on average. This would certainly accord with the prevailing policy narrative surrounding the UK's high-status professions. These fields are often cast as both historically elitist arenas but also as slowly and consciously opening up over time.[8] We can see from our data that people in our elite occupations tend to earn more the older they are (an average of £414 more for each extra year of their working lives). If privileged-origin people in top jobs are indeed older than working-class-origin people, their higher earnings could simply be based on their superior level of experience. However, our data contradicts this narrative. We find that people from working-class origins in top jobs are actually older, on average, than privileged-origin people in top jobs – about four years older, to be precise.[9]

This is not because people from working-class backgrounds somehow live longer (we are only looking at people aged 23–69 here). Instead, it is more likely the result of changes in the structure of the British workforce over time. The number of working-class jobs has been steadily declining since the beginning of the 20th century, while 'room at the top' (the number of jobs in the professions and management) has expanded substantially.[10] This means that if you were born 50 years ago, there's a much greater chance your parents had working-class jobs than if you were born 25 years ago.

We can also take into account other important demographic attributes. For example, is the class pay gap being driven by the fact that those from privileged backgrounds in top jobs are also more likely to be white English men? We noted in the last chapter that inequalities of ability, gender, and race and ethnicity often intersect and overlap with those based on class origin. Specifically we revealed the distinct double and triple disadvantages in earnings faced by women, people with disabilities, and people from certain racial-ethnic groups from working-class backgrounds. We can also look at where in the world people were born: whether they are immigrants to the UK, or born in England, Wales, Scotland or Northern Ireland.[11]

In Figure 3.1, we show how the size of the pay gap is affected when we take into account demographic factors. Essentially, we are showing what the pay gap would be if working-class and privileged-origin people were equally likely to be white, from England, the same age, and so on. Strikingly, we see that the class pay gap actually increases substantially. Working-class origin people who are otherwise similar to privileged-origin people in terms of their gender, racial-ethnic group, age, and country of birth earn on average about £8,300 less each year than their privileged-origin colleagues.

This increase is driven in large part by the relationship between age and class origin, which is somewhat hidden in our initial reporting of the class pay gap. Without controlling for age, in other words, the relative earnings of those from working-class backgrounds in top jobs look higher than they should, because we aren't taking into account their greater average age, and thus the fact that they have had more time to accrue experience and earnings. Put another way, when we compare people who are the same age, we see a much larger class pay gap.

Figure 3.1: The class pay gap is even larger after accounting for demographics

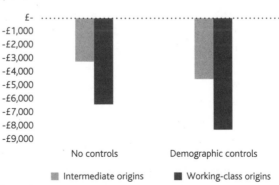

Note: Predicted class pay gaps between upwardly mobile and professional-managerial-origin people, with no controls, and in a regression model with controls for demographics – racial-ethnic group, country of birth, age, gender and disability status. Both class-origin pay gaps are statistically significant at $p<0.05$.
Source: LFS

see colour version in plate section

Is education really the 'great equaliser'?

Demographic differences, then, definitively do *not* explain the class pay gap. But what about differences in 'merit' or what Boris Johnson might call 'raw ability'? For many, particularly on the right and centre of British politics, this is the go-to mechanism when confronted with this type of inequality. Those campaigning to end the gender pay gap, for example, have spent decades working to dispel myths that women perform less well, are less ambitious, or less well-qualified.[12] Tellingly, most people in positions of power who we interviewed for this book also instinctively reached for meritocratic explanations when asked about the class pay gap. Of course it's easy to see why such explanations are popular. They provide legitimacy for both the status quo and for one's own career progression. In this way, class inequality can be cast as the unfortunate but ultimately fair result of highly competitive labour markets.

Perhaps the most widely used and widely agreed notion of 'merit' is educational attainment. Education has long been fetishised as the 'great equaliser', the most powerful institutional means of ironing out inequalities rooted in class origin.[13] In this view, a key function of the educational system, and the bestowing of educational credentials, is to sort people into different tracks within the labour market according to their perceived intelligence, ability or even IQ. And to some extent, education *has* had this effect. A classic US study carried out in the 1980s by the sociologist Mike Hout,[14] for example, found that the dogged association between class background and occupational success was almost completely eliminated once people obtained undergraduate degrees. Higher education, on this reading, serves to combat class-based inequities (albeit only for those able to enter university in the first place). Following this hypothesis, we next explore whether the class pay gap is neutralised when education is taken into account.

As outlined in the previous chapter, those from disadvantaged backgrounds who enter top jobs tend to have significantly lower levels of educational attainment than their privileged peers. There is also a large earnings premium for having a higher level of education; people in top jobs without a university degree, regardless of background, earn on average £9,350 less than those with a university degree or higher. Connecting these findings together, then, it is pretty clear that class differences in rates of educational attainment play an important role in driving the class pay gap.

However, when we look at the relationship between class origin, education, and earnings, there is one important additional thing to note. At every educational level there is still an earnings gradient by class origin. Put another way, even when people from working-class origins have the same level of education as their advantaged colleagues, they still earn significantly less.[15] This is important. It demonstrates that educational attainment, and even higher educational attainment, is not the great equaliser; a significant class pay gap persists even for those from working-class backgrounds who achieve the very highest educational credentials.

We can also examine more detailed measures of educational 'merit'. For example, it is often suggested that 'getting on' in top occupations is less about educational level (having an undergraduate degree is de rigueur in most professions) and more about the perceived 'quality' of one's university type, and one's academic record once there.[16] While nearly half of those from professional or managerial backgrounds attended the highly selective Russell Group universities,[17] only a little over a quarter of those from working-class backgrounds did so. This is important because attending such universities comes with a significant earnings premium – about £4,000 a year (and more like £7,000 for those who attend Oxford or Cambridge). Again it is possible to argue that this represents a further 'meritocratic' driver of the pay gap; the privileged are more likely to obtain the credentials needed to attend more prestigious universities, and therefore their higher average pay reflects their greater ability or talent.

Yet again, however, our results simultaneously confirm and puncture this assumption. Figure 3.2 demonstrates that even when those from disadvantaged backgrounds do get into Britain's most hallowed universities, they do not receive the same earnings premium as those from privileged backgrounds.[18] For example, among Oxbridge graduates, those from privileged backgrounds earn around £5,000 a year more than graduates from less advantaged origins. This echoes recent work showing that Oxbridge graduates from top private schools are twice as likely

Figure 3.2: Those from working-class backgrounds earn less even when they go to top universities

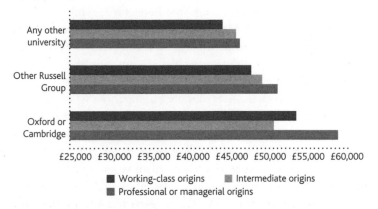

£25,000 £30,000 £35,000 £40,000 £45,000 £50,000 £55,000 £60,000

■ Working-class origins   ■ Intermediate origins
■ Professional or managerial origins

see colour version in plate section

Note: Average estimated annual earnings for each combination of class origin and university type, for people in our elite occupations.
Source: LFS

as those from any other school to reach the most elite positions in British society.[19] Both findings illustrate the distinct cumulative advantages that flow from following particular elite pathways. Elite universities, in other words, are not monolithic, and individuals entering from specific origins (in terms of class privilege and elite schooling) are clearly better able to capitalise on opportunities once inside. One has only to think about the enduring connection between elite backgrounds, elite schools and key Oxbridge clubs such as the Footlights, the Cambridge Apostles and the Bullingdon Club to see such elite channels in action.[20]

These findings also arguably represent another stark rejoinder to the 'great equaliser' thesis. Even educational institutions like Oxford and Cambridge, heralded as the ultimate meritocratic sorting houses, do not necessarily wash away the advantages of class background. In fact, in many cases, they accentuate and inflate them.

But we can even go further than this. We also have data showing how well respondents did in their undergraduate degree; this is called their degree classification, and is similar to a grade point average (GPA) in the US. As a measure of academic achievement, this is arguably an even more fine-grained measure of ability or 'merit'. People with higher degree classifications also earn more – about £2,000 more a year for a first as compared with a lower second class degree.

But two important things emerge here. First, while working-class people are less likely to get degrees, and less likely to attend the most prestigious universities, there is essentially no difference in how well they do at university. Yet, despite this, there is a very important difference in their ability to convert their academic achievement into earnings. Strikingly, among those who obtain the very highest classification – a hallowed first class degree – it is the privileged who tend to benefit more – earning on average £7,000 per year more than those with firsts who are socially mobile.[21]

Each of these factors – that those from working-class origins are less likely to have degrees, less likely to have gone to prestigious universities, and tend to earn less even when they have gone to the top universities and got the highest grades – are clearly sociologically telling in and of themselves. However, our main aim in this chapter is to formally assess their importance in explaining the class pay gap.

In Figure 3.3 we add all of these educational controls[22] together, and we can see that the class pay gap is reduced by a little less than half.[23] This is certainly a significant reduction. However, it also reveals a telling persistence; our model predicts

Figure 3.3: Differences in educational attainment account for about half the class pay gap

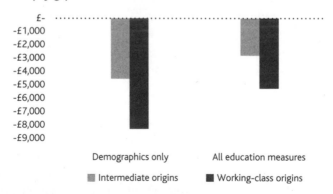

Demographics only   All education measures

■ Intermediate origins   ■ Working-class origins

Note: Predicted class pay gaps between upwardly mobile and professional-managerial origin people, with only demographic controls, and in a regression model with controls for demographics and educational attainment: highest degree attained, and for those who attained a BA or more, degree class and university attended. All class-origin pay gaps are statistically significant at p<0.05.
Source: LFS

that those from working-class backgrounds who have similar levels of educational attainment in every way we can measure to those from privileged origins still earn substantially less.

But what about hard work, skill and experience?

Of course there are other indicators of 'merit' or productive capacity beyond educational attainment. Here we look at three indicators that we can tap using the LFS: hard work or effort (measured in terms of hours worked per week); skill (in terms of level of job-related training); and experience (in terms of years in current job, and the existence of any past health problems that might have kept someone out of the workforce). All these dimensions of 'merit' are associated with higher pay.[24] Significantly, however, we find that none of these factors vary substantially by class origin. Those from privileged origins work half an hour more a week and are marginally more likely to have had recent training but are slightly less experienced. In other words, and as Figure 3.4 shows, many conventional markers of 'merit' do essentially nothing to explain the class pay gap.

Figure 3.4: Other measures of 'merit' do little to account for the class pay gap

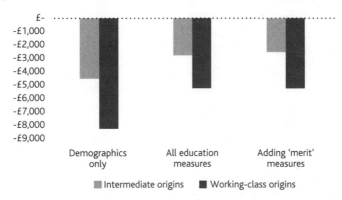

Note: Predicted class pay gaps between upwardly mobile and professional-managerial origin people, with only demographic controls, in a model with controls for demographics and educational attainment, and in a model that includes demographics, education and other measures of 'merit': hours worked, years at current job, recent training and past health problems (as an indicator of possible time out of the workforce). All class pay gaps are still statistically significant at p<0.05.
Source: LFS

The (reverse) Dick Whittington effect

So far we have shown that the class pay gap is not adequately explained by either the demographic make-up of people in top jobs or by a series of 'meritocratic' measures. In many ways these factors might be seen as ways of justifying or explaining away the pay gap, either via 'legitimate', 'fair' or 'natural' processes, or through more powerful inequalities of gender or ethnicity. We now need to shift our lens to start thinking about how class origin more directly shapes people's career trajectories. In this section we are particularly interested in examining the process of what sociologists call 'occupational sorting', that is, how a person's background affects where *specifically* they end up in the labour market. For example, what part of the country they work in, what particular occupation they take up, and what type of firm (in terms of size, industry, public vs private etc). These sorting effects are not necessarily 'innocent'; they are not always the result of an unconstrained and intentional 'choice' on the part of the individual. Instead, class origin, and the resources that flow from it, can be very important in shaping the courses of action available to people.

First, we look at where people work – their geographical region. This is because one of the biggest determinants of income in top jobs is simply where in the UK someone lives and works. Those working in elite occupations in Central London, for example, earn on average £16,000 or 36% more than the average elsewhere in the UK.

There are also big differences in the social composition of different regions, particularly in terms of class origin. Again, London stands out. Those working in the Capital's top jobs are disproportionately likely to come from privileged backgrounds.[25] This is driven in large part by patterns of domestic migration: 56% of domestic migrants to London are from professional or managerial backgrounds (compared to 36% on average across Britain).[26] These findings indicate that a key driver of the class pay gap is a geographical sorting effect, or what we might even term a 'reverse Dick Whittington effect'. Thus, rather than the poor flocking to the Big City to seek their fortune, like the protagonist in the famous 14th-century tale, it is actually those from privileged backgrounds who are much more likely, and able, to move and take advantage of the Capital's lucrative job opportunities. In this way, Figure 3.5 shows that the region in which people work explains about 23% of the pay gap.

Figure 3.5: Regional differences in pay also contribute to the class pay gap

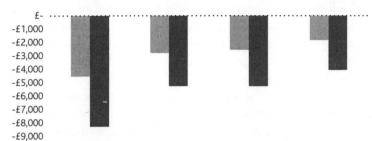

Note: Predicted class pay gaps between upwardly mobile and professional-managerial origin people, with only demographic controls, in a model with controls for demographics and educational attainment, in a model that includes demographics, education and other measures of 'merit', and in a model that includes all that plus which region of the UK respondents work in. All class pay gaps are still statistically significant at p<0.05.
Source: LFS

Finding a fit: Occupational sorting

But people do not just sort into different locations; they also work in different occupations, firms, sectors and industries. We address each of these sorting effects in turn.

First, as we have shown in the last two chapters, the class composition of different elite occupations varies enormously. While areas like medicine, law and finance are dominated by the privileged, other areas like engineering and IT are more socially open. Significantly, these patterns also map onto rates of pay with salaries in the more exclusive of our 19 elite occupations generally higher. For example, the average salary of doctors in our sample is £55,000, compared to £42,000 among engineers.

Second, people work in firms that vary significantly in size. This is important because generally speaking, in most fields, bigger companies tend to be more prestigious and more selective in whom they hire. They also pay better – on average those in top jobs in big firms (over 500 employees) earn £14,000 more per year than those in the smallest firms (with less than 25 employees). And significantly, working-class–origin people are under-represented in the biggest firms and over-represented in the smallest ones.

Finally, people also often make quite explicit and politically informed decisions to work in either the private or public *sector*. This has obvious ramifications in terms of pay as the private sector generally offers much higher salaries. Another potential driver of the class pay gap, then, may be that those from working-class origins tend to sort into top jobs located in the public sector rather than the private sector. It turns out, however, that the inverse is true; those from privileged origins are actually slightly over-represented within the public sector and those from working-class origins slightly overrepresented within the private sector.[27]

Figure 3.6: The privileged also sort into higher-paying occupations and bigger firms

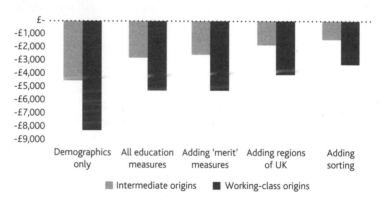

see colour version in plate section

Note: Predicted class pay gaps between upwardly mobile and professional-managerial origin people, with only demographic controls, in a model with controls for demographics and educational attainment, in a model that includes demographics, education and other measures of 'merit', in a model that includes all that plus region, and finally, in a model that includes all the preceding controls, plus the specific occupation the respondent worked in, the NS-SEC category for their job, whether they were in the public or private sector and the industry they work in. In this final model, the class-origin pay gap between those from intermediate class origins and those from professional-managerial origins is only statistically significant at the p<0.01 level, but the gap between working class/professional-managerial is still significant at p<0.05.
Source: LFS

These sorting effects have an important bearing on the class pay gap. As Figure 3.6 shows, when we add controls for the firm size, industry, sector, and specific elite occupation[28] a person works in, the difference in earnings shrinks further. Specifically, the specific elite occupation a person works in explains 18% of the class pay gap, and the size of their firm a further 9%.

Explaining the unexplained

These analyses reveal three key drivers of the class pay gap. First, those from privileged backgrounds have higher and more prestigious educational credentials; second, they are more likely to live in London and/or move to London for work; and third, they tend to sort into certain occupations and larger firms. Crucially, all of these factors are associated with higher pay.

Taken together, the drivers examined in this chapter, depicted in Figure 3.7, explain 47% of the class pay gap.[29] In this way, they provide invaluable insights into how class-origin structures career trajectories in Britain's elite occupations.[30] But at the same time, they also leave over half of the difference unexplained. To some extent this may reflect limitations in our data – there are no questions about private education or the region respondents were born in, for example, both of which are likely to be associated with class background *and* earnings. But there are also many features of work that large-scale survey research simply cannot capture – the internal hierarchies and divisions within firms, the culture inside workplaces and people's lived experiences of career progression. In pushing further to explain the 'unexplained', then, we need to change tack and actually enter the field, go inside elite workplaces and examine the working lives of those who work within them.

In the next chapter we start this process. Specifically, we introduce our case studies – a national television broadcaster, a large multinational accountancy firm, an architecture practice and a set of self-employed actors. In each case we began our fieldwork by collecting and analysing data on the social make-up of the firm (or occupation). This, as we go on to explore, was highly revealing. In particular it indicates that in many elite settings the class pay gap is less an issue of equal pay for equal work and more about the *horizontal* segregation of the socially mobile into less prestigious departments or functions, and/or their *vertical* segregation into lower tiers or positions.

Figure 3.7: The drivers of the class pay gap – what advantages the privileged?

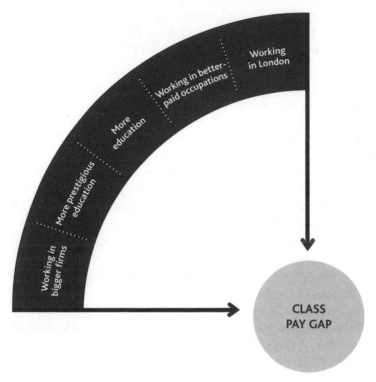

FOUR

Inside elite firms

"Hear that?" asks Dave, a senior manager at 6TV, as he leads us through the offices of the television broadcaster, on the way to our interview room. The layout of each department, we observe as we walk, is exactly the same. There is no spatial demarcation of grade or seniority, and the desks are arranged open-plan around a line of brightly coloured 'break-out' rooms in the centre of each floor. This gives both the impression of inclusivity and also, as we've just put it to Dave, means that it must be quite hard to remember which department you are in. He smiles knowingly. "Hear that?" he repeats, this time cupping his hand over his ear to listen on the third floor: "You just have to listen to know which floor you're in. You can tell by the accents. Posh, right? Yep, this is Commissioning."

So far in this book we have shown that those from privileged backgrounds not only enter organisations like 6TV at disproportionately high rates, but they also tend to earn significantly more once they get there. More worryingly, and as we explored in the previous chapter, this class pay gap persists even when we take into account an extensive battery of 'meritocratic' factors.

Yet a pay gap like this can imply two quite different issues. It might mean, for example, that those from working-class backgrounds are getting *paid less for doing the same work* (that is, for doing jobs at the same level, same company and same department).[1] Equally, however, it may also reflect the kind of workplace *segregation* implied by Dave's comment – that is, those from working-class backgrounds may be paid less on average because they are less likely to enter the most prestigious (and high-paying) departments, like Commissioning at 6TV. Moreover, and perhaps even more significantly, this segregation may also be *vertical*; it may be that even when those from a working-class background enter the most prestigious areas within the most prestigious firms, they still struggle to reach the top.

Adjudicating between these accounts means going beyond national survey data. Much as a large data set such as the Labour Force Survey (LFS) represents a powerful analytical tool, it also has important limitations. In particular, it lacks the granularity necessary to see such patterns of segregation *within* firms. To capture these dimensions, we argue in this chapter that we need to actually go behind the closed doors of elite firms and see how career progression operates in everyday life. In the remainder of the book we do exactly this. We draw on case studies of three (anonymised) organisations – a national television broadcaster, 6TV; a large multinational accounting firm, Turner Clarke; and an architecture practice, Coopers[2] – as well as an examination of self-employed actors.

We would not claim that these are necessarily representative of *all* elite occupations and *all* elite organisations (we discuss the strengths and limitations of our case selection extensively in the Methodological appendix). Here we simply emphasise that selection was motivated, above all, by the aim of making sense of the results outlined earlier in Chapters Two and Three. The class pay gap, as we have shown, is very high in accountancy and acting. Yet in architecture and film and television we found no evidence of a pay gap. In this way, our choices reflected a desire to explore the dynamics that both facilitate and hinder the development of class pay gaps.

In this chapter we introduce our case studies. Understanding the nature of these organisations – what they look like, their structure, their demographic make-up – is key for contextualising the chapters that follow.

These organisational x-rays are also highly revealing in their own right. They demonstrate that when it comes to the class pay gap, by far the most powerful issue is not equal pay for equal work. Instead, we find that the socially mobile very often face a *class ceiling* – they are less likely to enter the most high-paying departments and, even more significantly, rarely reach the top of the organisational structure.

6TV

6TV does not wear its visual identity lightly. Occupying a corner plot in an otherwise quiet and unassuming district of North London, its large purpose-built headquarters jut out loudly, dominating the surrounding built environment. The building itself, clad in powder-grey aluminium and glass, is an outlandish, futuristic creation. Arranged in a distinct L-shape, it addresses the corner of the street with a curved connecting space framed by two 'satellite towers'. In the middle is the entrance, the most dramatic aspect of the design. A stepped ramp leads from the street over a glass bridge towards a dramatic concave glazed wall. Here visitors are ushered into a loud, noisy, always-busy reception area.

This, in other words, is not your average office block – the abstraction and singularity of the design functions as an immediate visual signal. Visitors are reminded of both the intentions of the brand – edgy, confident, cool – but also, crucially, its *eliteness*. 6TV is one of the country's main television broadcasters. It is one of a number of 'publisher-broadcasters', meaning it commissions television programmes that are then produced by independent production companies ('indies'). This means that the channel's reach extends far beyond its own core workforce, commissioning several hundred indies ever year.

The channel is one of the five biggest producers of television content in the UK, broadcasting across multiple platforms and reaching millions of viewers each day. In the reception area multiple huge screens remind you of this, showcasing live outputs from across the channel's multiple platforms.

Most of the channel's approximately 1,000[3] staff are situated in the London headquarters (only 5% work outside the capital). 6TV compares favourably to the wider film and television industries in two areas of workplace diversity – gender and ethnicity. The channel contains twice the national average of Black and Minority Ethnic staff, and women form the clear *majority* of employees.[4]

This pattern is reversed, however, when it comes to class background. Figure 4.1 shows that the channel is significantly more socially exclusive than the wider industry. A clear majority of 6TV staff (67%) come from privileged backgrounds and less than one in ten (9%) were brought up in working–class households. To place this in comparative context, it is also possible to benchmark 6TV with two other sources – one of its main competitors, the BBC, and the independent television production sector (made up of what are colloquially called 'indies'), from which the channel commissions most of the TV programmes it broadcasts.[5] 6TV is significantly more socially exclusive than the BBC. More than twice as many BBC staff are from working–class backgrounds (27%), and significantly less (61%) are from professional and managerial backgrounds. Yet its make–up is very similar to the 'indie' sector, where 65% are from upper middle-class backgrounds.

6TV personnel are employed across six main departments that each occupy one floor of the building: Commissioning; Marketing and Communications; Legal and Commercial; Sales, Digital and Trading; Technical and Strategy; and HR, Finance and Estates.[6] The departments vary in size (from 75 to 150 employees), but as we described above, at first they all look roughly the same. However, we quickly learned that the office environment is not quite as egalitarian as it appears.

Figure 4.1: 6TV is much more socially exclusive than film and television nationally

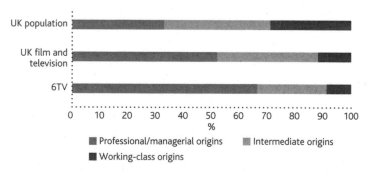

Note: Percentage of people in the UK labour force and in UK film and television, and at 6TV from each class background.
Source for first two groups: LFS; Source for 6TV: Survey of 6TV

Commissioning, with the 'posh' accents Dave mentioned, is by far the most prestigious and powerful department. It contains the most staff and also holds by far the largest share of top positions – more than a quarter of the 40 executives and heads of department are in Commissioning. The power is partly a reflection of the channel's remit as a 'publisher–broadcaster'. This means that Commissioners are both responsible for the creative direction of the channel and also, through the television projects they commission, the employment of a large portion of those working in the indie sector.

Significantly, as Dave indicated, Commissioning is also by far the most socially exclusive department. As Figure 4.2 illustrates, 79% of staff working here are from professional and managerial backgrounds versus 54% in HR, Finance and Estates. Similarly, only 7% of Commissioning staff are from working-class backgrounds, compared to 22% in HR, Finance and Estates.

Despite the spatial illusion of equality, the channel is also fairly hierarchical. Staff are structured according to six pay grades, from 'Assistant'[7] to 'Executive/Head of Department' (HoD). While the average pay of Assistants is around £20,000 a year, Channel Executives earn over £100,000 a year. Looking at

Figure 4.2: Commissioning is the 'poshest' department at 6TV

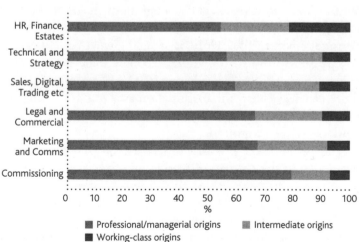

Note: Percentage of people in each 6TV department from each class background.
Source: Survey of 6TV

Figure 4.3: The class ceiling at 6TV

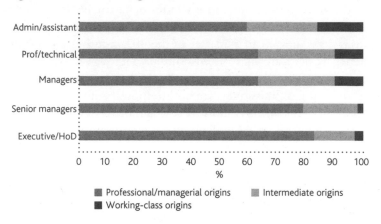

Note: Percentage of people in each level at 6TV from each class background.
Source: Survey of 6TV

the social composition of these different grades in Figure 4.3, a very striking class ceiling emerges. Those from intermediate and particularly working-class backgrounds tend to be found in lower and middle management, and only 2.5% of those in these top positions are from working-class backgrounds.

In contrast, the privileged dominate the upper echelons. While those from privileged backgrounds make up 63% of managers, at the level above – Senior Managers – this jumps considerably to 79%. Here it is again worth making the comparison to the BBC, where strikingly there is no ceiling effect. The backgrounds of senior BBC staff are only partially more privileged than the organisation as a whole – with 63% from professional and managerial backgrounds and 23% from working-class backgrounds.

Progression at 6TV works differently in each department but, much to the chagrin of many junior staff we spoke to, it is fairly rare to progress through the ranks. Instead, senior staff tend to be hired externally, having gained experience, and demonstrated expertise, elsewhere. This is particularly striking in Commissioning. Junior and senior 6TV Commissioners are normally recruited from indies or other broadcasters, and are typically Executive Producers, Series Producers, Creative

Directors, or Heads of Development with long and prominent track records (see Chapter Six for more on this). Connected to this, 6TV's class ceiling can be linked to its departmental segregation. *Startlingly, 90% of Senior Commissioners are from upper-middle-class backgrounds and none are from working-class backgrounds.*

In sum, it is clear that those from privileged backgrounds are considerably over-represented at 6TV. There is also a very clear class-ceiling effect within the organisation, with those from working-class backgrounds rarely making it to senior management positions. Significantly, this ceiling is particularly acute at the upper echelons of Commissioning, the department responsible for shaping the programmes the channel produces.[8]

Turner Clarke

Elite spaces come in very different shapes and sizes. If 6TV signals its prestige with architectural flair and abstraction, our second case study – multinational accountancy firm Turner Clarke (TC) – does so in a markedly more restrained manner. There are no screens, or even colour, as you enter the firm's rather austere London office. Instead it is remarkably quiet. Receptionists talk in hushed tones, and staff – all in formal business attire – pass in and out looking busy and serious. The aesthetic is clean and sparse. There is an abundance of open, uncluttered space. Yet there are also important signals of eliteness – on arrival, rather than being escorted upstairs to a meeting room, we are ushered into an informal, semi-hidden reception space full of comfortable furniture (yet in our experience always deserted), where a dedicated host offers guests an apparently limitless array of free drinks and snacks.

TC is one of the biggest accountancy firms in the world, employing tens of thousands of people across 130 countries. It has a turnover of several billion pounds a year. We focus here on its UK operation, which has several thousand employees.[9] The firm has offices throughout the country, but like many large accountancy firms its senior workforce is disproportionately located in Central London – 40% are based in the various London offices. Its staff are 16% Black and minority ethnic, and 48% are women – both marginally higher than the national average for accountancy.

At TC we use type of secondary schooling as a proxy for class background.[10] Although this is not as precise as parental occupation, it is highly correlated with class background.[11] Figure 4.4 distinguishes three main types of schooling: independent or private, selective state, and state comprehensive. Nearly 21% of TC employees were privately educated, a very significant over-representation compared to 7% in the UK population as a whole. It is also worth comparing this figure to KPMG, another very large accountancy firm and a competitor to TC in terms of size and prestige. Here TC compares somewhat favourably, with a slightly higher proportion of KPMG staff (23%) privately educated.[12]

Work at TC is organised into three distinct service lines: Tax, Audit and Advisory (as well as a smaller 'Support' department that incorporates Estates, IT, Admin, and so on). Those working in Audit and Tax provide material services for clients, and normally rely on significant technical expertise: auditors forensically assess a company's accounts to determine whether they are a true and fair representation of their financial affairs, and those working in Tax assist companies in the completion of complex tax returns and on national and international tax law. In contrast, Advisory contracts require TC employees to give advice rather than perform material client work.[13]

Figure 4.4: The privately educated are highly over-represented at Turner Clarke

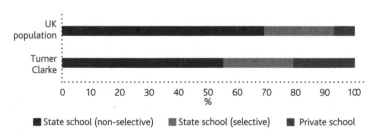

Note: Percentage of people in the UK population, and at Turner Clarke, who attended each type of school.
Source: For UK population: Department of Education; Source for Turner Clarke: Internal data from Turner Clarke

Advisory is the most prestigious and highly remunerated area of the business, and contains a higher share of staff in senior positions (37% of Partners and 44% of Directors are located in Advisory). Significantly, as Figure 4.5 shows, it is also more exclusive than the other service lines: 28% of those in Advisory are privately educated, whereas the figure within the other three lines is between 16% and 20%.

Like 6TV, there is no spatial demarcation of grade or seniority inside the TC office. Traditionally, as Audit Partner Cathy tells us, the division of space within the office – and in accountancy firms more generally – was strongly elitist. "Making Partner," she notes, also meant getting your own office, with lots of attendant politics about who got what office, on what floor, and with how many windows. "Now," she says, "things are very different; everyone hot desks and no one – even Partners – has a fixed workspace."

But again, this egalitarian organisation of space masks a very hierarchical career structure. Progression is arranged according to eight grades, from Trainee 'Associate' (approximately £25,000 a year) all the way up to 'Partner' (from £150,000-£500,000 a year). Progression through the first three or four levels is generally straightforward and largely based on accumulating the requisite experience and training.[14] Progressing through middle management and up to Partner level, in contrast, is much more competitive and uncertain. Only a select few will experience this trajectory – 3-4%, according to Senior Partner, Colin.[15]

Figure 4.5: Advisory is the most exclusive area of Turner Clarke

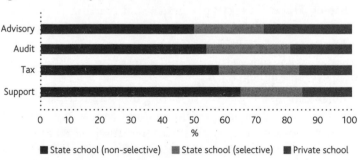

Note: Percentage of people at Turner Clarke in each department who attended each type of school.
Source: Internal data from Turner Clarke

Figure 4.6: The class ceiling at Turner Clarke

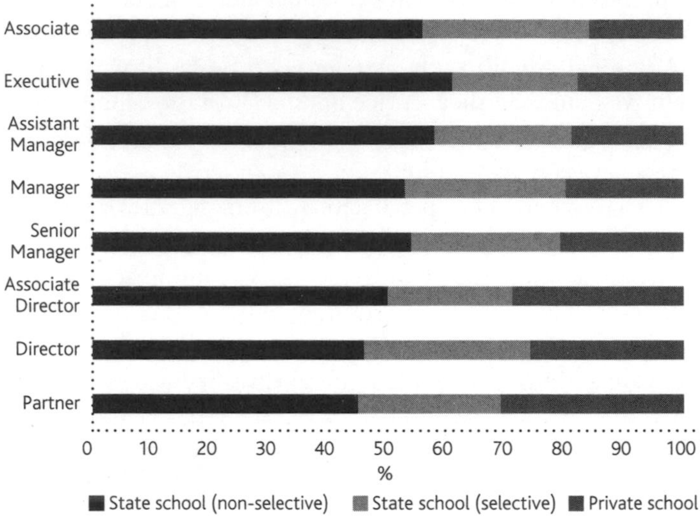

Note: Percentage of people at Turner Clarke in each organisational level who attended each type of school.
Source: Internal data from Turner Clarke

Figure 4.6 indicates that there is also a class ceiling at TC. While only 17% of Associates are privately educated, the figure among Partners is nearly double, at 30%. Those from (educationally) privileged backgrounds, in other words, are much more likely to reach the top echelons of the business.[16]

There are two further important observations to be made about the composition of TC. First, there is a very clear 'London effect' within the firm that strongly echoes our findings in Chapter Three. At every pay grade, staff based in London are much more likely to be privately educated. This distinction is particularly stark within the Partner group – 35% of London Partners were privately educated compared to 22% among Partners working elsewhere.

Finally, like 6TV, it is worth noting how these departmental, positional (and geographical) dimensions connect. For example, when we look at TC's highest earning group of employees – London-based Partners who work in Advisory – it is here we see by far the largest over-representation of the privileged, with

42% of this group privately educated – that is six times the rate of private education in the UK as a whole.

To summarise, those from privileged backgrounds (in terms of schooling, at least) are clearly over-represented at TC. There is also a ceiling effect within the organisation, with those from privileged backgrounds disproportionately dominating the Partner group – particularly the most lucrative and prestigious positions in Advisory and in London.

Coopers

Architecture firm Coopers is remarkably unassuming compared to our other case studies. Its principal studio covers two floors of a modern building that is nestled away on a quiet back road in Central London. The offices are open plan and stylishly furnished, but the atmosphere is warm rather than intimidating. The ground floor is dominated by a huge, rectangular, wooden table, on which are arranged design magazines and the firm's own 'manifestoes' on the future of architecture. Detailed, technical drawings from current projects compete for wall space with more imaginative visions of futuristic cityscapes. But the studio feels uncluttered and well ordered.

The office is a sociable, busy space. Site-based staff pop in for client and project meetings, and Junior Architects take lunch together in the office. Regular seminars are held to discuss the latest urban design issue. Partners sit next to Architectural Assistants: there is no obvious hierarchy on show. Staff adhere to a distinctly architectural 'uniform'. This is contemporary, but still professional: little formal business attire, lots of trendy eye-wear, even the odd discreet tattoo or piercing, but nothing too outré.

Coopers was established around 40 years ago by three Founder-Partners, who each took individual responsibility for leading one of the key service areas of the business – Commercial, Technical and Design. Over time the practice has grown, organically and fitfully, recruiting rapidly as major projects are commissioned, and making redundancies during economic downturns. The firm is now relatively large for an architectural practice, employing around 100 people, the vast majority of whom are based in London.[17]

The firm principally works in defence, education, healthcare, transport and residential development. It has been very successful in recent years, leading on a number of high-profile airport and bus terminal projects, and staff numbers have expanded rapidly. However, as a firm with a strong 'delivery' focus, it lacks both the cultural prestige of established 'starchitect'-led practices, such as Fosters, or the professional cachet of design-led boutique studios.

Employing many Architectural Assistants yet to complete all of their professional qualifications, Coopers is a young office, with an average age of around 30 compared with 46 for architecture nationally. It is also cosmopolitan, with nearly half of staff (43%) brought up outside the UK. In some ways, the firm compares favourably to the wider architecture profession in terms of gender and racial-ethnic diversity. Women make up 41% of Coopers staff (compared with 26% in architecture nationally) and people from racial-ethnic minority groups 20% (compared with 9%[18]). *Tellingly, however, only one of the 15 Partners is a member of an ethnic minority, and none are women.*

In terms of class background, the practice is significantly more elite than UK architects as a whole.[19] Figure 4.7 shows that a clear majority of staff (74%) are from middle-class professional or managerial backgrounds, and only 6% are from working-class backgrounds.

Figure 4.7: Staff at Coopers are unusually privileged

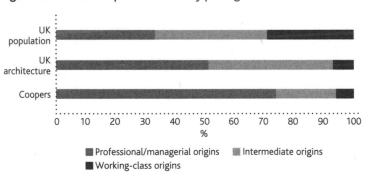

Note: Percentage of people in the UK labour force, in UK architecture, and at Coopers, from each class background.
Source for first two groups: LFS; Source for Coopers: Survey of Coopers

For much of its history, Coopers' organisational hierarchy was fairly loose, but it has made conscious efforts over the last few years to put more formal practice and staff management processes and systems in place. There are now 15 Partners, as well as Associate Partners, Associates, qualified Architects and Architectural Assistants. Compared to our other case studies, earnings between these levels varies less – approximately £25,000-£40,000 among Architectural Assistants to £60,000+ among Partners.

Despite being demographically skewed towards the privileged, there is *no evidence of a class ceiling at Coopers* – much like the wider architecture profession. Indeed, if anything, the inverse is more accurate at Coopers. As Figure 4.8 illustrates, around half the Partner group are from intermediate or working-class backgrounds, compared with just over a quarter of the most junior grade of Architectural Assistant.

Figure 4.8: There is no class ceiling at Coopers

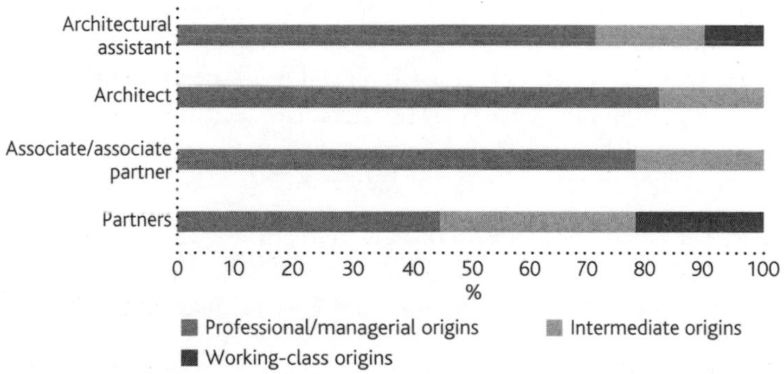

Note: Percentage of people at each organisational level at Coopers from each class background.
Source: Survey of Coopers

The size of the workforce at Coopers prevents us from breaking these findings down into more granular distinctions by project team or sector focus. But it is worth reiterating that, in contrast to our other case studies, there is no ceiling for the socially mobile.

Actors

Readers will notice that our final case study is not a firm or an organisation. Instead, we look at a whole field, acting. This is because actors rarely work in firms and are largely self-employed. As outlined earlier, our analysis has so far excluded the self-employed and therefore this case study was motivated primarily by a desire to plug this gap in our analysis. A focus on acting also made sense for other reasons. For example, a long line of high-profile actors have recently voiced their concerns about social mobility and what the actor David Morrissey has called the slow "economic excision of working-class actors". Acting also arguably has a heightened significance because of the role actors play in representing social reality, and how these representations, in turn, constitute and reproduce powerful 'common-sense' understandings of class (as well as race, gender, disability and so on).

British actors are broadly similar to the rest of the UK population in terms of race and ethnicity and are marginally more male. Strikingly, however, they are disproportionately drawn from privileged class backgrounds. As Figure 4.9 shows, 73% of actors come from professional or managerial backgrounds and only 10% have parents who worked in semi-routine and routine employment.[20]

Figure 4.9: Actors are disproportionately from privileged backgrounds

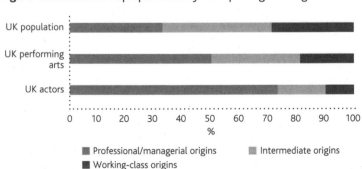

Note: Percentage of people in the UK labour force, in the UK performing arts as a whole, and in acting from each class background.
Source: For UK population and performing arts: LFS; Source for actors: GBCS

There is also a very clear class pay gap in acting. Those from professional or managerial backgrounds enjoy average annual (household) incomes of between £7,000 and £21,000 higher than other actors.[21] This pay gap remains substantial and significant even when we account for many of the variables explored in Chapter Three, such as schooling, education, location and age.[22]

From the class pay gap to the class ceiling

Profiling our case study firms reveals important insights about how class background affects career progression in specific organisational settings. Here, those from working-class backgrounds not only sort into less prestigious specialisms and/or office locations but they often also struggle to make it beyond middle management roles and are significantly under-represented at the top of their organisations. Yet the example of Coopers demonstrates that these effects are not universal, and that in some settings the socially mobile actively break the class ceiling.

These filtering effects – both horizontal and vertical – explain more about the class pay gap we introduced in Chapters Two and Three. As Figure 4.10 indicates, many of the drivers of the pay gap – including several we introduced in Chapter Three – may be taking place *within firms*. For example, prestigious educational credentials may help the privileged work in the biggest and best-paid London law firms but, once in, these credentials may also help them move into the best-paying departments and positions inside the firm. At the same time, the class ceiling effects we have uncovered in this chapter are clearly not adequately explained by the drivers outlined in Chapter Three – class origin may matter in other ways. Next, then, we must move beyond the explanatory language of statistics to interrogate the lived experience of career progression. How do people make sense of their own careers? Are the socially mobile less likely to benefit from the help of mentors or sponsors, are they more reluctant to ask for pay rises, and are embodied markers of class background – such as accent, pronunciation and self-presentation – unfairly misrecognised as markers of talent or ability?

Figure 4.10: The drivers of the class pay gap – what advantages the privileged?

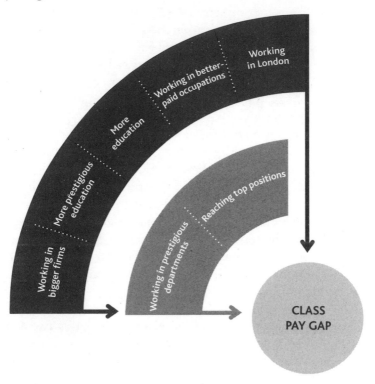

Note: This figure brings together the drivers of the class pay gap identified in Chapter Three with those identified in this chapter.

In the following chapters we draw on an extensive programme of 175 interviews with people from different class backgrounds, across our four cases, to answer precisely these questions.

The Bank of [...] and Dad

We interviewed Nathan at [...] ndon's most prestigious [...] he was the l[...] the venue's big budget autumn play and was enjoying [...] od reviews. It was only the latest accolade in an illustrious [...] ing career. Now in his [...] on. He has played ri[...] acclaimed roles on stage Compan[...] appeared [...] Holly[...] the Royal Shakespeare [...] A[...] award-winning [...] ockbusters and fronted [...] and prestigious talent. H[...] ecently profiled in the [...] he tells us [...] down [...] Nathan is celebrated as [...] making good [...] lf is more modest. Any [...] turn down acting projects [...] orking incredibly hard" No job is worth sacrificing yourself [...] rly crucial, he notes, has [...] t he hasn't believed in: [...] or," he tells us.

[...] ctor and also in his 40s. [...] interviewed Jim a few weeks later [...] at another top London [...] was not at crisis [...] inside. In fact, he wasn't [...] good indeed for som[...] x months. Yet Jim also had an impressive CV. Though in [...] and 30s he had worked consistently in television and theatre and a few years ago had accepted a prominent part in a television soap. But after four years his character was axed and, in the intervening years, he had struggled to re-adjust.

"I've just been going up for smaller and smaller parts, for less and less money," he says, explaining that he has recently decided to leave the profession: "The writing is on the wall. But it still hurts because ... because it sort of means I've failed."

Jim's story is not particularly unusual. Acting is widely considered one of the most precarious and competitive professions in the world.[2] Comparing these two men's careers at face value, then, many people might come to the conclusion that Nathan is simply a more talented actor. Or has worked harder. Or has made better decisions.

There may be some truth to this. But such routine judgements also reflect the fact that the explanatory tool that most reach for when making sense of who gets ahead is 'meritocracy'.[3] As we explained in the Introduction to this book, there is much ambiguity over the meaning and definition of 'merit'.[4] Yet in everyday life, meritocracy is regularly invoked to explain and justify the different outcomes experienced by people like Nathan and Jim; that talent, plus effort, will always shine through. The main principles of 'meritocracy' are often formalised by academics through the concept of 'human capital'. This is normally measured by calculating the sum of an individual's credentials, experience and training, and is seen by many, especially in economics, as the key determinant of a person's productive capacity and, therefore, their earning potential.[5]

But one of the biggest problems with the human capital thesis is that it implies that people operate in a vacuum, that their work life is cut off from outside influences and that their career progression is driven solely by their own skills, 'merits' and actions. In other words, it implies that we live in an era of meritocratic individualism where success and failure are solely matters of personal responsibility.[6]

This take is challenged by the results of our fieldwork. When we reflect on the stories of Nathan and Jim, for example, plotting in full how both had made their way in the acting profession, a competing narrative emerges. Take Nathan. The son of two successful cultural professionals, Nathan went to a very expensive private school in London. After university, Nathan was rejected from a number of drama schools. But, determined to pursue a career in acting, he moved back to the family home in London and began taking any acting work he could find – "working for free or just for food." Nathan tells us it was really these first few years that were most decisive for his future, when he worked hardest and where his decisions to work with "the best up and coming directors" paid real dividends.

But of course Nathan's *ability* to work hard, in terms of concentrating on (often unpaid) acting projects, and his *ability* to make good decisions, in terms of being able to reject jobs (even paying ones), were both heavily contingent on his parents' financial support. They were able to insulate him from the debilitating precarity of the acting labour market, providing free and well-located housing as well as substantial living costs.

It is possible to read Jim's trajectory in a different way too. Jim's father was a van driver and his mother worked in the local pub. Against his parents' advice, Jim attended drama school in Newcastle as a mature student before moving to London. Although he had spent the next 15 years building a successful career ("I was definitely doing better than most"), he explained that money was a constant source of anxiety. When he was offered a long-term job on a soap, he therefore faced a difficult decision. On the one hand, the soap represented his "first real chance of financial security," a period where he could "finally do normal things like get a mortgage." Yet on the other, it meant working on a programme he didn't like and didn't "respect".

Eventually the financial imperative won out and Jim took the role. But a struggle ensued with the production team over the depiction of his character ("a tough, very working-class character who was also gay"). For Jim this was the continuation of a long-running theme of being typecast in shallow, caricatured working-class roles – as "the drug dealer, the drug taker or the violent odd-ball". He explained:

> It is all these middle-class people making this working-class programme and some of the storylines are completely ridiculous: you go "my character did this, said this." But they're not interested. I remember they told me not to take things so seriously – "just go in front of the camera and say the fucking line."

For Jim these frustrations represented a difficult bind. While at odds, politically, with the role he was playing, the basic need to work, "to pay the bills", limited his ability to reject the work

– or even register partial objections or reservations. He told us: "You have to play by their rules. I found that you just couldn't say anything or you get this reputation of being problematic, of being difficult, and then people see you as a risk."

What was striking about talking to Jim was both his palpable anger at the constraints imposed on his acting career, and at the same time his profound sense of helplessness in tackling them. Money saturated this narrative. Like Nathan, it had fundamentally shaped what courses of action were available in his career. But unlike Nathan, it had not acted as an enabler. Instead, it had driven a series of decisions that were ultimately harmful to his career progression and had, eventually, forced him to leave the profession altogether.

We should reiterate that we don't present these stories to somehow undermine Nathan's success, or to suggest he is not a talented actor. Our aim is simply to highlight how Nathan and Jim's ability to realise, or cash in, their respective 'talents' rested strongly on the economic capital at their disposal. Indeed, across our case studies we find strong evidence that those who progress quickest and furthest in elite occupations very often do so with significant help from others. People's accumulation of 'human capital', in other words, particularly in their early careers, is highly contingent on their access to the 'Bank of Mum and Dad'.

As we explore in this chapter, this kind of financial patronage is particularly important in uncertain and precarious elite labour markets. We therefore primarily focus our attention here on our case studies of acting and television. Having said this, we believe such processes likely apply to many other self-employed elite professionals – to consultants, barristers, novelists, journalists, artists and even some academics.[7] In these fields, an economic cushion often shapes what courses of action are possible in people's careers – what type of work they specialise in, where they work, and how they approach things like risk-taking and creative self-expression.[8] For the privileged, in particular, inherited or gifted funds often act as a pivotal early-career lubricant, buying them a freedom of choice and allowing them to manoeuvre on to more promising career tracks, focus on developing valuable networks, resist exploitative employment or take risky opportunities – all of which may propel them in the long term.

We also argue that one reason these resources are so powerful is because they are largely hidden from public view; largely un-talked about (often even among close friends) or actively downplayed. This is partly conscious, part of wider-ranging efforts to play down one's privilege and emphasise one's 'ordinariness'.[9] Yet our interviews suggest that more frequently it simply goes unacknowledged as people fail to see how their agency is scaffolded by the resources of others.

Family fortunes

It is well established that careers in the UK cultural and creative industries (often called the CCIs) are marked by intense precarity.[10] An extensive body of research has documented how conditions of low or no pay and extreme competition are widespread across the sector.[11] Such insecurity is particularly acute in our case study of acting, a long-time forerunner of the 'gig economy'.[12] Experiences of uncertainty, exhaustion and anxiety dominated our interviews with *all* actors – regardless of age, gender, racial ethnic group or class origin. This was perhaps best illustrated when we asked, 'What represents success in the acting profession?' We expected actors to hold divergent views on this topic, but instead responses were strikingly uniform. Success, we were repeatedly told, simply equals 'working'. As John noted, "This must be one of the hardest professions in the world ... if you can make a living that *is* success." Amid widespread uncertainty, achievement hinged on the basic ability to work, and to work consistently.

Yet although actors faced a set of similar challenges, they did not do so on an equal footing. In particular, interviews revealed the profound occupational advantages afforded to actors who could draw on economic resources beyond their own income. Here there was a very stark acknowledgment that those with money "behind them" had it easier in acting. This ability to access, or call on, familial wealth shaped the experience of actors in myriad ways. First, it provided insulation from much of the precariousness of the labour market. While for Nathan this insulation was particularly important at the beginning of his career, when he was trying to establish himself, for all but the most successful actors it was a more permanent necessity. Parental support was important, in particular, in protecting many from the need to seek alternative work to support themselves between acting roles. Andy, whose parents are both doctors, explained that his existence as an actor was heavily contingent on the ability to "call mum" during lean spells for financial top-ups. "It's not great," he explained, "but I can't imagine how I would be able to do it if it wasn't for her. I really can't." For Andy, as with many privileged-origin actors, the significance of this safety net was not just about economic survival but also the ability to respond more rapidly to the demands of the labour market, fully prepare for roles, be immediately available for auditions, and not feel tired or burnt out from other work. He explains:

> It's like you get a phone call to audition tomorrow and they want you to be "off book" and then you have to spend every second 'til the audition working on the script. It would be impossible if I had no outside support.

Although familial support was often a somewhat sensitive topic, most of these actors acknowledged that they were fortunate. This was often revealed in moments of spontaneous comparison with less privileged colleagues. Tommy, for example, was from a very wealthy background and had attended an elite public school. He explained that he initially quit acting in his mid-20s after sustained periods of unemployment, but after a long period travelling had recently re-entered the profession – a luxury he recognised was not available to most of his peers:

> I am 30 and effectively dipping my toe back in the water because I have an apartment in Central London. I have another that pays rent. I have money, assets, capital. It's desperately unfair. My friend lives in a Peabody House and struggles finding all kinds of work. He has a degree from Cambridge but, you know, he sells maps and chewing gum and washes

cars. He sometimes turns down jobs because it doesn't make economic sense in terms of rent. If I go off and have a successful career now, [I know] it's unfair. Really unfair.

The stories of Andy and Tommy capture much of the security provided by economic capital – of being able to able to survive periods with little or no acting work, of having access to subsidised and well-located housing, and more generally, of ensuring one can be as competitive as possible when opportunities arise.

Here the contrast with actors making their way with little or no economic safety net was striking. Economic insecurity, for these respondents, was a chronic condition. Ray, for example, was from a working-class background in Northern England. After getting a good agent from his graduation showcase, Ray, like many actors, had moved to London. He had worked consistently during his first nine months but now, after several months without work, was suddenly "on his arse" financially. Without the luxury of financial help, and facing "impossibly high" rent, he had been forced to take a full-time non-acting job. But this, he explained, left him in a difficult bind. He knew that "exhausting" non-acting work was having a "knock-on effect", but he needed to survive. His predicament, he summed up, has "a massive element of chaos to it – I feel like I'm skydiving without a parachute."

Money talks: Responses to typecasting

Economic patronage provides the privileged with concrete advantages in forging many professional careers. But such advantages are not just about earning power or progression. In acting, financial support is often more significant in terms of shaping how actors respond to pernicious aspects of the labour market such as typecasting. We were particularly interested in how the practice of typecasting was negotiated by women and racial-ethnic minority actors from different class backgrounds.

It's worth saying that all actors are, to some extent at least, 'typecast' – that is, the roles they are encouraged to audition for, and that they tend to get, follow a set social 'type' that reflects their real-life demographic characteristics, particularly in terms of age, gender, ethnicity, region and class. Most acknowledged that this typecasting actually has a clear utility in the sense that it provides a set of defined roles where they have comparative advantage. However, there was also a prevailing sense that some 'types' are better rewarded in the acting labour market, particularly white, male, middle-class actors.[13] As others have noted,[14] such actors tend to benefit from a significant oversupply of roles for white, male, middle-class *characters*. Moreover, such roles are also, on average, broader, more complex and more multifaceted, and, flowing from this, more central and better remunerated.

In contrast, actors who deviated from this hegemonic 'type' described typecasting as a much more problematic process. This is for two main reasons. First, in terms of the labour market, these actors have a much smaller pool of roles to choose from, and the parts imagined for their 'type' tend to be secondary and less well paid. Moreover, these actors often expressed anger and dismay at the *nature* of the roles they were cast to play, roles that they often felt were caricatured and politically regressive. For example, Lily (intermediate origins), who was Chinese-British, described playing countless "offensive" Asian characters portrayed as "funny because they don't understand – me-speaky no-English – and you just think 'oh no, not again'." Similarly Derek, from a working-class background, explained: "I should have a police pension, I've played so many coppers."

What was particularly interesting to us, however, was how different 'othered' actors had responded to the constraints of their typecast. While most registered a certain resigned acceptance, a significant minority had made active efforts to resist or reject their typecasting. Here we were struck by the way economic resources that flowed from an actor's familial background often shaped their ability to resist. To illustrate, we explore the stories of three female actors from very different class backgrounds.

First, Molly. Molly is white; her father was a stockbroker, her mother an educational manager, and she grew up in an affluent area of London. She was educated privately before gaining a place at one of London's most prestigious drama schools. After finishing drama school, she spent three years working full time as an actor – auditioning for, and often being cast in, what she described as a "string of middle-class princess girl parts". These were often central roles but revolved around a narrow and reoccurring set of female characters:

> They were all slightly passive, functional, pretty, females continually being chased around by interesting, complex, hilarious, men – and that was very frustrating.

Molly decided she wanted to "challenge" this "pigeon-holing" and set out to start writing her own play. Moving back to her parents' house in London and relying on their financial support to live, she took a year out of acting to write (and perform in) her own one-woman play about female sexuality. She explains the premise:

> I just thought, wouldn't you just love it if you were sat in a theatre and a female character just walked on stage and said *that*. It was that need for female characters who contradict themselves and are surprising ... so it was definitely an experiment and the line was always – "Can we say that?" and then always "Yes – yes we absolutely should." And it did come out of a rage of, like, let's do something different, change the way people think about women.

Molly's play was thus a direct attempt to critique her restricted female typecast and to produce a lead female character that directly confounded traditional representations of middle-class women. The play was a huge critical and popular success. It also directly led to Molly being commissioned to write, and perform in, a primetime TV series. While she explained that she still auditions for the occasional outside acting job, she is now much more "picky" and writing has given her much more "control" and "autonomy" over the characters she plays:

> I love how powerful you feel when you are acting in something where people really listen to you. Stuff that

> you feel is significant and important and changing
> things … I sound like some twat [*laughs*]. But that
> is what is crazy about being an actor – people listen
> to you, they've paid to listen to you, they want to
> be affected. So yeah, once that really clicked – that
> if-you-build-it-they-will-come kind of idea – it had
> huge appeal. Rather than the [typecast] look-at-me-
> in-my-dress-running-around-a-lake-kind-of-thing.

It is clear that Molly has found a place in the acting labour
market where she can very effectively resist the narrowness of
her typecasting. This is undoubtedly the result of much hard
work and a writing talent widely recognised by industry peers.
However, what we are particularly interested in here is how
Molly could manoeuvre her career in order to express herself
politically and 'cash in' on this writing talent. Most significant
here are the familial economic resources that Molly could rely
on during this transitional period, which both covered her living
costs and the expense of staging her first play.

The contrast between Molly and Mia is striking. Raised
in Scotland, Mia's father was an electrician and her mother a
housewife. She went to drama school in Wales and had since
built a fragmented but financially successful career as a film actor.
However, Mia explained that her entire career had revolved
around playing a very one-dimensional type of character. It
began, she explained, when she played a heroin-addicted mother
in a big-budget film:

> After that I've always, always got cast as working-class
> victims. Always. Put it this way, if Downton Abbey
> was on then I would certainly be below stairs [*laughs*].
> I swear to god I have lost children about 15 times on-
> screen; the battered wife, the junkie or someone who
> has lost a child because of their badness or carelessness.

What was significant about Mia's typecast is that it was clearly
classed *and* gendered. While she shared Molly's exasperation
at continually playing passive female characters, as a woman
with a "strong Scottish accent", the working-class characters

she had been offered were even more restricted. Indeed, she expressed a particular anger at the way female working-class-ness was either connected to crime or victim roles, which are "invariably dreamed up by some posh male writer". Like Molly, Mia had taken active steps early in her career to resist typecast. She described countless auditions for more varied playing parts that had all been fruitless. This experience, she concluded, had left her with the sense that the only feasible form of resistance was to turn down the roles she was being offered, to start the slow process of changing casting agents' perception of her. But, unlike Molly, this option depended on outside financial support she simply did not possess:

> I wish I could be more brave, and say "I'm not going to do that anymore," or "I'm not going to take this unless you let me do it like this." But quite often you are not allowed to be as brave as you want to be – especially if you're trying to make a living in London. And I'm not exactly flooded with loads of other options at the moment, if you know what I mean …

Finally we turn to Deborah, 50, from an intermediate class background (her father worked in administration and mother as a retail assistant). Deborah went to drama school in Scotland before working for 10–15 years in the North of England. She explained that her typecast – which revolved around her Midlands accent, gender and mixed ethnicity – had come to be the defining, and ultimately limiting, feature of her acting career:

> I am a Black character actress and frankly there is not a lot out there for us. I've played a hell of a lot of nurses. I've played more nurses than there are in the whole of St George's Hospital.

In her mid-30s, Deborah decided to be more active in resisting her typecast:

> So yeah, I started to get bored of that and I wouldn't take it if all I was saying was "the doctor will see you

in a few minutes"... I just felt that kind of storytelling is not reflecting anything about my life as a mixed-race woman.

Like Molly, Deborah decided the best way to mount a challenge was through writing. Although she initially had some success as a playwright, she described hitting "a lot of brick walls". She described one telling turning point:

Deborah: [A major London theatre studio] asked me to write a play but then the reason the literary manager gave me for not even pursuing it was because another Black actor, a male actor, had written a play that he said had similar themes. But it was a Pentecostal musical! I had written about a very middle-class man and a working-class Black girl and their relationship and I just think that was too difficult for him to take whereas a Pentecostal musical ...

Sam: ... is what "we" expect from a Black voice?

Deborah: Exactly. And that has been my experience as a writer, because you see the people who are commissioning work and you get much closer to smelling that white elite. And you say, actually, I would like to do this story about a middle-class mixed-race woman who is having doubts about who she is, but the ones that are always getting commissioned are the sink estate dramas, tales of African war, American Black history.

For Deborah, resisting typecast was a clear political decision to reject the caricatured racialised and gendered roles that had dominated her career. Yet unlike Molly, this project had been largely unsuccessful and, in Deborah's mind, had actually had a negative knock-on effect on her career. In recent years she explained that work had "dried up" and she was now working almost full time in a supermarket:

> I do feel frustrated that my potential hasn't been completely fulfilled. It is the lack of people seeing that ability in me, but also – you know – I don't have that confidence that a certain level of class gives you. I don't ... I would rather squeak in a corner than go up to somebody and say "I have got this great idea." It is that quality of not being able to push myself forward.

We place Mia and Deborah's stories alongside Molly's here to underline the professional bind frequently faced by working-class actors, particularly those who are female and/or from a Black and Minority Ethnic (BME) group. While they often object to the gendered, raced or classed representations they are asked to portray, their ability to reject such work is weakened by both the restricted supply of roles available and the financial imperative to work. Molly, in contrast, represents an exemplar of how an economic cushion can embolden actors to challenge the terms of their typecasting. Of course we cannot say for certain that Molly would not have challenged her type, and been successful in doing so, if she had not had financial support. But what we can say with some certainty is that it would have been much harder.

The leaky pipeline: Sorting, segregation, stagnation

The broader point we wish to underline is that across elite occupations, material inequalities *between* people from different backgrounds had a profound impact on the courses of action available to them. Although in acting this often played out in fairly crude terms – in terms of who can actually survive day-to-day as an actor – economic advantage played a more subtle (but equally important) role in another of our case studies: television.

To understand this, it is important to recall the stark class ceiling we uncovered at 6TV in Chapter Four (Figure 4.3). This ceiling is most apparent in Commissioning, the department that holds creative control over what the channel broadcasts. Here 90% of senior staff are from upper-middle-class origins, and none are from working-class backgrounds.

To explain this extraordinary finding, our interviews suggested the need to first understand the 'creative route' in television, and who is able to follow it. The creative route typically begins with 'running'[15] jobs, which eventually graduate to producing or researcher roles and then, for those who succeed, jobs as series producers or directors. Significantly, it is only when individuals have accumulated years of experience along this creative pathway (where work is normally short-term and sporadic) that they reach the appropriate 'pool' to be considered for a commissioning role at somewhere like 6TV.

Nearly all our interviewees explained that their early ambitions had centred on this creative route – the dream of making, directing or producing television. However, although these initial orientations were similar, we were struck by the number of upwardly mobile interviewees who had then either deliberately chosen *not* to follow the 'creative' pathway, or who had left the track in the early or mid-section of their careers.

Trajectories began to diverge, in particular, as people entered the labour market. Here many from working-class backgrounds quickly recalibrated expectations away from the creative route as they began to understand the profound economic precarity it entailed. More specifically, the prospect of a string of unpaid or poorly paid entry-level running jobs or worries about negotiating extortionate London housing costs were frequently mentioned as key factors underpinning decisions to abandon the creative route for a more 'stable' role elsewhere in the industry.

Kate, a Communications Manager at 6TV, who was from a single-parent, working-class background, recalled dreaming of making television at university, but even after graduating with a first class degree from a Russell Group university, explained how this had felt "out of reach":

> I wouldn't change now, I love my job and it suits me. But if you're asking me whether I would have liked to have gone down that [creative] route originally – if I'd felt it was more within my reach – then yes, absolutely I would have. It would have been my dream job.

Others had started off on the creative route, often progressing well in the 'indie' sector, but had then taken sideways or downward moves into more economically secure positions at 6TV. Hannah, for example, who was Black British and from a fairly poor, lower-middle-class family in the North of England, had been on a very promising production trajectory in her 20s – racking up a series of credits on high-profile 'shiny-floor'[16] entertainment shows. But she explained how this was flanked by a "relentless" feeling of vulnerability amid the ruthlessness and instability of the freelance labour market. Without outside financial support, she explained, "you are always thinking about taking jobs for money and it is impossible to manage your career." After 10 years, Hannah saw an advertisement for a Human Resources (HR) role at 6TV and decided it was time to move on. Taking this horizontal move, however, was a reluctant decision. Hannah knew at the time that it offered little room for progression, and acknowledged that her career had subsequently stagnated: "It's definitely a dead end; once you've done this people just see you as the HR person and forget you've done anything else."

The advantage this leaky pipeline posed for those from privileged backgrounds was often openly acknowledged. As Dave, a Senior Commissioner from professional/managerial origins, explained:

> If you've got nothing to fall back on, and you're out of work for three months, you're fucked. Whereas if you come from a kind of relatively affluent background like me, and you understand the kind of machinations of the tax system, and you can always get bailed out by Mum and Dad if it all goes wrong in the early stages, then it's very different. I mean I … I mean I was very lucky.

There was a consensus, then, among nearly all our interviewees that the structure of the creative pathway in television meant the odds were overwhelmingly stacked in favour of those from advantaged backgrounds. This was perhaps summarised most effectively and articulately by Alice, who was from a working-class background in the rural South West of England. Like Hannah, she had reluctantly abandoned the creative pathway and taken a pay cut to accept a full-time role as a Junior Script Editor at 6TV (which she had now been in for six years). Discussing a set of senior colleagues in Commissioning, she explained how their class privilege had initiated a process of cumulative advantage[17] that they and others often misrecognised as talent:

> Like they are all really talented, it's not that. But … kind of the reason they are is because, you know, they've had that opportunity to get more and more experience, and learn through every project. So yes, they may have started almost where I am but now they are like a million times above where I could ever be because they have had all that experience, they were given that opportunity and they had that confidence to go for it … whereas I started out thinking I could do anything, but actually now I don't know if I've got the energy to fight my way there.

This process of occupational sorting represents a key driver of the class ceiling in television. It means that very few upwardly mobile individuals actually reach the appropriate 'pool' to be considered for senior creative roles in places like 6TV. Instead, their creative talents often go unrealised as they grudgingly self-select out towards less precarious parts of the industry.[18]

Downplaying privilege?

We have shown in this chapter that some people from advantaged backgrounds acknowledge their economic privilege, and recognise its role in facilitating their career progression. Yet we should stress that such acknowledgments were rare. People often recognised privilege in some areas of their life and ignored it in others. And as illustrated by Nathan at the beginning of this chapter, those from upper-middle-class backgrounds tended to narrate their career progression, and that of those around them, mostly in terms of 'merit', as the result of talent and, most importantly, hard work.[19] Notably, they were also much more likely than upwardly mobile interviewees to see their profession as 'meritocratic' and, unlike Dave, almost never questioned the legitimacy of their own success. Moreover, when these interviewees did talk openly about privilege, they were awkward exchanges.[20] They often looked visibly uncomfortable, avoiding eye contact or stumbling over their words.

The topic of parental money, in particular, was especially fraught. We noticed that even those who acknowledged the 'Bank of Mum and Dad' tended to do so in an abstract, generalised way, and almost never talked about specific figures. Peter, a Junior Commissioner at 6TV, was "fortunate" that his mum and dad were able to "help out" when he was trying to break into production. Similarly, actor Ellie continually used the words "support" and "contribution" when talking about her parents' gifting of capital to buy her London flat, but said she "preferred not to say" when we asked about the actual amount involved.[21] These interviewees often talked extensively about the financial reality of low- or no-paid work, or periods where they were out of work, while the privileged tended to gloss over such periods and focus more on the work itself.

This may be partly about simply not noticing one's economic advantage. Research suggests that people in advantaged groups often misrecognise their advantage because they compare themselves to those around them, who tend to be similar. They therefore see themselves as "normal", "average" or "ordinary".[22] Moreover, in uncertain and precarious worlds like television or acting, where parental support is often simply about providing a safety net, it is maybe not surprising that these interviewees did not see themselves as particularly fortunate or well-off.

Having said this, we think it is likely that at least some of these people do recognise, and think about, their own economic privilege, yet feel uncomfortable *talking* about it – particularly to an interrogative sociologist! This is because there is a fairly significant tension between benefiting from unearned wealth and adherence to dominant norms of meritocracy. The Bank of Mum and Dad arguably strikes right to the heart of the moral legitimacy of one's success. Sociologist Rachel Sherman calls this 'the anxieties of affluence'.[23] Like Sherman, we read the privileged as often working hard to downplay or justify their privilege, especially when we asked direct questions about the Bank of Mum and Dad. This orientation played out in three ways.

First, we were intrigued by the way participants deployed particular stories about the source of family money as a means of justification. This often meant narrating their own backgrounds in terms of upward mobility – based, curiously, not on their own origins but that of their parents or even grandparents. Patricia, an Executive at 6TV, had been privately educated. Her mother was a teacher, her father the managing director of a big manufacturing firm. Yet Patricia described her background as "working class".[24] Here, instead of talking about her own childhood, she spoke extensively about her parents' upward trajectories from poor working-class families in West Wales. Throughout the interview she continually described her own background in terms of her parents, seeing her identity as inextricably linked to theirs. This acted as a device to both downplay her privilege but also to present her parents' money (and by implication, their gifting to her via private schooling, a deposit for her flat and help getting "set up in TV") as having meritocratic legitimacy.

Others downplayed privilege by steering conversations towards colleagues who had received *greater* financial help. This was a way of normalising gifting as a general practice, while also drawing moral boundaries with more privileged others. Daniel, a Junior Commissioner at 6TV, was the son of two teachers. His parents had given him extensive financial help for two years when he first entered television as a runner, and he had also lived rent-free in his brother's London flat. But Daniel was very proud that since his mid-20s he had been "fully self-sufficient". He told us:

> I definitely feel like I'm in a slightly different category than most people in TV. So I hate the idea that people might look at you and go well you're quite privileged, from a middle-class background, and "Oh, of course, haven't you done well." And I have, to a certain extent, because my parents did help me out at the start with rent and stuff. But ... but I've got loads of mates in TV who, you know, have been given the deposit for a house or who still get their phone bill paid by their parents! So I'm there going

hold on ... I'm not ... this is all ... I've worked really fucking hard.

Finally, some interviewees deflected conversations about money by emphasising the constraints on their agency, that their hands were metaphorically tied. Many thus presented financial gifts or parental support as something they had little choice over, where the money was, in actor Jack's words, "thrown at them", or where, as 6TV Marketing Manager Ruth put it, their parents "insisted". Here, refusing financial support would offend or cause interpersonal problems. It wasn't that these people claimed that this somehow offset their privilege, but instead it was often followed with a more resigned, fatalistic mode. "I mean I could be like I won't accept," noted Kate, a 6TV Script Editor. "But it wouldn't change a thing."

Of course it is hard to pull apart the relationship between thinking about privilege and talking about it.[25] It is impossible for us to know, for example, whether people like Patricia and Daniel are strategic or unwitting in downplaying their privilege (although we suspect a combination of both). Yet either way, we would stress that this downplaying has important implications for the class pay gap. It means that the true value of the Bank of Mum and Dad goes largely unspoken in professional life, and its distorting influence on individual trajectories remains hidden from public view.

Money matters less at Coopers and Turner Clarke

We have seen various ways in which the Bank of Mum and Dad acts to shape the work trajectories of those in elite occupations from different class backgrounds. It is worth reiterating, however, that this varies very significantly by occupation. Readers will have noticed that two of our case studies – Turner Clarke (TC) and Coopers – have not featured so far in this chapter. This is not because the Bank of Mum and Dad is not important at all for understanding the professions of accountancy and architecture. Economic capital likely plays a pivotal role in understanding barriers to access in architecture, for example. Certainly, many staff at Coopers spoke of the prohibitive economic costs and risks involved in forging a career in architecture, and how this favoured those from wealthy backgrounds. Most notable here is the question of who can negotiate the student fees and living costs associated with a lengthy seven-year architecture education, as well as additional costs of materials and field trips.[26]

Similarly, our interviews suggested that the Bank of Mum and Dad may play a significant role in the geographical sorting effect that we see in accountancy – both in the wider profession and at TC – whereby the privileged filter into London (where salaries are higher). For example, while 13% of Trainee TC Associates outside London have been privately educated, the figure among Associates in London is 25% – nearly double. Our interviews suggested this is not just an innocent issue of 'personal choice'. Many TC trainees, for example, explained that their 'choice' to work outside London was largely based on worries about the cost of living – particularly in terms of housing.[27]

These dimensions of career building at Coopers and TC are certainly important. Yet at the same time we would stress that family wealth is comparatively much less powerful in these organisations, and only has minimal traction in influencing career progression. This is because architecture and, in particular, accountancy, represent fairly stable and secure professions that tend to offer permanent full-time jobs and above-average earnings. Put simply, once they've gained entry most practitioners – regardless of background – can comfortably pursue a career without the need for outside support. The contrast here with acting and television – along with many other precarious elite occupations – is striking. In these arenas, where work is often freelance, short-term, poorly paid and extremely competitive, the Bank of Mum and Dad fundamentally mediates how people can respond to chronic early-career conditions of precarity, offering an invisible hand to some while leaving many others, often unwittingly, at an unfair disadvantage.

Yet a helping hand does not always come from behind, or below. Similarly, it does not always have to come in the form of financial support or patronage. In many elite occupations, for example, particularly more traditional professions such as accountancy and architecture, support is more likely to come from above rather than below. And instead of economic it is social – in the form of informal sponsorship. As we explore in the next chapter, this form of sponsored mobility is often a prerequisite for those wishing to get to the top.

SIX

A helping hand

In 1960, the pioneering American sociologist Ralph H. Turner wrote a prescient article in the *American Sociological Review*.[1] In it, he introduced the concepts of 'sponsored' and 'contest' mobility. In contest mobility, success is the prize in an open tournament, and the contest is only judged to be fair if all players compete on an equal footing. Here victory must be won by one's own efforts, and the most satisfactory outcome is not necessarily the victory of the most intelligent, or most educated, but the most deserving. The tortoise that defeats the hare, he wrote, was thus both possible and appreciated in these contexts. In contrast, in sponsored mobility, individuals reach the top largely because they are selected by those already in senior positions and carefully inducted into elite worlds. Thus, upward progression is granted or denied based on whether established elites judge a candidate to possess the qualities they wish to see, or the 'merits' they value. As Turner notes, this type of 'upward mobility is like entry into a private club, where each candidate must be sponsored by one or more members.'[2]

Turner saw the UK as the exemplar of sponsored mobility.[3] His article conjured images of an antiquated old boy network, where elite appointments are contingent on a set of 'old school tie' connections who 'pull strings' for one another, and whose relationships are rooted in the shared experience of 'public'[4] schooling, Oxbridge and private members clubs. Yet the power of this old boy network is thought by many to have waned considerably in the last 60 years. Indeed, many have argued that a number of countervailing forces, such as the expansion of secondary and higher education, the decline of the landed aristocracy, rising absolute rates of social mobility, and the achievements of second-wave feminism, have fundamentally eroded this kind of elite closure.[5]

This is not to say that who you know is not considered important today; research showing the power of networks in elite professions is voluminous.[6] Yet in recent decades this has tended to focus on the power of what sociologist Mark Granovetter famously called 'weak ties'.[7] Here the emphasis is on the importance of forging a multitude of informal professional contacts, on being a good 'networker', especially with those in positions of power. Such weak ties have also been shown to be a source of 'social capital', instrumental in both facilitating job opportunities and establishing one's professional reputation.[8]

This model of networking, based on somewhat fleeting and shallow connections, certainly featured in our interviews. But it was often mentioned in a somewhat abstract sense, as one of a number of generic attributes people reached for when we asked what was necessary to get ahead. In contrast, when people actually told their own richer, more vivid, stories of career progression, or of those around them, we were struck by the importance of much stronger social ties. These relationships, as we explore in this chapter, function in a very similar way to that originally envisaged by Turner – those in senior positions act as sponsors and, after choosing sponsees early in their careers, actively scaffold their upward trajectory. Of course the operation of sponsorship varies in important ways by occupation. In some cases, sponsors hoist sponsees on to accelerated career tracks; in others, they subtly circumvent hiring or promotion protocols in order to secure advantage for their 'favourites'. Either way, we argue in this chapter that Ralph Turner's depiction of sponsored mobility remains highly relevant to understanding who gets to the top in the UK.

Contemporary sponsorship, however, is not a shadowy process premised on fitting some crude old boy mould. Instead, as we explain, it is often a normalised practice. This does not mean sponsorship is necessarily named as such (although in some fields the term is used). Instead, we find that it is usually practised under the guise of meeting vague buzzword objectives such as 'mapping talent' or identifying 'partner material'. And while such exercises are routinely presented as a neutral form of talent spotting, we find that sponsor relationships are rarely established on the basis of work performance. Instead, they are almost always forged, in the first instance at least, on cultural affinity.[9] This means that, inadvertently, important progression opportunities in many elite occupations do not just rest on competence but also a 'looking-glass' version of 'merit' rooted in class-cultural similarity.[10]

Hitting the partner track: Accumulating experience

'Talent mapping': this curious piece of corporate-speak featured in nearly every Partner interview we conducted at Turner Clarke (TC). When we asked what this actually meant, Advisory Partner Mark explained that it was about "finding the Partners of the future". But while the word 'mapping' implied some sort of formalised system, the reality was far more casual. Partners were encouraged,[11] we learned, to find and sponsor "promising" junior staff. But this process was neither registered nor regulated in any formal way. Instead, Partners were granted autonomy to "spot" talented junior accountants in their own way and encouraged to "bring them through" to Partner.

This was not a new practice. In fact, sponsorship was a key theme in Partners' own trajectories. Among those from privileged backgrounds in particular, sponsors featured heavily in career pathways. Such relationships had not only been sources of mentorship, advocacy and advice but had also often played a very active role in propelling or scaffolding career trajectories – allocating particular types of work, passing on particular clients or engineering situations that, in turn, provided the necessary *experience* to progress. James, a Tax Partner from professional/ managerial origins, provided a telling example:

> There was this guy, Martin, who was the Partner at the time, who said "I think you're quite good at this, try this, try that, have a go at this", and gave me lots of opportunities. I remember at one point he was like, "You're not ready yet, but I'll tell you what I'll do, we'll see if we can find someone who will do this role

for two to three years, possibly been at a large firm, has reached mandatory retirement but could come in and be a contractor for us, you could learn a lot from that, with a view to, not making any promises, bringing you through in three years' time …"

What is significant here is how sponsors like Martin were able to single-handedly change the course of a person's career, here placing James on an accelerated pathway – often referred to as the 'Partner track'. TC facilitated this kind of sponsorship by allowing Partners to intervene, influence or "game" promotion decisions. Many of our interviewees told us this was a fairly standard practice – an "open secret", as Jane, an Audit Partner noted – and involved Partners circumventing or bypassing "objective" performance metrics or ratings in order to secure promotions for those they wanted to promote – their "favourites", as Tax Partner Karen put it.

Significantly, when people told us about opportunities brokered by sponsors, they almost always narrated this in terms of rewarding skill or competence – of someone "spotting talent" or "believing in me". Yet we were particularly interested in how these relationships were established in the first place. What was the ingredient that transformed them from everyday work relations into bonds worthy of sponsorship? Here we found that connections rarely hinged on work. Instead, they were almost always established in the first instance based on a sense of cultural connection or affinity – shared leisure pursuits, shared tastes and shared humour. Let us return to James and his sponsor Martin introduced above:

> I would say there was a bond beyond just a working relationship. A friend would be a push because of the age difference. But it was nurturing, beyond just "what can we get out of each other?" And there were things which helped with that, I suppose. So on the marketing side it sort of started with this skiing trip, which we went on two or three times together. So there is a bonding … you go away with somebody for a week then you're bonding, it takes it beyond work.

Seeking out such commonalities in knowledge and interests does not sound particularly untoward or suspicious. In fact, research indicates that it is typically the first thing two people do on meeting. Discovering such similarities serves as a powerful emotional glue that facilitates trust and comfort, and bonds individuals together.[12] However, academic research has also long established a clear relationship between class background and such cultural tastes, distastes, interests and lifestyles.[13] Indeed, sponsors often acknowledged that these relationships were rooted in a process of 'homophily' – of like attracting like.[14] Nigel, for example, a privileged-origin Partner in Advisory, identified "drinking" as the key lubricant in his relationship with a recent sponsee:

> There's one guy that I've mentored all the way through and he got made Partner at Christmas, but he's very much in my mould. It wasn't difficult taking him out with me, suggesting things for him to do. It's easy for me to pass on the tricks of the trade. He's obviously a practitioner in that drinking mould so it wasn't difficult.

Joe, a Partner in Tax, and also from an upper-middle-class background, went further, acknowledging directly the connection between homophily and his willingness to sponsor:

> It's ironic; I guess the person that I think has done the best is the person that is most like me ... same sense of humour, same approach to work. But then that is maybe because I really forced that, took them down the same route.

Despite acknowledging these similarities, most were keen to distance themselves from any suspicion of deliberate favouritism. Most narrated sponsor relationships as evolving spontaneously, organically. Nevertheless, we would argue that, inadvertently, the widespread existence of such homophilous chains of sponsorship ensured that many progression opportunities at TC did not *just* rest on competence. As sociologist Lauren Rivera[15] has argued, 'cultural similarities are more than just sources of liking; they are also fundamental bases on which we evaluate "merit". Indeed, consciously or not, gatekeepers may use cultural similarities when evaluating others and distributing valued rewards.'

Upwardly mobile staff at TC, particularly those who were women and/or members of racial-ethnic minority groups, described very different pathways to becoming a Partner. As Table A.1b in the Methodological appendix shows,[16] they had usually 'made Partner' at a later age, and their average length of service to reach the partnership was, at every appointment grade, significantly longer. Notably, these interviewees tended to emphasise a more individualised approach to accruing experience – of "building one's own path" (Lola, working-class origins), of demonstrating an "expertise that speaks for itself" (Raymond, intermediate origins) or of continually "hitting targets" (Jess, working-class origins). Significantly, sponsors rarely featured in these accounts.[17] This is not to say that these interviewees did not understand the value of sponsored mobility. However, as the following accounts underline, it was often located as a mechanism that disproportionately favoured those from privileged backgrounds, and particularly men:

> They look right, they fit, and they've got the confidence, so you do see some of these bright young men come in and they're very self-assured and then the older guys will take them under their wing and they'll take them along to a presentation or something like that, so it's creating the opportunities. It creates the chance for them to shine. (Martina, Advisory, working-class origins)

> I know I can't compete with that. And I've never been able to. So I've had to work a lot harder in my opinion … to get where I am. Because I can't trade off of my father knew x or we went to school together. That just doesn't exist for me. (Bev, Advisory, intermediate origins)

Sponsors thus play a particularly important role at TC. They are both able to allocate work in ways that scaffold 'Partner tracks' and also often act as important senior advocates when a person is seeking induction to the Partner group. However, while these relationships are invariably premised on a genuine desire to identify and reward actual talent, they are also highly subjective and often reflect strong personal connections forged on the basis of cultural familiarity.[18]

'It's quite medieval in television': Sponsorship and lateral hiring at 6TV

The power of networks in forging a career in television is well documented.[19] Attention here often centres on the caricature of a shallow, superficial industry, where 'weak ties', to use Granovetter's parlance, play a particularly important role. Our research partly supports this, especially in terms of the early-career narratives of 6TV staff. Here a broad range of informal networks had clearly facilitated 'getting a foot in the door' via work experience or casual word-of-mouth recommendations. Yet when we discussed progression to senior positions, stronger ties were much more important. Certainly, the careers of those in senior management had often hinged on a few pivotal moments when close contacts had played a very active role in propelling them. As Mark, a Senior Commissioner at 6TV, explained in the Introduction of this book: "It's quite medieval in television; you sort of have a patron or you serve apprenticeships. I mean, I could almost give you my whole trajectory in sponsors."

Like TC, these sponsor relationships almost always rested on a process of class–cultural matching – on sharing leisure pursuits, tastes and humour. This was often facilitated by the informal nature of much television work, particularly short-term but intense production projects. Here two Commissioners, Sophie and Rachel, reflect on the genesis of sponsor relationships in these kind of environments:

> The show involved us travelling to Australia and New Zealand for 10 days and, erm, you know, we got talking and his interest in politics came out. So did mine. And it sort of went from there ... (Rachel, Commissioning, professional/managerial origins)

It's a big step from a Runner to Researcher, and I remember when I first got it saying to Jane after a few months, "How did you know I was going to be so brilliant?" [*Laughter.*] And she said, "I didn't know you were going to be brilliant; I just knew we'd have fun working together." So I think there's an expectation of sociability, of sort of out-of-work fun, in this industry … I mean my friend who is a surgeon doesn't expect to spend all his time with people he likes, but in this industry people expect that. (Sophie, Commissioning, professional/managerial origins)

As these quotes illustrate, sponsors were important to the career trajectories of nearly all Commissioners and Senior Executives at 6TV. Also, as at TC, sponsor relationships were premised in large part on cultural affinity. Yet there are some important differences, as Sophie illustrates: the informal yet intense nature of television work, combined with the overall ethos of 'fun' and sociability, makes the nature of sponsorship in television quite distinct.

Moreover, there were important differences in the *way* sponsors helped their sponsees at the two firms. Unlike at TC, where sponsors largely 'brought through' junior staff, Commissioners at 6TV were almost entirely appointed externally. They were 'lateral hires'. But readers will recall that the ceiling effect at 6TV is predominantly concentrated in the Commissioning department, where 90% of senior staff are from professional or managerial backgrounds. This is a particularly stark disparity considering that those in the most appropriate pool for filling Commissioning roles – executives at 'indies' – are three times more likely to be from a working-class background.[20]

How might we understand this? One explanation is that the process of senior hiring in Commissioning often inadvertently rewards those from higher socio-economic backgrounds. This is certainly not the result of any conscious discrimination – we found no evidence of open class snobbery at 6TV. Nor can this be reduced to the kind of 'unconscious bias' often associated with interview settings. Instead, we argue that sponsorship, or at least strong personal ties, is key.

Certainly, hiring practices in Senior Commissioning are strikingly informal. The process normally consists of Commissioners drawing up a small list of potential contenders, based on their own contacts and industry knowledge, or the headhunting suggestions of the channel's 'Talent Manager'. These candidates are then sounded out, often informally over coffee or a drink. Occasionally, these meetings are then followed by formal interviews, but often an individual is simply approached directly and offered the job. And significantly, the channel's HR Department – which normally oversees recruitment processes – are cut off from this type of hiring. Senior Commissioners have almost complete autonomy.

This was not without reason. In fact, interviewees offered three justifications for these practices: first, the extreme financial and reputational risk involved in commissioning programmes;[21] second, that programming projects are often very time-sensitive and therefore decisions about hiring senior personnel must be taken very quickly; and third, that the work of a Commissioner is highly collaborative and therefore a candidate's perceived interpersonal skills, of being able to get on with the team, is very important. One way to mitigate all of these risks, most therefore argued, is to turn towards trusted entities, people one can "rely on to deliver", as Senior Commissioner Roger noted.[22]

Yet one of the by-products of this is that, as Senior Commissioner Michael admitted, "reliability and likeability sort of get mixed up" and people inadvertently hire in their own image. The explicit language of sponsorship was more muted in these discussions than at TC. But most Commissioners did concede that those they appointed tended to have close industry ties – either to them or to someone else directly involved in the hiring process. As James, a Commissioner from professional/managerial origins, elaborated:

> I'm as guilty as the next man ... and part of it is when you've been doing it for a few years so many things can go wrong, you kind of want to put a brick

wall against things you can't control; and part of that
reassurance is working with established companies,
with people who are of a like mind, you know, similar
background, similar interests ... And to be honest I
think most of the time being competent and getting
on with someone go hand in hand so it's kind of a
vicious circle.

At both TC and 6TV, sponsorship therefore plays an important
role in getting into the most valued and highly paid positions. At
6TV, this is first because of the informality of hiring processes –
particularly in Commissioning – which allow personal networks
to play a powerful role in selection decisions and, second, because
the conditions of risk and uncertainty that characterise television
work increase the demand for loyalty and reliability. However,
while these traits are partially connected to 'meritocratic' or
measurable competencies such as track record, they also act to
accentuate and legitimate sponsors' tendency to recruit for 'trust'
and therefore, very often, to hire in their own image.

Turning the tables: Sponsorship at Coopers

So far, we have discussed the ways in which sponsorship from
above tends to advantage the privileged. Yet it is important to
recognise that there is no reason why this should necessarily be
the case. Ralph Turner's original model of sponsored mobility
was premised on the simple notion that those in positions
of power grant upward mobility on the basis of the qualities
they wish to see in others, or the qualities they perceive as
'meritorious'. For Turner this process *did* work to privilege
the already privileged, but arguably only because he assumed
that elite incumbents were themselves largely from advantaged
backgrounds. What happens in elite occupations or organisations
where this is not the case?

Here it is worth turning to architecture firm, Coopers.
Sponsorship has a long history in architecture, facilitated
by a particular one-to-one, 'master–pupil', model of career
progression.[23] Such chains of sponsorship remain common today,
and are assisted by the small size of most architecture firms where

first jobs often involve working directly with a senior architect.[24] Sponsorship was a key theme in the career narratives of staff at Coopers. We were struck both by the prevalence of such one-to-one relationships and, at times, their emotional depth.

Yet it is also worth recalling that around half of the Partners at Coopers are from intermediate or working-class backgrounds. Stories of sponsorship at the practice, told by both sponsors and sponsees, were therefore quite different from TC and 6TV. While they were often rooted in homophilic bonds of class-cultural similarity, this often worked to advantage those from less (rather than more) privileged backgrounds. Sometimes this was referred to in subtly classed ways, about connecting due to shared regional identities ("he's Northern as well"), or sharing out-of-work hobbies. However, in a number of cases the narrative seemed to follow the mould of fairly conscious sponsorship, of senior staff seeing themselves in a junior colleague and providing concrete forms of help and support.

To illustrate, here we probe one relationship in particular, that of Gary and Amin. Gary was one of the Partners and had come from a working-class family in Yorkshire. He was passionate about the topic of class, expressing palpable anger at how working class people are portrayed in the media and the boundaries imposed by social class on his family. Amin, who Gary described as his 'right-hand man', was now a partner at the firm and was also from a working-class background. While there were important differences between the pair – Amin was British Pakistani and from Glasgow while Gary was white British and from a rural background – they had both grown up in environments where money was tight and had both clearly made it into architecture against the odds. It was also clear that Gary had quite explicitly sponsored Amin's career, had "taken him on", as Amin put it. Amin had originally entered Coopers after struggling to complete his undergraduate degree. Some 15 years on, he has still not yet formally qualified[25] as an architect. Ignoring this formal limitation, Gary has consistently provided Amin with career opportunities, beginning with general office duties, moving into project management, and ultimately promoting him to Partner with special responsibility for commercial strategy.

But as important as the concrete work opportunities were, the most significant theme that emerged from this relationship was the sense of emotional and psychological backing provided by Gary, of helping Amin overcome insecurities and supporting him when he was struggling with stress. Amin described himself and Gary as "introverts" and talked at length about the need to follow Gary's example in forcing himself to become more extroverted. He also explained how Gary had encouraged him to finish his architectural training, and had intervened when he was struggling with the abstract aesthetic aspects of the course:

> I did my dissertation and Gary was absolutely brilliant in helping me through that. He introduced me to the world of art. So arts and architecture. It was all new to me and we went to galleries. It was such a brilliant journey and I had this appreciation by the end of it.

In the context of the wider arguments in this book, it might be easier to feel more sympathetic about this type of sponsorship. Gary was operating as what Annette Lareau would call a 'cultural guide',[26] helping Amin to navigate an elite profession and trying to use his own power to unilaterally promote social mobility.[27]

But at the same time, it is important not to romanticise or scrutinise in the same way the relational implications of this type of sponsorship. Such relationships are still rooted in homophily, still cemented by a 'natural' or 'organic' sense of cultural commonality. And for every sponsee successfully inducted and nurtured by a senior sponsor, there are several less fortunate others who must try to make their way on their own.

Indeed, the importance of a one-to-one bond is often illustrated most clearly when it is absent. At Coopers, this was particularly striking among the women we spoke to. It is widely acknowledged that architecture is one of the worst professions when it comes to the *glass* ceiling.[28] Although feted as one of the better practices for overall gender representation, Coopers was no different. None of the practice's 15 Partners were women. And while stories of mentorship and sponsorship were common in the career narratives of female staff, these were often told by younger architects still at the beginning of their career, and had yet to lead to material benefits.

Sarah provided a telling example. While Sarah's immediate background was middle class (she had been privately educated and her father had risen to become an engineer), this privilege had not aided her in forging relationships with senior figures in the profession. She narrated her career progression as entirely self-driven, and explained that throughout her 20-year career she had never had a mentor or any meaningful senior support. On the contrary, she described architecture, particularly at the start of her career, as an "egocentric boys' club".

Despite this, Sarah had forged a highly successful career path. In her 20s and 30s, she worked hard to develop demonstrable expertise in multiple areas of architectural practice, and – against the odds (she was working part time and raising a young child) – had made Partner at a prestigious firm six years ago. Ultimately, however, this success – exceptional as it was – was temporary. She recently "chose" to leave the firm due to the unethical behaviour of a tyrannical male partner, and had accepted a demotion to take up her current role at Coopers.[29]

In Sarah's story, we see the fragility of progression without advocacy and sponsorship. While she had worked demonstrably hard, built expertise and even arguably over-delivered, this success was always vulnerable without the security of personal support from senior (largely male) colleagues.

The example of Coopers thus provides important nuances to our arguments about sponsorship and the class ceiling. It illustrates that sponsored mobility is not necessarily the preserve of the class-privileged. While this is often the case, sponsorship is a process premised most often on homophily, which can form around many different demographic characteristics. In the case of Coopers, the clearest losers when it comes to sponsorship are not necessarily those from working-class backgrounds but women – of all backgrounds.[30]

Networks and inequality

Much academic and policy literature focuses on the power of networks for career success. Accordingly, many interested in tackling organisational inequalities have devoted their attention to strengthening the weak-tie networks of disadvantaged groups while simultaneously attempting to diversify the networks leveraged by the privileged. "We all just need to swap black books," the influential UK diversity campaigner Deborah Williams has argued.

While such aims are clearly laudable, our work suggests that network inequalities at the top may be rooted in the patterning of much stronger ties. We have shown in this chapter how these forms of sponsorship act to fast-track careers, often providing a 'back-door' trajectory that is neither transparent nor easily held to account. And, of course, although sponsorship does not guarantee success, it does offer significant advantages.

The opportunities brokered by sponsors are almost always rationalised on the basis of 'merit' – of 'spotting talent' or 'rewarding potential'. We have shown, however, that such helping hands are also very often rooted in cultural affinity and cultural matching. We do not mean to suggest that sponsors are being disingenuous when they talk of searching for talent. Instead, the issue here is that very often, cultural similarity is one of the fundamental bases on which we read 'merit' and talent. But this does not just mean the specific cultural similarities shared by individual sponsors and sponsees; it can often relate to broader behavioural codes that dominate in particular elite occupations. In the next chapter, we explore the operation of these behavioural codes in our different case study professions. These codes, we argue, often govern people's instinctive sense of whether certain people do or do not 'fit'.

SEVEN

Fitting in

"She was just good at selling herself ... without ... without looking like she was selling, do you know what I mean?" The Future Leaders panel murmur their agreement with Head Judge, Simon. They are discussing the relative merits of two interviewees, Sophie and Martin. Each are vying for a place on television's most prestigious mid-career scheme, a year-long programme that takes 'rising star' television professionals and provides them with the support, mentoring and network relationships to propel them into senior roles. "Whereas Martin," Mark continues, "... really impressive, definitely. But it just jarred a little, didn't it? I'm not sure that works for us ..."

On paper, Sophie and Martin have very similar credentials. They have both shone in the early years of their careers. Sophie, white British, privately educated and from an upper-middle-class background,[1] has racked up a series of impressive credits as a documentary producer. Martin, Black British, and from a working-class background, is already a multi-award-winning screenwriter. The panel agree that Sophie and Martin are both comfortably worthy of a place, but there's only space for one.

We are coming to the end of two intense days observing interviews on the Future Leaders scheme. Hundreds of applicants have been whittled down to 40 or so shortlisted candidates, most of whom have CVs that – while showcasing different specialities and knowledge – are hard to tell apart in terms of experience and achievement. Interviews, then, are key.

After a long discussion Sophie eventually gets the nod over Martin. "All in all, I think she's a better fit," Simon says, summarising the panel discussion. Simon doesn't elaborate on what he means by 'fit', but it's easy to read between the lines. Within seconds of entering Sophie had ingratiated herself, quipping about how the maze-like feel of the building reminded her of a popular '90s TV game show. Immediately the atmosphere changed. The panel, tense from hours of interview mode, visibly relaxed. The banter continued back and forth, Sophie swapping jokes with the panel about other obscure game shows. Sophie also clearly interviewed well. Her answers to the standardised questions were confident, articulate and knowledgeable. But it is the lasting impact of those first two minutes of interaction that is most striking. Here Sophie's informal demeanour, her knowing humour, forges an immediate affective energy with the panel, setting the tone for a friendly, sympathetic interview.

Martin's experience was very different. He came in wearing a suit and, eyeing that he was the only one dressed formally, looked visibly uncomfortable from the beginning. Like Sophie, Martin also tried to banter with the panel. But his jokes fell decidedly flat. And while his against-the-odds story impressed the panel, this same determination seemed to work against him in the interview. He spoke passionately, earnestly. His style, according to one panel member, was "a little aggressive". "He was just a bit serious," another concludes.

These kind of fuzzy, ambiguous notions of 'fit' do not feature on social sciences surveys. They are not in official employment data. And they're not found on job specs. Yet, as this example demonstrates, they can be tremendously powerful in understanding why some people progress ahead of others in the labour market. In fact, in this chapter we will argue that they are a pivotal driver of the UK's class pay gap.

Mastering behavioural codes is pivotal to 'getting on' in all the professions we examined. It is a key way of signalling that you are the 'right type' of person to get ahead, that you fit, and it is duly rewarded by senior decision-makers. Importantly, however, we find that these codes are often only tangentially related to the work that goes on in elite jobs and are not particularly credible measures of ability, performance or intelligence. Instead, we argue, they frequently represent metaphorical 'glass slippers', rendering workplaces a natural fit for some and uncomfortable for others. In particular, they often act as cultural barriers for those from working-class backgrounds, who often struggle to fit, or adapt, to these cultures of work.

The glass slipper

Most of us recognise that different professions have different identities – that academics look different to bankers, and that behaviours considered acceptable in an audition might not wash in a boardroom. The more pressing question is why – where do these codes come from and, of particular significance to us, do they unfairly advantage some over others? To explore these questions it is first helpful to introduce the concept of the 'glass slipper', a metaphor that builds on, and develops, insights related to the 'glass ceiling'. The glass slipper metaphor, developed by American scholar Karen Ashcraft, captures the way in which particular occupations come to appear possessed of inherent characteristics that have little to do with the actual work yet render them a natural fit for some and a stretch, if not an impossibility, for others.[2] Like Cinderella's slipper, then, the collective understanding of many elite occupations was made in the image of certain people who are then considered 'naturally' more suitable, even if they are not necessarily the most able, skilled or competent. Why, after all, is the size of the shoe elemental to the princess role? Cinderella's tiny foot only hails her the best candidate because the job was defined around a shoe that was *made for her.* In contrast, through the figures of the 'Ugly Sisters', the metaphor also captures the difficulty of fitting in, or faking it, when the culture of work was not made for you. The particular 'glass slippers' for different occupations, then, are about their histories, about what type of people tended to do this kind of work in the past and how their ideas about the 'right' way to act at work have become embedded, even institutionalised, over time.[3]

The value of the glass slipper concept has also grown in recent decades as management guidance in many professions has moved away from an emphasis on rationality and self-control and instead championed the importance of self-expression, 'personal qualities' and authenticity at work.[4] As Peter Fleming explains, employees nowadays face a 'just-be-yourself' management policy in which 'permitting employees to be themselves is presumed to result in higher motivation and productivity levels'.[5] But the glass slipper offers a useful corrective to such 'common-sense' mantras, demonstrating that some expressions of authentic identity are more readily rewarded than others. Not everyone is necessarily permitted to be oneself at work.

Of course the significance of the glass slipper is that by shaping who feels they do and do not 'fit' in a given occupation it can have a tangible impact on who gets ahead. It enacts what Nicola Ingram and Kim Allen, drawing on Bourdieu, see as a sort of 'social magic', whereby those whose structural privilege provides a kind of cultural symmetry with what is valued in the workplace appear 'naturally' to be a 'fish in water', possessed of inherent or objective skills that are unrelated to the social world in which they were developed.[6]

Ashcraft's work mostly explored the way in which occupational identities in the US have tended to advantage white men. Recently, however, the pioneering work of management scholar Louise Ashley has introduced the glass slipper concept to UK audiences. Ashley has begun to show how the concept also applies to class background. Looking at access to the investment banking profession, she shows that certain dress codes remain very powerful in signalling whether an aspirant banker is the right fit for the profession. Aspirant bankers need to 'look the part' – in terms of the right suit, tie, even shoes (black, not brown, apparently) – and hiring managers acknowledge that this often weighs heavily on their judgements in graduate job interviews or during internships. Equally, aspirant bankers can be ruled as unfit for the profession on the basis of specific behaviours, speech patterns or dress, even where their technical aptitude is exceptional.

Ashley shows that these elements of 'cultural competency' are rooted in middle-class socialisation and inculcated disproportionately via a privileged, white, family milieu. In turn, those outside this white, middle-class 'norm' must 'devote particularly high levels of energy to deciphering and navigating these quite complex codes, which may detract from their ability to perform at the highest level'.[7] Ashley's research is thus pivotal in showing how issues of identity that seem at first glance superficial and easy for everyone to adopt play a significant role in reproducing class inequality.

Ashley has certainly been formational in beginning to unravel the way in which 'glass slippers' enact social magic in Britain's elite workplaces. Yet her work is confined to access – to those labouring to 'get in'. In this chapter we argue that the concept is as, if not more, important for understanding who 'gets on'. While notions of fit are clearly important in concrete moments of entry or recruitment (such as a graduate interview), we would argue that they are just as pervasive in structuring the more mundane operations of a workplace. It is here, in everyday office interaction, in client presentations, in auditions, or pitch meetings, that the power of the 'glass slipper' – of fitting, or not fitting, the dominant image of your field – is revealed most clearly. This chapter is chiefly concerned with exploring such settings. In doing so, we reveal what the 'glass slipper' looks like in our case study occupations – its contours, its boundaries and, importantly, the way it impacts the careers of those from different class backgrounds.

Are you Partner material? The power of corporate 'polish'

At Turner Clarke (TC) one phrase marks nearly all conversations about getting on: 'Partner material'. This consecration tends to take place quite early in an accountancy career, usually the first five-to-six years, and normally leads to rapid fast-tracking through the various tiers of middle management.

For those identified as 'Partner material', then, there is a near-guaranteed pathway to the top. But this begs an obvious question – what does 'Partner material' look like and how is it recognised and assessed? Here many existing TC Partners began by making a distinction between the competencies needed to be an Accountant and those necessary to go further and reach the top of the firm. This distinction often centred on those who can transcend the technical, who can move beyond the 'nitty-gritty' computational and arithmetic skills (knowledge of accountancy standards and complex tax codes, for example) necessary to qualify as an Accountant. While such tangible skills are important at the early-career stage, as one moves up in the business they give way to the need for a more ambiguous set of 'soft' skills – of being personable, trustworthy and charming.[8] As Colin, an Audit Partner from professional/ managerial origins, explained:

> To start with it's all technical stuff, you have to become technically exceptional and basically, cover the backsides of Partners. But then there comes a point where actually you know all the technical stuff, and it becomes less important ... there comes a point, about manager grade, where you have to go beyond that ...

Going beyond the technical, we learned, often hinges on a person's self-presentation and style of communication; of "looking and sounding the part", as Tax Partner Matthew put it, or "projecting an image of competency", in the words of Advisory trainee Rebecca (both from professional/managerial origins). This set of attributes is frequently summarised as an overall sense of 'polish'. And this notion of polish, we argue, gets to the heart of understanding the 'glass slipper' in accountancy.

Polish has multiple dimensions. First, it involves certain expectations around a person's accent and style of speech, particularly a preference for RP (Received Pronunciation).[9] As Robert, an Advisory Partner from an upper-middle-class background, told us:

> Language and articulation is a huge differentiator and it's probably one of the few things that makes me go ... When I hear people using inaccurate grammar or things like that, it's a very obvious identifier of something, a regional dialect that hasn't been tempered ...

Polish is also about appearance, dress and 'etiquette'. TC – like most large corporate firms – has an explicit 'modern professional' dress code. Its guidelines suggest that the 'guiding principle is "dress for your diary, dress for the brand"'. But this is, of course, extremely vague advice. This was particularly challenging for women, where expectations around dress were both more opaque and scrutinised more carefully. Bev, who had recently made Partner (with intermediate origins), explained how she had struggled for years with a sense that she was being judged on the 'appropriateness' of what she wore by senior men at work:

> Once upon a time, I would have gone in to Jigsaw or Reiss and bought a suit and then tried to … I don't know. But I've given up all that crap. I'm just like, this is what you get.

Most importantly, however, polish is about a particular *style* of communication. Here our findings strongly echo the work of Lauren Rivera, who writes about the power of 'polish' in US professional service firms. Reflecting on graduate interviews, she writes: 'Polish consists of seeming at ease while putting the interviewer at ease. Taking the reins in conversation while maintaining adherence to conversational and turn-taking norms, displaying excitement but keeping it within bounds, seeming confident but not cocky'.[10] This aspect of polish – interactional poise, understatement and embodied ease – was also integral to success at TC. In fact, we would argue that the power of this kind of diffuse communication style might be stronger in terms of progression than access. Certainly, it appeared central to successful everyday office life, smoothing interactions in meetings, appraisals, client pitches and networking events. And significantly, those most articulate in explaining its importance were often those who felt they lacked it. Philip, an Advisory Partner from a working-class background, explains:

> But in a meeting environment some people just automatically know when to pitch in … Like, you need to be trained in the game to actually sort of contribute. So this is one thing I have found I am incredibly bad at. If I've got something to present I am good at that. But if I actually have to sit with my peers around a table of 10 to 12 people – it's kind of when do you chip in, when do you bring in the

personal anecdote? Invariably the guy who has had the, for want of a better word, the posher upbringing is the one who is more comfortable talking. It's not necessarily the subject matter, it is actually the delivery of it and how you converse and interact, the sort of verbal cues and how you present yourself.

Polish is not reducible to any one of the areas discussed so far. Instead, as Philip describes here, it is seen more as a package, something others discern instinctively, or a capacity that 'just radiates outwards', as Audit Partner Martin (professional/managerial origins) put it. He explained that he often 'tests' polish by asking junior staff to lead meetings with key clients: "If you take somebody out with you to a lunch, how do they get on ... do they participate, are they confident, comfortable? I want people who've got some spark about them, people who are engaging, polished, who can develop a rapport."

Possessing polish, then, was a prerequisite for 'bringing someone through' to partnership. It was a key aspect of 'fit'. However, most also recognised that it wasn't (and indeed couldn't be) assessed in any formal or transparent way. Instead, as James, an Advisory Partner with professional/managerial origins, confided, it is typically evaluated in a tacit manner, and often in informal settings:

> It's a little bit ... can you go and have a pint with him? Or her, for that matter. And actually, I think it's interesting, there is a kind of ... there's a kind of shorthand if we're thinking about bringing someone through but haven't quite made up our mind. There is a kind of shorthand that says, "You'd go for a beer with them, but only a half" [*laughs*]. That's about as much as you could put up with! So it's a kind of shorthand for a whole load of other stuff.

Polish may be pivotal to becoming a partner, but how does it relate to class background? Many think of these kinds of social skills as qualities that some naturally possess and others don't.[11] However, a number of sociologists have strongly disputed this. Rivera, for example, has argued forcefully that the traits underpinning a polished corporate self-presentation, for example, can be closely traced back to a privileged upbringing.[12] This is also clear in our data. Nearly all TC interviewees from working-class backgrounds described struggling to adapt to dominant expectations around polish, or feeling a sense of inferiority in this regard.[13] Many specifically picked up on the irony between the firm's stated encouragement 'to bring your whole self to work' and their experience of having to manage or conceal their difference. Moreover, many believed that this perceived deficit had worked against them in important workplace settings.[14] The stories of two Partners from working-class backgrounds are telling here.

Raymond had recently made Partner but at 45, this was approximately 10 years later than average – and on his second attempt. The first time, after his application was rejected, he was told in confidence by one Senior Partner that he "just didn't feel like a partner". This colleague had then gone on to give him advice about dress:

> I can remember him saying, "Don't do dress down, just don't do it, Ray. If you want to be a bit more informal then take your tie off, it will just help people's perception of you" … what was the other one? Oh, because you carry around laptops and bags, we all get given a rucksack. "Ray, ditch the rucksack, you need a proper briefcase," he said.

In contrast, Paul *had* made it to partner on his first attempt. However, he explained that when he was 'brought through', his lack of polish had been 'noted'. In an attempt to remedy the situation, he explained, the partner group decided he should have an external 'presence coach':

> I am sure it was phenomenally expensive. And I used to joke that I felt a bit like Crocodile Dundee, used to go, "I bet [the coach] checks I haven't nicked anything after I've gone!" You know I am a Partner in one of the largest accountancy firms in the world

> but you still wonder ... now is that just me having a
> laugh or is there something deeper?

Of course, projecting an aura of polish is not necessarily a 'given' for every privileged-origin person and, as we've explained, often has important gendered and raced elements.[15] Yet the key point here is that for those from working-class backgrounds, mastering the appearance of polish frequently proves especially elusive. They start from a clear disadvantage, and are often unsettled by a lingering anxiety that they are making 'mistakes' in their execution of dominant behavioural codes.

We can look to history to understand the roots of this 'glass slipper'. Certainly, in the case of accountancy, it is possible to locate notions of polish running through a much longer history of the profession. Here, polish has particular antecedents in the understated, cultured figure of the 'gentleman'. Strongly linked to a privileged class background, mastery of such gentility – with its attendant set of appropriate behaviours, values and recreations – was key to progressing in Britain's finance sector in the 19th and early 20th centuries, particularly in the City of London.[16] It acted as a key way to signal one's elite status to employers, a dispositional shorthand that communicated to already anointed gentlemen 'that he is, of course, one of us', as C. Wright Mills famously wrote.[17] Such gatekeepers would then use their informal networks to grant advantages to these 'old boys' in the labour market.

Many of the coordinates of this gentlemanly motif have, of course, been eroded in the contemporary era, particularly those associated with the comportment of the aristocracy.[18] In the 1980s and 1990s, for example, several commentators argued that the 'Americanisation' of the City led to a conscious shift towards more meritocratic recruitment procedures and the eschewal of the traditional 'blue-blooded' image of the sector; a 'newly classless City', as historian David Kynaston proclaimed.[19] However, a clear division between an old and new City of London is too simple.[20] While there might be an *increased* emphasis on concrete educational credentials and/or technical skills, success at the top echelons – as we have already outlined – remains closely connected to less transparently relevant attributes.

In this context, it is possible to see polish as constituting a distinct reimagining of gentility – deftly combining modesty, understated yet professional dress, and an embodied ease.

It is worth adding that although polish was important across the board at TC, it had a heightened significance among those working in Advisory. This was for two key reasons; first, those in Advisory are not required to pass the same kinds of technical exams (which often have very low pass rates) as those working in Tax and Audit and second, self-presentation and impression management are particularly important in Advisory as clients lack other forms of reliable information to assess the quality of the advice they are being given. This 'ambiguity of knowledge'[21] (in contrast to technical skills that may be more straightforward to evaluate) can have important ramifications. As Ashley has argued,[22] such uncertainty places a heightened emphasis on nurturing an *image* of competency, of cultivating a belief in one's expertise. To that end polish becomes a pivotal weapon, an effective substitute or proxy for demonstrable competence. As Neil, an Audit Partner from intermediate origins, put it:

> What are Advisers, what are Consultants? People that can talk about having been there and done it. It is all sort of airy-fairy, head-in-the-clouds stuff, which lends itself to someone that can talk very well and doesn't necessarily have the depth of … the deep understanding and the technical knowledge that sits behind it. In Audit you couldn't get away with that because immediately people expect you to be an absolute technical specialist.

Presenting the appropriate image works here, at least in part, as an act of persuasion, where markers of polish become signals of the provision of high-quality advice.[23] This demonstrates a further, very important, dimension of the 'glass slipper'. In elite occupations, it's not just *what* you know that matters, but *who* you are and *how* you present yourself. And that, in turn, shapes what you are *perceived* to know. In areas like Advisory where knowledge, and therefore performance, is particularly hard to evaluate, there is a particular premium on image, rhetoric and the mastery of behavioural codes.[24]

Studied informality

Polish may be easier for some to embody than others, but at least behavioural codes in accountancy tend to be relatively formal and involve some clear-cut expectations governing dress, appearance and behaviour.[25] Elsewhere, such norms are often less transparent.

At 6TV, notions of corporate polish hold little sway. Indeed, many interviewees told us they had chosen 6TV precisely because there were *no* formal expectations around dress and appearance. Instead, most stressed the distinct informality of 6TV, with many in senior positions heralding this informality as a distinct sign of the channel's openness, where "everyone is welcome", as Executive Lizzie noted, or where "you can be who you want to be", according to Marketing Head of Department (HoD) Nigel. This was certainly borne out in our initial observations of the working environment. Here the contrast with TC was palpable. There was not a business suit in sight at 6TV. Instead we saw bucket hats, Hawaiian shirts, Dr. Martens, oversize glasses, jumpsuits, winklepickers, and shell-suits.

But this 'hip' informality was not the social leveller many presumed; on the contrary, it functioned as a subtle, intricate and highly 'knowing' code. We call this *studied informality*. And like polish, it has many dimensions. First, it involves dress. This does not take the form of a conventional uniform but – as these three interviewees describe – instead revolves around a more opaque *style* of dress:

> Someone from another channel once said to me, "Oh, you can tell when you're getting close to 6TV." I said, "What do you mean?" She was like, "Oh, just the way everyone's dressed." So there's definitely a 6TV way, a certain creative ... like notice the trainers [*points to her feet*]; trainers, but smart trainers, that's very 6TV. (Martha, Commissioning, professional/managerial origins)

Like, you can turn up in a T-shirt and jeans, but people have to know you're doing it for style, not laziness ... I can't tell you how to get that on the nail, but I'll know when I see it. (Peter, Marketing and Communications, professional/managerial origins)

There's a bit of, like, trying to fit with the tribe. I mean, I don't know why I dress like this. It's a uniform, isn't it? Like, in the same way you wear a suit, you work in the City ... I think it is my own taste but also I'm trying to be fashionable and not look like a weird stand-out-geek in the middle of a bunch of people dressed one way. (Mark, Commissioning, professional/managerial origins)

Studied informality, then, cannot be reduced to particular clothes. It is more an approach, *a way of dressing*, an indefinable style that these individuals – who are all from upper-middle-class backgrounds – know when they 'see it'. But studied informality extends far beyond just dress. It also demands a particular knowing mode of self-presentation – including humour, way of speaking and non-verbal communication. This was clear in the way people approached our interviews, which was distinct from other occupations we researched. We were struck by the number of interviewees who swore during interviews, made jokes, put their feet up on tables or sofas, or who finished interviews with a hug rather than a handshake. Studied informality, in other words, implies a level of interpersonal familiarity not normally associated with the professional workplace. Such a code may seem relatively superficial but many, like Senior Commissioner Rachel (professional/managerial origins), were quick to emphasise that its mastery represented a very real asset in the industry:

... it is really important to be able to chat and yes, have a bit of humour and for it to be jolly. There's a certain lightness of touch and it's really tiring, because you are performing. You are on. It sort of looks open but it's actually quite careful and not like ... it's actually a skill.

Studied informality, we argue, constitutes a central component of television's glass slipper. And like polish, its importance can be directly connected to the ambiguity of knowledge inherent to television production. This was apparent, for example, in the wide diversity of responses we received when we asked interviewees 'What makes a good 6TV Commissioner?' Answers were often vague or rambling, and there was little agreement on the core skillset necessary. This was underlined in discussions about training, expertise and credentials, particularly the snobbery directed towards film and television degrees. "If I saw that on someone's CV that would probably put me off them, to be honest," Commissioner Josh (professional/managerial origins) acknowledged. "This is a trade, not a profession. You can't 'learn' how to be good at TV."

Indeed, one of the key challenges for Executives and Commissioners at 6TV is that the potential success of a new programme is very hard to foretell, because most of the industry's final 'products' (that is, documentaries, drama serials, sitcoms) must be produced well before eventual audience consumption. Key staff such as Commissioners are therefore employed to address and (ultimately reduce) this uncertainty by assessing potential programmes' worth and potential, and by deciding which to select and promote for further development.[26] In the absence of concrete or reliable knowledge, many Executives acknowledged that the way Commissioners present their ideas, how they're packaged, becomes especially important. A command of studied informality is integral to this packaging. A candid discussion with one of the channel's Senior Creative Executives, Kerry (professional/managerial origins), illustrated the point:

> This is an absolutely insane place to work because in any given day you jump off a cliff 20 times. So I might decide I'm going to make a show about the history of jelly – I have no idea if that's going to work! I mean, I might look at data and the insights team might suggest it'll work. But actually the things that catch fire are often the least expected. So the risk profile of what we do is extremely high, and against

that backdrop you can do a few things to mitigate the risk ... one of them is to work with people who ... well ... well, the people I struggle with tend to be incredibly introverted, or who have an inability to be clear, articulate ... and I'm sure sometimes that maps quite well with different social backgrounds. I mean, this is probably very unattractive given that I'm Oxbridge, but there is a shorthand of ... or it is certainly easier for me to talk to people who are from that background because we understand each other.

This passage neatly illustrates how in this uncertain, time-sensitive, high-pressure, decision-making environment, sharing the command of a seemingly innocuous behavioural code such as studied informality can actually be pivotal for lubricating communication, for feeding a sense of mutual understanding. Kerry's frank reflections also reveal how studied informality, like polish, is classed in important ways. She was not alone in this. Many, for example, described how they had noticed that those from working-class backgrounds found it particularly hard to adopt such codes, and that this worked against them in important workplace settings. James, a Commissioner (professional/managerial origins), explains:

There is a kind of unwritten code and, whether you're kind of consciously adhering to it or not, you kind of recognise it, so that when someone, for example, comes in to pitch an idea, if it's not pitched in a certain way, then you kind of ... your gut reaction, your instinct is to dismiss it, because it's not ... I don't know, couched in the right language, or it's, you know, being pitched by someone who isn't playing the game ... or who doesn't understand the game, so you're kind of ... you trust people that understand the rules of the game. And I absolutely hold my hands up to being part of that.

This illustrates how interviewees often struggled to explain precisely *how* and *why* the socially mobile struggled with studied informality. Instead, they all grappled with an instinctive sense of cultural disconnection – that such individuals just didn't 'understand the rules of the game' or 'talk the same language'.

This barrier was felt both ways. Those from working-class and intermediate backgrounds found it similarly hard to explain but often described a general feeling of being on the outside, or of being shut out socially and culturally. Here two describe their experiences:

> There's just a thing of when people are from that kind of background, there's sometimes a bit of a ... a style of banter or something that sometimes makes me a bit ... in meetings ... like little in-jokes ... or like there's just a bit of a kind of club of people that all know each other. (Kate, Marketing and Communications, working-class origins)

> It tends to be walking into a room and thinking "I'm some kind of imposter here." It's like they all know each other ... I know they don't, but there's this sense ... I can't bear those meetings. It's like they all went to Hogwarts or something ... this posh club that I can't be in. (Claire, Strategy, intermediate origins)

Significantly, these accounts do not point towards a particularly clear and coherent barrier. Instead, they attest to a subtle but very powerful way-of-being in television that feels fundamentally alien. Moreover, when this behavioural code is executed successfully it seems to give the impression of familiarity – a sense, as many interviewees expressed, that everyone 'knows each other' (even if, in reality, they don't).

Also integral to these accounts was an underlying anxiety about making 'mistakes' in one's execution of studied informality, of not knowing the appropriate moment to swear in a meeting, how to deploy the right kind of joke, or when to put your feet up. Many interviewees explained how these mistakes often resulted in them being read by senior staff as too 'pushy' or 'aggressive'.

As Script Assistant Kieran (working-class origins) explained, "the irony is that I had to fight to get in the door but now that same fight holds me back!"[27]

The peril of misinterpreting informality at 6TV was most keenly felt among those we talked to who were from working-class backgrounds *and* racial-ethnic minority groups.[28] Here there was a strong sense that the colour of their skin increased the visibility of their class-cultural difference. "I was easier to read because I was brown, you know," Javid, Indian British, recalled of his first year at the channel, only half-joking: "I had really bad shoes, I get that [*laughs*], but if I was white and had really bad shoes ... maybe it would take them longer to notice." Others like Mary, who was Black British, explained this in terms of feeling "exposed", of insecurities around accent and vocabulary being accentuated by racial-ethnic difference: "There is one thing about the language, the way they argue their points, but as I was often the only Black person, as soon as I started talking, people used to kind of lean forward in this big boardroom."[29] These intersections between race and class were perhaps most aptly illustrated, however, by the example of one Black British former Commissioner who was from a working-class background but who had left the organisation a few years prior. This person was mentioned in multiple interviews, with each interviewee giving a similar account of someone whose style, behaviour and mode of informality was somehow incompatible with 6TV:

> He wandered round in tracksuit bottoms with a baseball cap on backwards all the time ... and everyone thought he was really cool. Genuinely. But he lasted about six months ... it was like he spoke another language, he just couldn't find a way in and it wasn't because there was a lack of willingness to integrate him. We genuinely wanted him here, people really wanted him to flourish. But in the end it was as though he was walking one way and we were all walking the other and we couldn't find the moments where we intersected. And I don't know what the solution to that is ... because I can't stop

the train to let people on, do you know what I mean?
(Lizzie, Executive, professional/managerial origins)

This final quote demonstrates the difficulty of tackling studied informality as a barrier to social mobility. As Lizzie illustrates, even if many within 6TV may be aware that such codes bear little or no relation to intelligence or ability, they remain dominant in the wider industry and this, in turn, stymies both the willingness and commitment to "stop the train".[30]

'Seeing through the bullshit': Coopers as 'pragmatic' architects

It is worth recalling that, unlike the other occupations we have explored, there is little evidence of a class ceiling in architecture – both in the UK as a whole, and within our case study firm, Coopers. Recall that half of the partners at Coopers were actually from working-class or intermediate backgrounds. Let us consider the reasons for this striking difference.

One clue might lie in the status of technical knowledge and skills. While highly ambiguous forms of aesthetic knowledge are very important in architecture, they must jostle for prominence with more technical dimensions of building design, construction and delivery. Significantly, these more practical skills are particularly important at Coopers. The commercial focus of the firm (which concentrates on large-scale defence and transport projects) ensures that technical skills enjoy an elevated status. In the words of Senior Partner, Paul (professional/managerial origins), Coopers is ultimately a firm made up of "pragmatic architects":

> Yes we're very creative, yes we're architects. But we're practical about it. We solve practical problems as well. We're not just dreamers.[31]

Mastery of these technical dimensions is often connected to a wider emphasis on 'perfectionism' within the firm (and architecture more broadly), of a heightened attention to detail, or, as ambitious Architectural Assistant Martin put it: "spending extra time even though nobody's asked us to."

The contrast here with TC is striking. Where in accountancy we described a clear ceiling in terms of how far technical knowledge will take you, at Coopers such competence was key at all levels. Indeed, in setting up the firm, technical expertise represented one of the three pillars for which the trio of Founder Partners took individual responsibility (the other two being commercial issues and design). Tellingly, the Technical Partner remains arguably the practice's most acclaimed figure, described by one founder as the "supreme detailer".

The currency of deep technical skills, or what we would call technical capital,[32] was most clearly revealed in the narratives of early-career staff. Elena spoke enthusiastically about her plans to develop a particular "scripting tool" to aid with "complex geometrical modelling", while Martin explained his aspiration to become an expert in "hyperloop transportation". Both explained that partners were actively encouraging them to develop these kinds of technical expertise, to find their 'niche' or master a 'specialist area'. Similarly, when explaining who he looked up to, and why, Connor, an Architectural Assistant from intermediate origins, foregrounded technical expertise:

> Sometimes I'm working on a project with some of the [Partners] upstairs and you just stand back and you're like, "Wow!" When I'm their age, in 10 years' time, I'd love to be able to do that … just the amount of stuff they memorise in their heads, how the building works, the intricate details of everything – I think, "How is he doing that?!"

Why is this significant for social mobility? We would argue that this kind of technical knowledge is significantly more transparent, learnable and evaluable than the competencies foregrounded in television Commissioning or financial Advisory, and less likely to be passed on via a privileged background.[33] In fact, it may even act to militate against the development of classed behavioural norms such as polish and studied informality. For example, Coopers staff often describe a fairly straightforward process of mastering architectural skills, of investing time and effort and subsequently developing a demonstrable expertise. There is little talk of opaque behavioural codes.

Of course, technical know-how is not solely about the application of knowledge.[34] As Connor's comments illustrate, it can also play a highly symbolic role, signifying wisdom and magisterial expertise. But this less tangible aspect of technical knowledge is again not so clearly connected with a privileged background. When asked what first sparked an early interest in architecture, for example, many at Coopers would recall a practical interest in how to put things together, or a childish amazement at discovering the intricacies of building construction. The symbolic elements of this kind of technical knowledge, in other words, do not appear particularly socially exclusive.

There is an additional point to consider here. While at TC clients rarely had detailed knowledge of the areas they were being advised on, the opposite is the case at Coopers. Here clients are typically themselves practising architects or engineers, frequently share the same knowledge base, and are therefore in a strong position to reliably evaluate performance. In this sense, the artful deployment of polish or informality can actually backfire. As Eamon, an experienced Associate, summed up succinctly: "[clients] can see through any bullshit."

There was even some evidence that it can be an advantage to be read as working-class, particularly 'on site'. Here many described battling to evade the caricature of the 'precious architect'. One Partner, Paul, from a professional/managerial background, admitted dirtying up his rarely worn luminous protective equipment before setting foot on a new build site, while Architectural Assistant Martin explained that he proudly deploys his Northern[35] accent: "I think it gives me an edge, to be honest," he explained.

It is clear, then, that the technical dimensions of the glass slipper at Coopers lend it a more socially open feel than our other case study firms. But it is important not to overstate this celebratory narrative. The overall make-up of the firm is still strongly skewed towards the privileged, as is architecture more broadly (see Chapter Two).[36]

It may also be that a class ceiling *does* exist in some parts of the profession outside our case study, especially in the more prestigious design-led[37] firms.[38]

More starkly, readers will remember that a profound *glass ceiling* exists at Coopers. None of the firm's 15 Partners are women. This is an inequality echoed in the wider architecture profession, where the litany of problems faced by women – including a huge gender pay gap[39] – are well documented.[40] Accordingly, the glass slipper at Coopers is more gendered than classed.[41] More specifically, and perhaps reflecting the historical mythology of architecture as a vocation (rather than an occupation),[42] interviewees were unanimous that the key ingredient of success at Coopers was hard work. But this was a particular formulation of hard work. It was about demonstrating devotion rather than careerism, the sense that a virtuous 'vocational' trajectory is necessarily slow and based on an intense, uninterrupted commitment to seeing projects through to completion. We characterise this here as 'patient diligence'.

Yet we also saw very clearly how this emphasis on patient diligence works to favour men. Male staff had found it much easier to commit to long hours and full-time work, while many women struggled to perform patient diligence while also negotiating family caring responsibilities. Sofia, for example, who was from an upper-middle-class background, had recently returned to work after a short maternity leave, explaining that this was a necessity if she wanted to maintain her position as Project Architect. Paula, an Associate with intermediate origins, added ruefully:

> There are a few [female] colleagues that have children now, and you can see that they've given up even trying to progress when they're part time.

Classed markers, then, may be largely absent from this notion of the glass slipper. However, it is important to stress that codes like patient diligence still disrupt any sense that career progression at Coopers was driven purely by neutral technical competence or learnable business skills. Breaking the class ceiling, in other words, does not necessarily imply breaking the glass ceiling.

'Merit' is tricky: The tyranny of 'fit'

When most people think about pay gaps, whether by gender, race or indeed any category, the key issue is often discrimination – are some people suffering prejudicial treatment in the labour market? This is often conceived in fairly individualised terms, of gatekeepers either consciously or unconsciously rewarding some over others. This chapter complicates the issue. Was Martin being discriminated against by the judging panel of Future Leaders? Perhaps. But what we've tried to show in this chapter is that Martin's fate was shaped more by the judges' 'gut feelings', about who felt right, who fitted, who they sensed to be 'one of us'. We have also demonstrated, however, that notions of fit are often 'field-specific', and behavioural codes do not necessarily cross over from one elite occupation to the other.

Yet across all our occupations, we see evidence that such codes are routinely *misrecognised* as markers of 'objective' skill, talent and ability – of 'merit'.[43] While it may be possible to argue that some of the codes we have explored may be correlated with job performance, most are definitively not. Expectations around dress, accent, taste and etiquette, for example, clearly do not stand up as robust measures of talent or intelligence.

Most importantly we also see a clear pattern in terms of *who* tends to 'fit' and therefore who gets ahead. Again and again, our data reveals that it is the privileged who are most comfortable adopting, mastering and playing with dominant behavioural codes, who feel most able to 'bring their whole self to work', to borrow the corporate mantra of Turner Clarke. This is because these individuals are frequently able to give the impression that such norms are 'naturally' embodied, that they are known without ever having been learned. And just like Cinderella's glass slipper, we would argue that this is rooted in the fact that the collective images of many elite occupations have been made in their image, magically allowing them to appear more 'naturally' suitable and able. This may not constitute discrimination. But it is certainly unfair.

EIGHT

View from the top

At 6TV, there is one meeting that trumps all others. The 'Creative Assembly', as it's termed by its architect, the Chief Creative Officer (CCO), has, in many ways, become the channel's *key* decision-making forum. Held once a week, its aim is to review programmes that have been pitched to, or piloted by, the channel, and to discuss and debate the relative merits of each. Its principle players are the Senior Commissioning team, but a revolving group of junior staff from throughout the channel are also invited to join and their input encouraged. The aim, according to the CCO, is to initiate a "collision of different perspectives and ideas". She explains: "It's about finding a collective intelligence and creativity by bringing in different types of people, from different backgrounds, rather than versions of the same person."

The idea behind the Creative Assembly is certainly laudable. It represents a genuine attempt to break down barriers and bring in different voices – particularly those from different class backgrounds. Yet our interviews revealed that, in many ways, the concept has dramatically backfired. Far from disrupting existing hierarchies, the Creative Assembly has become a crucible of the already anointed, a gladiatorial encounter where the discussion of television programmes often acts as a vehicle for Senior Commissioners to underline their cultural prowess to the Executive team. Success here rests on the demonstration of a particular highbrow sensibility, with participants jockeying to drop legitimate cultural references, or showcase an ever-more arcane and lyrical mode of aesthetic appreciation. "It's sort of a game of showing off," Rachel, a Senior Commissioner (professional/managerial origins), explains:

> I'm like, how ... why are we talking about *Of Mice and Men* in relation to a programme about lie detectors? You don't need to know about the Great American Novel to make shows on 6TV.

For those from working-class backgrounds, the Creative Assembly is a visceral reminder of the ceiling they face at 6TV, a pageant for the performance of an elite culture they mostly find impenetrable and alienating. Bill, a Commissioner, summed up the sentiments of many. He explained that these meetings always provoke the most acute feelings of otherness: "There is always this moment where I look around and think, 'I'm not part of this club.' Like at the last one, I remember these two Commissioners suddenly started making references to classic literature ... I think it was Greek ... and then there was some Latin, and I was like ... I'm not, this is not my gaff!"[1]

It is perhaps not surprising that we detect distinct barriers at the upper echelons of 6TV. As outlined in Chapter Four, there is a very stark class ceiling at the channel with those from working-class backgrounds rarely reaching the top tiers of the organisation. This ceiling effect is echoed at Turner Clarke (TC), where a similar invisible barrier separates middle management and the hallowed partner group. These are unlikely to be isolated cases. Indeed, the national class pay gap outlined in Chapters Two and Three is likely driven – in many cases – by similar 'top-level' effects, of vertical segregation by class background that becomes more and more acute as people approach the boardroom or executive suite.

In this chapter we focus specifically on the drivers of this *ceiling*. Clearly, many mechanisms already discussed are relevant here. Behavioural codes (Chapter Seven) and familial financial cushions (Chapter Five), for example, both have cumulative effects that will enable some and disenable others to reach top-tier positions. Similarly, sponsorship (Chapter Six) plays a pivotal role in reaching magic circles,[2] especially in corporate environments where making it to Partner is often contingent on being 'brought through' by others.

But our fieldwork suggests that there are also distinct *organisational cultures* that exist at the top of many elite occupations that tend to work against those from working-class backgrounds. Less constrained by formal and explicit recruitment guidelines,[3] and with an abundant oversupply of appointable candidates, access to these top positions is often heavily dependent on 'signalling' one's familiarity with existing executive cultures, which is then recognised and rewarded by those already in elite positions.

In this chapter we look at two key dimensions of executive cultures. First, we explore the power of *internal* cultural norms that pervade executive environments. Looking specifically at the highbrow culture within 6TV Commissioning and the expectations around classed accents in acting, we show how these norms often function as 'fences', strongly advantaging those who have been socialised or schooled into a command of highbrow culture. Second, we explore the *outward*-facing dimensions of executive cultures, of who is considered best suited to represent their organisation in public or with clients, who has the requisite 'gravitas'. Here, we look specifically at processes of client matching in Advisory at TC. This, we argue, also advantages the privileged, as existing partners tend to bring through junior staff whom they believe are culturally similar and therefore familiar to clients – who instinctively reach for the appropriate communication style to adopt, the right cultural or sporting settings to entertain with, or the manner in which to approach sensitive issues like tax.

How elites close off the top

Scholars have long discussed the exclusionary nature of executive environments. The issue at stake in much of these discussions is the degree to which processes of recruitment to elite positions enact forms of what sociologists call 'social closure'.[4] This idea of closure is normally understood as a process whereby those already in elite positions, who often act as the gatekeepers of these roles, restrict access to opportunities to a limited circle of those they deem eligible. Eligibility here is often based on an individual possessing certain traits, dispositions or knowledge that function as 'signals' of perceived eliteness.[5] As C. Wright Mills famously remarked of the US power elite, 'time and time again, in close-ups of the executive career, we observe how men in the same circles choose one another'.[6]

This is often called 'opportunity hoarding', in the sense that it implies that opportunities are allocated in a fundamentally anti-competitive or unmeritocratic way, that is, the decisive signals gatekeepers rely on are often wholly unrelated to an individual's performance or job-related skills and experience. Instead, they simply indicate, in the words of C. Wright Mills, 'conformity with the criteria of those who have already succeeded ... to be compatible with the top men is to act like them, to look like them, to think like them.'[7]

In a UK context, as explored in the previous chapter, such elite signals were traditionally connected to the figure of the upper-class 'gentleman'. This cultural identity was in part simply a matter of having the 'right' pedigree, of hailing from a 'good family'. But it was also more purposively inculcated through a particular elite education at one of Britain's prestigious elite private schools (confusingly often called 'public schools' in the UK[8]). Family and schooling then combined to produce a distinct set of behaviours, values and recreations, a distinct way of being in the world that, while irreducible to any one particular trait or practice, was nonetheless unmistakeable to existing elites and allowed them to identify potential recruits.[9]

Recent work has found that Britain's public schools do indeed retain an extraordinary ability to propel their 'old boys' into elite positions. Even today, the alumni of the nine top public schools (known collectively as the 'Clarendon Schools') remain 94 times more likely to reach *Who's Who* – a longstanding catalogue of the British elite – than those who attended any other school. These individuals also retain a striking capacity to enter the elite even without passing through supposedly 'meritocratic' educational institutions, such as Oxford or Cambridge Universities.[10] This ability to achieve, even without the highest academic credentials, indicates that such schools continue to pass on distinct non-educational resources that function as elite signals in the workplace.

However, while the alumni of Britain's public schools may maintain enduring advantages, they still only represent a very small minority of Britain's occupational elite – less than one in ten. In other words, the operation of the class ceiling extends far beyond the advantages of the very wealthy. Here we echo the work of policy analyst Richard Reeves in pointing towards the importance of more 'ordinary' forms of upper-middle-class privilege in oiling one's life chances.[11] Reeves identifies a range of ways that the US upper-middle-class hoard opportunities unfairly, including legacy admissions at elite universities and the informal allocation of internships.[12] However, Reeves and other academics are fairly quiet on how such forms of ordinary class privilege play out later in life, especially as people seek to enter top occupational positions.

One source of insight here is the work of sociologist Omar Lizardo, and specifically his analysis of how culture is implicated in processes of elite social closure.[13] Drawing on the theory of Bourdieu, Lizardo looks at how different cultural tastes shape and sustain personal networks in the US. He is particularly interested in the idea of social capital – how possessing connections to high-status individuals can be mobilised to attain desirable resources, or in the context of this book, advance one's career. An orientation to popular culture, he argues, can act as a source of social bridging – providing interactional tools that facilitate weak ties across a range of social backgrounds. This kind of cultural material, in short, 'provides fodder for least common-denominator talk'.[14] In contrast, Lizardo shows that highbrow tastes – particularly those characterised by a more intellectual orientation – act less as a social bridge and more as a fence. These more 'legitimate' tastes – which tend to be 'scarce' in terms of only being available to those who have had the kind of privileged upbringing (and/or education) that provide the aesthetic tools to enjoy it – is necessarily more exclusive and tends to strengthen ties among restricted groups, particularly those in senior or high-status occupational positions. In this way, Lizardo provides a useful explication for how the seemingly innocuous expression of personal cultural identity – what one likes and does not – can be a pivotal means by which those from privileged backgrounds solidify networks of power and close off the upper echelons of elite occupations.

It's not Hegel! The highbrow culture of Commissioning

We begin our interrogation of UK class ceilings by returning to 6TV. Readers will recall that the ceiling effect at 6TV is predominantly channelled through the Commissioning department, which contains a disproportionate share of 6TV's Executive team and where 90% of Senior Commissioners are from professional or managerial backgrounds. As we explained in Chapter Five, this is partly about those from working-class backgrounds lacking the financial resources to stay on the television production tightrope and sorting out of creative roles early or mid-career. It is also partly about the informality of hiring practices in Commissioning, where those appointed often have strong personal ties to existing Commissioners. Here we introduce a third driver, a highbrow culture that dominates the upper echelons of Commissioning.

During interviews, we were struck by the way that interviewees categorised the culture in Commissioning, whether they worked there or not. While studied informality was pervasive throughout the company, there was a more distinct set of norms in Commissioning. If there was one attribute that all Commissioners shared, we were told, it was a particular command of, and preference for, highbrow culture. This didn't necessarily mean that all Commissioners had exactly the same cultural tastes, but they shared a particular way of talking about culture, a set of linguistic tools and a commitment to what Bourdieu calls the 'aesthetic disposition' – that is, that the consumption of culture should be difficult, demanding and require intellectual deliberation.[15] This, in turn, informed a very particular way of talking about television in work settings, or as Lindsey, a Senior Commissioner, put it, "being able to talk in the right way, in a sophisticated, artsy kind of way." Daniel, a Junior Commissioner from professional/managerial origins, elaborated:

> We are very highbrow ... and there's an expectation
> that you need to be that bit more highbrow to come

and work here, need to think highbrow ... there is that snobbery ... you can sort of see if you make a slightly populist suggestion and people just kind of recoil.

This expression of executive culture – or what Commissioner Mark characterised more as a "monoculture" – was most clearly demonstrated, as already outlined, during the Creative Assembly. But its importance extended far beyond this one setting. Commissioning, by its very nature, is a deliberative process, and therefore key decisions are normally subject to multiple meetings before final sign-off – from pitch, to initial development, to pilot, to production and broadcast. The experiences of one interviewee, Rachel, perfectly underlined the power of this highbrow sensibility. Rachel had recently been appointed to a Senior Commissioning role from the 'indie' sector. She had been headhunted for the role, and had gone through no formal recruitment process. She was also, significantly, from what she described as a "solidly middle-class background" (both her parents had been high-achieving professionals). Fairly new to Commissioning, Rachel was very conscious of the cultural particularities of the department:

> After my first big Commissioning meeting, I remember a few people sending me emails saying, "God it's just brilliant to have you here. You fit in straight away." And that's the thing. I did really enjoy it because I'm like, I'm in this room with all these clever people. They're all really lovely, it's a really nice environment. It doesn't feel intimidating to me. But then, that's because I speak the same language. I get the references. And I'm confident enough to say, "Do you know what, I didn't even notice that that drama was full of clichés. I just cried." And they laugh and that's okay. Do you know what I mean? Because I don't feel I need to prove that. But somebody else might.

Now it is important to acknowledge that for many Executives we spoke to, a command of this highbrow aesthetic is not simply about reflecting and reinforcing a relatively arbitrary taste profile. On the contrary, many saw it as a very important skill, a productive competency. Such a culture of "intellectual critique," as one Senior Commissioner, Jack (professional/managerial origins) put it, is "critical to good TV commissioning." We would not necessarily dispute that view here. As researchers, we would not pretend to have the industry-specific experience to pass judgement on the validity of a highbrow disposition as a skill or source of tangible productivity.

However, there are two points we wish to underline in response to this sentiment. First, regardless of its relationship to skill or productivity, our fieldwork suggested that the value placed on highbrow culture was strongly connected to the class ceiling at 6TV. This was largely because those from working-class backgrounds felt alienated from this way of discussing television. For many it epitomised an executive culture in which they didn't belong. This often manifested in terms of feelings of intimidation, or of not feeling able to contribute, in key settings. Alice, for example, was a Script Editor in Commissioning. She had been brought up on a council estate by her parents, a cleaner and a hospital porter. She had been at the channel for a few years and had worked her way up from an entry role as a Drama Assistant. Despite some progression, though, she expressed a strong sense of cultural distance from her senior colleagues in Commissioning. One telling conversation summed up this feeling of difference:

Alice:	Okay, so I have had a few different Commissioning Editors. And I guess at an early stage I thought, "I'll never be quite good enough to do that," just sort of accepted that subconsciously. That I'd never be the right person.
Interviewer:	Why?
Alice:	Well, I suppose I do feel a little bit intimidated. I think at a certain level in our department we are all a little bit nervous about being laughed at, like, in a big meeting. Whereas you know of course Commissioning Editors

	would never … they could come up with anything and they could all laugh and it would be fine. But if you are going to say one thing every week, it needs to be something good. So you can't freely sort of brainstorm. Like sometimes I think something about a script but I can't articulate it in the way that they do. Like they have these words.
Interviewer:	What, in terms of articulating their taste?
Alice:	Yes, a lot of it is taste. You need to be able to articulate, know your feelings, the right feelings about various film dramas that are currently out. You need to be aware of what's going on, you definitely need to be up with current affairs. So you just need to have like lots of points of reference. And yes you need to watch the right things, what is cool to watch, and then if somebody at the top, who is very respected, says actually it is cool to be watching this reality TV thing then everyone would be like "Oh yes, that's cool," and then you can relax and say "Actually, I love that too."

Alice conjures a vivid image of the organisational hold that a highbrow aesthetic possesses at 6TV, and the paralysis that flows from feeling locked out, of missing the nuances, the linguistic fluency and instinctive understanding of when to play with the rules of legitimacy or 'cool'. We strongly connect this highbrow cultural orientation to class background. Many readers may legitimately ask why. Well, here we draw on a formidable body of research, again rooted in the work of Bourdieu, that highlights how preferences for legitimate 'high' culture, as well as a command of the vocabulary and mode of aesthetic appreciation that accompanies it, are strongly tied to class background.[16] This begins during the process of primary socialisation, whereby middle-class parents inculcate in their children certain valuable cultural 'tools', such as knowledge and experience of the 'high arts'. For example, they are more likely to talk about cultural topics at home, or take their children to museums, theatres or art galleries. But they don't just *introduce* their children to legitimate culture; they also teach them to *look* and *listen* in specific ways, to employ a particular aesthetic lens, to "articulate" a particular critical lexicon, as Alice puts it, and ultimately to exude a seemingly natural confidence when speaking about culture. These capacities are together commonly termed 'embodied cultural capital' in academic literature (that is, they appear so intrinsic to the individual that they seem almost like physical traits[17]). And in our analysis it was very clear that this embodied cultural capital acted as a very strong 'signal' that someone could slot into the culture of Commissioning.[18]

But there is also an important second point to stress here. Highbrow culture not only acts as a barrier for those from working-class backgrounds, but the majority of our interviewees – including many from privileged backgrounds – also questioned or even disputed the value it added to the creative decision-making process. Here it is worth returning to Rachel, the Senior Commissioner introduced earlier in this chapter. Rachel was highly sceptical of this kind of highbrow signalling, and argued that it often actually acted to divert programming conversations away from "what real people care about":

> You don't need to know about the Great American Novel to make shows on 6TV. You really, really don't. What you need to know to make telly here is you need to be interested in the world; what actual real people care about and how you're gonna reflect it to them.

Rachel was not alone. Ten of fourteen Commissioners we spoke to mentioned at some point in their interview that this highbrow orientation, or mode of discussion, is largely irrelevant to effective decision-making around making or commissioning programmes. "We're talking about TV … it's not Hegel!", Executive Rowland exclaimed. Many felt that this shared aesthetic sensibility instead fulfils a largely "posturing" function, as Karen, a Senior Commissioner (intermediate origins), explained:

> Something about the deconstruction of how you say something … I feel like people are speaking so that they can be heard to be intelligent rather than necessarily … I think it's a bit of posturing probably … so there's a lyrical tone to the way that things are put, there's a definite, you know some people round the table might not understand some of the words used and that, and that's the sort of innate way of saying "I'm not sure if you are aware but I did go to Cambridge" which is, which is fine but there's sort of no need for it in a way …

This demonstrates the way a highbrow aesthetic functions more as an elite 'signal', an (arbitrary but powerful) marker that allows those from privileged backgrounds to recognise one another. Others, like Dave, a Commissioner (professional/managerial origins), went even further, arguing that this "pointless intellectual grandstanding" acts as a needless barrier to those from working-class backgrounds:

> You have to talk the same language. I genuinely, honestly, think that if you're Black or you're disabled, you can still be middle class and you will be okay here. Because nobody here is racist, they're just not. If you are middle class, you will still be able to talk that same language whatever your ethnicity is. Whatever your disability is. But class is a completely different thing. If we want to change the stories that we tell, we need to get working-class people in, poor people. You need to get poor people in. That is what we need. And it's the hardest thing because they are the most "other".

Of course this is a complicated issue – producing television is about producing culture, and therefore discussions of why you make one programme over another, and how one programme compares to others, are demonstrably important to being a television Commissioner. However, interviews indicate that there is a fairly strong swell of feeling that *what* cultural forms are valued in such creative discussions, as well as the *way* discussions are conducted (and then evaluated by senior staff), acts to significantly and arguably unfairly advantage those from more privileged backgrounds.

Voicing class distinction: The power of RP in British acting

So far we have explained how a command of highbrow culture and aesthetics acts as a potent signalling tool at the upper echelons of television, even when the production decisions being made at such levels bear very little connection to such high art culture. Yet it is also worth recognising that sometimes elite signalling is less about what someone knows and likes and more simply about how they speak and sound. It is here that we must return to the issue of accent. Language and accent have long been associated with class division in Britain,[19] with different working-class regional accents traditionally counterposed to the more standardised Received Pronunciation (RP)[20] – also known colloquially as the Queen's English or BBC English[21] – of the upper-middle classes.[22] Indeed, as we explained in Chapter Seven, RP is an important component of the dominant behavioural code at both TC and 6TV.[23]

Yet it is in the acting profession where accent generally, and RP specifically, has the most direct impact on who gets to the top. This is because RP is generally considered the vocal starting point of classical acting practice. This process of legitimation, our respondents told us, begins in drama school, where the importance of RP "is constantly hammered into you", as Fraser (working-class origins) put it. It then extends into the labour market, where many high-profile job adverts – particularly in theatre – will specify the need for a 'natural RP speaker', or else will strongly imply it in the audition process.

This, of course, presents a clear barrier for working-class actors who are perceived as lacking 'natural' RP intonation. Aiden, who spoke with a broad North East 'Geordie' accent, had experienced the normative power of RP as a recurring obstacle in his career. He explained that in classical theatre, and particularly in Shakespeare productions, regional accents like his own tended to be reserved for supplementary characters, as a counterpoint, a foil, for "the smaller comedy roles where you have to take the piss out of yourself to get the audience on side." Aiden told us that over time he had come to see this as deeply offensive, a process through which he was continually asked to "mock" his heritage to get work, where "it just feels like prostitution". Moreover, while Aiden had never explicitly been advised not to use his accent when auditioning for larger roles, 10 years of experience had taught him, "if I do my own accent I am actually doing myself out of the job." Derek (working-class origins) elaborated a similar point:

> They don't want to hear you spouting Shakespeare, they want someone with a "clear voice". You still get that now – "must be RP" or "genuine RP speaker." Not that you can't do RP. Most actors can. No, it has to be your accent. No reason why. But if you see a Shakespeare character with a regional accent it's always ... like a gimmick.

Significantly, however, the power of RP was not just about the skew of leading roles for middle-class *characters*; it was also about what type of actors were seen to be able to 'play against type', to evade their typecasting. This is often seen as a key signal that an actor has reached the top of the profession, that their acting talent transcends their own demographic coordinates. Yet we would argue that this is also where the institutionalisation of RP in 'classical' acting training is important. As RP is often seen as the 'neutral' voice of the British actor, this means 'natural RP' is often seen as the appropriate starting point from which to move beyond RP or play against type. This was evident from scrutinising the CVs of our acting interviewees. Here it was overwhelmingly 'natural RP speakers' from privileged backgrounds, particularly white men, who had played most consistently 'against type'.

Tommy was a case in point. Tommy's father was a CEO of a large company and his mother a retired dancer. He was educated privately, had studied at a top London drama school, and began acting professionally in the Capital's top West End theatres aged four. A highly varied career had followed. He had played a range of leading roles in an array of settings, including the Royal Shakespeare Company, London's West End, primetime television drama, cult television comedy, fringe physical theatre and even a handful of operas. These parts also covered a wide array of characters – from a king's wayward confidant in a Shakespearean play, to a gay Russian prisoner of war, to a housewife's teenage lover. Olly, also from London, had similarly diverse credits. The son of two high-profile actors, he had worked extensively in Hollywood and the West End, with leading roles including a lower-middle-class clerk, a Bohemian king, an abusive husband and a cocky schoolboy.

The CVs of actors we spoke to from working-class backgrounds looked very different. As Table A.1d in the Methodological appendix illustrates, most had not reached the same levels of success as our more privileged interviewees. And, as we explored in detail in Chapter Five, the roles these actors had played were often restricted to working-class characters that were heavily caricatured and politically regressive.

So while the construction of RP as the 'neutral' voice of British acting may appear an innocuous professional practice, what these interviews indicated is that over time it has become what the scholar Nirwal Puwar has called a 'somatic norm'.[24] The somatic here refers to the bodily, the physical, and so the somatic norm refers to the way that RP tacitly designates middle-class voice, pitch and tone as having a greater 'natural' right to occupy both a higher proportion, and a more prominent array, of roles within the profession. In contrast, the regional accents of working-class actors often act as a cultural barrier to getting work, marking them out as outsiders, as 'space invaders', to use Puwar's words again, that lack the 'natural' linguistic resources to be legitimately recognised.

Client matching: Flattery will you get you everywhere

The class ceiling is certainly a lot to do with the internal cultural norms that dominate in senior settings. Yet the outward-facing dimensions of top roles can also advantage certain types of people. For example, at TC, while a great many employees will pass the exams, hit the performance targets and assemble the requisite experience to 'make Partner', only a select few will be 'brought through'[25] – as few as 3-4% (of entrants), according to Colin, one of the Managing Partners. Beyond being identified as 'Partner material' early in their careers, as discussed in Chapter Seven, *the* key competency for 'making' Partner, we were told, was the ability to win and retain business. This reflects wider shifts in the accountancy profession since the 1990s, particularly what Chris Carter and Crawford Spence call 'the inexorable embrace of commercialism' and the attendant emergence of a 'client as king' ethos.[26] Thus while in the past there were various routes to Partner at TC, including via the development of specialist, technical expertise (known as 'Technical Partners'), this has now been superseded by a more entrepreneurial imperative. In this way, Partners at large multinational firms like TC increasingly function as revenue-generators, on a perpetual quest to sell services and find new clients.[27] Fundamentally this means 'making Partner' is tied to a practitioner's external profile, and in particular their relationships with clients or potential to build such relationships in the future. Accordingly, the judgement that an aspiring Partner is 'good with clients' or 'front office material'[28] is pivotal in ensuring a successful passage to the top – particularly in Advisory, where most work is 'client-facing'. Yet it is also worth remembering that it is among Advisory Partners that we see the highest over-representation of those from privileged backgrounds: 42% had been privately educated versus 24% within the company as a whole. These two patterns, we argue, are not unconnected.

To some extent, being seen as 'good with clients' is linked to the kind of self-presentation outlined in Chapter Seven – the premium placed on exuding a certain level of 'polish'. However, an additional presentational attribute frequently mentioned in more specific discussions about what it takes to look and sound like a partner was 'gravitas'. Descriptions of gravitas had much in common with polish, but the emphasis was less on a generalised aura of professionalism (serious, well-groomed, articulate) and more on commanding what many referred to as a certain 'presence' with clients. "It's about being able to communicate authority and wisdom," Nigel, a Senior Advisory Partner noted. Roger, also an Advisory Partner (professional/ managerial origins), expanded:

> The gravitas bit is the ability to command respect. He is going to be able to look after this business for me because he has that within his personality. He looks, feels and sounds like a Partner. So, yeah, how you speak and come across will affect your gravitas. It comes less from being earned, it's more about presence.

What is significant here is both Roger's fundamentally gendered conception of gravitas – as a 'he' competence[29] – as well as his insistence that gravitas is an intrinsic capacity that some simply have and others cannot 'earn'.[30]

But successful client relationships are not just about projecting gravitas. The secret ingredient, many interviewees told us, was about being able to connect, to relate – to "read [clients] quickly and understand their needs", as Audit Partner Jason explains. This is often couched in a particular business-speak, of "knowing how to reflect the marketplace", as Judy, an Advisory Partner, puts it. But, when pressed, most Partners acknowledged that effective 'reflecting' often rested on a fairly straightforward process of 'cultural matching' between Partner and client. Matthew, a very experienced Tax Partner (professional/managerial origins), explained:

> … [client relationships] can't jar, at the end of the day people have to relate to people. So it's almost, I was going to say two-way, but actually our clients are the people who pay our bills so actually there's more of an onus on us in terms of adapting to their needs, their styles.

This very calculated process of adaptation ensured that Partners who are looking to bring someone through often screened potential candidates on the basis of the type of clients they might be dealing with. Jane, a Senior Advisory Partner (professional/

managerial origins) talked us through the last few Partners she had brought through:

> If I am looking at somebody and thinking "are they Partner material?" am I thinking about that in the context of a certain type or group of clients? Probably. We are here as a business to make money and to do that we need to get the trust of our clients. So we do make conscious decisions in terms of who deals with a particular type of client. Because, you know, whether that is right or wrong, ultimately it's about the best interests of the business.

Although we detected a culture of client matching in all areas at TC, it was most openly acknowledged among those working here. Of course clients are particularly important in Advisory as the work is almost entirely client-facing. Yet the premium on client matching here is also linked to the nature of advisory work. As we explored in Chapter Seven, Advisory clients often lack reliable information to assess the quality of the advice they are being given; there is, in Ashley's words, heightened 'ambiguity of knowledge'.[31] Previously, we explained that to manage this ambiguity those in Advisory are expected to exhibit a particular self-presentational polish and gravitas. In this way, organisations are effectively recruiting a particular aesthetic experience for their clients that they see as integral to the act of persuasion involved in winning and retaining their business.[32] As well as polish, however, this ambiguity is also addressed by cultivating strong interpersonal relationships with clients. As Jane elaborates:

> You need the ability to develop a relationship which goes beyond the formal. Because it is not only gaining people's trust which is key, but also an understanding of the person. Okay fine, you may be advising the business, but actually you need to understand the individual as well, the ability to have those conversations, the ability to connect, is very important. Because with the scale of what we do you will inevitably get into some quite personal stuff.

Significantly, this process of matching was rarely explicitly linked to class by interviewees. As this quote illustrates, it was often described in more individualised or psychological terms as being able to establish "trust", "rapport" or "go beyond the formal". Nonetheless, there were also important signs that this ability to develop emotional closeness with clients was often linked to a shared class–cultural background. For example, most acknowledged the importance of using culture to cultivate strong connections, of converting cultural capital into social capital, to use Lizardo's terminology.[33] As the following examples illustrate, a sense of cultural similarity and familiarity can help when instinctively reaching for the appropriate communication style to adopt, the right cultural or sporting settings to entertain with, or the manner in which to approach sensitive issues like tax:

> We have a client base that's predominantly white, middle-aged, middle-class, privately educated, so if you've got people going up for Partner there will be soundings around the client basis ... so if it's banking or investment banking then, I'm sorry, but you need to fit. So a similar background will definitely help, especially if you want to fit that role as a trusted advisor. (Nigel, Advisory, professional/managerial origins)

> People often use the phrase "They go down really well with clients" and interestingly that could go both ways. Because a lot of the work you're doing early doors is with purchase ledger clerks, desk ledger clerks, you know, working-class professions. If you go in very plummy there you're going to die. Equally, if they go down very well with [higher status] clients and the chief exec likes them it may well be because they have the right accent, they were dressed right and they use the right terms. (Ben, Advisory, working-class origins)

> [Clients] will seek out people they can talk to on the same level. Because you are getting things that are very, very personal. It could be the family business

that's been around for a couple of generations or even, you know, things like inheritance tax. They are going to want to speak to somebody who perhaps understands that sort of thing in their life as well. (Colin, Audit, professional/managerial origins)

What is significant here is that while Partners do not necessarily know the class backgrounds of their senior clients, there is a fairly common assumption – as illustrated here – that the majority come from privileged backgrounds. Indeed, this assumption is largely supported by our nationally representative data, which shows that the backgrounds of typical TC clients (that is, medium and large business owners, and senior managers in finance and banking) are highly skewed towards the privileged.[34]

Again, however, this premium on client matching restricts Partners, and aspiring Partners, who cannot call on this sense of familiarity. Culture, in other words, acts as a fence that keeps them out. They are thus often considered 'more risky', their ascent curtailed such that they often only achieve 'next best' positions, as Directors or Senior Managers, well thought of and well remunerated, but just outside the magic circle of the Partner group. This was particularly clear among socially mobile women. Beth, a Director (intermediate origins) explained that she simply couldn't "trade off" the same cultural touch points as her privileged male colleagues, of elite sports rooted in "the posh school you went to" or "the stuffy members' club you drink at". With many clients, she went on, "I had to learn to tell a story that would resonate with them. Because they just don't get me."

Moreover, even when the socially mobile had made Partner at TC, there was a sense that class–cultural difference still acted as a barrier in client-facing interactions, as was the case for Paul, an Advisory Partner (working-class origins):

Later on this afternoon I am meeting [name of key client]. I fully expect him to be surprised when he meets me because I will not be what he's expecting. He will be expecting someone that looks older, that's got more grey hair, that talks with a posher accent, and so that will be the starting point. So I know that when I walk into that room, I am starting from an inferior position from the guy that's been in before me from a different firm. Now what that means is that what I say has to be that bit better than what somebody else would get away with.

There is little doubt that highbrow culture at 6TV, the emphasis on RP in acting, and client matching at TC all act as classed barriers to progression. They each represent examples of how the privileged exchange cultural capital for social capital in ways that directly aid their ability to get to, and stay at, the top of elite occupations. However, the more complex issue is whether they constitute forms of opportunity hoarding or social closure. A key question here is whether they lead to opportunities in an anti-competitive way. Or, put simply, are they justifiable practices in terms of what is needed to do these jobs effectively? We should stress here that among our respondents there is much contestation on this front. In the minds of existing top-level people, there is a clear rationale for their hiring decisions that concern who will be a more successful partner or commissioner. They feel they have important informal information about the demands of the job and so can bring forward applicants who fit these requirements. Yet we would stress that in all the cases explored in this chapter, it is very difficult to see any association between the attributes necessary to reach the top and any reliable measure of intelligence, ability or 'merit'.

Room at the top

Finally, we again return to Coopers, our case study with no discernible class ceiling. In earlier chapters we explained the more equitable outcomes achieved at this firm by exploring the absence of class-laden behavioural codes, or via chains of sponsorship that tend to advantage men from disadvantaged rather than privileged backgrounds. But here we argue that another important driver is also worth considering – executive culture. In particular, and to bring Coopers into dialogue with particularly 6TV and TC, we examine how aspects of internal *and* external culture differ in important ways at the architecture firm.

Certainly, reflecting on our fieldwork as a whole, it was clear that the in-house culture at Coopers differed significantly from our other case study settings. It was more inclusive, more open, more collaborative. These virtues were, of course, proclaimed by executives across all three organisations. However, such celebratory rhetoric was normally punctured once we encountered more junior staff, and particularly when they were able to speak freely in an anonymised interview. At Coopers, in contrast, these sentiments chimed with both our own observations and that of the staff we interviewed:

> In terms of the vibe, it's probably the reason I came back to be honest, I didn't feel intimidated, I felt we were all getting work and I knew it was a good place to learn rather than just produce output. (Amir, Architectural Assistant, working-class origins)

> When the project bays are all set up you've got brand new starters sitting next to Partners and the Planning Partners come around regularly to make sure everyone is getting on and talk to you about projects. I felt very much, from the start, I felt included in what's going on. (Dan, Architectural Assistant, professional/managerial origins)

> It is very inclusive, if you come up with some idea the management actually really listens and tries to ... not please everyone ... but if you have a good idea they are actually listening, regardless if you are part two, part one, or anything. (Elena, Architectural Assistant, professional/ managerial origins)

This inclusivity may be partly rooted in the size of the firm (where most staff are on first-name terms), the open plan layout of the office (where Partners sit alongside more junior staff) and the collaborative nature of much of the firm's work. However, the most heavily cited factor was actually one individual, Gary. One of the three founding Partners, and now the Managing Partner, Gary emerged as very much the driving force behind the practice. He was the public 'face' of the business, the lead on recruitment, and also the senior figure most visible to staff in an everyday sense. In this way, Gary was clearly seen as setting the tone of the organisational culture.

We can hypothesise how Gary's own class background and worldview impacted his management approach. Gary came from a working-class single-parent family in Yorkshire. Growing up on a rural council estate, he passed the 11-plus and attended the local grammar school. With money in the family tight, he had assumed that his education would finish at age 16, and that he would take a job and help support the family. His mother angrily rejected this idea, and made sacrifices so that he could continue his education and attend university. In this way, he experienced a social mobility journey since mythologised as classic, as a working-class 'grammar school boy' who benefited from the widespread expansion of professional and managerial positions in the post-war era.[35]

At work Gary certainly did not wear his politics or class background on his sleeve,[36] but clearly had greater insight into issues of class than many others we spoke to. Certainly, as we saw in Chapter Six, he had been fundamental to the career progression of a number of male staff from less privileged backgrounds.

The point we want to stress here is that when it comes to the class ceiling, executive culture matters. Those at the top demonstrate the values of an organisation, both as gatekeepers of who progresses, and also through their everyday style of management. And when such individuals are genuinely open to a range of talents of people from different social backgrounds, and when they embody the complexities of 'doing' rather than just 'saying', it can have a tangible impact on others. In terms of social mobility, policy interventions often focus on trying to 'fix' the individual, on how to 'nudge' those from disadvantaged backgrounds towards more aspiration and ambition.[37] However, paying close attention to executive culture reveals the weaknesses of this deficit model. As we have seen in this chapter, the culture of an organisation – particularly at the top echelons – can act as both a profound enabler and disabler of different people's ambitions. The highbrow culture of commissioning at 6TV, for example, produces an environment where some feel at home but many others, particularly those from working-class backgrounds, feel excluded and disempowered.

In contrast, Coopers represented an example of an organisation where the executive culture appeared to act as an enabler, regardless of class background. Gary, in particular, creates 'room at the top' and consciously or not, acts to ensure access does not require the artful deployment of classed ways of knowing. Of course, it is important not to over-emphasise this contrast or romanticise Coopers. The firm was certainly not inclusive in all areas of diversity, and clearly did not facilitate the equitable progression of female staff. It is also worth noting that the firm benefited strongly from comparisons to other architectural practices, particularly elite design–led firms, some of which were seen to demand long hours or contain tyrannical directors and unpleasant blame–cultures. In this way, we should be careful to again distinguish Coopers from architecture in general.

But it's not just internal culture that set Coopers apart from other firms. Client relationships are central to Coopers in much the same way as they are at TC. However, as we explored in Chapter Seven, there is an important difference in their occupational (and therefore demographic) make-up. While Partners at TC are largely interfacing with business owners or senior figures in finance, Coopers Architects are normally interacting with more technical clients such as senior engineers or built environment professionals, often in large collaborative teams. The nature of these relationships was also different. Interactional ingredients key at TC such as emotional connection and cultural familiarity were barely mentioned by senior Coopers staff. Client relationships were more functional, and far less intimate.

In Chapter Seven we explored how these kinds of differences, as well as the emphasis on technical skills, ensured that the premium on image and polish was reduced at Coopers. But here we also argue that it has implications for client matching. Not only does the collaborative nature of such projects make matching individuals in this way unnecessary, but the social composition of both groups also militated against it. One only needs to return to the class composition of different elite professions, detailed in Chapter One, to see that the average Coopers client is likely to come from a significantly less privileged background than the average TC client. As Partner David (intermediate origins) told us:

> We don't have that super-rich developer, or Lord Rothschild, kind of client base. Our clients are mostly government or align to a very engineering based discipline. And engineering is probably even more narrow in terms of socio types, blue-collar workers.

This compositional difference is also significant in terms of how culture functions as a source of connection. As Lizardo notes, the highbrow culture being exchanged between executives and clients at firms like TC is likely to establish exclusive, strong-tie networks among the privileged. In contrast, at Coopers relationships with clients are based much more on the technical content of the work and the interactional function of cultural taste, if any at all, was simply to lubricate small talk and pleasantries.[38]

Looking-glass 'merit'

What emerges from this chapter, and the one that immediately precedes it, are the difficulties in straightforwardly identifying 'merit' in elite occupations. This is not to say that conventional indicators of 'merit' are not valued in our case studies. They are – individuals undoubtedly need to possess strong educational credentials, amass relevant experience and work hard, in order to get ahead. Yet what also emerges in all these occupations, particularly in the upper echelons, is that these seemingly 'objective merits' have to be *activated* in a particular way; they have to be performed in a manner that is recognised and valued by those in positions of power. And this, as we have demonstrated, is very often about packaging one's 'merits' in a way that 'fits', that reflects the organisational culture cascaded downwards from the very top – from leaders who, in the case of TC and 6TV, are from very privileged backgrounds and, at Coopers, are disproportionately male. This, then, is often about a thinly veiled 'looking-glass' version of 'merit', of demonstrating an ability to embody relatively arbitrary (and highly classed) behavioural norms, or cultural preferences and tastes, that then function as signals of suitability among senior decision-makers.

Both chapters have also touched on what happens when people's performances of 'merit' are not recognised, the anxieties and ambivalences that flow from feeling that one is continually making 'mistakes' in the execution of dominant behavioural codes. Yet so far we know fairly little of what follows, in terms of the decisions or actions taken by the upwardly mobile, when they feel their performances don't *land*. This is the subject of our final empirical chapter.

NINE

Self-elimination

We are talking to Giles in the gigantic boardroom at Turner Clarke's (TC) London headquarters. Giles is one of the firm's most senior Partners. He was privately educated and his parents are both doctors. We are coming to the end of our interview and have reached the section where we ask Giles for his reflections on our findings so far. We explain that a profound class pay gap persists in UK accountancy, we outline the class ceiling at TC, and we then run through the drivers explored so far in this book – informal sponsorship, behavioural norms and exclusive executive cultures. Giles looks distinctly unconvinced. As we finish, he takes a deep breath and pauses, as if debating whether to say what he's thinking. Eventually he does:

> I understand what you're saying but ... but I do think you're missing something important. People might be afraid to say it but there is definitely an element of self-censorship. So how do you disentangle what you've been telling me from the "I didn't feel I had the same chops so I took a sideways move."

For Giles, the problem with our analysis so far is that it tilts too far towards issues of 'demand' rather than 'supply'. We have thus interrogated various barriers that hold the upwardly mobile back but have neglected how the mobile themselves may be implicated in the class ceiling. What about *their* actions, decisions, aspirations? In Giles's experience it is this 'supply' issue that is more important. To reach the partnership, he goes on to tell us, people need to "really want it", need to be "comfortable asserting themselves", need to handle "robust discussion". But the upwardly mobile, he argues, "sometimes, not always, but sometimes shy away from that."

This is not an isolated view. Over the course of this project we spoke to many, particularly those in senior positions (often white men from privileged backgrounds), who shared Giles's take on the class ceiling. This kind of sentiment is also echoed strongly in the political and policy domain. Here the go-to strategy in tackling social mobility is often to focus on 'fixing' the individual, to focus interventions on 'raising aspirations' among those from disadvantaged backgrounds, to build their confidence and self-esteem.[1] The implication here, whether consciously intended or not, is that if only the upwardly mobile were to 'lean in'[2] in the same way as those from privileged backgrounds, then outcomes would be far more equitable. Read in a certain way this can be used to legitimate the class ceiling – those from working-class origins simply lack the same drive, ambition and resilience, and therefore it is no surprise that they tend to earn less or fail to reach the top. This was certainly the way we read Giles's views on the topic.

We did find some empirical support for 'supply-side' explanations of the class ceiling. In particular, we found evidence that the upwardly mobile do fail to seek out leadership positions as readily as those from privileged backgrounds. This did not necessarily apply to all, or even the majority. But there was a sizeable minority of our interviewees – particularly those who had experienced very long-range upward trajectories – who had not pushed their career forward in the way we might expect considering their experience, performance and skills.

Yet we strongly challenge the idea that this points towards intrinsic class differences in confidence or aspiration. Instead we argue in this chapter that the upwardly mobile often commit acts of 'self-elimination' in elite occupations. This term is normally associated with Bourdieu, and specifically his analysis of class inequalities in the French education system. Bourdieu argued that the dispositions inculcated in one's childhood, that are primarily shaped by the class-infused conditions of our existence, guide people's actions through their perceptions of their chances of success in the future. A key illustration of this, he argues, is the way in which working-class children internalise negative feelings of self-worth that lead them to reject the education system. Bourdieu argues that such students 'anticipate' failure and therefore their subsequent 'self-elimination' from the education system is rooted in an 'unconscious estimation of their objective probabilities of success'.[3] In this way, those from working-class backgrounds 'become the accomplices of the processes that tend to make the probable a reality',[4] because they distinguish what is accessible and what is inaccessible (what is and is not 'for us').[5]

The key point here, then, is that class background does affect people's actions and future strategies in fairly fundamental ways, but this does not constitute, in the case of a working-class background, a 'deficit' of aspiration or ambition.[6] Instead, people from disadvantaged backgrounds often make calculations to self-eliminate from upward mobility based on an instinctive anticipation of very real 'demand-side' barriers. And significantly this anticipation is felt emotionally, as an impending anxiety or insecurity about what may lie ahead.

While Bourdieu largely applied the concept of self-elimination to education, we argue that it is equally important for understanding the decisions and strategies of those negotiating the elite labour market. Here the upwardly mobile tend to self-eliminate in three ways. First, in some cases, they simply *opt out* of concrete progression or promotion opportunities. Second, in other instances, a more subtle risk aversion slows their career trajectory or leads them to sort into less prestigious career tracks. And third, in some cases, they successfully enter the most prestigious executive spaces but then refuse to play by the rules of the game.

We therefore see self-elimination as an important driver of the class ceiling. Yet we stress that this supply-side mechanism does not represent a simple personal 'deficit' that can be somehow corrected or 'topped up' via training or coaching. Instead, self-elimination is inextricably linked to the barriers erected on the demand side; it is a reaction to, or an anticipation of, many of the issues explored so far in this book.

The issue of self-elimination also highlights, more broadly, the profound emotional imprint that goes hand-in-hand with upward social mobility. While this impact is sometimes worn lightly, as a reminder of how far one has come or what they have achieved, for the majority we interviewed 'success' came at a considerable psychological price. Upward journeys, we found, had often been difficult, uncomfortable, painful even. These emotional costs, we contend, are very important to understand. Not only do they constitute hidden injuries[7] that may explain why some prefer not to reach for the top, but they also reveal the limits of the current political fetish for social mobility.

Opting out ('I don't belong *there*')

Across our case studies there were many instances where socially mobile interviewees had rejected, ignored or avoided clear-cut opportunities. This often took place early in people's careers, where the mobile had chosen not to take paths that would have placed them on the most lucrative or prestigious career tracks. Karen and Frank, for example, had both "avoided" applying to prestigious architectural schools at University College London (UCL) and Cambridge – associated with lucrative design careers – on the basis that they were not for people "like me". Similarly, Raymond (intermediate origins), an Audit Partner at TC, explained how he had "messed up" a number of opportunities to work with key Partners on high-profile clients early in his career at TC because he had a "chip on his shoulder". He told us: "I thought they were so arrogant, so stuck up, and I used to think 'you're judging me, aren't you?' But looking back those were missed opportunities, it was all in my head."[8]

Such spurned opportunities also featured later in people's careers, especially when interviewees were on the cusp of entering key executive environments or roles. Gary, the founding Partner at Coopers, widely credited with making it such an inclusive environment for working-class architects, provided a notable example. Gary, as we mentioned, was from a working-class family in Yorkshire. He had had a long and successful career in architecture and was one of the most senior figures at the firm. Yet despite his success within Coopers, Gary was more uncertain about his standing within the wider architecture field. In the last few years, he explained, he had increasingly begun to rub shoulders with the upper echelons of the profession via his dealings with architecture's professional body, RIBA. Gary had a key ambassadorial role at RIBA, and through this had been invited to join several clubs frequented by the country's leading architects. Gary was fully aware that accepting such invitations would be key to furthering his career, in terms of forging valuable networks; yet he had repeatedly declined:

> You do meet some very posh people and, you know, I do feel sometimes like I'm out of place. Like I was invited to join the Chartered Company of Architects and a Gentleman's Club or something, but I've always said "no" because I don't really feel as though I belong there … you know those sorts of places, it's not me. So there must be a part of me that does think … even now, everybody has their place, I suppose.

Significantly, Gary's decision here was not motivated by a lack of aspiration or ambition. Instead, it was an act of self-elimination that seemed more borne out of emotional self-protection. Gary anticipated that reaching the very top of architecture – through membership at the profession's elite clubs and associations – would bring with it a distinct sense of discomfort, a feeling of being "out of place", and therefore he rejected progression on these grounds.[9]

Playing safe ('Have I ever gone there? No. And that probably tells you a lot')

Self-elimination is not always about opting out of concrete opportunities, however. In some cases it manifested more as a general risk aversion and caution that had flanked people's careers. This was often bound up with the kind of 'sorting' effects discussed in Chapters Three and Five. Thus, the upwardly mobile often chose to take what they described as 'safer' career routes. This was sometimes about economic security (as explored in Chapter Five) but also often about 'rising up the ranks' in one organisation rather than moving on. Bridget, an HR Executive at 6TV, was originally from South Wales, where her father was a welder and her mother a nursery nurse. Bridget, now in her early 60s, was very proud of her career and explained in detail how she had manoeuvred "up the ranks" in HR departments at two large companies before being headhunted by 6TV. During most of our interview, she gave the impression she was very satisfied with her career. Yet towards the end of our interview, as she became more comfortable, she began to talk more candidly about her background and how she felt it had impacted her career strategy. Her tone completely changed. She began to retell her career story, telling us that, actually, she "should have gone further", that she'd always been "too cautious", had always chosen "mid-level companies", and berated herself for not "just going for it". She summed up:

> I do wonder if there's something about willingness to take risk. I mean have I taken some of the risks I could have? You know, I'm not a group HR Director of a FTSE 100 company. Do I have the capability? I don't know, I've certainly thought about it. But have I ever gone there? No, no I haven't. And that probably tells you a lot …

This is clearly a very different form of self-elimination to that expressed by Gary. Bridget has not necessarily rejected opportunities so much as not sought them out. In her mind, the residue of her background is a risk aversion that has led her to sort into 'mid-level' roles and fail to reach the heights that, privately, she has always aspired to.

For Ben (working-class origins), a Tax Partner at TC, the issue was more one of speed. Ben was well into his 50s, and although he had recently made Partner, this was at least two decades beyond the average age his colleagues had done so at TC. Ben saw this as entirely his own "fault". He explained an enduring sense of discomfort with some of the more strategic aspects of the job, of how to navigate "the business end of promotion-seeking":[10]

> It's this feeling of sort of not being worthy. So, if I go, if I go to a black-tie event at the Grosvenor I would certainly feel more connected to the waiting staff than

I would the other guests. So, while I don't think it's ever stopped me getting on, it has certainly always made things feel harder, if that makes sense? And I do sometimes think, sometimes I do, that I could have been Managing Partner of TC by now if everything had been a bit cleaner, if you know what I mean.

A step too far ('You can sort of change yourself but that only gets you so far')

Of course not all interviewees had chosen to opt out or sort out of top positions. Indeed, as Tables A.1a–1d show, many socially mobile interviewees had reached what appeared to be the apex of their professions. Yet interestingly, even here we often detected elements of self-elimination at play. Bill, for example, was a Senior Commissioner at 6TV. His father worked as a draughtsman at a local factory, and his mother was a clerk at the bus depot. He explained that as his career developed, and particularly in the pursuit of becoming a Commissioner (at 6TV and previously at another broadcaster) he had learned that he needed, in his words, "to become middle-class, and play the game where necessary." He explained that "playing the game" had involved a fairly intricate process of cultural mimicry, of changing his accent, "never talking about his background", and generally imitating the highbrow executive culture outlined in Chapter Eight. He explained: "It's sort of like you have to understand that there are certain rules of the game and you have to play by those rules, learn the lingua, wear the clothes, and then that becomes almost a cloak of respectability."

In many ways this strategy had been successful – Bill was now one of the channel's most well-respected Commissioners.[11] Yet this process of assimilation was not without its limits. Bill had been in the same position for nearly a decade now and, as he explained in this remarkably lucid passage, he felt he had reached a clear ceiling in his career:

> You can sort of change yourself in terms of how you present yourself. But that only gets you so far. So I've found myself talking and thinking about

[my background] a lot more now than I have ever done, and perhaps that was one of the reasons I was keen to talk to you. Like there is this thing … and I wonder if it mirrors other people from similar backgrounds … I don't socialise much, and never have, with people in the industry. I don't go to the parties, the clubs, and there's part of me that thinks actually … they're all cunts [*laughs*] … you know, I'm not going to waste my time with them. I've got my friends from the past, my family, and that feels real and important. Whereas this often feels like a game … because I've assumed a role. And so, yes, I don't have a desire to go and get drunk with people I've spent the day working with and if I'm brutally honest I'd say I'm not a real member of the club; I've sort of blagged my way in and so in the end, although I'm saying I learned to play the game, to this day I still don't really feel a member properly, a properly signed-up member.

Here we see self-elimination emerging again, even within the context of the upper echelons of 6TV. Although Bill has been successful in entering this magic circle, he explains that reaching the *very top* is contingent on assimilation in one's personal as well as professional life, of fully embracing the "clubbable" aspects of the television profession. Yet for Bill extending this performance into his social life is simply a step too far, one that requires an existential betrayal of all that he describes as "real" and "important" in his life. In this way, Bill underlines the limits of class–cultural assimilation, a sense that such mimicry "will only get you so far". But, significantly, others do not enforce this limit. Instead, it is the result of Bill's own reluctance to embrace full-blown identity mutation.[12]

There is also an additional point to consider about Bill's story. Not only does it underline the limits of assimilation, but it also illustrates the exhausting emotional labour involved in maintaining this "blag", as Bill describes it. This emotional imprint is important to understand in its own right, as we go on to explore now.

Figure 1.1: How we measure social mobility into elite occupations (see page 30)

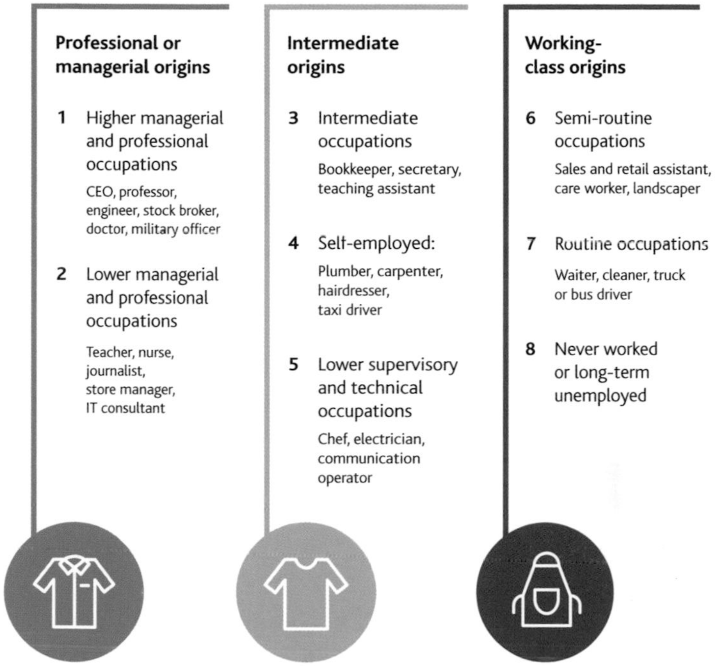

Professional or managerial origins	Intermediate origins	Working-class origins
1 Higher managerial and professional occupations CEO, professor, engineer, stock broker, doctor, military officer	**3 Intermediate occupations** Bookkeeper, secretary, teaching assistant	**6 Semi-routine occupations** Sales and retail assistant, care worker, landscaper
2 Lower managerial and professional occupations Teacher, nurse, journalist, store manager, IT consultant	**4 Self-employed:** Plumber, carpenter, hairdresser, taxi driver	**7 Routine occupations** Waiter, cleaner, truck or bus driver
	5 Lower supervisory and technical occupations Chef, electrician, communication operator	**8 Never worked or long-term unemployed**

Figure 0.1: Flows from origins to destinations in the UK (see pages 12-13)

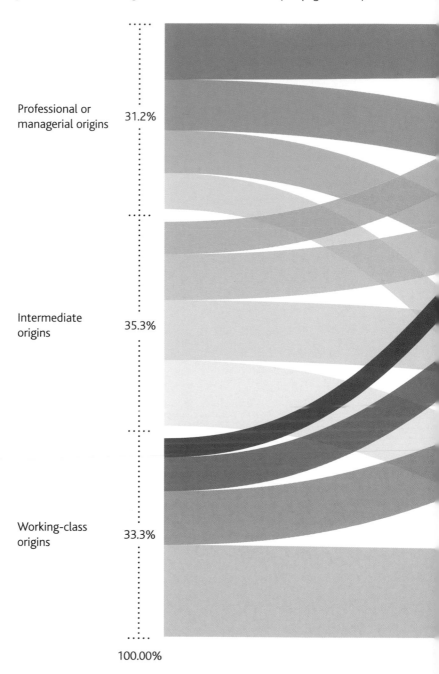

Professional or
managerial origins — 31.2%

Intermediate
origins — 35.3%

Working-class
origins — 33.3%

100.00%

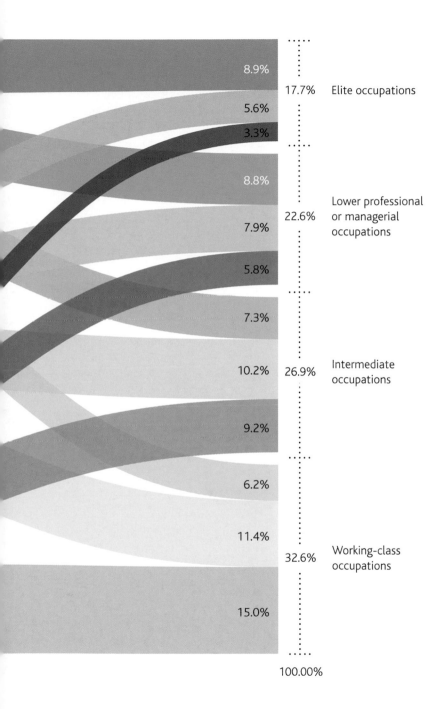

8.9%

17.7%　Elite occupations

5.6%

3.3%

8.8%

　　　　Lower professional
22.6%　or managerial
　　　　occupations

7.9%

5.8%

7.3%

10.2%　26.9%　Intermediate
　　　　　　　occupations

9.2%

6.2%

11.4%

32.6%　Working-class
　　　　occupations

15.0%

100.00%

Figure 1.5: Class matters for who gets a degree (see pages 36-37)

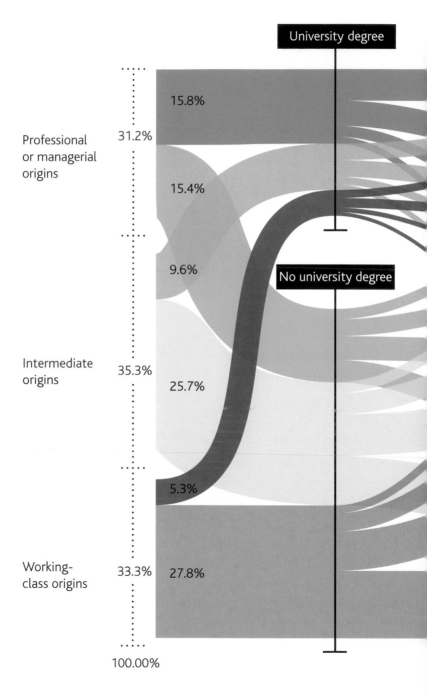

University degree

Professional
or managerial
origins

31.2%

15.8%

15.4%

9.6%

No university degree

Intermediate
origins

35.3%

25.7%

5.3%

Working-
class origins

33.3%

27.8%

100.00%

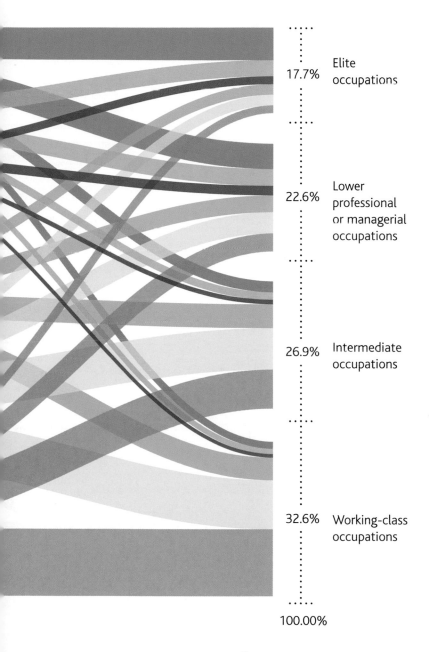

17.7% Elite
occupations

22.6% Lower
professional
or managerial
occupations

26.9% Intermediate
occupations

32.6% Working-class
occupations

100.00%

Figure 1.3: Some elite occupations are a lot more closed than others (see page 33)

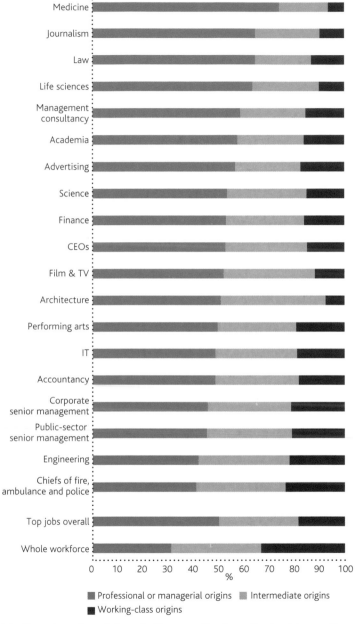

Note: Percentage of people in each elite occupation (as well as top jobs overall, and the whole workforce) who are from each class origin group.
Source: LFS

Figure 1.6: Even when working-class students outperform the privileged, they are less likely to get top jobs (see page 39)

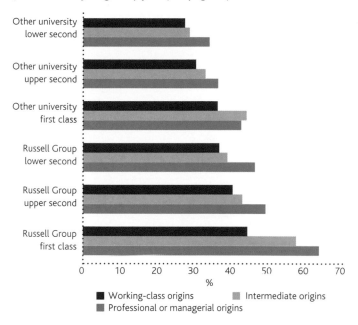

Note: Percentage of people from each combination of university type, degree class and class origin who make it into our set of elite occupations.

Source: LFS

Figure 1.7: Many racial-ethnic groups are under-represented in many top fields (see page 41)

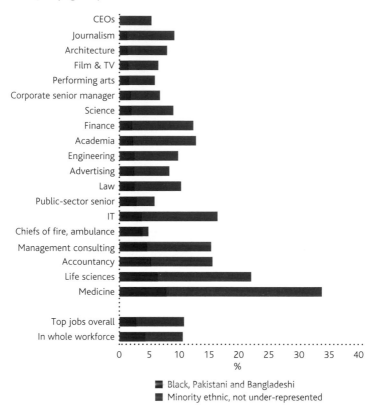

Note: Percentage of people in each elite occupation who are members of under-represented racial-ethnic groups (Black, Pakistani or Bangladeshi) or other racialised groups that are not under-represented in UK elite occupations (people who are categorised as Chinese, other Asian, Indian, Mixed or Multiple races, or other racial groups).

Source: LFS

Figure 1.8: Women are also under-represented in most top jobs (see page 42)

Note: Percentage of people in each elite occupation who are women.

Source: LFS

Figure 1.9: The privileged are more likely to get into top jobs in every racial-ethnic group (see page 43)

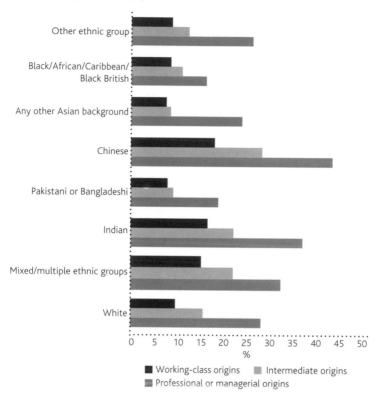

Note: Percentage of people from each combination of racial-ethnic group and class origin who work in our elite occupations.

Source: LFS

Figure 2.1: The class pay gap (see page 48)

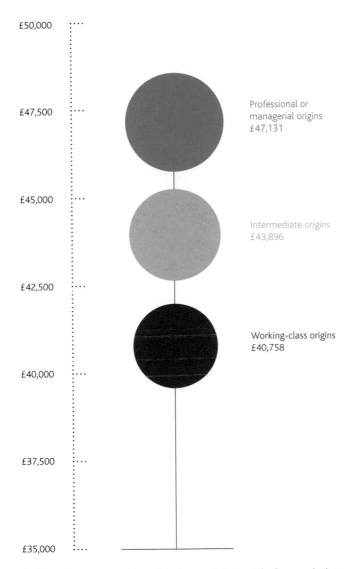

£50,000

£47,500 — Professional or managerial origins £47,131

£45,000 — Intermediate origins £43,896

£42,500

Working-class origins £40,758

£40,000

£37,500

£35,000

Note: Estimated average annual earnings for people in top jobs from each class-origin group.

Source: LFS

Figure 2.4: Many socially mobile racial-ethnic minorities also face a double disadvantage (see page 52)

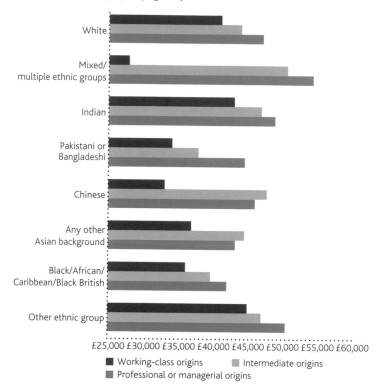

Note: Average estimated annual earnings for each class-origin and racial-ethnic group.

Source: LFS

Figure 2.5: The class pay gap is biggest in law, medicine and finance (see page 53)

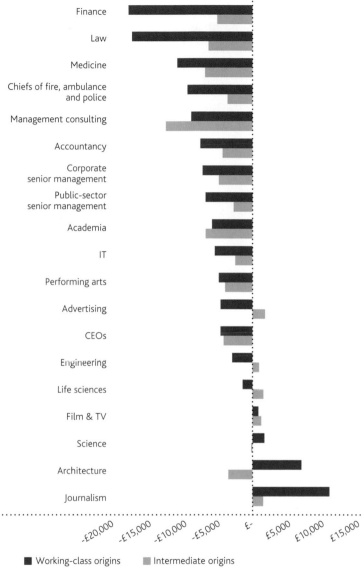

■ Working-class origins　■ Intermediate origins

Note: Class pay gaps between upwardly mobile (working-class or intermediate origin) and professional-managerial-origin people in each of our 19 elite occupational groups. Average earnings differences are statistically significant at p<0.05 for one or both upwardly mobile groups in finance, law, medicine, chiefs of fire, ambulance and police, management consulting, accountancy, corporate senior management, public sector senior management, and IT.
Source: LFS

Figure 2.3: Socially mobile women face a double disadvantage in earnings (see page 50)

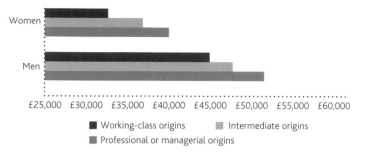

Note: Average estimated annual earnings for men and women from each class origin.

Source: LFS

Figure 3.2: Those from working-class backgrounds earn less even when they go to top universities (see page 63)

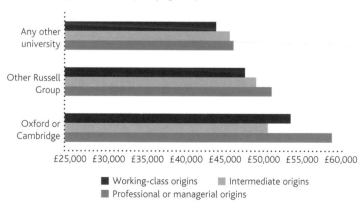

Note: Average estimated annual earnings for each combination of class origin and university type, for people in our elite occupations.

Source: LFS

Figure 3.1: The class pay gap is even larger after accounting for demographics (see page 60)

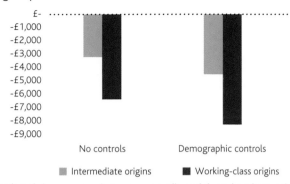

Note: Predicted class pay gaps between upwardly mobile and professional-managerial-origin people, with no controls, and in a regression model with controls for demographics – racial-ethnic group, country of birth, age, gender and disability status. Both class-origin pay gaps are statistically significant at p<0.05.

Source: LFS

Figure 3.6: The privileged also sort into higher-paying occupations and bigger firms (see page 68)

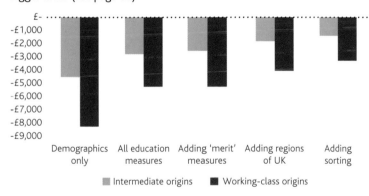

Note: Predicted class pay gaps between upwardly mobile and professional-managerial origin people, with only demographic controls, in a model with controls for demographics and educational attainment, in a model that includes demographics, education and other measures of 'merit', in a model that includes all that plus region, and finally, in a model that includes all the preceding controls, plus the specific occupation the respondent worked in, the NS-SEC category for their job, whether they were in the public or private sector and the industry they work in. In this final model, the class-origin pay gap between those from intermediate class origins and those from professional-managerial origins is only statistically significant at the p<0.01 level, but the gap between working class/professional-managerial is still significant at p<0.05.

Source: LFS

Figure A.7: Class pay gaps for each racial-ethnic group and class background (see page 283)

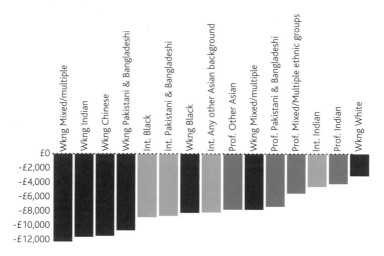

Note: From the model with controls for everything; all class-origin/racial-ethnic gaps are statistically significant when compared with white professional or managerial-origin people at p<0.05.

The price of the ticket

Many tend to presume that upward social mobility is a positive experience. The upwardly mobile are routinely presented as the 'winners' of meritocracy, romanticised figures who have made it 'against the odds'. Popular culture abounds with such heroic tales, particularly exemplars of the gendered trope of the 'working-class boy done good', such as Alan Sugar, Dr Dre or Joe Biden. Influential academic research has also cemented this idea of upward mobility as smooth and straightforward.[13]

Yet among our interviewees we found evidence that upward mobility often made for a distinctly bumpy emotional ride. Significantly, among long-range upwardly mobile interviewees – the group most celebrated in prevailing political rhetoric – mobility had often been particularly emotionally difficult. These individuals routinely reported battling feelings of insecurity and inferiority in the elite workplace. Philip, a newly made Managing Partner at TC, was from a fairly poor working-class background. He told us that ever since he made the initial move from working for a small rural accounting firm in his Midlands hometown to a middle management role at TC, he had experienced crippling self-doubt:

> I used to have, until probably relatively recently, this voice on my shoulder almost saying you're going to get found out, you know, eventually. And I used to have a recurring dream that I hadn't passed my exams. I vividly remember it – it was the day I qualified and I hadn't passed, I'd been found out. And it was only when I finally told someone about it, a career coach here, they were like "you really need to get on top of this".

Such lingering feelings of insecurity, a kind of extreme form of 'imposter syndrome', were relatively common among the long-range upwardly mobile. As with Philip, these feelings were often initiated by an abrupt 'moment'[14] of upward mobility, of being catapulted into an elite firm or in the aftermath of a significant promotion. These sudden life events had often left an enduring emotional residue, a suspicion that they somehow "aren't good enough", that they are a "fraud", or that a fall was just around the corner. This was mainly rooted in a sense of dislocation from the culture of their new workplace or colleagues, of being a 'fish out of water' and feeling anxious about failing to assimilate or mimic the kind of behavioural norms outlined in Chapters Seven and Eight.

But it was also strongly gendered.[15] Jenny, for example, had just begun as a trainee at TC. She was white British, her mum was a housewife and her dad was a taxi driver. Initially Jenny told us she was enjoying life at TC. Yet as our interview progressed she outlined an ever-growing list of anxieties. This ranged from dress ("I go to other offices and never know what to wear – I don't want to misrepresent the brand") to client relationships ("I'm always worried about boundaries, do they want me to ask about their family or their holidays? I don't want to overstep the mark"). Jenny's everyday work life demanded a gruelling programme of self-regulation. Most significant were her attempts to modulate her self-presentation in the pursuit of polish:

> I don't have the best social skills. I definitely have to consider what I say in front of certain people. Like some people just come out with words, and have such a vocabulary, whereas I am always very conscious about what I say to those people, and how I say things; my pronunciation. Like I get to the point where I've tried to make conversation and just run out of things to say and then there's an awkward silence. And in my head I'm thinking what do I possibly have in common with this person, what am I going to say that's going to make them think I'm not a complete idiot. And it is those topics, what they did at the weekend, how are the children, where I sort of let myself down … and I've got all these thoughts running through my head as the silence rolls on.

What is striking here is how Jenny accepts this cross-class conversational awkwardness as an issue of personal failure ("I know it's my problem," she tells us) and shoulders the emotional burden of lacking what she sees as objective social "skills".

Others were less accepting and more angry (at the power of such arbitrary behavioural norms). Natalia, who was Black British, was in an entry-level role at 6TV and had been for several years. She was one of our few interviewees who felt she had been actively discriminated against based on her working-class background (she had been brought up on what she described as a "rough council estate" in Birmingham[16]). She was proud of her background and felt it represented an unchangeable aspect of her identity. "This is who I am", she explained. "I can't change it." She told us that the reason she had twice been refused promotion over the last five years was because "who I am makes [her line managers] uncomfortable and people like what they're comfortable with." Unlike Jenny, Natalia refused to assimilate: "A lot of people are faking it until it works for them, adapting culturally … accent, dress, you know, social situations, just so they can have more to talk about with those people. Again it is all about making them feel comfortable. And I'm sick of it, frankly." Natalia was clearly very angry and soon after this, tearful, she stopped the interview: "Sorry I don't mean to get emotional but it hurts. You know [6TV] talk about championing diversity but … but it really doesn't feel that way."

While the emotional costs of upward mobility tend to cluster around negotiating similar travails of occupational 'fit', the challenge is often intensified by a simultaneous feeling of not fully belonging in the cultural world of one's origin. This was often expressed as a feeling of being caught between two worlds, or of being culturally homeless.[17] Douglas was an actor from a working-class family in the north of Scotland. Now living in London, he made most of his living working in West End theatre. He explained that despite the obvious gains in status and money that had flowed from his career, he still felt "somehow stuck in the middle":

> You are living in this strange zone. You are not part of that world, the acting world, the middle-class world, and you are also not part of where you came from any more. So you are a very isolated kind of figure.

> The people that really love you and care about you
> are delighted for you that you got away but they
> don't understand you. So there is a kind of isolation
> in that respect, you are in this strange zone where it
> is difficult to find identification or, you know, solace
> or safety. You are pretty much on your own.

Again what emerges most clearly here is the emotional labour required to reconcile these contradictory sources of identity – to "find solace", as Douglas notes. This represented a sort of emotional juggling act where, facing upwards, these individuals often expressed feelings of insecurity or self-doubt, but then when they faced down towards their origins they were often hit with feelings of guilt and estrangement.[18] In fact, many noted that our interview had constituted a somewhat cathartic experience, bringing to the fore thoughts and emotions normally left unexplored or deliberately repressed.

Our aim in foregrounding these emotions is not to somehow suggest that these people were entirely unhappy, or suffered from psychological disorder. If anything, we would suggest the people we spoke with were juggling this multitude of emotions valiantly, even successfully.[19] Indeed, some even told us that this dual identity sometimes carried distinct advantages, giving them a chameleonesque capacity to 'code-switch' with different types of clients or colleagues.[20] Yet whether successfully managed or not, we would simply stress that reconciling such an array of emotions is an exhausting burden to carry, especially while trying to navigate a high-pressure career.

Understanding how people actually experience social mobility is important for two reasons. First, it is possible to argue that there is a significant 'opportunity cost' involved that is directly relevant to the class ceiling. Seen through a relational lens, the mobile are very often expending emotional energy battling a headwind that those from privileged backgrounds simply do not have to. This is both unfair and puts the mobile at a further disadvantage.

Second, however, and beyond its role as a driver of the class ceiling, this emotional imprint is important to register in its own right. As we mentioned in the Introduction, prevailing political rhetoric tends to fetishise upward social mobility as a sort of panacea for society's ills. In fact, some may even read the central concern of this book – through its focus on elite occupations – as cementing this agenda. Yet we would stress that our research reveals very clearly that, despite the prevailing political rhetoric, upward social mobility is not the unequivocally positive force often assumed in wider society. Indeed, examined through the lens of emotional wellbeing rather than simply economic and occupational achievement, the 'success' of mobility is much more uncertain – even when it involves successfully breaking the class ceiling.

TEN

Class ceilings: A new approach to social mobility

We hope that over the course of this book we have made our key findings eminently clear: that people from working-class backgrounds earn less in top jobs than their privileged colleagues; that this can only be partially attributed to conventional measures of 'merit'; and that more powerful drivers are rooted in the misrecognition of classed self-presentation as 'talent', work cultures historically shaped by the privileged, the affordances of the 'Bank of Mum and Dad', and sponsored mobility premised on class-cultural homophily.

But we also want to stake out what we think is important and innovative about our *approach*, not only our findings. We should say from the outset that a discussion of this kind necessitates a sustained engagement with sociological theory and literature, and therefore a somewhat different writing style. While the bulk of this book has been addressed to those who are not specialists in the sociology of class, mobility and work, here we allow ourselves to write more directly for fellow scholars. In this way, we have structured the book so that non-academic readers can easily move from here to the Conclusion (Chapter Eleven) if they wish. However, at the same time, we would urge *all* readers to stay with us. Academic discussions about class and mobility can be dense but, at root, they address questions that we think everyone invested in this area is interested in: what we mean by class, how we should measure social mobility, and why our class origins appear to matter more in some areas of the labour market than others.

To address these foundational questions, we argue in this chapter that Pierre Bourdieu's central concepts of habitus,[1] capital[2] and field[3] provide a powerful set of tools to think with.[4] In fact, as we go on to explain, a Bourdieusian lens has flanked this entire book, informing both our research design and the manner in which we analyse our results. Yet (to improve readability!) this framing has been left largely implicit until now. Here, then, we sketch out more explicitly our Bourdieu-inspired 'class ceiling' approach to social mobility, and how we believe it offers a way of addressing some of the limitations that currently impair mobility analysis. The chapter is structured in three parts. First, we explain how our class ceiling approach is strongly informed by two research traditions that normally lie outside mainstream mobility analysis. Specifically, by synthesising elements of standard mobility analysis with both the feminist concept of the glass ceiling and an older tradition of elite recruitment studies, we are able to provide a large-scale, representative analysis of social mobility while also maintaining a conceptual focus on processes of closure at the top of the class structure.

Second, we argue that to shift mobility analysis in this way – that is, away from the conventional focus on who 'gets in' to who 'gets on' – requires a Bourdieusian theoretical lens. Here we make two specific points. First, we argue that adopting a Bourdieusian approach allows us to properly register the resources or 'capitals' that individuals carry with them into occupations, and then show how (and explain why) these often have long-lasting effects on people's mobility trajectories. Second, in making this move from access to progression, we also explain how our approach involves moving beyond single-variable indicators towards a more multidimensional measurement of both class origins and destinations.

Finally, in the third part of the chapter, we change tack to explain how we understand social mobility not only through a prism of *individual* resources or agency, but also as an experience that is also *mediated* by the particular occupational spaces or Bourdieusian 'fields' that individuals move into and through. Although these specific occupational settings are often ignored in standard mobility analysis, we argue that they are essential for understanding the class ceiling. This is because capitals that individuals inherit from their class backgrounds don't *automatically* confer advantages in the labour market. Instead, they have to be converted into more field-specific forms. For that to happen, their currency has to be recognised and valued by gatekeepers and/or those in positions of power. This is often contingent, our results suggest, on the extent to which occupational environments reward two types of cultural capital: embodied and technical.

Embodied cultural capital – widely valued tastes, categories of judgement and bodily self-presentation – is primarily inculcated via a privileged upbringing and therefore acts as a powerful (yet hidden) means through which those from upper-middle-class backgrounds secure advantage in elite occupations, as we have showed in Chapters Six, Seven and Eight. In contrast, technical capital – forms of practical and specialised knowledge, expertise, know-how and hands-on skill – can be more transparently acquired in education or the workplace, and therefore has less inherent capacity to advantage the already advantaged, as illustrated through the example of Coopers.[5]

While we think our Bourdieusian approach has a lot to offer, we are *not* arguing in this chapter for a war of paradigms, in which Bourdieu-inspired work offers a fundamental critique of the work done by more traditional social mobility researchers. These kinds of paradigm wars rarely allow cumulative knowledge to develop; nor do they allow researchers to collaborate to develop collective understandings. Moreover, we see much utility in standard approaches to social mobility. Occupational class remains, in our view, the best single proxy mobility analysis has at its disposal, as well as providing a measurement tool that can be easily and affordably adopted by organisations wishing to monitor the class origins of their staff, or by researchers – like us in this book – hoping to do so on their behalf.

Nonetheless, if we want to take seriously the full range of ways that origins matter for destinations, we need an approach to class that goes beyond single-variable, discrete time-point analyses. We believe that the Bourdieusian-inflected approach we articulate in this chapter (and operationalise throughout this book) – which takes into account income as well as occupation, and uses qualitative methods to get at individual trajectory, inherited and accumulated capital and occupationally specific notions of 'merit' – goes some way towards realising this.

The class ceiling: A synthetic mobility analysis

The systematic study of social mobility is arguably one of sociology's major contributions to social sciences, and public life more generally.[6] Here the standard quantitative approach involves comparing a person's origin and destination at two points[7] in time; first locating a parent's occupation within a set of socio-economic classes and then comparing this to the position of their own occupation. This grouping of origin and destination occupations into big classes then allows for the construction, and inspection, of what are called 'standard mobility tables'.[8] These provide an essential platform for analysis: a simple and reproducible means for assessing how many people have moved class position compared to their parents, and a basis for staging complex statistical procedures that model mobility patterns over time and/or across national contexts.[9]

This standard approach to mobility not only dominates academic discourse but, in the UK, has also been adopted by government[10] and most recently, recommended as the key measure for organisations when assessing the class composition of their workforces.[11] Our work has been strongly influenced by this approach and we draw on it throughout this book, particularly in Chapter One. To reiterate, we believe occupational class remains the most practical *single* indicator of class position and social mobility.

Yet readers will notice that as this book has progressed, it has moved further and further away from the standard approach to social mobility. In this section, we explain how our *quantitative* approach in particular – illustrated in Chapters One, Two, Three and Four – synthesises elements of the standard approach with two research traditions that normally stand outside the field of mainstream mobility analysis.

We begin our remarks here by explaining how our approach forges a critical link between contemporary mainstream mobility analysis and what is often called 'the sociology of elite recruitment' – a long and rich research tradition that has largely been forgotten in recent decades.[12] Studies of elite recruitment were central to sociological inquiry through much of the 20th century. In the 1950s and 1960s, in particular, a number of classic studies – particularly in the UK and US – investigated social mobility in a range of elite domains such as the senior civil service, the clergy, corporate management and politics.[13] The key issue at stake in this work was the degree to which processes of elite recruitment enact forms of social closure,[14] or how social collectives restrict access to resources and opportunities to a limited circle of the eligible.[15] This issue of closure was also seen as having particular significance in terms of elite formation. When elites are drawn from narrow backgrounds, for example, it is often hypothesised that they are more likely to develop 'a unity and cohesion of consciousness and action' which, in turn, may have profound implications for the exercise of power.[16]

However, from the 1980s onwards, this tradition of elite studies was somewhat eclipsed by class-structural approaches to social stratification,[17] particularly in the UK. There were several reasons for this. First, these studies were seen as empirically limited. Most relied on small-scale and unrepresentative data sources, looked only at a single elite occupation, and often relied on proxies for class background such as elite schooling. More conceptually, Goldthorpe also argued that by focusing on the social composition of 'who gets ahead', these approaches failed to place patterns of elite recruitment within the context of broader shifts in the class structure, particularly the post-war expansion of the salariat. The class-structural approach instead emphasised mobility rates between 'big social classes' and used nationally representative survey data. But, given the relatively small sample sizes of these 'gold standard' surveys, and the corresponding invisibility of elite groups within them, empirical scrutiny of those in elite occupations has largely died out.[18,19]

We therefore see our approach as powerfully renovating the sociology of elite recruitment, while also synthesising this tradition with more dominant elements of mobility analysis. Thus our analysis upholds many of the central tenets of current mobility analysis, in terms of using the representative Labour Force Survey (LFS) and by drawing on robust class-origin data. But at the same time, we also capitalise on the increased sample size offered by the LFS to aim our analytical lens upwards, at those in elite occupations.[20] Not only does this revive an analytical focus on elite closure, but it also insists on a more granular understanding of social mobility and a sensitivity to how class background may be particularly significant in structuring who gets to the very top.

Second, we also want to reflect on our adoption in this book of the feminist concept of the glass ceiling, albeit recast in terms of a 'class ceiling'. We should make it clear, here, that we are in no way asserting that the class ceiling has somehow replaced the glass ceiling, or implicitly suggesting, like many in the past, that class is some sort of 'master-category'.[21] Put simply, class-origin differences in the labour market do not operate in all the same ways as gender and ethnicity, and therefore retaining the specificity of the glass ceiling concept is clearly critical.

Yet at the same time we believe that mobility analysis has much to learn from this literature.[22] This is very clear from the results of this book. For example, many of the mechanisms that we have identified as drivers of the class ceiling – homophily, sponsorship, self-elimination, microaggressions[23] – echo those long identified in studies of white women and people from racial-ethnic minority groups in traditionally male and white occupations.[24]

Of course synthesising the glass ceiling with mobility analysis also necessitates a sustained engagement with the concept of intersectionality.[25] Traditionally, intersectionality has been at best under-theorised and at worst completely ignored in class and mobility analysis – both in standard approaches[26] and in Bourdieusian scholarship.[27] Yet as we explored in the Introduction, there is now a significant body of qualitative literature exploring the distinct psycho-social travails, and occupational barriers, experienced by upwardly socially mobile women and people of colour.

Drawing on these insights, we have tried to build intersectionality into the very fabric of our analysis. This has acted to productively complicate and disrupt class-only explanations of the inequalities we have uncovered in this book. For example, we have uncovered clear evidence – both quantitative and qualitative – that women and racial-ethnic minorities from working-class backgrounds face a distinct 'double disadvantage' in Britain's elite occupations, and that this inequality is often multiplicative rather than simply additive. In this way, we might see the barriers facing these groups as often more accurately constituting a denser, and less easily shattered, 'concrete ceiling'.[28] However, we also acknowledge here that our intersectional focus is in no way exhaustive. Not only are the complex classed experiences of our interviewees who were women and/or ethnic minorities probably deserving of a book in their own right, but we are also acutely aware that there are many axes of social division, such as sexuality, disability and migration, that we are not able to examine here.

Finally, we also hope that our incorporation and adaptation of the glass–ceiling concept may act as a means of sharpening the tools of class analysis. Here in particular we see the 'class ceiling' as providing a new *analytic tool* with which researchers of class and mobility can begin, as we have done here, to examine the pay gaps and other barriers that people from lower-class origins may face within particular occupations, sectors, geographical areas and national contexts. While some others have identified similar effects in other places and times,[29] we hope that by organising this work under an umbrella term like 'the class ceiling' will enable a clearer research tradition to emerge, cumulative knowledge to accumulate and political action to follow, in much the same way as has been achieved under the banner of the glass ceiling.

Beyond snapshots: Capturing the long shadow of class origin

As we have explained, our approach to social mobility partly represents a synthesis of standard quantitative approaches with insights from elite recruitment studies and glass ceiling research. The key issue that unites both these strands is a focus on not just who 'gets in' to elite occupations but who 'gets ahead'. Yet to fully conceptualise social mobility in this way, in terms of the long shadow cast by class origins on more granular occupational destinations, demands more than simply adapting or adjusting existing approaches.

To explain this we need to return to the issue of the standard mobility table. As we outlined, most quantitative mobility research begins by inspecting such tables, comparing a person's origin and destination class at two points in time. Yet to render class mobility in this way, as measured by one variable at each of two discrete time points, is clearly a simplification of much more complex trajectories.[30] This problem can be understood in quite simple terms – imagine we are analysing two 45-year-old accountants, one who has remained in an entry-level role at a small firm and therefore earns £30,000 a year, and one who has reached partner at a large multinational firm, and so earns £250,000 a year. Despite the vast differences in their career trajectories, standard analysis considers the class destinations of these accountants to be exactly the same. Similarly, imagine we also learn that both grew up with a breadwinning parent who was also an accountant. However, while one had another parent who was an academic, grew up in a £2 million home, and attended an expensive private school, the other had an unemployed second parent, lived in rented accommodation, and went to a non-selective secondary school. While it is easy to recognise that these constitute very meaningful differences, the standard approach again categorises both these accountants as hailing from the same class origins.

It is not that mobility researchers do not recognise these limitations; they do.[31] Yet despite this, most have remained doggedly attached to standard mobility tables. The most high-profile debate within the field, for example, revolves around how best to measure mobility – with economists focusing on income[32] and sociologists favouring occupational class.[33] Yet despite the voluminous and often heated methodological and empirical disagreements between these two camps, both still agree that mobility is best understood through the lens of a simple two-point inter-generational focus. Even recent innovations have failed to dislodge this consensus. Weeden and Grusky's micro-class concept,[34] for instance, has been important in registering class destinations at a more specific occupational level, while Chetty's recent mapping of US income mobility using tax and census data has introduced staggering new empirical scope.[35] Again, however, these projects, along with the vast majority of others in the field, remain focused on capturing a single time-point snapshot, symmetrically measured, of a person's mobility destination.[36]

There are, we believe, two main problems with this standard approach: first, its depiction of class as measurable using only a *single variable* and, second, its depiction of mobility destinations as measurable using only a *single time-point*. Addressing these limitations, we argue in this section, demands a different theoretical lens. Here, our ideas are deeply influenced by the work of Pierre Bourdieu.

Bourdieu, time and trajectory

We begin with the issue of time, or more specifically, what we would call mobility *trajectories*. The fairly simple problem with standard approaches is that they elide the ways in which *intra-generational* mobility (that is, mobility within one's own career) can complicate measures of inter-generational mobility. In sociological work, this means that social mobility is conceptualised as an issue of occupational *access*, with the implication that entry into an occupation is the sum total of a person's mobility trajectory. Yet, as the results in this book have demonstrated, although some of those from working-class backgrounds do secure admission into top occupations, they do not generally have the same kinds of career trajectories or levels of success as their colleagues from more privileged origins.

To take this linger of class origin seriously, we therefore need to move away from the fixation on measuring mobility between two fixed time-points and instead develop a richer conception of how past forces affect mobility in the present and future. We might see this as understanding the different propulsive forces associated with coming from different kinds of origins and their effects in projecting people into future positions. As Mark explained in the Introduction of this book, the resources that he brought with him into television represented a powerful "following wind" that, in turn, helped him reap significant rewards once inside.

In thinking through the way classed pasts shape career paths, we argue that Bourdieu's social theory can help us move forward. At first glance this might seem an unusual line of argument.

Certainly, Bourdieu rarely addressed social mobility head on[37] and was not involved with research communities that focused directly on the topic. Indeed, within the dominant arena of quantitative mobility research he is often characterised as a sociologist of 'reproduction' who denies the significance of mobility.[38] This view is normally associated with a critique of Bourdieu's notion of habitus, which many argue is almost antithetical to social mobility.[39] It is certainly true that Bourdieu[40] saw the dispositions flowing from primary socialisation as so robust that in the vast majority of cases the habitus stayed unified over the life course, meaning those who inherited strong reserves of economic, social and cultural capital were the most likely to accumulate further, and vice versa.[41]

However, what many of Bourdieu's detractors fail to recognise is that his conception of social space was constructed along *three* dimensions – volume of capital, composition of capital *and* 'change in these properties over time'.[42] Thus he viewed social mobility as effectively the third axis of social space,[43] with each individual possessing a 'band of more or less probable *trajectories*' based on their volume of inherited capital. In this way, contrary to his critics, Bourdieu did acknowledge that the dispositional architecture of the habitus was subject to change, according to both new experiences,[44] and also via conscious, intentional self-fashioning or pedagogic effort. Yet he saw the nature of this change as gradual and fundamentally limited[45] by the childhood dispositions that always act as the scaffolding of habitus.[46] We would argue that this conception of habitus – which is both structured by the capitals that flow from one's class origin but also that act as a structuring force in guiding action in the present – allows for a much more nuanced and joined-up understanding of the role of history and trajectory in understanding mobility. Specifically, it demands that we turn our analytical focus to the prior endowments that people bring with them into their careers and how these accumulated assets then act to structure their possibilities of action (and career progression) in the present and future.[47]

In this book we have explored a new way of conducting mobility research that draws directly on these insights. In particular, we have tried to push beyond mobility as occupational access and better engage, quantitatively, with mobility *destinations*. Specifically, by analysing occupation and earnings in tandem, we have tried to engage with not just who 'gets in' but also who 'gets on' in Britain's top occupations. Our results illustrate the importance of this kind of conceptual innovation. Specifically, our discovery of a significant class pay gap[48] demonstrates the powerful ways in which class origin tends to linger throughout the life course. It also provides a stark illustration of how standard approaches to social mobility obscure our understanding of the long shadows cast by class backgrounds.[49]

Of course it is important to acknowledge that our quantitative analyses only partially realise a Bourdieusian approach to social mobility. We are still reliant, for example, on a temporal snapshot of class destination, using earnings as a proxy for trajectory rather than examining career pathways in detail. There *are* ways to address this. Indeed, it was exactly this issue that led Andrew Abbott to champion sequence analysis in the 1990s, an approach that measures an individual's occupational position on a regular basis and then clusters the different trajectories that are revealed.[50] This allows a much richer understanding of the sequences of people's career pathways. More recently, Maren Toft has demonstrated the potential of this method for capturing the stickiness of class origin. Examining career trajectories within the Norwegian upper class, Toft shows that the upwardly mobile tend to have much less stable careers at the top, arriving later than their privileged colleagues and often failing to 'stay up'.[51] Unfortunately, the kind of large-scale data needed to do this kind of analysis (that is, that can measure the sequencing of mobility trajectories while also maintaining a granular focus on those at the top) is rare. Indeed, despite a handful of innovative studies,[52] it is telling that sequence analysis has not been used widely in mobility research.[53]

In moving towards a Bourdieusian analysis of trajectory, then, we would stress the distinct advantages of the mixed-methods approach we employ in this book. In particular, in each of our case studies we have triangulated survey data with in-depth interviews. This allowed us to directly probe people's career trajectories, asking all of our 175 interviewees to walk us through the key moments and critical junctures in their work histories.

This was particularly important in allowing us to assess the *speed* and *linearity* of people's careers, and how this was patterned according to class origin. For example, as we explained in Chapter Seven, where those from privileged backgrounds had made Partner at Turner Clarke, they had largely done so via an accelerated 'Partner track' that was facilitated by the advocacy of senior sponsors. This meant they had usually become Partners at a much earlier age than Partners from less privileged backgrounds. At 6TV, career trajectories were also systematically stratified by class origin. As we explained in Chapter Eight, senior personnel from privileged backgrounds had largely been recruited laterally from outside the firm, and often from fairly junior positions. In contrast, socially mobile senior staff were more likely to have risen up the ranks – a longer and more unlikely route to the top. In these ways, interviews allowed us to see how patterns in types of career trajectory, what Bourdieu[54] called their 'slope and thrust', map onto class origins. We include a categorisation of each participant's career trajectory in Tables A.1a-1d, in the Methodological appendix.

Towards a multidimensional approach to social mobility

The second limitation of conventional mobility analysis is the one-dimensional way in which it conceptualises class. Here class origins and destinations are normally reduced to a single indicator of occupation. While we agree that occupation is probably the best single proxy for class, and certainly the most practical to operationalise, we are sceptical that it (or indeed any single indicator) is sufficient on its own.

Drawing on Bourdieu again, then, we believe class should be understood as multidimensional[55] – that origins *and* destinations can only be fully understood as the sum total of capitals at a person's disposal: most centrally economic and cultural, as well as social, symbolic and field–specific forms. Yet most quantitative data is fundamentally limited in its ability to capture such capitals. Not only do most standard surveys lack the necessary questions to measure all forms of Bourdieusian capital, but even when they are constructed with this aim in mind they tend to prove blunt instruments for measuring complex dispositional configurations such as embodied cultural capital.[56]

In this way, quantitative analysis is a necessary but not sufficient step towards realising a truly Bourdieusian approach to social mobility.[57] In order to move towards more accurate measurement we would argue that survey data should be supplemented with qualitative enquiry. In the context of our case studies, this allowed us to more fully capture participants' stocks of inherited and accumulated capital. Interviews thus began with an extensive mapping of inherited capital, including detailed questions about parental income, wealth and property assets, as well as type of schooling. Moreover, we also tapped inherited embodied cultural capital by initiating a lengthy and open-ended discussion about the role of culture in interviewees' upbringings. Here, following Bourdieu, we specifically probed the extent to which interviewees had been exposed to, and had repeated experiences with, legitimate and/or canonical culture in their early years, and therefore the degree to which they may embody and deploy what Bourdieu calls the 'aesthetic disposition', a key aspect of embodied cultural capital (as we explain later in this chapter).[58] We include individual-level information about inherited economic and cultural capital in Tables A.1a–1d in the Methodological appendix.

This provided a much more detailed and nuanced understanding of mobility than looking solely at a single indicator of parental occupation. In many cases, for example, interviewees who were coded as having a particular class origin based on their initial survey response looked very different once information about both parents' occupations, and/or their inherited cultural and economic capital, were added. Take Roger at 6TV. The survey revealed him to be one of the only individuals from the executive team to come from a working-class background and therefore, naturally, we were keen to interview him. Yet although Roger's father had been a pipe fitter when he was 14 and his mother unemployed, he elaborated during our interview that his father had subsequently gone on to become a senior manager at his firm and his mother, while not working, was a keen amateur artist who inspired his interest in becoming a television and film director. Moreover, his grandparents had paid for him to go to an expensive private school and his parents had provided money for both rent and living costs in his early years in television. As he quipped when we mentioned his survey response, "A working-class hero I certainly am not!" Many similar instances of miscategorisation are revealed in Tables A.1a–1d in the Methodological appendix.[59] This demonstrates the productive dissonances that can emerge from triangulating analysis across different methods, and specifically how examining class multidimensionally can reveal what is missed when mobility is measured based only on single variables.[60]

Capitals in context

So far we have explained the importance of properly registering the resources that individuals bring with them into occupations and, in so doing, have demonstrated how these prior endowments often have long-lasting effects on mobility trajectories. We might think of this as the 'supply-side' of social mobility – how a person's passage is affected by both the assets, inherited and accumulated, that they possess, as well as their own voluntaristic agency and action. But a Bourdieusian perspective insists that we also look at the 'demand-side' of social mobility, how trajectories are also mediated by the particular contexts and settings in which a person's mobility takes place, as well as by the others they encounter once there.[61]

In Bourdieusian terms this is, of course, about the interplay between habitus and *field*[62] – the dynamic social spaces in which individuals compete for position and power. Fields can exist at many scales, but in terms of the top of the class structure, the most pertinent unit of analysis is what Bourdieu called the 'field of power'. Rather than seeing the upper layer of society as composed of a coherent and cohesive group, as in the 'big-class' categories of standard mobility analysis imply (as did work on the power elite), Bourdieu identified it as a site of internal struggle and contestation between those in different elite sectors (business, the state, media, culture and so on) who jostle for overarching power.[63] This usefully directs us not only towards important fractures *between* dominant groups, but also what Bourdieu called 'occupational effects',[64] the ways in which firms and organisations (within elite occupations) operate as distinct *sub-fields*, each with their own specific set of stakes and localised version of 'merit' or value.[65] To get ahead in a particular elite occupation or organisation, in other words, one must accumulate what Bourdieu calls 'field-specific capital'.

This is critical for understanding the class ceiling we have identified in this book. It emphasises that while individuals may enter elite organisational environments with various kinds of capital derived directly from their class origins (as we detail in Tables A.1a–1d in the Methodological appendix), such inherited resources will not necessarily confer advantage in the same way in every setting. We therefore need to interrogate how different capitals operate *in context*, and if and how they are *converted* into more 'field-specific' forms in particular workplaces.[66] In this regard, and as we go on to explore in the next section, our qualitative case studies revealed the distinct but uneven power of (inherited) embodied cultural capital, and the hidden ways in which this is 'cashed in' in certain settings.

Cashing in (embodied) cultural capital

Bourdieu distinguished three main forms of cultural capital: *institutionalised* in the form of educational and other credentials; *objectified* through the possession of legitimate cultural objects such as paintings and books; and *embodied* via particular long-lasting dispositions.[67] Of these, he considered embodied cultural capital to be the most 'fundamental'.[68] This is partly because he saw the acquisition of institutionalised capital, or consumption of objectified capital, as (at least partially) contingent on possessing the dispositions that constitute embodied capital. But more than this, and of particular significance for this book, he also saw embodied cultural capital as carrying the greatest 'weight' in terms of class reproduction.[69] This is because, he argued, it is the 'best hidden form of hereditary transmission of capital', inculcated and transmitted by upper-middle class parents during their children's primary socialisation and thereafter 'misrecognised as [a] legitimate competence' in social life.[70] Our analysis very much supports this formulation. Indeed, we would argue that the successful activation of embodied cultural capital represents *the most significant driver* of the class ceiling in Britain's top occupations.[71]

To understand this, it is first useful to distinguish between what Bourdieu saw as two connected but distinct manifestations of embodied cultural capital. First, he pointed to class-specific and durable modes of *comportment* that are imprinted during early childhood. He stressed that these are inculcated less through any explicit teaching and more through a prolonged immersion in, and experience of, a particular set of socio-economic conditions.[72] This process of transmission and encoding leaves physical traces *in* and *on* the body – in accent, inflection, gesture and posture, as well as styles of dress, etiquette and manners.[73]

Second, he then connected these styles of comportment or *hexis* to particular ways of thinking and feeling. The material affluence of the educated upper-middle classes, he argued, afford them a certain distance from necessity that is then reflected in the way they socialise their children. In particular, they have the time and space 'freed from [economic] urgency' to inculcate a propensity for what he called 'symbolic mastery'. This includes a certain mode of using language, including an elaborate vocabulary and 'correct' grammar, as well as more generally an ease and familiarity with abstraction, theoretical ideas, and concepts transcending concrete things and events.[74] But symbolic mastery was most clearly discerned, Bourdieu argued, in the taste profiles of dominant groups, and – crucially – how they *express* their tastes aesthetically. Here he pointed to the way the privileged not only introduce their children to legitimate culture but also inculcate particular ways of *seeing* and *listening*. He calls this the 'aesthetic disposition' – a refusal of cultural objects or experiences that are considered easy, facile or sensational, and instead an insistence on a 'disinterested'[75] aesthetic lens, where true artistic beauty can only be experienced if one separates oneself from any physical, emotional or functional investment in an art work.[76] And significantly, he emphasises that while the early acquisition of this aesthetic disposition is first honed through exposure to traditional highbrow culture, the deeper this early exposure the more assured the individual will be in then extending and transposing the aesthetic disposition to other, less canonical cultural forms.[77]

For Bourdieu, the key point about the aesthetic disposition, as well as other aspects of symbolic mastery and embodiment associated with a privileged upbringing, is that they tend to be (mis)recognised as legitimate in social life. They may only constitute, he is at pains to stress, one way of knowing the world. But nonetheless, in most Western societies they are assigned high value; they function as widely recognised signals of cultural distinction, 'natural' sophistication, even intelligence.[78] In this way, they operate as a 'symbolic capital' that can be 'cashed in'[79] in multiple settings, including in the labour market.

We see this process of capital conversion very clearly in the data presented in this book. In Chapter Seven, for example, we reveal how the specifically bodily aspects of cultural capital confer advantage in the workplace. Here, in particular, we see the alignment between particular modes of privileged embodiment and the unwritten behavioural codes that prevail in occupational settings.[80] Significantly, however, these codes are not uniform. In fact, they are strongly 'field-specific' – from the formal expectations of corporate polish at Turner Clarke to the studied informality demanded at 6TV. Yet while these codes are different in important ways, our analysis indicates that they tilt similarly towards the bodily schemas inculcated in privileged families.[81] This, we argue, is strongly connected to the legacy of those who have traditionally dominated these fields, and who – over time – have been successful in institutionalising particular 'doxic' or taken-for-granted behavioural codes (what we called the 'glass slipper' in Chapter Seven) that masquerade as neutral but in fact reflect their own embodied praxis.[82]

Our analysis also shows the profits that can be gleaned from the more aesthetic aspects of embodied cultural capital. In Chapter Eight, for example, we explore how legitimate forms of cultural taste can be 'cashed in'. This is exemplified most clearly at 6TV, where the ability to transpose the aesthetic disposition to popular television confers significant value, particularly at the upper echelons of Commissioning. But it is also relevant at Turner Clarke, where an instinctive sense of the right cultural or sporting setting to entertain clients can be pivotal. Here, notably, the embodied cultural capital of certain employees is not only profitable for them, individually, but is also converted into economic capital by the organisation itself, with the partners playing a pivotal role in communicating the company brand and winning external business.[83]

The convertibility of both these forms of inherited cultural capital, our analysis suggests, is strongest in areas of work characterised by heightened ambiguity of knowledge and where performance is especially hard to evaluate, such as Commissioning at 6TV or Advisory at Turner Clarke. In these environments, where the success of the final product is uncertain, the expertise of the professional is particularly contestable. And what is often deployed to plug this uncertainty, our results show, is the self-presentational baggage of a privileged class origin. This embodied cultural capital becomes integral to the act of pitching a programme idea or selling a financial service, a proxy for a competence that cannot be reliably demonstrated or verified.

Finally, our analysis also captures the difficulties of successfully activating embodied cultural capital if it has not been inculcated early in life. Here it is worth reiterating Bourdieu's argument that while the aesthetic disposition *can* be acquired later in life (via education or in the workplace), those who incorporate it in primary socialisation will always possess a head start, particularly in terms of their ability to transpose their disinterested orientation to areas of popular culture.[84] This is echoed in the uncertain testimonies of many socially mobile interviewees at 6TV. Here, as Alice illustrated in Chapter Eight, there is an enduring anxiety that one has missed certain cultural references, or lacks the confidence to play with the rules of aesthetic legitimacy. Indeed, even when these individuals describe consciously aligning their presentation of self with those that their social mobility has brought them into contact with, elements of their bodily 'hexis' – accent, pronunciation, vocabulary, posture, taste – tend to mark them out as 'other' – of only ever being able to partially 'fake it'.[85]

In all of these ways our analysis shows the distinct ways that those from privileged backgrounds convert their embodied cultural capital into *field-specific capital* (and subsequently economic capital) in Britain's top occupations. We would argue that this is not only significant in explaining the class ceiling but also has wider implications. Bourdieusian scholars interested in embodied cultural capital, for example, have tended to confine their enquiries to the patterning of cultural consumption, either by analysing *what* types of legitimate culture people consume,[86] or *how* they consume it.[87] This has, of course, been pivotal in helping us understand how taste is stratified, but our analysis indicates the need for this literature to engage further with how people actually deploy their tastes in different spheres of social life, and specifically, if and how they act to confer tangible forms of advantage.[88] Similarly, we also believe this analysis may be useful for scholars of work and occupations. Discussions of the economic returns to cultural capital in this field are largely confined to discussions of educational credentials,[89] or more recently occupational access,[90] and we know of very little work that uses embodied cultural capital to understand the specific issue of career progression.[91]

Embodied versus technical capital

The value of our Bourdieusian-influenced approach not only lies in helping us better understand the mechanisms driving the class ceiling, but also in unravelling why we see important *variations* in these ceiling effects. In this final section we argue that by developing the under-theorised Bourdieusian concept of technical capital, and contrasting it with embodied cultural capital, we can begin to understand a key cleavage in the way class origin plays out across Britain's top occupations.

Technical capital can be simply defined as forms of practical expertise, knowledge, know-how – or what Bourdieu called 'hands-on skill' – that is amassed in occupational settings and can be leveraged to progress one's career, or more generally converted into other forms of capital.[92] Yet compared to the other capitals theorised by Bourdieu, technical capital is far less well known. This is partly because Bourdieu only began to develop it in later works, and even then left it tantalisingly under-theorised.[93]

However, we want to argue that the relative neglect of technical capital, both by Bourdieu himself and among Bourdieusian scholars more generally, may also have something to do with the fact that the very idea of technical capital, although posited by Bourdieu as 'a particular kind of cultural capital',[94] arguably poses a (partial) threat to his account of class reproduction. This is because technical capital has a much more uncertain relationship to the kinds of inherited dispositions that Bourdieu saw as pivotal to the reproduction of class advantage.

It is true that Bourdieu himself never explicitly addressed this issue. However, he did concede that technical capital was distinct from embodied cultural capital in two important ways. First, there are much lower barriers to the *acquisition* of technical capital. Individuals, he explained, can learn and amass technical expertise in a fairly linear fashion by following 'formalised, rationalised procedures'.[95] Of course this is very different to the logic of embodied cultural capital, which, as we have explained, is much harder to acquire and accumulate if it is not inculcated during primary socialisation.[96] Second, Bourdieu saw technical capital as connected to a very different set of inherited dispositions, to principles of 'practical mastery' (rather than symbolic mastery), inculcated in dominated rather than dominant groups, and celebrating a more realist valorisation of technique, pragmatism and scientific truth, rather than a disinterested Kantian emphasis on the abstract and symbolic.[97]

These distinctions are central to understanding how and whether different forms of 'merit' land in different workplaces, especially in terms of their relationship to class origin. In particular we read Bourdieu's conceptualisation of technical capital as both less heritable than embodied cultural capital, in terms of the greater likelihood that it is obtained from personal engagement with the labour market[98] and, even where it is inherited, more likely to align with dispositions inculcated in working-class or intermediate families.

Yet while we might infer this reading of technical capital from Bourdieu, it is clear from his own empirical work that he viewed it as a fairly marginal form of capital. A key reason for this is that, in the French context he was working in, he located the exchange value of technical capital as confined to the context of skilled manual work and the self-employed tradesman of the intermediate social classes.[99] In a contemporary UK context (and likely beyond), the significance of technical capital is arguably more wide-ranging.[100]

To understand this, it is important to understand the way in which class relations in the UK evolved over the course of the 20th century. As Savage[101] explains, during the Second World War there was a considerable surge in demand for newer, more technically oriented, professions such as science and engineering. This continued in the post-war period, with many such professions beginning to rival – in size and status – traditional 'gentlemanly' fields such as law, medicine, accountancy and finance.[102] This, Savage argues, signalled a sea-change in the nature and formation of middle-class identities. Many of these new professionals were upwardly socially mobile men, particularly from the kind of skilled manual backgrounds that Bourdieu saw as the incubators of technical capital. This set up an important cleavage within the middle classes, with the ethos of this new, largely male, technical middle class very much pitted against the hidden, implicit and 'arty' class-cultural codes of the gentlemanly professions. But rather than showing deference or what Bourdieu would call 'cultural goodwill' to such traditional modes, these new identities confidently drew on 'a long tradition of a skilled working class, steeped in practical skills and its own form of craft intellectualism',[103] to champion a new rational, scientific orientation to expertise. The strength of this technical orientation persists to the present day. A number of studies have shown its centrality to organisational cultures within areas of the civil service,[104] the IT sector,[105] and engineering.[106]

The key point for us here is not just that these occupational areas tend to be more socially open, and have a particular representation of those from skilled manual class origins. It is also that what is championed in these areas is a distinct 'ethic of expertise', one that is proclaimed as more transparent, more 'meritocratic', and that self-consciously repudiates the shadowy aesthetic principles associated with Bourdieusian embodied cultural capital.

We argue that it is possible to see a distinct residue of this division throughout the data in this book. It first emerges, albeit tentatively, in the patterning of our quantitative data. The traditional 'gentlemanly' professions of law, medicine, journalism and accountancy, for example, remain significantly more socially exclusive than certain technical professions such as engineering and IT. This is further reflected in variation in the class pay gap. Notably more technical professions such as engineering and science have negligible pay gaps and contrast strongly with law, finance and medicine.[107]

But it is really in our qualitative data where this distinction emerges most clearly. This is perhaps most evident in comparisons between television broadcaster 6TV and architecture firm Coopers. Here there is a gulf between what type of behaviours and skills are valued in the workplace as a whole (Chapter Seven) and specifically in executive environments (Chapter Eight). At 6TV, as we explored in the previous section, we see the power of embodied cultural capital playing out very clearly, both in terms of its alignment with dominant organisational modes of bodily praxis and through the value of a highbrow aesthetic orientation. In contrast, the ethos of Coopers couldn't be more different. This, we are continually told, is a "pragmatic" firm where staff and clients alike can "see through" the "bullshit" of embodiment masquerading as "merit". Instead, there is a strong emphasis on technical competence, perfectionism and project delivery. And, as several interviewees outline in Chapter Seven, staff are rewarded for developing highly specialised forms of technical expertise.

However, we should be clear that we don't see this distinction as always, or necessarily, mapping onto areas where the work is 'objectively'[108] more technical. Take Turner Clarke, for example. The core skills required to become an accountant are arguably just as technical as that of an architect. However, as we show in Chapters Seven and Eight, technical competency tends to only confer advantage at Turner Clarke in early-career roles, and as one moves up the business, the emphasis shifts more to polish, gravitas and the demonstration of entrepreneurial flair. The point here, then, is that it is not necessarily the nature of the work that matters, but more which competencies, real or imagined, are *valued* in different occupational environments, and then how these ideas about the 'right' way to work become embedded over time. In this way, it is no surprise that at Turner Clarke the shift in the competencies valued as one ascends the business maps onto the shifting class profile of the firm, with those from privileged backgrounds much more likely to reach the partnership.

Our overarching point here, then, is that we see a clear association between work environments where technical capital is *rewarded* and the class ceiling. Put simply, in environments that strongly value technical expertise, there appear to be smaller class pay gaps, less pronounced class ceilings and the socially mobile (albeit men – more on this later) appear to feel more comfortable and ambitious.

We should stress, however, that we don't see the foregrounding of technical (or cultural) capital as necessarily confined to specific occupations or firms.[109] We have highlighted throughout this book that Coopers, for example, is unlikely to be representative of the wider architecture profession, and that a more abstract highbrow aesthetic may be much more highly valued in design-led firms. Similarly, we also demonstrate that the distinction between the aesthetic and the technical often plays out *within* firms. For example, departments where embodied cultural capital is most clearly foregrounded, such as Commissioning at 6TV or Advisory at Turner Clarke, are much more socially exclusive than more 'technical' departments such as Tax at Turner Clarke or Technical and Strategy at 6TV (see Chapter Four).

This attention to what is valued in different environments brings us on to an important caveat to our findings concerning the relative ease with which those from disadvantaged backgrounds can accrue, and be rewarded for, technical capital – *this ease of access does not appear to extend to women*. Many of the professions that appear more open in terms of social mobility, such as engineering, are profoundly skewed in favour of men. Similarly, at Coopers it is striking that the socially mobile architects who have been successful are all men. Here it is instructive to return to Savage's historical account. He explains that while the emerging technical identities of the 1950s and 1960s posed as more open and meritocratic, their roots in skilled manual work were profoundly male, and thus there was a macho, even 'chauvinistic' tenor to many of these newly made men.[110] In this way, we should be very cautious before pronouncing the acquisition of technical capital as necessarily or definitively more socially open and 'meritocratic'. After all, technical capital – like all capitals – still has to land to be effective. And our findings suggest this is much less likely among women than men. Breaking the class ceiling, to reiterate, does not necessarily dovetail with breaking the glass ceiling.

It is important to remember that, as Wacquant famously remarked, 'Bourdieu's work is not free of contradictions, gaps, tensions, puzzlements, or unresolved questions, and therefore thinking with Bourdieu can necessitate thinking against and beyond Bourdieu where required.'[111] Following in this vein, we believe the findings discussed in this chapter point towards a more nuanced contemporary understanding of cultural capital, particularly in terms of its currency in occupational settings, how it may have changed form over time,[112] and how it manifests in a particular national context like the UK. Our findings suggest that distinct historical shifts in the occupational structure and formation of middle-class identities have elevated the importance of a particular technical form of cultural capital. This, in turn, has acted to at least partially challenge the ability of those from privileged backgrounds to cash in more inherited modes of embodied cultural capital in *some* areas of the labour market.[113]

ELEVEN

Conclusion

In contemporary Britain it quite literally pays to be privileged. Even when individuals from working-class backgrounds are successful in entering the country's elite occupations they go on to earn, on average, 16% less than colleagues from more privileged backgrounds. And more significantly, this class pay gap is not explained away by conventional indicators of 'merit'. A substantial gap remains even when we take into account a person's educational credentials, the hours they work and their level of training and experience.

In many ways this one relatively simple finding constitutes *the* central contribution of this book. We tend to assume that people get ahead in their careers on the basis of their own individual skill, experience and effort. These principles, both morally and pragmatically, underpin Britain's 'meritocratic ideal',[1] and have long dominated discussions about economic growth and social mobility. Yet the existence of a 'class pay gap' provides a sobering corrective to this lofty aim. When even institutions like Oxford and Cambridge, widely championed as the ultimate meritocratic sorting houses, do not wash away the advantages of class background, as we show emphatically in Chapter Three, this surely constitutes a stark rejoinder to even the most strident believers in Britain's meritocracy. The class pay gap, in other words, reveals a powerful and previously unobserved axis of inequality that clearly demands urgent attention.

Still, we always wanted to do more than just diagnose a problem. In this way, most of this book has been devoted to unravelling the *drivers* of the class pay gap, the mechanisms that explain precisely *why* the upwardly socially mobile, even when they are as 'meritorious' as their privileged colleagues (in every way we can measure), still fail to progress equally. One theme, in particular, runs throughout our analysis. This relates to the idea of 'merit' itself. We would not dispute that conventional measures of 'merit' – skills, qualifications, expertise, effort, experience – are important to career progression in Britain's elite occupations. But what our analysis indicates is that people do not necessarily have an equal capacity to 'cash in' their 'merit' or 'realise' their talent. This is because for 'merit' to land it has to be given the opportunity to be demonstrated, it has to be performed in a way that aligns with dominant ideas about the 'right' way to work, and it has to be recognised as valuable by those holding the keys to progression. And in all of these ways, as we go on to explain, it is the privileged who enjoy a critical head start.

The invisible hand (up)

In most elite occupations, and certainly among the people we interviewed, there is a strong belief in the meritocratic ideal – the idea that career progression should be based on the abilities, skills and achievements of the *individual*. Yet we find that people rarely progress in elite occupations based *only* on their own efforts. Instead career trajectories are shaped in important ways by the supporting actions of others. Very often when our interviewees narrated decisive moments in their careers – key decisions, new jobs, big promotions – there were other actors in their stories, sources that provided a pivotal *hand up*. Such help, our analysis indicates, tends to come from two directions.

First, in Chapter Five, we identified sources of support flowing from a person's class background, namely, the 'Bank of Mum and Dad'. This kind of financial patronage, we argue, is pivotal in propelling careers forward, particularly in precarious elite labour markets such as the cultural industries. Here money acts as an important early-career lubricant, allowing the privileged to manoeuvre into more promising career tracks, to focus on developing valuable networks, resist exploitative employment and take risky opportunities – all of which increases their chances of long-term success.

Yet a helping hand does not always push from behind or below. In Chapter Six we showed that in many traditional elite occupations, support is more likely to come from above rather than below, a pull rather than a push. And instead of economic help it is often social – in the form of informal sponsorship. In Britain such sponsored mobility is often associated with a bygone era, a relic of a now outdated 'old boy network'. But our fieldwork suggests sponsorship remains rife across a range of elite occupations – and continues to disproportionately advantage those from advantaged backgrounds. It may operate in subtly different ways in different occupations, but the key function is the same: a senior leader identifies a junior protégé and then fast-tracks their career by brokering job opportunities, allocating valuable work or advocating on their behalf. This, we argue, is social capital in the Bourdieusian sense, not necessarily being a 'good networker', but networking with the 'right' people and crucially, knowing them well enough to leverage their backing.

These helping hands rig the game of progression in favour of the privileged. And the main reason they are so effective, we argue, is that they are largely hidden from public view – they operate as *invisible hands*, helping to propel some and simultaneously disadvantage others. In terms of sponsorship this is partly about a particular species of management jargon – the use of empty terms such as 'talent mapping' – that give a misleading impression of formalised performance management and obscure the autonomy enjoyed by senior leaders in advancing sponsees through the organisational ranks.

There are also wider issues around whether such support is acknowledged. We find, for example, that both sponsors and the Bank of Mum and Dad are perennially downplayed in people's career narratives. Of course this strikes to the heart of the moral legitimacy of success; most *want* to believe they deserve their good fortune, as Weber famously argued.[2] But at the same time such muting, concealing and obscuring means that others working in elite occupations, and the public as a whole, are prevented from knowing the true extent to which elite careers rest on the support of others. This fundamentally complicates our understanding of 'merit' as individual. It suggests that to be effective, a person's 'merit' – in terms of demonstrable skills, qualifications and efforts – needs to be given a particular *platform*. As Alice (working-class origins) astutely observed of Senior Commissioners at 6TV: "Like, they're all really talented, it's not that. But kind of the reason they are [so successful] is because they've had the opportunities to be, kind of, *seen as* talented."

'Merit', then, needs to be showcased in the right setting or in front of the right people – *it needs to be seen* – and it is often the resources and/or opportunities brokered by others that provide this platform.

The performance of 'merit'

'Merit' is not only assumed to be the sole property of individuals. It is also thought to have a fixed nature – conventional indicators are widely considered 'objectively measurable' and equally recognised by all.[3] But a key theme running through this book is that 'merit' has to be continually and actively demonstrated in the workplace, and others – especially senior decision-makers – have to recognise and be persuaded of its value. In many ways we might see this as akin to a performance – in carrying out job-related tasks one has to activate what might be considered their objective stocks of 'merit' – qualifications, experience, expertise – via a particular embodied self-presentation that encompasses dress, accent, language and comportment. And the key point here is that supposedly objective measures of 'merit' are often actually received, assessed and valued very differently according to how they are performed. Some performances 'fit', in other words, and others do not.

To understand why some performances of 'merit' 'fit' in elite occupations, we need to understand what we refer to in Chapter Seven as the 'glass slipper' effect. This captures the way in which particular occupations come to appear possessed of inherent characteristics that have little to do with the actual work yet render them a natural fit for some and a squeeze for others. In professions such as accountancy, for example, and more specifically in certain spaces like the City (of London), the historical legacy of an overwhelmingly privileged (white, male) majority is that their ideas about the 'right' way to act and work have become embedded. This means that particular performances of 'merit', especially those that demonstrate a command of classed behavioural codes, have come to shape perceptions of who is appropriate to promote and progress – even though such codes arguably have little connection to the expertise required to do the job effectively. Decision-makers largely expressed this sense of fit as an instinctive 'gut' feeling, an intuitive sense, as Raymond from Turner Clarke put it, that some people simply "feel like a Partner".

Our book is peppered with examples of such 'looking-glass' versions of 'merit'. In Chapter Seven, for example, we explore the power of 'polish' in accountancy and 'studied informality' in television. While different in important ways, these both pivot on a package of expectations – relating to dress, accent, taste, language and etiquette – that are strongly associated with, or cultivated via, a privileged upbringing, what Pierre Bourdieu called *embodied cultural capital*. We also find that behavioural codes are particularly important in *certain* elite environments. For example, we argue that they take on a heightened significance in areas of work, such as Commissioning at 6TV or Advisory at Turner Clarke, where performance is especially hard to evaluate, and where notions of 'merit' are therefore particularly uncertain and contestable. In both these environments, the success of the 'final product' – whether financial advice or a television programme – is very hard to foretell, and therefore the knowledge and expertise of the professional is inherently ambiguous. Presenting or performing the right image, then, when advising a client or pitching a programme idea, becomes integral as an act of persuasion, a proxy for a competence that cannot be reliably or definitively demonstrated in the moment.

Notions of fit are also particularly important in senior management. Again this is partly about the inherent ambiguities in identifying and recognising leadership 'skills' and 'potential'. But in Chapter Eight, we argue that it is also a tool through which those already in executive positions restrict access to a limited circle they deem eligible. In the case of 6TV, for example, a command of highbrow aesthetics is considered a prerequisite for entry into senior management – despite most within this magic circle admitting privately its irrelevance to the mainstream programmes the channel produces.

In all of these settings, then, we find evidence that the self-presentational baggage of a privileged class origin is routinely misrecognised as a marker of talent or potential. *These are classed performances, in other words, masquerading as objective 'merit'.* And it is no surprise that it is precisely these areas – Commissioning, Advisory, Senior Management – where we find the highest concentration of people from privileged backgrounds in our case studies.

Birds of a feather

We have demonstrated that for someone to capitalise on their skills, credentials and expertise they not only need a particular platform, but they must perform their 'merits' in a way that aligns with dominant notions of fit and is valued by those holding the keys to progression. But the recognition of such decision-makers does not just rest on the way someone performs in meetings, presentations or interviews; it is also, we argue, very often about *relationships*.

Here we start from the basic observation that similarity breeds connection. This principle – known as homophily[4] – structures relationships of nearly every kind. People gravitate towards people like themselves and this, in turn, has powerful implications for the information they receive, the attitudes they form and the interactions they experience. While this has been shown to be powerful in explaining inequalities of race and gender, a key theme running throughout this book is that homophily, rooted in class origin, is also a key driver of the class ceiling.

Most straightforwardly, homophily is central to understanding the relationships of career support we have already outlined. Sponsorship ties, as we explained in Chapter Six, are rarely rooted solely in work. Instead, they are almost always forged on the basis of an organic-feeling connection, which, when traced to its genesis,[5] is often rooted in cultural affinity – of sharing tastes, interests, lifestyles and humour. While this cultural matching does not always map onto shared class origins, a formidable body of research suggests that it very often does.[6] This was certainly the case in the majority of our interviews. Here senior leaders, themselves disproportionately from privileged backgrounds, most often sponsored in their own image. This matters. It means that the significant career opportunities brokered by sponsors do not just rest on talent or ability, but also on class-cultural commonality.

At the same time it also helps to understand the more negative 'gut reactions' of senior figures when faced with those who have very different demographic coordinates. Such moments of awkwardness can be telling in foreclosing the cultivation of sponsorship ties, delineating, in Turner Clarke partner James's blunt terms, those who "you might go for a pint with but only stay for a half".

Of course it is very hard to prevent such bonds being established at work. Discovering cultural similarities serves as a powerful emotional glue, facilitating intimacy and trust.[7] Yet the more pressing question is, why is this kind of class homophily so consequential for career *progression*? Again our analysis provides some clues. First, senior hiring and promotion processes tend to be more informal and less transparent than those at lower levels. This increases the ability of sponsors to secure advantage for their sponsees, either by actively propelling them or by influencing the decisions made by others. Connected to this, work at the upper echelons is also characterised by significant uncertainty.[8] As top 6TV Executive Lizzie described it, "every day we jump off a cliff five times." Faced with such heightened uncertainty, senior figures tend to gravitate towards those they can rely on, those who they feel will be loyal – "people who are of a like mind," as James from Turner Clarke put it. Yet this increased demand for loyalty and trust, and the sense of risk aversion that runs alongside it, only accentuates the tendency to hire in one's own image. "Reliability and likeability get mixed up," as Michael at 6TV notes, and there's a sense, as Lizzie later acknowledged, that "you can't stop the train [to] let people on" who might be less familiar and therefore more risky.

When 'merit' does not stick

What happens when people don't get the platform to showcase their 'merits', or when their performances of 'merit' are not recognised by decision-makers? Over the course of our research we heard from many people who reported these kinds of experiences. Not all were upwardly socially mobile. But most were. These narratives underlined the uncertainties that flow from *not* having an economic safety net, the extra labour required if one does *not* have the advocacy of a sponsor, or the lingering anxiety that stems from failing to convincingly mimic dominant behavioural norms – to "crack the code", as Martina at Warner Clare put it.

They also provide striking illustrations of what follows, in terms of individual decision-making, when performances of 'merit' don't stick. Here the term 'sorting' is pivotal. Put simply, this describes the process whereby those from working-class backgrounds filter *horizontally* into certain elite sectors, occupations and departments that then lead to lower rewards in terms of earnings and status. Specifically, in Chapter Three we saw that the mobile tend to sort into less lucrative occupations, smaller firms and workplaces situated outside London. In Chapter Four we explored how this sorting also takes place within firms, with those from privileged backgrounds funnelling into departments where there is significantly more room for progression, such as Advisory at Turner Clarke or Commissioning at 6TV. And finally, in Chapter Nine we outlined how this sorting also has a *vertical* dimension. Specifically, we explored how the mobile often self-eliminate from pushing forward in their careers. But this is not because they somehow lack ambition or aspiration, as is sometimes presumed in policy circles.[9] Instead, it is largely a reaction to, or an anticipation of, the kinds of barriers already outlined – economic uncertainty, feeling less supported, or anxieties and ambivalences about 'fitting in'. All these factors profoundly impacted the 'career imaginations'[10] of our upwardly mobile interviewees, of what they saw as possible in their careers.

In Figure 11.1[11] we return to the heuristic diagrams that closed Chapters Three and Four. Now, however, we can add the drivers of the class pay gap identified in our case studies – the Bank of Mum and Dad, sponsorship, behavioural codes and self-elimination. While our analysis here is in no way definitive, and inevitably tilts towards the specific elite domains where we carried out our fieldwork, we do believe these drivers together go a considerable distance towards unravelling the class pay gap.

Figure 11.1: All drivers of the class ceiling – what advantages the privileged?

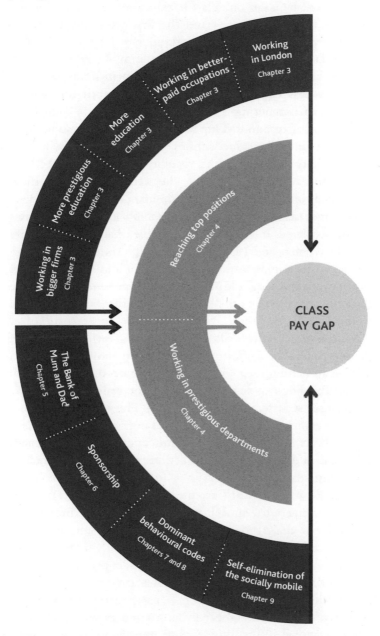

Working in London
Chapter 3

Working in better-paid occupations
Chapter 3

More education
Chapter 3

More prestigious education
Chapter 3

Working in bigger firms
Chapter 3

The Bank of Mum and Dad
Chapter 5

Sponsorship
Chapter 6

Dominant behavioural codes
Chapters 7 and 8

Self-elimination of the socially mobile
Chapter 9

Reaching top positions
Chapter 4

Working in prestigious departments
Chapter 4

CLASS PAY GAP

Note: In this diagram we bring together all the sets of drivers of the class ceiling we have identified throughout the book.

Of course, the performance and recognition of 'merit' is not just affected by a person's class background. On the contrary, we find strong evidence – and the first we know of – that *upwardly mobile* women and (certain) racial-ethnic minority groups face a double (and even sometimes triple) earnings disadvantage in elite occupations. Black British women from working-class backgrounds, for example, earn on average a somewhat staggering £20,000 less than white men from privileged backgrounds. Our interview data sheds some light on these intersectional inequalities, particularly the way gender and ethnicity can increase the visibility of class difference (and vice versa), and in turn increase the scrutiny placed on these individuals in their execution of dominant behavioural codes.

Our understanding of this type of mobility experience remains highly restricted. It is telling, for example, that it was upwardly mobile women and Black and Minority Ethnic actors who described their typecast as most offensive and caricatured, of trotting out the same old stereotypes – the battered wife, the Shakespearean jester or the 'Black nurse' – that bear no relation to their lived experience.

Moreover, as the voluminous glass-ceiling literature demonstrates, these groups also face many non-class-related hurdles in getting their 'merit' to stick. Indeed, we in no way intend this book to suggest that the class ceiling is somehow replacing or superseding the glass ceiling. This kind of assertion is fundamentally short-sighted. Class does not operate in a vacuum, and understanding the way inequalities interact to the detriment of people at demographic intersections, we argue, is pivotal to unravelling the class ceiling.

Finally, we also want to underline the importance of understanding what mobility *means* for those experiencing it. Here our analysis disrupts common-sense assumptions that upward mobility is an unequivocally positive experience. We find that when the mobile enter elite occupations, the lack of fit is deeply felt, and often generates a sense of unease that lingers throughout their careers – particularly among those who have experienced especially long-range upward mobility.[12] This emotional toll is important to register in its own right. As mentioned in the Introduction, prevailing political rhetoric tends to fetishise upward social mobility as a sort of panacea for society's ills. In fact, some may even read the central concern of this book – through its focus on elite occupations – as cementing this agenda. Yet we would stress that when examined through the lens of emotional wellbeing rather than simply economic and occupational achievement, the 'success' of mobility is much more uncertain, even when it involves successfully breaking the class ceiling.

Why this matters

In August 2017, after we had completed our fieldwork, we returned to 6TV to outline our findings to the senior leaders who had commissioned the research. It was a tense affair – the results were clearly very critical and the atmosphere, at times, strained. The senior leadership generally accepted the results, with many reacting thoughtfully and reflexively to our analysis. However, when we began to critique the highbrow culture of Commissioning, things changed. This clearly hit a nerve. One very senior figure, Josh, interrupted our presentation to protest. His first point was well made. "It's a bit rich," Josh joked, "for a bunch of academics to come in and tell us we're too intellectual!" Touché. His second point, however, was more serious. A command of highbrow culture, he told us, was not some pointless affectation – it was central to good programme-making:

> The products of 6TV are cultural artefacts and therefore they don't sit outside the books or paintings on people's walls. We judge them like that and so do our viewers. So if your argument is that it's not useful to make an intellectual critique of *Big Brother*, or take popular culture seriously, and give it the level of critique I think it deserves, I'd push back really hard on that.

Josh makes an important point here. We are sociologists, not television commissioners, and therefore there are clearly limits to our capacity to pronounce the precise skills and attributes needed to do elite jobs effectively. And it is worth acknowledging that some interviewees (incidentally, almost always white, privileged men in senior positions) did counter, like Josh, that what we identified as arbitrary behavioural codes or performances of 'merit' are actually entirely legitimate *components* of 'merit', that aspects of self-presentation or reserves of cultural knowledge *are* necessary to do elite jobs well.

We concede that this is not a straightforward issue, particularly if these things are valued by the kinds of clients that elite professionals rely on for business or funding. Yet we would stress that we do not see any clear association, or convincing rationale, connecting these attributes to credible measures of skill, intelligence or ability. Moreover, the majority of the people we interviewed – speaking within the safe confines of an anonymous interview – acknowledged this themselves.

We also want to be clear about our view on 'merit'. We do not want to be understood as saying there's no such thing as talent, or that career success is unrelated to individual skill or effort. We think it's likely that most of the successful people in the fields we studied are indeed smart, hardworking and talented. Instead, our key point is that the identification of 'merit' in these fields is intertwined with the way 'merit' is executed, how it is facilitated and who the decision-makers are who recognise it. It is nearly impossible to evaluate 'merit' in any purely objective way, separate from our various biases. Even standardised tests often incorporate racial, class and gender biases, or test experience as much as innate abilities.[13] Too often, then, evaluations of 'merit' are subsumed by other forms of social evaluation, which means that the privileged are more readily rewarded than those who are (at least) equally deserving but come from more disadvantaged backgrounds.

This has implications, we argue, for a whole range of those working in elite occupations – from HR professionals to diversity officers to senior managers. In the Epilogue, we distil these into a set of 10 practical recommendations aimed at exactly these kinds of practitioners. We intend these to provide both organisations and individuals with tools to tackle the class ceiling. Here we would simply add two points central to all of these interventions. First, our work underlines the need for those working in elite occupations, particularly at the upper echelons, to critically interrogate the 'objective' measures of 'merit' they rely on, and think carefully about whether such measures have a subjective, or performed dimension. Second, we would stress the need for direct political action to tackle the class ceiling. The UK government has recently led the way in tackling the gender pay gap – compelling large organisations to publish details of their internal pay divide. While this kind of mandatory reporting certainly does not represent a panacea for gender inequality, it has proved an effective way to very publicly call companies to account. Some significant change has also followed. Many big companies, for example, have rushed to take action in an effort to counter the fallout from embarrassing data. We believe a similar approach to tackling the class ceiling is possible, particularly as more and more companies begin collecting data on the social origins of their staff. We would urge politicians to be bold and mandate reporting of the class pay gap.

Why this matters for sociology

We have tried to write this book in a way that (hopefully) appeals beyond the academy. Yet of course we also want it to be read by, and useful to, colleagues in sociology. Here we summarise what we think are our main contributions (we explore these in detail in Chapter Ten).

First, we believe that our approach and findings have implications for how scholars think about social class. Most research on social mobility, for example, proceeds with the presumption that once a class 'destination' – in the form of entry to a particular occupation – has been achieved, class origin ceases to matter. However, our analysis shows that class origin is deeply 'sticky'. The resources that flow from class origin often shape individuals' life courses well beyond occupational entry.

To some researchers of class, this may seem a somewhat banal observation. After all, a wealth of qualitative research indicates that class identities tend to always carry – in some form at least – the symbolic baggage of the past, and this historical imprint often has important consequences for how people act in the present.[14] However, in the dominant quantitative arena of class analysis, sensitivity to how class origin lingers is often absent, and no one, to our knowledge, has yet demonstrated the ways economic and cultural capital rooted in social origin systematically shape how well people get *on* in their careers, not just which careers or firms they are able to get *in* to.

Second, and very much relatedly, we believe our analysis advances a new way of conducting social mobility research. Our work demonstrates that a person's class destination is never fully captured by large, aggregate occupational classes. These 'big classes' simply hide too much pertinent information. Occupations within the National Statistics Socio-Economic Classification (NS-SEC) 1,[15] as we show, are characterised by enormous variation in rates of mobility. Understanding this variation surely sheds important new light on the precise *channels* through which intergenerational class inequality is reproduced. Indeed, here our analysis points towards the importance of different forms of knowledge and 'merit' across different elite occupations, and how these may be implicated in different rates of mobility. In particular our analysis suggests that in elite occupations where notions of 'merit', or demonstrable expertise, are more ambiguous and harder to evaluate – such as in TV Commissioning or Advisory – the cultural trappings of a privileged class background may provide more concrete advantages. Under such conditions of heightened uncertainty, the classed performance of 'merit' is arguably imbued with an elevated currency.

Yet we would also go further. Even specific occupations, we would argue, are not sufficient for understanding a person's class destination. Take the example we gave in Chapter Ten, of two accountants working in different-sized firms, with different class backgrounds and very different salaries. While they are certainly in the same *occupation*, it is not clear that they are meaningfully in the same *class position*. Single occupations provide a *more* accurate indication of class position than big classes – their members are likely to be closer in earnings and other resources than are those in their wider macro class – but even they can mask important differences. Indeed, following Bourdieu and more recently even Goldthorpe,[16] we argue here that a full understanding of class destination must take into account multiple indicators of social position and resources.

Third, we would tentatively add that our analysis might also be useful to those working outside class – specifically, scholars of gender and race and ethnicity. Our work is the first we know of that shows systematic intersections between class, gender and ethnicity in terms of pay inequality. While we in no way intend this to suggest the revival of class as some sort of overarching 'master variable', we do think that future work on glass ceilings and pay gaps may yield valuable intersectional insight by taking class origin into account where possible.

Finally, we also see our work as extending the reach of a growing body of research exploring the 'long shadow of class origin'. This work, much of it inspired by Bourdieu, has long elucidated the stickiness of class background in shaping our experiences of primary and secondary schooling, and university.[17] More recently, the ground-breaking work of Lauren Rivera and Louise Ashley has shifted the focus to the labour market, and specifically, how the hiring practices of elite firms work to advantage those from privileged backgrounds.

We see our work as continuing in this vein, but adding to our understanding of the 'long shadow' in three key ways. First, our work echoes many of the processes so skilfully outlined by these scholars – including sponsorship and class-cultural matching – but shows that such classed mechanisms operate beyond just banking and law into many other elite fields. Moreover, these drivers are pivotal not only at the hiring stage, but also throughout elite careers. Indeed, we would argue that they are *more* powerful in structuring progression, as it is precisely through the more everyday operations of a work environment that sponsors are able to scaffold 'back-door' trajectories, or via seemingly mundane office interactions that decision-makers generate a more lasting 'feel' of 'fit'. Third, our analysis also points to *additional* ways in which class origin shapes occupational trajectories. In particular, our work emphasises the role that outside economic support can play in people's career trajectories. We find that these familial resources, often invisible in hiring processes and more generally downplayed in narratives of success, are nonetheless pivotal in shaping careers – particularly in more precarious labour markets such as the cultural industries. Here financial help, or even its theoretical availability, often help the privileged pivot on to more lucrative or prestigious career tracks, while shunting those without help on to more secure but lower-paying trajectories.

Some clarifications

We also want to be clear about what we are *not* saying in this book, and do not mean to imply. First and foremost, we cannot say for certain how class ceilings work beyond the evidence we have. Our evidence allows us to make the case that there is an overall class ceiling in top occupations, and in many specific occupations, with a fair degree of confidence. We can also say that there is a class ceiling in three of our four case studies, and that it works through the mechanisms we have outlined. We think it is likely that many of these same mechanisms operate in other accounting and television companies, and indeed elsewhere in elite occupations, but without further research, it is not possible to know for sure.

Just as we can't say that the barriers we've identified operate outside the firms we've studied, we also can't be sure that we have identified all the mechanisms that might be at play, even in those firms. Many people, for example, have suggested to us that people with working-class origins might be more reluctant to ask for pay raises, or less likely to leverage promotions by threatening to leave. We know that there are important and consequential gender differences in these areas,[18] and it seems plausible that there would also be class-cultural differences. But we did not find systematic evidence of this in our fieldwork. This may have something to do with the methodological choices we made. Such practices arguably carry a particular moral stigma, and may therefore be better revealed by observing behaviour, ethnographically, rather than asking people in interviews.

Similarly, many readers may be wondering about the issue of class *discrimination*. Here it is worth saying that we observed very limited evidence of what might be called overt discrimination. For example, while there are class-origin pay differences across top jobs and within three of the fields we studied, we did not find any evidence that people from different class backgrounds were doing the same work for unequal pay. Having said that, there were multiple examples of what we might call 'microaggressions'

– of people's working-class accents being mocked by colleagues or jokes being made about 'chavs'[19] or other stereotypes of the working class. These microaggressions were most marked in acting, as explored in Chapter Eight, particularly during auditions where, as Ray noted, "people just make a snap judgement about you". As Grace recalled, "Someone asked me once whether I could speak 'properly' if I wanted to. They actually said that to my face!" Jim recounted a similar incident at drama school: "One of my lecturers said to me, 'Have you ever considered going back and being a plumber?' This is what he said to me. 'Go back and be a plumber'."

However, these were isolated examples. Most of those we spoke to from privileged backgrounds were keen to stress their desire to work in class-diverse settings, and expressed support for colleagues from working-class backgrounds. Again, however, this doesn't mean no such class-origin discrimination exists in any of the firms we studied, or elsewhere in top jobs; once again, it may very well be happening in ways we simply didn't, or couldn't, pick up on. For example, recent research suggests that the privileged continue to privately harbour strong feelings of class snobbery in the UK, yet such expressions of judgement are constrained in interview settings by a strong moral imperative to appear open, tolerant and respectful of others.[20]

It is also important to emphasise that our findings are about overall patterns and themes in the experiences and earnings of people from working-class origins. As with all sociology, and all claims about averages or what is typical, this does not mean that *all* working-class origin people who become actors or doctors, accountants or CEOs will face any or all of the barriers we outline here. In other words, none of this should be understood to mean that working-class people never reach the top, or that every working-class person in an elite occupation will face great difficulty in their career. Many people with working-class origins we interviewed had achieved very highly (as evidenced by Tables A.1a–1d in the Methodological appendix).

Here it is also worth underlining, in particular, the findings that emerged from our case study at architecture firm Coopers. Notably, we found no class ceiling at Coopers. In Chapters Seven and Eight we suggest that one important reason for this is that classed performances of 'merit' are less important at Coopers; they are less valued by both senior leaders and clients, who, in the words of Eamon, "can see through the bullshit". At the same time, we also find that conventional markers of 'merit' – in the form of technical expertise – are easier to demonstrate; as "pragmatic architects", Gary notes, the Partners believe that quality work is identifiable largely through the work *product*, not the character of the person doing the work.

But this doesn't necessarily mean Coopers were immune to other inequalities. The lack of female Partners, depressing although not atypical in architecture, suggests the performance of 'merit' is still gendered in important ways.

Prevailing winds

We began this book with Mark, one of the most Senior Commissioners at 6TV. Mark characterised the linger of privilege as a 'following wind' that had swept him forward throughout his career. This idea of a prevailing wind neatly captures, we think, the subtle propulsive power provided by an advantaged class background – how it deftly acts to shape career trajectories, delineating what courses of action are possible, what kind of support is available and how one's 'merits' are perceived by others. Privilege, in other words, acts as an energy-saving device, allowing some to get further with less effort. Equally, the metaphor also visualises the experience of those upwardly mobile individuals operating 'against the wind'. It is not that such individuals cannot move forward, or never reach the top; just that, generally, it takes longer, happens less frequently and often represents a markedly more labour-intensive, even exhausting experience.

The other useful dimension of thinking about class privilege as a prevailing wind is that it has ramifications that extend far beyond elite occupations. This book is, of course, primarily about social mobility, or lack thereof, at the top of British society. But we are keen that our findings are not read simply as a further fetishisation of the top; our class backgrounds do not matter *only* in relation to who has the top salaries, or the most powerful jobs. Instead, we see our findings as illustrating one of many ways in which privilege affects all sorts of life outcomes, in all parts of the class structure.[21] And in all of these domains, when the following wind of privilege is misread as 'merit', the inequalities that result are legitimised. This leads those who have been fortunate to believe they have earned it on their own, and those who have been less fortunate to blame themselves. We hope that by shedding light on the ways in which 'merit' is, at best, an insufficient explanation for career success at the top, we can raise wider questions about the legitimacy of an economic system that too often allocates profoundly unequal rewards based on the accident of social origin.

Epilogue: 10 ways to break the class ceiling

with Nik Miller, Chief Executive, The Bridge Group

Academics are good at diagnosing problems. Where we tend to be less effective is when it comes to converting our critical insights into concrete, realisable policy recommendations. This is partly about the questions we tend to ask. For example, the drivers of the class ceiling, as we have shown, are in large part societal. They are about fundamental inequalities in the resources (economic, cultural and social) that flow from a person's family background. And there are no simple, silver-bullet policy tools to address this kind of systemic inequity. But it is also an issue of expertise. Sociologists like us are not normally trained to think about policy solutions. But there are many people who are. A good example is Nik Miller, Chief Executive of The Bridge Group, a charity that researches and promotes socio-economic diversity in the higher education and employment.[1] Since its inception in 2008, The Bridge Group has established itself as the UK's leading policy voice on social mobility. This reputation has been forged, in large part, by providing a unique offering, producing critical, independent research, but doing so alongside employers, and then crafting insights into practical recommendations that organisations can actually implement. In the remainder of this Epilogue we team up with Nik to think about how we might begin to tackle the class ceiling.[2] Together, we have come up with 10 practical steps to support meaningful change.

Before we outline our recommendations, it is worth briefly reflecting on the contemporary policy terrain surrounding social mobility and elite occupations. As we outlined in the Introduction to this book, political concern about the exclusivity of the UK's most prestigious professions is longstanding. Yet this has largely not transferred onto the organisational agendas of employers. Certainly, action to promote social mobility lags many years behind allied interventions on gender and ethnicity (as well as disability and sexual orientation). There are three key reasons for this: first, there has not been a robust evidence base on social mobility into elite occupations for organisations to draw on; second, there have been longstanding concerns among firms about how to effectively measure class background – or what most employers call 'socio-economic background'; and third, there is no legal imperative compelling organisations to act – class background is not a protected characteristic in the UK.

But things are changing. Ever since the Social Mobility Commission's (SMC) 2009 Milburn Review, which highlighted the need to 'open up' the professions, political pressure has been slowly building. The establishment of the Social Mobility Business Compact by the coalition government, in particular, signalled an important move from research and rhetoric towards action. While the Compact did not prescribe policies that employers should adopt, it was nonetheless important in bringing together employers to debate and share the imperatives and opportunities associated with driving social mobility. Certain high-profile employers have also led the way. For example, the seminal report from The Bridge Group, *Socio-economic diversity in the Civil Service Fast Stream*,[3] was the first in-depth analysis of a large national recruiter, from which a series of practical recommendations were made and crucially, implemented: the Fast Stream doubled its intake of candidates from 'lower socio-economic backgrounds'. The professional services sectors have also broken new ground in terms of transparency, with firms such as KPMG championing the collection, publication and use of comprehensive workforce data to better inform diversity and inclusion strategies.[4]

Employers' investments have of course been partly driven by a belief that diversity will result in improved business performance, but peer pressure has also played a critical[5] role, as evidenced by the growth of the Social Mobility Employer Index (which ranks employers based on action taken to promote socio-economic diversity).[6]

We now move to outline our 10 recommendations for employers. These draw on both The Bridge Group's experience of what is possible, and what works, in improving social mobility across a range of organisational settings, as well as ways to tackle the specific drivers of the class ceiling identified in this book.

1. Measure and monitor class background

The first step towards meaningful change in elite occupations, we believe, is accurate *measurement*. At present there is little consensus across sectors about the measurement and monitoring of class or socio-economic background. Many organisations still don't collect data in this area and, among those that do, a range of different measures are used. The latest evidence highlights that class background is the only diversity characteristic where more employers claim to have a strategy than are actually measuring it within their workforce.[7] This suggests that many employers are attempting to tackle challenges that are not fully understood, and the lack of measurement has stymied progress and prevented organisations from benchmarking their data with others in their sector and beyond. But there are important signs that this is changing. In June 2018, after consulting with stakeholders including ourselves and The Bridge Group, the UK government published recommendations on how employers should measure class background in their workforce.[8] This recommends that organisations collect data from employees in four areas – parental occupation, type of schooling, free school meal eligibility and parental experience of higher education. Many large organisations, such as the BBC, KPMG and the Civil Service, have already collated these data and others are poised to follow suit.[9] To this end, we would urge all employers to follow The Bridge Group guidance on how to collate workforce diversity data with respect to class background (available on their website[10]). This provides detailed guidance on the precise survey questions organisations should ask, the answer categories they should provide, communications that can help drive high response rates, and how the resulting data should be presented.

We understand that some organisations may be hesitant about introducing four new measures to already extensive and time-consuming staff surveys. Following the approach taken in this book, we would stress our view that the best *single measure*, if only one can be used, is *parental occupation*. Unlike the other recommended measures, parental occupation is useful in pinpointing the relative degree of both class advantage *and* disadvantage experienced in a person's upbringing, as well as being accurate and clear, easily comparable, and likely to elicit a response.

2. Find out whether our organisation has a class ceiling

Effective measurement has two dimensions. Certainly, organisations need to understand the overall class composition of their workforce, but it's also important that they do not stop there. We would urge firms to investigate whether they too have a *class ceiling*. This can be achieved by both looking at how socio-economic composition varies by grade or position (see Chapter Four), or by investigating whether there is a pay gap by class background, and whether this can be explained by any indicators that are clearly connected to job performance or skills, such as training, job tenure or appraisal ratings (see Chapters Two and Three). Where firms do uncover ceiling effects, we encourage them to undertake qualitative research to understand the factors contributing to this. As our book underlines, many drivers of the class ceiling are firm-specific and will therefore require firm-specific solutions.

3. Start a conversation about talent

Among the drivers of the class ceiling outlined in this book, the most significant relates to how talent and 'merit' are defined and rewarded within organisations. Our key point here is that the identification of 'merit' is often intertwined with the way 'merit' is performed (in terms of classed self-presentation and arbitrary behavioural codes) and who the decision-makers are whose job it is to recognise and reward these attributes. This is a thorny and provocative issue that is very hard to tackle, especially where there is contestation about what talent looks like within an organisation or sector. But we would urge organisations to embrace this contestation, to critically interrogate the 'objective' measures of 'merit' they rely on, and to think carefully about whether such measures have a subjective or performed dimension, whether there are contextual factors that may underpin how 'merit' is recognised, and to what extent it can be reliably connected to demonstrable output or performance. It is critical that organisations create opportunities for these kinds of open and frank conversations to take place, and that they ensure those at all levels contribute. There are various ways this type of conversation might be achieved. It might take the form of a conference,[11] online engagement via blogs and webinars (often anonymity can be useful here), a set of public events,[12] or an internal away day. In any case, it should pit authoritative but purposively opposing voices against one another to discuss and debate evidence, research and data, and should be aimed at creating practical responses, drawing on suggestions outlined in this section.

4. Take intersectionality seriously

Equality and diversity provision within organisations is very often organised one-dimensionally along a single axis of social inequality, such as gender or ethnicity. Yet people's work lives are better understood as being shaped by many axes of inequality that often work together and influence one another, or create distinct types of disadvantage that are experienced in different ways. As our analysis in this book shows, for example, white women and people of colour from working-class backgrounds face a very clear 'double disadvantage' in earnings, which can be multiplicative rather than simply additive. This is often rooted, for example, in the different ways that markers of women and men's class backgrounds are 'read' by decision-makers. In this way, we urge organisations to examine intersections between different strands of diversity, both in terms of how they analyse their employee data, and also in their design of 'diversity' interventions.

5. Publish social mobility data

Positive change with respect to social mobility requires *collective responsibility* and collaborative action *across sectors*. To achieve this, individual organisations need to be bold and transparent about the issues they face. This means publishing data regarding the class backgrounds of all staff and senior leaders in particular. This will allow for benchmarking across firms and sectors, as well as for sector-wide drivers to be identified and collective solutions sought out. Where data are published, firms should also include details about what actions they are taking to drive improvements; publishing data alone could have the effect of deterring the very audience – candidates from working-class backgrounds – that organisations are trying to encourage.

6. Ban unpaid and unadvertised internships

One of the clearest drivers of the class ceiling is the way in which those from privileged backgrounds use the 'Bank of Mum and Dad' to help them establish their career. Perhaps the most direct way this takes place is via unpaid, or very low-paid, internships – which can often only be undertaken if one has outside financial support. These kinds of internships remain commonplace in many elite occupations and can be important stepping-stones in accessing highly competitive graduate employment opportunities. For example, over 60% of university students who undertook an internship with a legal firm in 2016/17 went on to secure a graduate position at the same firm.[13] An associated, and similarly unhelpful, practice is unadvertised internships, which are available only to those within a closed network, who are often connected to existing employees. We would urge all organisations to cease altogether the practice of unpaid and unadvertised internships, and to advocate a four-week legal limit on all internships; the use of apprenticeship levy funding to generate quality placements;[14] and the publishing of accessible national guidance on the rights of interns.

7. Senior champions are necessary but not sufficient

If organisations are going to take social mobility seriously there needs to be meaningful buy-in from senior management. In the best examples that we have seen, this means that a very senior individual (or more than one) acts as a visible champion for forwarding the agenda. Accountability and ownership are essential here; targets for social mobility should have equal status, and be managed in the same way, as other corporate targets. While senior advocacy is critical, so, too, is the engagement of those in positions where change is typically most needed. This will clearly vary by firm, but in much of our research, and the wider studies conducted by The Bridge Group, it is often middle and senior managers (that is, those below the senior executive team, but on the trajectory to those positions) who are most responsible for enacting and 'socialising' dominant work cultures, and who make routine decisions about how talent is defined and identified. It is also the case that it is often those in these middle and lower senior positions that perceive themselves as having most to lose in efforts to drive forward inclusion and equality. Based on The Bridge Group's experience, engaging this audience usually requires a compelling case for change built on both advancing business performance and social equality; collation and presentation of internal and benchmark data to highlight the nature of the challenge; and the collation of voices from within the organisation (most usefully sourced through independent research) that animate the issues at stake in a way that resonates.

8. Formalise the informal

In all of our case study firms we found a culture of informal sponsorship. Here senior staff, often operating outside of formal processes, were able to fast-track the careers of junior staff whom they were drawn to on the basis of cultural similarity. While it is both difficult and problematic for organisations to try to dictate who builds relationships with whom in the workplace, they do have the power to decide the autonomy that senior staff have in bypassing, circumventing or 'gaming' formal processes regarding hiring (especially experienced hires rather than entry-level roles), promotion, progression and work allocation. We believe that properly articulated, and properly enforced, guidelines are key to shutting down informal progression tracks (that we have shown disproportionately reward the privileged). With respect to informal sponsorship, one way to achieve this would be to formalise (through transparently designed and communicated programmes) and democratise (by making opportunities available to all) these sponsorship opportunities. More generally, it is important that employers understand that it is not the sole responsibility of the HR departments to design and decree policies relating to pay and progression. The expertise and experience of colleagues working in this area are clearly essential, but decision-makers across the workforce must be invested in, and given time to implement, these policies routinely, and exceptions actively justified and accounted for.

9. Support those who want it

Our results reveal that those from working-class backgrounds often self-eliminate from pushing forward in their careers, or sort into less prestigious or lucrative specialisms. This is rarely about a lack of ambition. As we have shown, it is more to do with rejecting expectations to assimilate, battling feelings of 'otherness' or negotiating low-level but constant microaggressions in the workplace. These issues should be approached sensitively. At present we believe the dominant narrative about socio-economic diversity tends to misinterpret self-elimination through the lens of individual deficit ("there are less advantaged people out there who lack certain attributes, who need our help to succeed"). For example, Bridge Group research has revealed that, in the legal sector, the notion that those from working-class backgrounds voluntarily sort into less-prestigious areas of practice appears to be normalised and largely goes unchallenged. In this way, practical initiatives are often designed to help under-represented groups assimilate into unfamiliar professional cultures, rather than interrogating whether the cultures themselves (see Recommendations 3 and 8 above) should be reimagined to enable diverse groups of people to thrive and contribute equally. We believe that there has been a disproportionate focus on the former, and that progress will continue to be painfully slow without reflection and meaningful action to tackle the latter.

Having said this, we do think it is important that those with working-class backgrounds are at least offered specific support by employers. There is no universal formula here. In some cases, support networks or advocacy groups of the kind that have proven effective in supporting white women and people of colour in elite workplaces may work. The Opportunity Network in the Civil Service[15] provides one successful example of this. Yet it is also important for employers to recognise that coming from a working-class background is not always an 'identity' that people want to wear or own in the workplace in this kind of public way. For many, then, less public support mechanisms may be more appropriate, such as mentoring or buddying, or it may simply be that induction processes need to recognise better that candidates from different backgrounds can have markedly different levels of familiarity with working cultures and behavioural norms on arrival. Either way, it is important that organisations consult with staff from disadvantaged backgrounds about how to best support them, and prevent them from self-eliminating.

10. Lobby for legal protection

The Equality Act 2010 ensured legal protections for a range of minority groups but, as mentioned, did not include class or socio-economic background. Yet what is less known is that the Act actually contains a section entitled the 'Socioeconomic Duty', which requires government and all public bodies to have due regard for 'reducing the inequalities of outcome which result from socio-economic disadvantage'. Notably, successive governments have declined to bring this section into effect, which (among other ramifications) would provide a clear mandate for making class background a protected characteristic. But momentum is gathering around furthering this legal agenda. Scotland recently introduced the 'Fairer Scotland Duty', modelled on the Socioeconomic Duty. And in England Harriet Harman has instantiated Early Day Motion 591, which calls on the government to enact the Socioeconomic Duty. To date, 78 MPs have pledged their support for the motion. We would urge readers to support this further by writing to their MP and calling on them to support the Early Day Motion, using a template written by *#1forequality*,[16] a campaign led by Just Fair and The Equality Trust.

Improved diversity and inclusion depend on reducing inequalities at every stage of an individual's journey. The effects of inequality are manifest long before individuals access the labour market, taking hold in early years and often exacerbated via a higher education system that is remarkably efficient at perpetuating inequality. However, while recognising these important upstream effects, we have also shown in this book that employers are often very effective at introducing barriers of their own making.

The rewards of effectively tackling these barriers are significant. They include more inclusive and diverse workforces, higher levels of productivity and, most importantly, a more socially just approach to the workplace, where individuals can thrive irrespective of background, and where differences of class origin are a virtue on which to draw rather than a challenge to be addressed. We hope that this book can contribute to positive movement in this direction – both in elite occupations and in any other environment where class inequality is reproduced through the misrecognition of 'merit'.

Methodological appendix

Academics often tell suspiciously neat stories of the research process. Most often we package our methodology into a few formulaic paragraphs within an article or book and narrate fieldwork and decision-making as linear, rational and seamless. But research rarely plays out like this. In practice it is usually profoundly messy and disjointed. This project certainly was. The book you have in your hands is the result of a sprawling, often unwieldy, research collaboration that has spanned over four years. It was always an expansive, ambitious project, but also one that has suffered multiple false starts and wrong turns, and which is flawed in important ways. In this Appendix we aim to tell *this* story. And we try to do so as honestly and transparently as possible, giving readers a chronological picture of exactly how our fieldwork unfolded. At the end we also explore a number of more technical and conceptual issues, including how our own class backgrounds (and other demographic coordinates) affected our research, how we conducted interviews, how we define 'elite' occupations, how we measure social mobility, how and why we selected our case studies, how we constructed our statistical analysis, how we fed our research back to our case study firms, and the key limitations of the study.

Stumbling across a class ceiling

This project began entirely serendipitously. It was September 2014 and we had both recently started jobs at the London School of Economics and Political Science (LSE). Our offices were directly opposite one another. Initially working together on the BBC's Great British Class Survey (GBCS), we were asked to contribute to a special issue of *Sociological Review*. While Daniel's paper sailed through peer review, Sam's did not. The paper, an attempt to use the GBCS to examine the experience of social mobility, received three reviews – two lukewarm, one savage. 'In my view this is just bad science,' concluded Reviewer 3, 'and will ultimately damage the reputation of the author.' Ouch.

The journal Editor, reacting, was tactful but direct – completely rewrite the paper, or withdraw. On the verge of accepting defeat, Sam shared the article with Daniel. Could something be salvaged? Daniel wasn't sure. But he did agree that the paper contained one intriguing finding. Among those who had entered the GBCS 'elite', those from working-class backgrounds had incomes far lower than colleagues from more privileged backgrounds. Why might this be, we asked ourselves? A long, sprawling, excited conversation ensued. Within two weeks we had written an entirely new article (with the help of Andy Miles) and had only become more intrigued. We knew that pay gaps by gender, racial-ethnic group and sexuality were well documented, but what about a class pay gap?

But there was a snag. The GBCS was a rich data source, but it was also a self-selecting web survey, and its respondents were strongly skewed towards the privileged. Mindful of the critiques already levelled at the GBCS,[1] we needed a 'gold standard' nationally representative source to corroborate our findings.

We began to scan the sources available. Mobility research in the UK has, for a long time, been hampered by the limitations of nationally representative data. Most existing studies rely on longitudinal sources such as the Birth Cohort Studies, where respondents were born in 1958 and 1970. These have been very useful for understanding how national mobility rates have changed over time, but their limited sample sizes have left a number of important questions unanswered.

Then there was another piece of serendipity. Within days of our search it was announced that the UK's largest employment survey, the Labour Force Survey (LFS), had just published data from a new 'social mobility module', including data on respondents' (parental occupational) class background. The newly released data file had a huge representative sample of nearly 100,000[2] (more details on this data is included later in this Appendix, in 'Analysing the Labour Force Survey').

What we found inside the LFS – a profound 16% class pay gap in Britain's elite occupations – was both shocking but also somewhat reassuring; it fitted closely with what we had found in the GBCS, but gave us a more robust and representative platform from which to make claims. Armed with this new data source, we began to present the results at academic conferences and seminars. Reactions were striking. Some were outraged, others sceptical, but everyone encouraged us to go further. And one question kept coming up – *why?* What mechanisms may be driving the class pay gap? People suggested a range of hypotheses – maybe the upwardly mobile are the victims of class discrimination, maybe they have lower aspirations, maybe they are less likely to negotiate over pay, or maybe they enter less-prestigious occupational specialisms or firms?

Many of these mechanisms, we reflected, are things that are indiscernible using national-level data, however large and rich. They are processes that take place in specific occupations or within particular firms. To understand these drivers, then, we needed to actually enter the field, to go inside elite workplaces and examine the everyday working lives of those inside.

Going 'inside' elite organisations

Our aim was to conduct a set of case studies of elite firms. To do this we needed time and research support. In January 2015 Sam applied for an Economic and Social Research Council (ESRC)[3] Future Research Leaders Award[4] to conduct case studies in three firms across three elite occupations. The aim was to look at one occupation with a small, statistically insignificant class pay gap, and two with larger gaps, but that differed from each other in other ways (later in this Appendix we explain the process through which we came to our particular case study occupations and organisations).

Going inside organisations made sense for understanding most elite occupations, but what about professions where people tended to be self-employed or employed on freelance or short-term contracts? The so-called 'gig economy' has grown rapidly in recent years and, as Dave O'Brien from Goldsmiths College explained to us late in 2014, it is particularly important for understanding

Britain's cultural industries. Working with Dave, and while we waited to hear about our research grant, we therefore decided to make the acting profession our first case study.

Researching actors

The case study first involved analysis of 402 actors within the GBCS. Even the large-sample LFS only contains 61 actors, so using the GBCS was essential for getting a more detailed demographic overview of the profession. As a self-selecting web survey, the GBCS by no means provides a representative sample of the acting profession. However, no other survey offers such a large sample of actors alongside details of their class background. We also compared, where possible, GBCS actors to their counterparts in the LFS.

The second part of the project involved 47 semi-structured interviews with actors conducted between December 2014 and March 2015. We wanted to interview GBCS respondents, but due to BBC data protection policy, this was not possible. We therefore placed an advert on social media asking for interviewees to take part, and shared this with a range of acting websites, news outlets and unions. This yielded 31 interviewees. We then used snowball techniques to complete the sample and match it to the demographic make-up of the British acting profession in the representative LFS. We also wanted a broadly equal proportion of actors from different class backgrounds, resulting in 19 respondents from professional and managerial backgrounds, 10 from intermediate backgrounds and 18 from working-class backgrounds (more details on all interviewees are included in Table A.1c).

Researching 6TV

In December 2015, another chance encounter opened the door to a second case study. After presenting our analysis at a diversity conference a card was passed to us by Louise, Head of Diversity for one of Britain's biggest television channels, 6TV. "Class is always the elephant in the room when we discuss diversity," Louise confided. "But to be honest, we just don't know how to measure it. Can you help?"

This was an opportunity too good to miss. Louise brokered an initial meeting at 6TV, but it was clear from this early stage that management were torn on letting sociologists 'in'. On the one hand, most suspected 6TV had a fairly socially exclusive workforce, were genuinely concerned to address the problem and wanted to ground such longstanding assumptions in reliable evidence. Yet at the same time, many were also cautious about the negative publicity that would inevitably flow from research that substantiated these suspicions. "Ultimately it's my job to protect my Executives", one senior HR figure exclaimed at a particularly heated planning meeting. Negotiating this sensitivity proved difficult. Gaining access was long and somewhat torturous. But finally, after around nine months of discussion, the research began in earnest in September 2016.

Fieldwork took place in three stages. The first involved sending a short, anonymous questionnaire via email to all 6TV staff – which received a very robust response rate of 76%.[5] The questionnaire asked about respondents' age, gender, ethnicity, education and region of origin, as well as their department and position within 6TV. To measure social mobility we adopted the same question used in the LFS, which asks respondents the occupation of their main income-earning parent when they were 14.

As we explained in Chapter Four, 6TV is one of a number of 'publisher-broadcasters' that commission programmes that are then produced by 'indies'. To get an understanding of the indie sector, we circulated an identical follow-up questionnaire to those working at independent television production companies. This was achieved via circulation to members of the Producers Alliance for Cinema and Television (PACT), the trade association representing the commercial interests of UK independent television companies. This garnered a response rate of 75% (1,373 responses).

The second part of the project involved conducting 50 in-depth interviews with 6TV staff. Although the questionnaire was anonymous, respondents were asked to include their email address if they were willing to be interviewed; 49% indicated that they were willing to be interviewed, and from this we constructed an interview sample that was representative of the overall 6TV workforce in terms of gender, racial- ethnic group, age and region of origin (see Table A.1a for further details of all interviewees). The survey results, detailed in Chapter Four, led to a focus on three sets of interviewees – those working in a specific department (20 interviews in Commissioning), those at a particular level of seniority (27 interviews with Senior Managers and Executives/ Heads of Department) and those from different class origins (14 from working-class origins; 11 from intermediate backgrounds; 25 from professional/managerial backgrounds). Most interviews were conducted at the London Head Office, although we did conduct five interviews in the Glasgow office.

The final part of the case study involved participant observation of interviews for the mid-career talent scheme, Future Leaders, which is part-funded by 6TV along with other broadcasters. The scheme is a highly prestigious year-long programme that takes 'rising star' television professionals and provides them with the support, mentoring and network relationships to propel them into senior roles. The organisers invited us to sit in on interviews and wrap-up sessions conducted in June 2016 in central London. Future Leaders attracts approximately 500 applicants, 100 of whom are then shortlisted for interview. There are 30 places on the scheme. The interview panel consists of a group of senior television executives selected by the Future Leaders organisers. Before each interview, the panel are provided with the CV and supporting statement provided by each applicant, which includes information about their type of schooling and parental occupation.

Researching Turner Clarke

Our choice of two final case studies was more deliberate. But again, neither took place entirely as planned. Our accountancy case study began with talks with one of the world's largest multinationals. The firm in question has been active in addressing the issue of social mobility and was initially very positive about taking part in the research. Yet, as with 6TV, we sensed from early meetings that there was also significant fear, panic even, about what might emerge from the research. After nearly six months of discussion, and countless meetings and email exchanges, they finally decided against taking part. The reasons given – "not the right time" – were relatively thin. Indeed, we have since been informed, off the record, by one former employee, that the project was ultimately torpedoed by senior staff afraid of allowing sociologists access to results (even fully anonymised) that may generate negative publicity. We think this episode illustrates the clear anxieties of those in positions of power about what might be revealed in explorations of class ceilings.

We were lucky. In the immediate aftermath of losing this firm, and after hearing about our experience, a policy contact put us in touch with a gatekeeper at Turner Clarke (TC). Accountancy has been one of the most closely scrutinised professions in terms of social mobility, and TC has been very active in responding to this agenda. It has piloted a range of initiatives aimed at increasing access, including introducing 'contextual' academic data and school and university-blind graduate applications, and is widely considered an industry leader on social mobility. Our case study was therefore pitched to management as an opportunity to cement this reputation by looking beyond access to issues of progression. On this basis the CEO agreed to allow us begin a case study in February 2017.

Our fieldwork at TC was organised in two stages. In the first stage we analysed internal staff data relating to gender, ethnicity, office location, service line and performance. In terms of social mobility, the firm does not currently collect data on parental occupation and was unwilling to subject their staff to a further survey. Instead, the firm asks its employees a number of questions to measure what it calls 'socio-economic background' – whether the employee received free school meals, whether they were educated at private or state school, and whether either of their parents went to university; 79% of the workforce responded to these questions.

In the second stage of the case study, between March and July 2017, we conducted 42 in-depth interviews. The interview sample was constructed to reflect the demographic diversity of the firm. Like 6TV, it was also based on the results of the questionnaire. The findings from the survey, detailed in Chapter Four, led to a focus on three sets of interviewees – those working in a specific department (20 interviews in Advisory), those at different ends of the organisation (24 Partners and 18 Trainees) and those from different class backgrounds. We also examined different office locations, conducting interviews at TC offices in London, Oxford, Manchester, St Albans, Milton Keynes, Cardiff and Birmingham. While the staff data lacked information on parental occupation, interviewees were recruited via an email that was sent to all Partners and all Trainees, and which included a question about parental occupation. We conducted 18 interviews with those from professional and managerial backgrounds, 10 from intermediate backgrounds and 14 from working-class backgrounds (see Table A.1b).

Researching Coopers

Our final case study, carried out in large part by our research assistant, Ian McDonald, was more straightforward. We began by contacting a number of firms about taking part in the research, and Coopers was the only firm to respond positively – which again underlines that the firm may not be representative of the wider profession.

One of the founding Partners, Gary, acted as the key gatekeeper. After a simple email exchange he invited us for a short meeting at the firm's offices and immediately agreed to take part. This was not because he thought social mobility was a particularly live issue in architecture. Instead, he felt the problem of social exclusivity had been effectively resolved some decades ago, with the Thatcher-led deregulation of the profession and the abolition of fee scales effectively producing a level-playing field.[6] Nonetheless, he was interested in wider issues of social class, expressing concern about rising university fees and frustration at negative media portrayals of the working classes.

The research took place between April and June 2017 and comprised a staff survey (response rate 64%) and 36 follow-up interviews. We carried out a follow-up interview with every available staff member who volunteered within the research time frame. The follow-up interviews included a spread by seniority, age, gender and project team (see Table A.1d). In line with the composition of the firm measured in the staff survey, we carried out 28 interviews with staff from a professional/managerial background, five from intermediate backgrounds and three from working-class backgrounds.

How we conducted interviews

Across our case studies, interviews[7] were structured across four sections. First, we began with a set of questions that probed interviewees' class background. This included questions about both parents' occupation (when the interviewee was growing up), schooling, an open-ended discussion about inherited economic capital (including questions about parental *income*, *wealth* and *property*), and an open-ended discussion about inherited cultural capital (including questions about parental art *ownership*, *participation* in art activities in childhood, degree of formal *education* and degree of parental art *encouragement* and art *exposure* during childhood[8]). Second, we asked interviewees to describe their own career trajectory to date, allowing them to narrate the key moments and critical junctures in their own words.[9] Third, we asked a number of more specific questions about their career, about the specific culture in their firm, how talent is defined in their firm and occupation more widely, and whether they feel their career has been held back in any way. Finally, we ended each interview by briefly explaining our findings regarding the class pay gap, and asking for their reactions and reflections.

In Tables A.1a–1d we draw on the questions we asked in the interviews to provide information for each interviewee on measures of class background, current position and career trajectory. We indicate respondents' parents' occupations, the type of schools they attended, and make subjective (but informed) judgements about interviewees' levels of inherited economic and cultural capital (high, medium or low on each), and the rate of progress through their career (accelerated, steady or impeded). The 'Position and salary' column gives somewhat different information for each case study: for TC, 6TV and Coopers we give the firms' categorisation of each interviewee's position; for TC and 6TV we give the salary range associated with that job description, while for Coopers we have self-reported income in ranges, and for actors we simply asked them about how much they earned in a year and report that here.

Table A.1a: 6TV interviewees

Name	Gender	Ethnicity	Age	Father's occupation	Mother's occupation	Inherited economic capital	Inherited cultural capital	Schooling	Position and salary range	Department	Interview location	Career trajectory
Aika	Woman	Mixed/ multiple	30s	Taxi driver	Shop assistant	Low	Low	State	Prof/tech, £25k–70k	Legal and Commercial	London	Steady
Aila	Woman	White British	40s	Actor	Nurse	Medium	Medium	State	HoD/exec, £100k–500k	HR, Finance, Estates	London	Accelerated
Aisha	Woman	Black British	20s	Teacher	Police officer	Medium	Medium	State	Prof/tech, £25k–70k	Marketing and Communications	London	Steady
Alex	Woman	White Other	20s	Factory worker	Secretary	Low	Low	State	Prof/tech, £25k–70k	Legal and Commercial	Glasgow	Impeded
Alice	Woman	White British	40s	Hospital porter	Cleaner	Low	Low	State	Assistant/admin, £21k–60k	Commissioning	London	Impeded
Bill	Man	White British	50s	Factory machine operator	Housewife	Low	Low	State	HoD/exec, £100k–500k	Commissioning	London	Steady
Bridget	Woman	White British	60s	Steelworker	Housewife	Low	Low	Grammar	HoD/exec, £100k–500k	HR, Finance, Estates	London	Steady
Catherine	Woman	White British	30s	Senior manager	Secretary	Medium	Medium	State	Senior manager, £60k–120k	Technical and Strategy	London	Steady
Claire	Woman	White British	50s	IT technician	Admin assistant	Medium	Low	State	HoD/exec, £100k–500k	Technical and Strategy	London	Steady
Cora	Woman	White British	40s	Senior civil servant	Housewife	High	High	Private	Senior manager, £60k–120k	Legal and Commercial	London	Steady
Daniel	Man	White British	20s	Teacher	Teacher	Medium	High	State	Senior manager, £60k–120k	Commissioning	London	Accelerated
Dave	Man	White British	50s	FE teacher	Office manager	Medium	High	Grammar	Senior manager, £60k–120k	Commissioning	London	Steady

Name	Gender	Ethnicity	Age	Father's occupation	Mother's occupation	Inherited economic capital	Inherited cultural capital	Schooling	Position and salary range	Department	Interview location	Career trajectory
Dean	Man	White Other	30s	Shopkeeper	Shop assistant	Medium	Low	State	Senior manager, £60k–120k	Sales, Digital, Trading	London	Steady
Esme	Woman	White Other	30s	Builder	Dressmaker	Medium	Low	State	Prof/tech, £25k–70k	Technical and Strategy	London	Steady
Gemma	Woman	White British	30s	Labourer	Cleaner	Low	Low	State	Prof/tech, £25k–70k	HR, Finance, Estates	London	Steady
George	Man	White British	30s	Barman	Admin assistant	Low	Low	Private	Prof/tech, £25k–70k	Commissioning	London	Steady
Hannah	Woman	Black British	50s	Plasterer	Hairdresser	Medium	Low	State	Manager, £35k–80k	HR, Finance, Estates	London	Impeded
Holly	Woman	Chinese British	20s	Cook	Waitress	Low	Medium	State	Assistant/admin, £21k–60k	Commissioning	London	Impeded
James	Man	White Other	60s	Medium-size business owner	Housewife	High	High	Private	HoD/exec, £100k–500k	Commissioning	London	Accelerated
Javid	Man	Indian British	20s	Factory worker	Factory worker	Low	Low	State	Senior manager, £60k–120k	Sales, Digital, Trading	London	Impeded
Josh	Man	White British	40s	Headteacher	Care worker	Medium	High	Private	HoD/exec, £100k–500k	Commissioning	London	Accelerated
Kate	Woman	White British	20s	N/A	Cleaner	Low	Medium	Grammar	Senior manager, £60k–120k	Marketing and Communications	London	Steady
Katie	Woman	White British	50s	Dentist	Housewife	High	Medium	Private	Manager, £35k–80k	Technical and Strategy	London	Steady
Keir	Man	White British	50s	Scientist	Housewife	High	Medium	State	Senior manager, £60k–120k	Technical and Strategy	London	Steady
Kerry	Woman	White Other	60s	Senior civil servant	Housewife	High	High	Private	HoD/exec, £100k–500k	Commissioning	London	Steady

Table A.1a: 6TV interviewees (continued)

Name	Gender	Ethnicity	Age	Father's occupation	Mother's occupation	Inherited economic capital	Inherited cultural capital	Schooling	Position and salary range	Department	Interview location	Career trajectory
Kevin	Man	White Other	50s	Large business owner	Senior business manager	High	High	Private	Senior manager, £60k–120k	Commissioning	London	Accelerated
Kieran	Man	White British	20s	Labourer	N/A	Low	Low	State	Assistant/admin, £21k–60k	Commissioning	London	Impeded
Kylie	Woman	White British	40s	Factory worker	Primary school teacher	Medium	Medium	Private	Senior manager, £60k–120k	Sales, Digital, Trading	London	Steady
Leon	Man	White British	20s	Soldier	Shop assistant	Low	Low	State	Manager, £35k–80k	Sales, Digital, Trading	Glasgow	Steady
Lizzie	Woman	White British	40s	Professor	Housewife	High	High	Private	HoD/exec, £100k–500k	Commissioning	London	Accelerated
Maisie	Woman	White British	30s	N/A	Home help	Low	Low	State	Manager, £35k–80k	HR, Finance, Estates	London	Steady
Mark	Man	White British	30s	Scientist	Teacher	High	High	Private	Senior manager, £60k–120k	Commissioning	London	Accelerated
Martha	Woman	White British	40s	Headteacher	Social worker	Medium	High	Private	HoD/exec, £100k–500k	Commissioning	London	Steady
Mary	Woman	Black British	20s	N/A	Catering assistant	Low	Low	State	Prof/tech, £25k–70k	HR, Finance, Estates	London	Impeded
Michael	Man	White British	40s	University lecturer	Pharmacist	High	High	State	Senior manager, £60k–120k	Commissioning	London	Steady
Mo	Man	Mixed/ multiple	20s	Taxi driver	Shop assistant	Medium	Low	Private	Prof/tech, £25k–70k	HR, Finance, Estates	London	Steady
Monica	Woman	White British	30s	Teacher	Office manager	Medium	Medium	State	Senior manager, £60k–120k	Commissioning	London	Steady

Name	Gender	Ethnicity	Age	Father's occupation	Mother's occupation	Inherited economic capital	Inherited cultural capital	Schooling	Position and salary range	Department	Interview location	Career trajectory
Natalia	Woman	Black British	20s	N/A	Porter	Low	Low	State	Assistant/admin, £21k–60k	Commissioning	London	Impeded
Nigel	Man	White British	40s	Management consultant	Secretary	High	High	Private	HoD/exec, £100k–500k	Marketing and Communications	London	Accelerated
Nish	Man	Asian British	50s	Architect	Nurse	High	High	State	HoD/exec, £100k–500k	Legal and Commercial	London	Accelerated
Patricia	Woman	White British	40s	Managing director	Teacher	Medium	Medium	Private	HoD/exec, £100k–500k	Technical and Strategy	London	Steady
Peter	Man	White British	30s	Teacher	Radiographer	Medium	Medium	State	Senior manager, £60k–120k	Marketing and Communications	London	Accelerated
Rachel	Woman	White British	40s	Professor	Editor	High	High	State	Senior manager, £60k–120k	Commissioning	London	Accelerated
Roger	Man	White Other	50s	Senior manager	Housewife	Medium	High	Private	HoD/exec, £100k–500k	Legal and Commercial	London	Accelerated
Ruth	Woman	White British	50s	Large business owner	Teacher	High	Medium	Private	Manager, £35k–80k	Marketing and Communications	London	Steady
Sam	Man	White British	30s	Plumber	Missing data	Low	Low	State	Prof/tech, £25k–70k	HR, Finance, Estates	Glasgow	Steady
Sophie	Woman	White British	30s	Senior manager	Translator	High	High	Private	Senior manager, £60k–120k	Commissioning	London	Accelerated
Suzy	Woman	Black British	40s	Unemployed	Waitress	Low	Low	State	Manager, £35k–80k	HR, Finance, Estates	London	Impeded
Theo	Man	White British	30s	Farmer	Secretary	Medium	Low	State	Manager, £35k–80k	Technical and Strategy	Glasgow	Steady

Table A.1b: Turner Clarke interviewees

Name	Gender	Ethnicity	Age	Father's occupation	Mother's occupation	Inherited economic capital	Inherited cultural capital	Schooling	Position and salary range	Department	Interview location	Career trajectory
Ally	Man	White British	20s	Missing	Missing	Missing	Missing	State	Trainee, £25k–50k	Tax	London	Steady
Barbara	Woman	White British	20s	Missing	Missing	Missing	Missing	Private	Trainee, £25k–50k	Advisory	London	Steady
Ben	Man	White British	60s	Carpenter	Shop assistant	Low	Low	State	Partner, £100k–500k	Advisory	London	Impeded
Benedict	Man	White British	20s	Missing	Missing	Missing	Missing	State	Trainee, £25k–50k	Audit	London	Steady
Beth	Woman	White British	30s	Shop owner	Housewife	Medium	Low	State	Director, £75k–125k	Advisory		Impeded
Bev	Woman	White British	30s	Builder/estate agent	Secretary	Low	Low	State	Partner, £100k–500k	Advisory	London	Impeded
Cathy	Woman	White British	40s	Legal executive	Secretary	Medium	Medium	Grammar	Partner, £100k–500k	Audit	London	Steady
Charlotte	Woman	White British	20s	Missing	Missing	Missing	Missing	State	Trainee, £25k–50k	Tax	London	Steady
Christopher	Man	White British	20s	Missing	Missing	Missing	Missing	State	Trainee, £25k–50k	Tax	London	Steady
Colin	Man	White British	40s	Tax inspector	Middle manager	Medium	Medium	Private	Partner, £100k–500k	Audit	St Albans	Accelerated
Eugene	Man	White British	20s	Lawyer	Marketing executive	High	High	Private	Trainee, £25k–50k	Tax	London	Steady
Fraser	Man	White Other	20s	Missing	Missing	Missing	Missing	State	Trainee, £25k–50k	Audit	London	Steady
George	Man	White British	20s	Missing	Missing	Missing	Missing	State	Trainee, £25k–50k	Audit	London	Steady
Georgia	Woman	White British	20s	Missing	Missing	Missing	Missing	Private	Trainee, £25k–50k	Advisory	London	Steady
Giles	Man	White British	50s	Doctor	Doctor	High	High	Private	Partner, £100k–500k	Advisory	London	Accelerated

Name	Gender	Ethnicity	Age	Father's occupation	Mother's occupation	Inherited economic capital	Inherited cultural capital	Schooling	Position and salary range	Department	Interview location	Career trajectory
Graham	Man	White British	40s	Actor	Actor	High	High	Private	Partner, £100k–500k	Audit	London	Accelerated
Hayley	Woman	Black British	20s	Missing	Missing	Missing	Missing	State	Trainee, £25k–50k	Tax	London	Steady
Imogen	Woman	White British	20s	Missing	Missing	Missing	Missing	Private	Trainee, £25k–50k	Advisory	London	Steady
James	Man	White British	40s	Politician	Housewife	High	High	State	Partner, £100k–500k	Advisory	Cardiff	Accelerated
Jane	Woman	White British	50s	Accountant	Nurse	High	High	Private	Partner, £100k–500k	Advisory	Manchester	Accelerated
Jason	Man	White Other	40s	Teacher	Teacher	Medium	Medium	State	Partner, £100k–500k	Audit	Manchester	Impeded
Jennifer	Woman	Chinese British	20s	Missing	Missing	Missing	Missing	State	Trainee, £25k–50k	Advisory	London	Steady
Jenny	Woman	Pakistani British	20s	Taxi driver	Housewife	Medium	Low	State	Trainee, £25k–50k	Tax	London	Impeded
Jess	Woman	White British	50s	Factory worker	Cleaner	Low	Low	State	Partner, £100k–500k	Tax	Cardiff	Impeded
Joe	Man	White British	40s	Environmental health officer	Teacher	Medium	Medium	Private	Partner, £100k–500k	Tax	Milton Keynes	Steady
Joshua	Man	Black British	20s	Hotel manager	HR manager	Medium	Medium	Private	Trainee, £25k–50k	Audit	London	Steady
Judy	Woman	White British	40s	Finance manager	Housewife	High	Medium	Grammar	Partner, £100k–500k	Advisory	London	Accelerated
Karen	Woman	White British	40s	University professor	Housewife	High	High	State	Partner, £100k–500k	Support	Milton Keynes	Steady
Lola	Woman	White British	50s	Toolmaker	Seamstress	Medium	Low	State	Partner, £100k–500k	Audit	London	Impeded

Table A.1b: Turner Clarke interviewees (continued)

Name	Gender	Ethnicity	Age	Father's occupation	Mother's occupation	Inherited economic capital	Inherited cultural capital	Schooling	Position and salary range	Department	Interview location	Career trajectory
Martin	Man	White British	40s	Large business owner	Housewife	High	High	Private	Partner, £100k–500k	Audit	Leicester	Accelerated
Martina	Man	White British	20s	Barman	Cook	Low	Low	State	Trainee, £25k–50k	Advisory	Milton Keynes	Impeded
Matthew	Man	White British	40s	Engineer	Shop owner	Medium	Medium	State	Partner, £100k–500k	Tax	Manchester	Steady
Neil	Man	White British	30s	Senior manager	Middle Manager	High	High	State	Partner, £100k–500k	Audit	Milton Keynes	Accelerated
Nigel	Man	White British	30s	Senior manager	Housewife	High	High	Private	Partner, £100k–500k	Advisory	London	Accelerated
Paul	Man	White British	50s	Salesman	Housewife	Low	Low	Grammar	Partner, £100k–500k	Advisory	Birmingham	Impeded
Philip	Man	White British	40s	Gardener	Shop assistant	Low	Low	State	Partner, £100k–500k	Advisory	Manchester	Impeded
Raymond	Man	White British	40s	Electrician	Housewife	Low	Low	State	Partner, £100k–500k	Audit	Cambridge	Impeded
Rebecca	Woman	White British	20s	IT manager	Nurse	High	High	State	Trainee, £25k–50k	Advisory	Leicester	Accelerated
Robert	Man	White British	40s	Senior manager	Office manager	High	Medium	Grammar	Partner, £100k–500k	Advisory	London	Accelerated
Roger	Man	White British	50s	Middle manager	Secretary	Medium	Medium	Grammar	Partner, £100k–500k	Advisory	London	Steady
Terry	Man	White British	20s	Missing	Missing	Missing	Missing	State	Trainee, £25k–50k	Audit	London	Steady
Will	Man	White British	20s	Doctor	Lawyer	High	High	Private	Trainee, £25k–50k	Advisory	London	Accelerated
Yasmine	Woman	White British	20s	Missing	Missing	Missing	Missing	State	Trainee, £25k–50k	Tax	London	Steady

Table A.1c: Actors interviewees

Name	Gender	Ethnicity	Age	Father's occupation	Mother's occupation	Inherited economic capital	Inherited cultural capital	Schooling	Salary	Interview location	Career trajectory
Abigail	Woman	White British	30s	N/A	Teacher	Medium	High	State	£16.5k	London	Steady
Aiden	Man	White British	20s	Unemployed	Care assistant	Low	Low	State	£60k	London	Steady/impeded
Alaina	Woman	White British	20s	Chef	Admin assistant	Low	Low	State	£15k	London	Steady
Andy	Man	White British	20s	Doctor	Doctor	Medium	High	State	Missing	London	Steady
Archie	Man	White British	50s	Farmer	Housewife	Medium	Low	State	Negligible	London	Impeded
Brian	Man	Black British	40s	N/A	Singer	Low	Medium	State	£10k	London	Steady
Carrie	Woman	White British	30s	Architect	Housewife	High	High	Private	£18k	London	Steady
Carter	Man	White British	50s	Engineer	Housewife	Medium	Medium	Grammar	£12k	London	Steady
Charlotte	Woman	White British	30s	N/A	Civil servant	Medium	High	Grammar	£30k	London	Steady
Daisy	Woman	White British	30s	Teacher	Teacher	Medium	High	State	Missing	London	Steady
Dani	Man	Asian (mixed)	30s	Teacher	Teacher	Medium	High	Private	£36k	London	Accelerated
Daniel	Man	White British	20s	Technician	Admin assistant	Low	Low	State	Negligible	London	Impeded
Deborah	Woman	Black British	40s	Office clerk	Shop assistant	Low	Low	State	£8k	Newcastle	Impeded
Derek	Man	White British	50s	Labourer	Secretary	Low	Low	State	£27k	London	Impeded
Douglas	Man	White British	30s	Small business owner	Housewife	Medium	Medium	Private	£18k	London	Steady
Ella	Woman	White British	40s	Draughtsman	Hairdresser	Medium	Low	State	£12k	London	Impeded
Ellie	Woman	White British	30s	Headteacher	Senior manager	High	High	State	£20k	Birmingham	Steady

Table A.1c: Actors interviewees (continued)

Name	Gender	Ethnicity	Age	Father's occupation	Mother's occupation	Inherited economic capital	Inherited cultural capital	Schooling	Salary	Interview location	Career trajectory
Faith	Woman	Mixed/multiple	40s	Priest	Social worker	Low	Low	State	£20k	London	Impeded
Fraser	Man	White British	20s	Maintenance man	Admin assistant	Medium	Low	State	Negligible	London	Impeded
Grace	Woman	White British	30s	Builder	Housewife	Medium	Low	State	£27k	Liverpool	Steady
Imogen	Woman	Asian (mixed)	30s	Actuary	Housewife	High	High	Private	£24k–27k	London	Steady
Isabelle	Woman	White British	20s	Kitchen fitter	Sales buyer	Medium	Medium	Grammar	£20k	London	Steady
Jack	Man	White British	30s	Musician	Arts administrator	Medium	High	State	£40k	Edinburgh	Accelerated
Jane	Woman	White British	40s	Office clerk	Office clerk	Medium	Low	State	£100k–200k	Glasgow	Accelerated
Jim	Man	White British	50s	Van driver	Barman	Low	Low	State	£35k	London	Impeded
Joan	Woman	White British	30s	Medium-sized business owner	Teacher	High	Medium	Grammar	Negligible	London	Impeded
John	Man	Chinese British	40s	Teacher	Teacher	Medium	Medium	State	£20k	London	Steady
Leah	Woman	Black British	20s	Engineer	Teacher	High	Medium	Private	Missing	London	Steady
Leon	Man	White British	30s	Teacher	Secretary	Medium	High	State	£25k	London	Steady
Lewis	Man	White British	40s	Mechanical engineer	Cleaner	Medium	Low	State	£4k	London	Steady
Lily	Woman	Chinese British	50s	Medium-size business owner	Primary school teacher	Medium	Medium	State	£34k	London	Steady
Lloyd	Man	White British	40s	Mechanic	Care assistant	Low	Low	State	£17k	London	Steady
Lola	Woman	White British	40s	N/A	Unemployed	Low	Low	State	Missing	Glasgow	Impeded

Methodological appendix

Name	Gender	Ethnicity	Age	Father's occupation	Mother's occupation	Inherited economic capital	Inherited cultural capital	Schooling	Salary	Interview location	Career trajectory
Lucy	Woman	White British	20s	Labourer	Housewife	Low	Medium	State	Negligible	Liverpool	Impeded
Mark	Man	White British	Teens	Company director	Marketing assistant	High	Medium	State	£12k–15k	London	Steady
Mason	Man	White British	40s	Factory worker	Factory worker	Low	Low	State	Missing	London	Steady
Mia	Woman	White British	40s	Electrician	Housewife	Medium	Low	State	£30k	London	Steady/impeded
Millie	Woman	White British	50s	Stockbroker	Education manager	Medium	Medium	State	£12k–20k	Portsmouth	Steady
Mollie	Woman	White British	30s	Large business owner	Office manager	High	High	Private	£45k	London	Accelerated
Nathan	Man	White British	40s	Actor	Actor	High	High	Private	£50k	London	Accelerated
Olly	Man	White British	30s	Actor	Actor	High	High	Private	£35k	London	Accelerated
Peter	M	White British	20s	Cleric	Barrister	Medium	Medium	Grammar	£14k	London	Steady
Ray	Man	White British	20s	N/A	Care worker	Low	Low	State	Negligible	London	Impeded
Sandy	Man	White British	20s	Senior manager	Housewife	High	High	Private	£24k	London	Accelerated
Sophie	Woman	White British	30s	Labourer	Housewife	Low	Low	State	Negligible	Manchester	Impeded
Ted	Man	White British	50s	Cleric	Primary school teacher	Medium	Medium	Grammar	£20k	Skype	Steady
Tommy	Man	White British	30s	Large business owner	Housewife	High	High	Private	£40k	London	Accelerated

Table A.1d: Coopers interviewees

Name	Gender	Ethnicity	Age	Father's occupation	Mother's occupation	Inherited economic capital	Inherited cultural capital	Schooling	Position and salary category	Interview location	Career trajectory
Alan	Man	White British	30s	Architect	Osteopath	High	High	Private	Associate, £40k–59,999	London	Accelerated
Amin	Man	British Pakistani	30s	Taxi driver	Housewife	Low	Low	State	Partner, £60k+	London	Accelerated
Amir	Man	British Pakistani	20s	Unemployed	Housewife	Low	Medium	State	Architectural Assistant, prefer not to say	London	Steady
Anna	Woman	White Other	20s	Solicitor	Nurse	Medium	Medium	State	Architectural Assistant, £25k–39,999	London	Steady
Christine	Woman	White British	30s	Retail manager	Engineer	Medium	Medium	State	Office Team, £40k–59,999	London	Steady
Claire	Woman	White British	30s	IT manager	Headteacher	High	Medium	State	Architect, £25k–39,999	London	Steady
Clive	Man	White British	40s	Architect	Shop manager	High	Medium	State	Partner, £60k+	London	Steady
Colm	Man	White other	20s	Engineer	Nurse	Medium	Medium	State	Architectural Assistant, £25k–39,999	London	Steady
Connor	Man	White British	20s	Sales representative	Physiotherapist	Medium	Medium	State	Architectural Assistant, £25k–39,999	London	Steady
Daffyd	Man	White British	20s	Purchasing manager	Retail manager	Medium	Medium	State	Architectural Assistant, £25k–39,999	London	Accelerated
Dan	Man	White British	20s	Engineer	Small business owner	High	High	State	Architectural Assistant, up to £24,999	London	Steady
David	Man	White British	40s	Potter	Primary school teacher	Medium	Medium	State	Partner, £60k+	London	Steady

Name	Gender	Ethnicity	Age	Father's occupation	Mother's occupation	Inherited economic capital	Inherited cultural capital	Schooling	Position and salary category	Interview location	Career trajectory
Eamon	Man	White Other	30s	Sales representative	Primary school teacher	Medium	Medium	State	Associate, £40k–59,999	London	Steady
Elena	Woman	White Other	30s	Engineer	Physiotherapist	High	Medium	State	Architectural Assistant, £25k–39,999	London	Steady
Finola	Woman	White Other	20s	Business owner – construction	Housewife	Medium	Medium	State	Architectural Assistant, £25k–39,999	London	Steady
Fran	Woman	White Other	20s	Company director	Receptionist	High	Medium	State	Architect, £25k–39,999	London	Impeded
Gabriella	Woman	White Other	20s	Senior company manager	Housewife	High	High	Private	Architectural Assistant, £25k–39,999	London	Steady
Gary	Man	White British	50+	Mason	Canteen worker	Low	Medium	State	Partner, £60k+	London	Steady
Helen	Woman	Mixed Other	20s	Doctor	Social worker	High	Medium	Private	Office Team, up to £24,999	London	Steady
Jessica	Woman	White British	20s	Craftsman	Local authority manager	High	Medium	Private	Architectural Assistant, up to £24,999	London	Steady
John	Man	White British	40s	Local authority manager	Charity administration	Medium	Medium	State	Associate, £60k+	London	Steady
Kirsten	Woman	White Other	20s	Hotel manager	Public relations manager	High	Medium	Private	Architectural Assistant, £25k–39,999	London	Steady
Kristof	Man	White Other	40s	Engineer	Secretary	Medium	Medium	State	Architect, £40k–59,999	London	Impeded
Luke	Man	White British	20s	Hotel manager	HR manager	Medium	Medium	State	Architect, £25k–39,999	London	Steady

Table A.1d: Coopers interviewees (continued)

Name	Gender	Ethnicity	Age	Father's occupation	Mother's occupation	Inherited economic capital	Inherited cultural capital	Schooling	Position and salary category	Interview location	Career trajectory
Martin	Man	White British	20s	Graphic designer	Local authority manager	Medium	Medium	State	Architectural Assistant, £25k–39,999	London	Accelerated
Miguel	Man	White Other	40s	Doctor	Housewife	High	Medium	State	Associate, £40k–59,999	London	Steady
Mike	Man	White British	40s	Architect	Canteen worker	Medium	Medium	State	Partner, £60k+	London	Impeded
Paolo	Man	White Other	20s	Lawyer	Nurse	High	Medium	State	Architectural Assistant, £25k–39,999	London	Steady
Paul	Man	White British	40s	Engineer	Researcher	Medium	Medium	State	Partner, £60k+	London	Steady
Paula	Woman	White Other	30s	Clerical	Clerical	Medium	Medium	Private	Associate, £40k–59,999	London	Impeded
Pauline	Woman	White British	20s	Entrepreneur	Entrepreneur	Medium	Medium	State	Architectural Assistant, £25k–39,999	London	Steady
Sara	Woman	Black African	20s	Dentist	Housewife	Medium	Medium	State	Architect, £25k–39,999	London	Steady
Sarah	Woman	White Other	40s	Engineer	Personal assistant	High	Medium	Private	Associate, £60k+	London	Impeded
Seamus	Man	White Other	20s	Public-sector senior manager	Physiotherapist	Medium	Medium	State	Architectural Assistant, £25k–39,999	London	Steady
Simon	Man	White British	30s	Architect	Civil servant	High	High	State	Associate Partner, £40k–59,999	London	Steady
Sofia	Woman	White Other	30s	Business owner	Teacher	High	Medium	State	Associate, £40k–59,999	London	Impeded

Check your privilege! Our class origins and the research process

When we read books like this we often find ourselves wondering who the researchers are. Yet most sociologists tend to leave themselves out of the methodological stories they tell. There are some good reasons for this – an over-reliance on the first-person, for example, can often smack of self-indulgence. But at the same time we are mindful of the need to reflect on the way in which our own social coordinates inevitably impacted the research in this book.

At first glance we (Sam and Daniel) look very similar as researchers. We are both white men in the high-status occupation of academia, and therefore highly privileged in many ways. This positionality is significant and it is important to recognise that it may have affected how comfortable certain interviewees – particularly women and racial-ethnic minorities – felt in sharing their experiences of work with us.

Yet we are also different people in various ways. Most obviously Daniel is American while Sam is British, and this gives us quite different perspectives and assumptions about class, mobility and elite work. Less obviously, Daniel is a transgender man he identified as a queer woman and worked in LGBT and women's organisations before going to graduate school and later transitioning.

But the difference that is most relevant for this book is that we actually have very divergent class backgrounds. Sam is from a fairly conventional upper-middle-class background. While his parents are both from intermediate or lower-middle-class backgrounds, they were themselves upwardly mobile, and when Sam was growing up they worked as an economist and a social worker. The family lived in a big house in an affluent enclave of Bristol and Sam was privately educated. Daniel, in contrast, was raised by a self-consciously (if not entirely uncomplicatedly) working-class single mother, who had not quite finished college and worked as a union organiser and a secretary while he was growing up. His family lived in a number of different rental houses, mostly in the poorer 'South End' of Seattle, Washington, before finally buying a house when he was 14. He attended public (in the US sense)/state schools until university.

These divergent class backgrounds have played an important role in our research collaboration. In both explicit and implicit ways they have acted to animate our research, providing a constant, productive tension in the ways we each read the data the project has produced. We have also reflected extensively on how our own backgrounds have affected our respective career trajectories. One of the first discussions we had, for example, involved a very intense deconstruction of how and why Sam had got a permanent job at LSE. Here Sam reflected on his sense that the recruitment process, which involved a series of informal one-on-one meetings with existing staff (who were then able to vote on their chosen interviewee) and also a dinner with staff and other shortlistees, had probably acted to unfairly advantage him. Specifically (with a father in the academy) the behavioural codes and implicit 'rules of the game' required to successfully navigate this kind of process came fairly instinctively to Sam. In contrast, other interviewees, Sam notes, recalling the intensely awkward candidate dinner, were clearly disorientated. Daniel, on the other hand, knew no one who was a professor, besides those he had met while at university/in college, before he started graduate school. His sense is that many of his career successes have come *despite* his lack of intuitive understanding of the rules of the game or behavioural codes. It's hard for any one individual to parse how much of what feels strange or uncomfortable is simply due to their own idiosyncrasies, and how much is really about class and class cultures. But Daniel recalls being mystified by many of the professional rituals of academia when he first encountered them; he feels he is especially bad at the kinds of chit-chat expected at the wine-and-cheese receptions that often follow academic talks, for example, and first encountered a place setting with more than one fork sometime in his mid-20s.

How do you measure social mobility?

Measuring social mobility can simply involve looking at a person's origin and current position (or 'destination') in life, and then calculating the movement or mobility between the two.

However, deciding precisely what social category or variable to use in measuring class origins and destinations is anything but simple (we explore these conceptual issues in Chapter Ten). Traditionally economists have tended to use income while sociologists have favoured occupation. In both cases origin is calculated in terms of *parental* occupation or income and destination in terms of people's *own* occupation or income. While income is fairly easy to measure, occupation is normally aggregated into occupational classes. In the UK the most widely used schema was developed by sociologist John Goldthorpe and is entitled the National Statistics Socio-Economic Classification (NS-SEC). Over the last 20 years a bitter debate has raged about which of these approaches is more valid and accurate, particularly in terms of understanding changes in mobility rates over time.[10]

However, there are important signs that the sociological approach is beginning to win out, particularly in the UK. In particular, the UK Cabinet Office has recently recommended that all large organisations and government departments foreground measures of parental occupation when monitoring social mobility.[11] We also use the NS-SEC here. In terms of destination, we are, of course, only interested in respondents who have a particular occupational destination in an 'elite occupation'. As we explain in the following section, we define this in terms of all higher professional and managerial (NS-SEC 1) occupations plus a set of cultural and creative jobs. Together these occupations constitute a sample of 18,413 respondents in the LFS.[12] At various points we also distinguish 19 individual professions within this group. While these are not all recognisable 'professions', our goal was to create occupational groupings with broadly similar training, skills and work contexts,[13] while also having a sufficiently large *sample* within each group to allow for meaningful inference. It is important to note that not every person included in the analyses of the full 'elite' destination is within one of these 19 occupational groups; 2,177 have an NS-SEC 1 categorisation but no specific occupation recorded, and 1,492 are in occupations that have sample sizes too small to analyse individually and that could not be sensibly grouped with other elite occupations. We give the number of respondents in each top occupation (and those uncategorised) from each origin group in Table A.2.

Table A.2: Number of LFS respondents in each elite occupation by origin

	Professional and managerial origins	Intermediate origins	Working-class origins	Total
Performing arts	184	123	74	381
Film & TV	185	139	43	367
Journalism	244	107	39	390
Architecture	92	70	16	178
Academia	298	137	87	522
Science	269	166	81	516
Life sciences	269	123	46	438
Medicine	520	146	47	713
Law	313	124	66	503
Accountancy	384	272	155	811
Engineering	451	401	250	1,102
IT	1,027	717	433	2,177
Advertising	612	311	203	1,126
CEOs	103	62	31	196
Management consulting	240	114	71	425
Finance	321	245	115	681
Corporate senior management	1,494	1,152	767	3,413
Public-sector senior management	281	212	133	626
Chiefs of fire, ambulance services	74	63	42	179
Any other top job	1,542	1,256	871	3,669
Total	8,903	5,940	3,570	18,413

To measure the class origins of respondents we refer to the LFS question that asks respondents, 'When you were 14 what was the occupation of the main income-earner in your household?' (Notably, in over 80% of cases, this means the occupation of the father.) Based on answers to this question we then group people's origins into the seven classes of NS-SEC; those with no income-earning family member are coded into an eighth category for the long-term unemployed. Figure 1.1 highlights examples of occupations in each NS-SEC origin class.

In most sections of the book we show results using the simplified three-class scheme of NS-SEC for ease of presentation. We refer to those from NS-SEC 1 and 2 origins as hailing from 'professional and managerial', 'upper-middle-class' or 'privileged' backgrounds. Those from NS-SEC 3, 4 and 5 backgrounds we refer to as either from 'intermediate' or 'lower-middle-class' origins. Finally, we write about those from NS-SEC 6 and 7 backgrounds and those from no-earner families as coming from either 'routine and semi-routine' or 'working-class' backgrounds. We acknowledge that there is some conceptual ambiguity surrounding these terms, particularly categories such as upper-middle class and lower-middle class. However, we think these terms are useful in clarifying the relational distinction between the three origin groups we examine here.

It is also worth noting that one limitation of our analysis is that it does not register the short-range mobility of those from NS-SEC 2 backgrounds who then move into NS-SEC 1 jobs – the children of teachers who become academics, for example. Around 3% of the population experience this trajectory, and about 21% of those in our elite occupations are from NS-SEC 2 origins. In other published work we have examined whether these people face a class pay gap compared to the children of higher professionals and managers (NS-SEC 1). We find that they do earn, on average, around £2,900 a year less than the very privileged. However, once all controls are applied, this pay gap loses statistical significance.[14]

What is an 'elite' occupation?

The polysemic nature of the term 'elite' makes it difficult to define a set of uncontested 'elite occupations'. In a UK context we primarily draw on the guidance of David Rose, one of the architects of the NS-SEC classification, who argues the best existing measure is the top class of the NS-SEC.[15] This distinguishes a set of 'higher professional, managerial and administrative' occupations. We also include a number of cultural and creative occupations routinely associated in policy discourse with top professions but categorised elsewhere in the NS-SEC scheme rather than NS-SEC 1. This includes journalists, and those working in film and television, the performing arts, and advertising. While earnings in some of these occupations may be, on average, lower than other elite occupations, their 'eliteness' emerges in other important ways. Careers in these areas are among the most competitive of all our elite occupations. They are also highly prized, promising (even if not necessarily delivering) creativity, self-expression and glamour. Finally, the leaders in these occupations – who are of particular interest to us in this book – wield meaningful influence in public life, playing a pivotal role in shaping the nation's cultural identity via film, media and the performing arts.

We should stress here that we are not claiming that everyone employed in our elite occupations is elite in all senses of the term. Instead, we would argue that our respondents are employed in occupations that promise, if one reaches the upper echelons, disproportionate access to exactly the kind of 'pivotal positions'[16] in British society that most would agree qualify as elite.

Analysing the Labour Force Survey

As outlined, we pool data from the 2013 waves through the 2016 waves of the LFS.[17] The LFS conducts surveys every quarter, using a rolling sample of respondents who are contacted across five quarters, or 15 months. In any given quarterly survey, about a fifth of respondents are participating for the first time, another fifth for the second time, and so on, but not all questions are asked of all respondents in all quarters; the social origin questions were only asked in July-September surveys, so we combined data for any respondent who answered the social origin questions in July-September 2014, 2015 or 2016. This means that respondents could have started the survey as early as July-September 2013, or as late as July-September 2016. Pooling data this way gives us the largest-possible sample sizes, and also allows us to use data for individual respondents from different quarters where necessary.

We then restrict our sample in various ways. First, we restrict our sample to those aged 69 or younger to minimise the effects of retirement. Second, we remove all individuals under age 23 or in full-time education from the analyses as they are unlikely to have stably transitioned into professional jobs. In this regard, it is worth noting that mobility analysts normally look only at people aged 30 or 35 or older.[18] However, we include the widest reasonable age range because we are interested in the composition of professional and managerial jobs, not mobility chances by origin.

To analyse progression within the professions, we use the earnings of LFS respondents. Of course earnings do not necessarily provide a definitive measure of occupational position, but they are the best available proxy and an important marker of success in their own right. These measures were only collected for each participant in their first and fifth quarters participating in the survey (which not all respondents participated in), and not all respondents were willing to answer the earnings question. This resulted in a sample of 8,563 respondents working in our set of elite occupations who also have earnings information, and 8,325 with data on all covariates used in regression models. While there are a lot of respondents with missing earnings data, we explain our confidence in the results in the online appendix at https://www.classceiling.org/appendix.

Given the large sample size in the LFS, we are also able to consider differences in social mobility by gender, age and ethnicity. We use the variable in the LFS that includes a racial–ethnic category for the most people, which distinguishes White, Black/ African/Caribbean/Black British, Indian, Pakistani, Bangladeshi, Chinese, Other Asian, Mixed or Multiple Ethnicities, and any other ethnic group. We sometimes combine Bangladeshi and Pakistani groups where sample sizes would otherwise be too small, as both groups are predominantly Muslim, tend to face similar levels of disadvantage in the British labour market, and also experience similar levels of social fluidity.[19] Migrants and the children of white European origins from Europe, North America, Australia, New Zealand (white other) and from the Republic of Ireland (white Irish) are included in the White category; we capture some of this variation with the question about country of origin, which distinguishes those born in England, Wales, Scotland or Northern Ireland, as well as those born outside of the UK.

Using regression to understand the class pay gap

In Chapter Three we presented a series of figures based on regression models. This allowed us to check whether differences in work-related attributes among people from different class origins explain the pay gap we see in top jobs. More specifically, regression models estimate how much a 'dependent variable' (in this case earnings) increases (or decreases) due, separately, to each potential factor included in that model by the researcher. If two variables tend to both be associated with increases in the dependent variable, and are also associated with each other when we include them both, we normally see a smaller independent effect of each one. This is commonly referred to as 'controlling for' additional variables.

One way to visualise how this works is to picture going up a mountain slope. If the peak is to the south-east, for every step you take in that direction, some of your rise up the slope is due to your movement to the south, and some to your movement to the east, and it is possible to measure these separately. If you were only measuring your south–north movement, it might look like all your gain in elevation was due to moving south. Looking only at class origin and pay is like only measuring only southward movement – think about the 'slope' visible in the graphs of pay by class in the last chapter. Figure A.1 shows the earnings 'mountain' for class origin and education. For each step 'up' in the north–south class-origin slope, earnings increase, but they *also* increase for each step in the education/eastward direction. Adding education to our understanding of the earnings slope makes our estimate of the slope due to class smaller, because some of the class slope was actually due to educational differences between the groups – the east–west slope.

In Chapter Three we attempt to disentangle potential sources of class-origin income difference. To do this we conduct a series of nested linear regressions that control for four sets of factors that we identified from previous research as key sources of income inequality. We use the LFS variable indicating weekly earnings, multiplied by 52, for an estimate of annual earnings as the dependent variable. In the demographics model, we include controls for gender, ethnicity, disability and age, as well as the quarter in which the respondent gave earnings information. In the education model, we add three measures of education: the highest degree or qualification the respondent achieved, the type of university they attended and their degree classification. The other 'merit' model adds additional measures of human capital – training, job tenure, usual number of hours worked and past health. We next add the region of the UK in which respondents worked, then the specific occupation they worked in (using the SOC10 codes for occupations in our elite jobs), then the industry their job was in, whether they worked in the public or private sector, and the size of the firm at which they worked.[20] The results we get from these models are substantively identical to those we see when we use logged earnings as the dependent variable,[21] or earnings percentile, or earnings percentile by region.[22]

We describe the percentage of the total pay gap explained by each set of controls based on the results of a Blinder-Oaxaca decomposition model,[23] a type of regression analysis designed specifically for this purpose (we explain this approach in previous work and give more complete details of our analysis in the online appendix at www.classceiling.org/appendix).[24]

Comparing case study occupations

As we have already explained, our four case studies are not necessarily representative of *all* elite occupations, and our choices were partially informed by serendipitous opportunities to research particular elite organisations.

However, our decision to compare these particular occupations does have a rationale. They all share a number of important features. First and foremost, they are all widely considered high-status professions. Accountancy and architecture, for example, promise both material rewards (by way of comparatively high salaries) and symbolic rewards of prestige.[25] Careers in television and acting are also highly prized, promising (even if not necessarily delivering) creativity, self-expression and glamour. Second, these all represent highly competitive professions that occupy top positions in national league tables of the most prized graduate employment destinations. Finally, the leaders of each of these professions – who are of particular interest to us in this book – wield particular influence in public life. Executives in accountancy preside over some of the UK's largest and most powerful corporations, whereas leaders in television, architecture and acting play a pivotal role in shaping the nation's cultural identity via the media, performing arts and built environment.

While these occupations share important characteristics, they also differ in four important ways. First, employment tends to be structured in very different ways. Accountancy and architecture are old and traditional professions, and jobs tend to be stable and permanent. Acting and television are, in contrast, exemplars of what is now called the 'gig' economy. Employment in television, for instance, often relies on negotiating a series of short-term contracts – particularly for those following the 'creative' pathway through television production (see Chapter Five for more on the significance of creative pathways in television). Acting is arguably even more precarious, and most actors are self-employed. Our choice of acting, then, was partly motivated by a desire to probe this association between self-employment and the class ceiling.

Second, careers and career progression work differently in these fields. Accountancy, first of all, is dominated – in terms of economic output – by a small number of multinational firms. These companies tend to be very large with career progression ordered vertically along up to seven or eight grades. As illustrated in Chapter Four, there are relatively established pathways in such firms, with many employees 'rising up the ranks'. Television broadcasting is similarly dominated by a small number of terrestrial television channels (although there are approximately 480 smaller free-to-air, free-to-view and subscription channels). These main broadcasters are, like 6TV, fairly hierarchical, although progression to top creative positions is normally contingent on amassing experience in the independent production ('indie') sector. Acting is an example of a 'winner-takes-all' labour market. Here a very small number of top professionals receive very high rewards, in terms of income and status, whereas the vast majority make do on fairly low earnings. Architecture, in contrast, is less hierarchical. Many UK architects work as sole practitioners or in tiny practices of five employees or fewer. In this context, occupational grades are less meaningful. Early-career, the impetus is to complete all three parts of an architectural education, which typically takes seven years or more, so as to be allowed to use the protected term 'architect'. Thereafter, gaining experience as a project architect is key.

Third, these professions all occupy distinct positions in terms of current policy debates around social mobility. For example, social mobility has been a key issue within accountancy ever since it was singled out as having particularly acute problems in Alan Milburn's influential 2009 report *Fair Access to the Professions*. Many large firms have subsequently led the way among the traditional professions in introducing 'contextual' academic data and school and university-blind applications in graduate recruitment processes (although there has been much less emphasis on progression). More recently, both television and acting have also come under scrutiny, with a number of celebrities and policy-makers using a media platform to decry barriers to access and progression.[26] Architecture, despite its history as an elite profession, has largely avoided this policy focus, with only sporadic debate and activity to promote social mobility. Instead, the diversity agenda has been dominated by issues of gender discrimination and a lack of women within the profession, particularly in more senior positions.

Finally, and as we outlined in Chapter Four, the impact of class background on career progression varies strongly across these professions. Our LFS analysis demonstrates that the class pay gap is comparatively high in both accountancy (particularly among large City [of London] firms) and acting. Yet in architecture and film and television we find no evidence of a class pay gap. In this way, our choice of case study occupations was fundamentally connected to our aim to understand what potential factors aid *and* thwart the class pay gap.

Comparing elite organisations

As explained earlier in this book, we believed many potential drivers of the class pay gap were operating at the firm level, in terms of the culture and structure of particular organisations.

To interrogate these mechanisms we chose to look at elite occupations through the lens of organisational case studies rather than examining a cross-section of individuals from different firms. These case study firms were 6TV, a national television broadcaster, Turner Clarke, a large multinational accountancy company, and Coopers, an architecture practice.

In addition to our reasoning for selecting particular occupations, we also thought through the particular kinds of *firms* we wanted to study. First, we were interested in further exploring the London effect uncovered in Chapter Three. In this way, we selected three organisations with significant workforces located in Central London. We also wanted at least one organisation whose national workforce is spatially distributed in ways that allowed us to do meaningful comparative analysis. Turner Clarke provided this opportunity – 60% of employees are based outside the capital, whereas over 90% of those at Coopers and 6TV work in London.

Second, we wanted to explore differences related to firm size. Recall that in Chapter Three we explained that the pay gap was more accentuated in larger firms. To explore this further, we selected one medium-size firm, Coopers, one medium-to-large firm, 6TV, and one very large firm, Turner Clarke.

Finally, we also wanted to compare firms where there is a varying degree of within-firm specialisation. Chapter Three showed very clearly the power of sorting *between* elite occupations. However, we were interested in whether there are similarly pertinent forms of horizontal segregation *within* elite occupations – do people from different class origins sort into different areas or departments, and does this have a bearing on their progression prospects? As we explain in Chapter Four there are very important forms of specialisation within 6TV (especially Commissioning versus the other five main departments), at Turner Clarke (especially Advisory versus Audit and Tax), and Coopers (especially between staff focusing on Design, Technical and Commercial).

Feeding back to case study organisations

Each of our case studies was carried out in partnership with the organisation in question. After completing the fieldwork we fed our results back to senior leaders within each firm – first, via an oral presentation and then, after absorbing and incorporating their feedback, in the form of a formal report. We felt this process of feeding back was important in allowing each organisation a 'right to reply'. Moreover, our aim was also always to produce research that could actually be used by the organisation to address issues of social mobility and career progression.

Feeding back was not an entirely smooth process, however. In the case of 6TV and Turner Clarke, our results were highly critical. For the most part leaders at both firms accepted these findings. However, there were also some strong objections from certain individuals. At Turner Clarke, for example, as we were explaining the prevalence of informal sponsorship, one Senior Partner interjected angrily, "I just don't buy this. In my experience this does not go on here." In other cases, objections were rooted more in our interpretation of the data. For example, as explained in the Conclusion (Chapter Eleven), there was particular push-back on our critique of the culture in Commissioning at 6TV.

Our work has also had a tangible impact on our case study organisations. At 6TV, for example, a steering group (which Sam was a member of) was set up to address our findings. This eventually yielded an extensive social mobility strategy that includes an ongoing commitment to measuring and monitoring the class backgrounds of staff, targets for increasing the representation of socially mobile staff at upper echelons, and the ring-fencing of the majority of the firm's trainee places for those from socially mobile backgrounds. At Turner Clarke, our research has also initiated change, including a similar commitment to the monitoring of the class composition of its staff. The firm has also made a number of changes to its graduate trainee selection process, including the removal of the emphasis on relevant work experience and extra-curricular achievements, and adapting its aptitude test so it now takes a more holistic approach to identifying talent and cultural fit.

A note on confidentiality

We are extremely concerned about preserving the anonymity of both our case study organisations and individual interviewees. For firms, the aggregate information about staff composition is commercially sensitive. For interviewees the questions we asked were intimate and provocative, and being identifiable could have a serious bearing on their careers. Our main concern was thus not that interviewees would be identifiable to the general reader, which we think is almost impossible, but rather that they may be recognisable to colleagues within their organisation. For these reasons we take a number of steps towards ensuring anonymity. First, we refer to all participants with pseudonyms. Second, we also modify the characteristics of some interviewees, or details about their lives, in order to ensure they are not identifiable. However, in masking certain details, we have avoided making changes that are likely to affect the reader's capacity to evaluate our arguments (such as major changes to demographic characteristics). Finally, readers will notice that occasionally we refer to individuals with certain characteristics but do not attach a pseudonym. We do this when the comment is fairly provocative and where the respondent may be identifiable if readers follow their pseudonym throughout the book. In Tables A.1a–1d we provide details of the gender, ethnicity and parental occupation of each interviewee.

Limitations and future research

There are many important limitations to this project. Some are fairly obvious. For example, a key question remains – is the class ceiling a new phenomenon? In this book we claim that the class ceiling has not been meaningfully uncovered before. But that is very different from saying it didn't *exist* in the past. Specifically, we know that the status attainment approach to mobility studies, dominant in the US and in much comparative research through the 1970s, found a direct effect of class origins on pay, net of the effect of occupational destination itself.[27]

Unfortunately, the cross-sectional data at our disposal simply do not allow us to address the issue of change over time. One fruitful line of future enquiry, then, might be to try to find longitudinal data that are able to examine whether the UK class pay gap existed in the past and whether it has increased or decreased over time.

There are also limitations inherent in case selection. Put simply, if we had looked at other top occupations and other elite organisations, we may well have uncovered different drivers of the class pay gap. Notably, our case study organisations are unrepresentative in one important way; they were willing to open their doors and let researchers examine a sensitive issue like class. It is hard to know exactly how this affected our results, but it is plausible that wider issues of class inequality were better understood and acknowledged at these firms than at others. Most others, including some we tried and failed to access, may well be more fearful of what might be uncovered in discussions of class. In this way, our results may actually underestimate the scale of the class ceiling, especially if the firms who refused us access contained more severe class–origin barriers.

Another key limitation of our approach is that it is hard to meaningfully adjudicate between the relative salience of, and relationship between, the different drivers of the pay gap we have identified. This reflects, in many ways, the bumpiness of employing mixed methods in the way we do. For example, while we find a class pay gap across all 'elite occupations' in Chapters Two and Three, our analysis from Chapter Four onwards examines four specific case studies rather than continuing to look at all elite occupations.[28] There is, in many ways, an imperfect analytic connection between these two parts of our project. First, as we have just explained, we cannot be sure that the mechanisms we have identified in our case studies hold for all elite occupations. Second, many of the drivers identified in Chapter Three are about (or, in the case of education, happen before) which occupation or firm people *enter*, and that is largely happening outside of, or temporally before, our analyses of what happens to people *within* firms (although we can, of course, detect the residue of some of these earlier drivers in people's career narratives, especially at 6TV). Finally, some of the people in our case studies, while working in an elite *firm*, are not doing work that would be classified as part of our 'elite occupations'. For example, the Administrative Assistants at 6TV, and many of the 'support' staff at TC, are not clearly employed in elite occupations.[29]

Other limitations relate to our methodological decisions. This project has been largely interview-based because we needed to understand people's career trajectories and their experiences in their jobs. However, it is important to recognise that there is often a disconnect between what people say they do and what they actually do in practice. 'Talk is cheap,' as Jerolmack and Khan[30] note, and does not always match behaviour. This is particularly relevant in terms of a mechanism such as class discrimination. Although we found little evidence of this in our research, this may well be an artefact of the interview setting, where people tend to foreground less judgemental, 'honourable' selves.[31] Moreover, the use of more ethnographic observation methods may also be useful to further elucidate many mechanisms we cite in this book, such as the power of behavioural codes, the establishment of sponsorship relationships and the expression of exclusive executive cultures. There are also important gatekeeping encounters, such as pay negotiation, interviews or promotion appraisals, that are crucial for understanding the class ceiling and that are better tapped using ethnographic observational methods.

We have spent much of this book, particularly in Chapter Ten, arguing that researchers must move beyond broad occupational categories to utilise more detailed measures of class *destination* – be it earnings or occupational position. Yet at the same time we ourselves use this same conventional measure of occupation when looking at people's class *origin* (in the LFS). This double standard has not escaped us, and we would note that future work should also use more fine-grained measures of origin; we are limited by the information available in the LFS, but hope more large-scale studies (possibly even the LFS itself) will include multiple measures of class origin in the future.

Additional table and figures

In the process of doing the analyses presented in the first part of this book, we created far more figures than we could fully discuss in the main text. However, we mention a number of analyses that interested readers might like to understand further; we present some of the figures we find most compelling in the table and figures overleaf, and describe our analyses with yet more detail and figures in the online appendix at www.classceiling.org/ appendix. We present these figures here with minimal discussion, as they are referenced in the main text.

Table A.3: Origins and destinations in the LFS (%)

Parents	Higher managerial and professional	Lower managerial and professional	Intermediate	Small employers	Lower supervisory and technical	Semi-routine	Routine occupations	Never worked	Total
Higher managerial and professional	3.8	4.6	1.7	1.1	0.6	0.9	0.5	1.1	14.3
Lower managerial and professional	3.5	5.4	2.1	1.4	0.9	1.4	0.8	1.5	16.9
Intermediate	1.7	2.9	1.5	0.8	0.5	1.1	0.7	1.0	10.1
Small employers	1.4	2.9	1.5	1.9	0.9	1.7	1.3	1.8	13.4
Lower supervisory and technical	1.5	2.9	1.6	1.1	1.0	1.5	1.0	1.5	12.0
Semi-routine	1.1	2.5	1.5	1.0	1.0	1.9	1.4	1.8	12.3
Routine occupations	1.3	3.0	2.0	1.4	1.3	2.5	2.2	2.8	16.6
Never worked	0.3	0.7	0.5	0.3	0.3	0.8	0.6	1.0	4.4
Total	14.6	24.8	12.3	8.9	6.5	11.7	8.6	12.5	100.0

Figure A.1: Earnings mountain – explaining regression

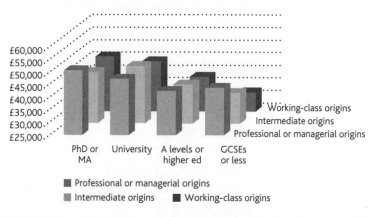

Note: This figure uses real data from our analyses to illustrate conceptually what regression models are doing.
Source: LFS

Figure A.2: Percentage of each racial-ethnic group from each class origin, whole UK labour force

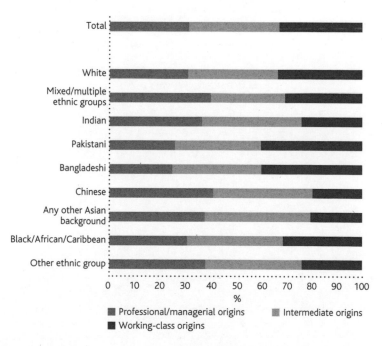

Figure A.3: Percentage with a BA or more from each racial-ethnic group and class origin

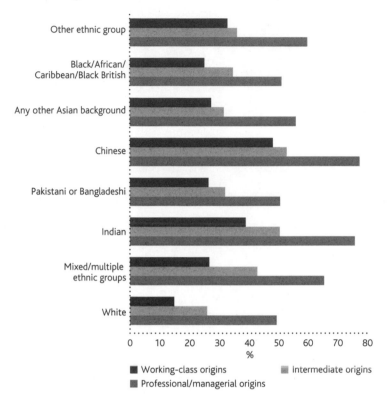

Figure A.4: Percentage of people from each racial-ethnic group and class origin in top jobs, among those with a BA or higher

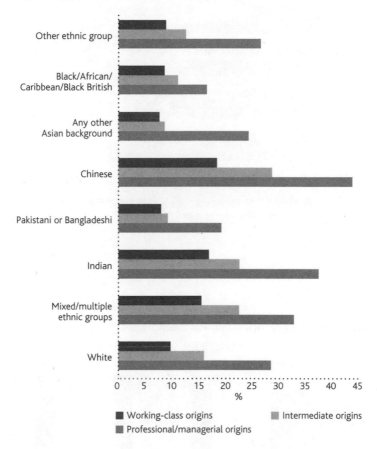

Figure A.5: Earnings by class origin and educational attainment

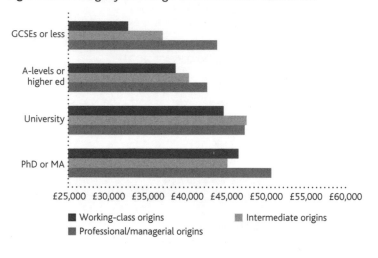

- Working-class origins
- Professional/managerial origins
- Intermediate origins

Figure A.6: Class pay gaps within education levels

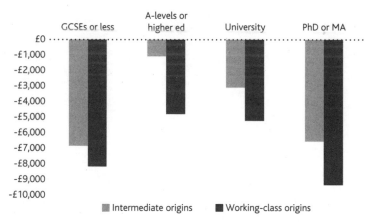

- Intermediate origins
- Working-class origins

Note: These are from regressions including the same controls as those in the demographic models in Chapter Three. All class pay gaps are statistically significant at p<0.05 except for between intermediate- and professional or managerial-origin people with A-levels or higher education (HE).

Figure A.7: Class pay gaps for each racial-ethnic group and class background

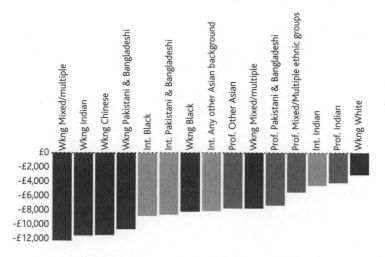

Note: From the model with controls for everything; all class-origin/racial-ethnic gaps are statistically significant when compared with white professional or managerial-origin people at p<0.05.

Notes

Introduction

1   'Mark' and all names used throughout the book are pseudonyms. We have also modified certain details about some interviewees' lives in order to ensure anonymity. We outline our approach to confidentiality in the Methodological appendix (see p. 239).

2   6TV and the other case study firms we refer to in the book, Turner Clarke and Coopers, are all pseudonyms.

3   In the UK, final undergraduate and Master's-level projects are called 'dissertations', while to get a PhD you complete a 'thesis'. This is the exact opposite of the usage of these terms in the US. As this book is about the UK, we use British English in the text, but provide translations for Americans as needed throughout.

4   Isaac Hayes was a critically acclaimed African-American soul singer-songwriter.

5   *Private Eye* is a long-running UK satirical and current affairs magazine.

6   *Have I Got News For You* is a long-running BBC television comedy current affairs panel show.

7   We include a list of all interviewees, including extensive demographic and career details, in Tables A.1a-1d in the Methodological appendix.

8   Throughout the book we put the word 'merit' in quotation marks because, as we show, 'merit' is tricky. When someone is said to have 'merit', we usually mean that they deserve their success, through hard work, talent, skill or some other kind of genuine, objectively measurable attribute or action. However, most sociologists agree that it is unlikely that evaluations of this kind of 'merit' can be made fully independent of social biases (see also Littler, 2017; Mijs, 2016). Even intelligence tests, for example, are often racially biased, and/or gauge the quality of someone's education rather than their innate ability (Fischer and Voss, 1996). Yet it is also unlikely that skills, talents, motivations or effort have *no* bearing on career success; of course firms and managers try to reward those who are the most effective in their jobs. Much of the book is dedicated to attempting to disentangle the ways class origin, and other attributes, shape how 'merit' is evaluated.

9   Weber (1992, p 271).

[10] The term 'meritocracy' was popularised by Michael Young in a dystopian novel meant to critique the vision of a society based entirely on 'merit' (Young, 2001).

[11] Major (1990).

[12] Blair (1999).

[13] Beck (1992, 1996); Beck and Willms (2003).

[14] Giddens (1991).

[15] Bauman (2000).

[16] First quote: Beck (1992, p 128); second quote: Beck et al (1994, p 13).

[17] These scholars were careful not to argue that the end of class meant that everyone had become middle class or affluent. They were clear that inequalities remain. Nonetheless, their sociological narratives chimed with political manifestos evoking the idea that class was bound up with a past whose hold had been shattered by the forces of globalisation and modernisation.

[18] Lindert (2004).

[19] Payne (2017).

[20] In the UK, a 'grammar school' is akin to some magnet schools in the US, a highly selective state secondary school where admission is based on performing well in an examination, known as the '11-plus', administered to 11-year-olds. In the post-war period there were over 1,200 state grammar schools in the UK, but this number has now dwindled to 164.

[21] Goldthorpe et al (1980). For an excellent overview of UK trends in absolute and relative mobility, see Goldthorpe (2016).

[22] Bukodi et al (2015).

[23] Piketty (2014).

[24] Savage and Friedman (2017).

[25] Piketty (2014) and Dorling (2014). The Gini coefficient is the dominant approach to measuring and comparing levels of economic inequality; Piketty's work generally examines the share of income going to the top 1% of earners in a country. By either measure, there was a slight dip in inequality around the 2008 financial crisis, but the overall trend since the 1970s has been towards higher inequality.

[26] McKenzie (2015); Savage et al (2015b); Bloodworth (2016); Major and Machin (2018); Wilkinson and Pickett (2018).

[27] Elliott (2017).

[28] Doherty (2016).

[29] Payne (2017).

[30] Blanden et al (2004); Blanden and Machin (2017).

[31] For example, 2011 research by YouGov for Policy Exchange found 85% of the UK public agrees that 'in a fair society, people's incomes should depend on how hard they work and how talented they are.' Fairness was second only to economic competence as an important value voters look for in a political party. Similarly, the 2016 British Social Attitudes survey finds that 95% of the public agrees 'in a fair society every person should

have an equal opportunity to get ahead' (Elitist Britain, 2016; Milburn, 2014).

[32] This leaves out the broader question of who decides which jobs are most important, and whether the most important jobs actually end up being the highest paid. This is a classic debate, going back at least to Davis and Moore's (1945) 'Some principles of stratification' and Tumin's (1953) 'Critical analysis' response.

[33] Goldthorpe and Jackson (2007). In the US this is, of course, encapsulated in the belief in the 'American Dream'.

[34] Wilkinson and Pickett (2009).

[35] Piketty (2014).

[36] Dorling (2014).

[37] IMF (2017).

[38] The World Bank (2016).

[39] Jeremy Corbyn, for example, the leader of the UK Labour Party, has recently revived the issue of class inequality. As he noted in a speech at Unite in 2018: 'For 30 years, the media and the establishment tried to tell us the class doesn't matter anymore and that we should ditch any idea of representing and advancing the interests of the working-class' while 'a tiny minority at the top of society have become ever more wealthy' (Corbyn, 2018).

[40] Watson (2017).

[41] The key issue at stake here is the degree to which processes of elite recruitment enact forms of closure that restrict access to resources and opportunities to a limited circle of the eligible (Parkin, 1979; Tilly, 1999; Weeden, 2002).

[42] 'Council estates' are called public housing or colloquially 'projects' in the US.

[43] Lancaster University (nd). www.lancaster.ac.uk/alumni/news/archive/features/alan-milburn---from-council-estate-to-cabinet/

[44] Cabinet Office (2009).

[45] There are some studies that look at this issue in relation to single elite occupations such as law (Ashley, 2010; Ashley and Empson, 2013), and the bar (Freer, 2018), or a small subset of elite occupations such as banking and life sciences (Moore et al, 2016) or elite professional services (Rivera, 2012, 2015; Ashley and Empson, 2017). While the SMC and outlets like the Sutton Trust have published reports looking at exclusivity in different elite sectors, these have largely relied on imperfect proxies for class origin such as type of schooling, and have only focused on the very upper echelons of elite occupations. In contrast, the last meaningful discussion of mobility across a wide range of elite occupations was in Heath (1981).

[46] Some notable works include Stanworth and Giddens (1974); Heath (1981); Dahl (1989); and Domhoff (2002).

[47] Typically these 'big' social classes group together 30-100 individual occupations each.

[48] Bukodi et al (2015); Goldthorpe (2016).

[49] Breen and Jonsson (2005).

[50] ONS (2016).

[51] Based on the UK's National Statistics Socio-Economic Classification (NS-SEC) scheme.

[52] The words 'higher' and 'lower' are not our own value judgements but are taken from the NS-SEC classification.

[53] This was developed in consultation with John Goldthorpe and other sociologists, and is based in large part on the dominant class scheme across sociology, commonly called the 'EGP' for Erikson, Goldthorpe and Portocarero's foundational 1979 article.

[54] As Banks (2017, p 89) notes: 'a job in culture is not just a material opportunity, it also provides the chance to secure status and recognition, as well as to participate in the shared making of social and political life.' The perceived glamour of the culture and creative industries has also been extensively discussed, and critiqued, in recent sociological literature (Friedman et al, 2016; Oakley et al, 2017; O'Brien et al, 2017; Campbell et al, 2018).

[55] Such as Mills (1999); Pareto et al (2014); and Davis (2018).

[56] Heath (1981).

[57] We explain our definition of elite occupations in more detail in the Methodological appendix (see the section titled 'What is an "elite" occupation?', p. 265).

[58] Our analysis; this is in line with the finding in Bukodi et al (2015), based on birth cohort studies, of symmetrical odds ratios between roughly 4 and 8 for women and men in three birth cohorts (their Table 5), although for somewhat different class origin and destination configurations.

[59] These patterns are broadly similar to the US, as demonstrated by Chetty et al (2014a). For a comparison of different measures of social mobility across different countries, see Blanden (2013).

[60] Capital, for Bourdieu (1986, p 241), 'is accumulated labour (in its materialized form or its "incorporated", embodied form) which, when appropriated on a private, ie, exclusive, basis by agents or groups of agents, enables them to appropriate social energy in the form of reified or living labour.'

[61] Bourdieu (1977, p 94, 1984, pp 437, 466-8), and more generally, Jenkins (2002, pp 74-5).

[62] Bourdieu (1984, p 291).

[63] Lareau (2011).

[64] Devine (2004); Reay (2017).

[65] McCrory Calarco (2018); Reay (2017).

[66] Carter (2007); Reeves et al (2017); Ingram (2018).

[67] Reay et al (2009); Jack (2014, 2016); Armstrong and Hamilton (2015); Abrahams (2017).

[68] Bennett et al (2009); Lizardo and Skiles (2012); Friedman (2014); Jarness (2015).

[69] Bourdieu viewed such change through the prism of what he called the 'improvisations' of the habitus. Contrary to his critics, Bourdieu did

acknowledge that the dispositional architecture of the habitus was subject to change, according to both new experiences and also via conscious, intentional self-fashioning or pedagogic effort. Yet, he saw the nature of this change as gradual and fundamentally limited by the childhood dispositions that always act as the scaffolding of habitus (Bourdieu, 2000). In other words, primary dispositions are 'long-lasting; they tend to perpetuate, to reproduce themselves, *but they are not eternal*' (Bourdieu, 2005, p 45, emphasis added).

[70] Kuhn (2002, p 98).

[71] Of course, the 'glass ceiling' has itself been subject to substantial critique as well as theoretical refinement. There is a danger that the metaphor wrongly suggests gendered inequalities are apparent only in the upper reaches of women's career progression. Eagly and Carli (2007) propose the metaphor of the labyrinth to connote the different barriers, anticipated and unseen, which are apparent from the outset of women's careers.

[72] Collins (1993, 1997); Kanter (1993); Weyer (2007); Gorman and Kmec (2009); Wingfield (2009, 2010); Woodson (2015); Brown et al (2016).

[73] Ruderman et al (1996).

[74] Reeves et al (2017).

[75] The essential insight about intersectionality is that when we think about only one axis of discrimination or oppression at once, we miss the ways a given type of inequality works for all those who face it. Kimberlé Crenshaw's (1991) seminal article made this point with regard to the way efforts to stop domestic violence failed Black and immigrant women because they were premised on the experiences and needs of white women. A host of research has since shown how intersectional approaches strengthen our understanding of inequality (see Collins, 1986; Steinbugler et al, 2006; Choo and Ferree, 2010; Dubrow, 2015; Collins and Bilge, 2016; McMillan Cottom, 2016; Ferree, 2018).

[76] Lawler (1999, p 12).

[77] hooks, in Tokarczyk and Fay (1993); Hey (1997); Skeggs (1997); Hanley (2017); Bhopal (2018); Reay (2017); and for more in this genre, see Dews and Law (1995); and van Galen and van Dempsey (2009).

[78] Some studies have also reversed this focus, looking at the specific experiences of upwardly mobile men. This work has underlined the significant emotional, intellectual and interactive work men from working-class backgrounds must produce to combat the misalignment between masculine dispositions forged in the family and those needed for educational and career success (Reay, 2002; Ingram, 2011).

[79] Skeggs (1997).

[80] There is also a growing body of literature examining the social mobility of ethnic minorities. Work here has focused on how ethnic bonds can actually act to inhibit (or de-incentivise) social mobility (Srinivansan, 1995; Bourdieu, 1987b). Nicola Rollock, for example, describes how upwardly mobile Black Caribbean people are often forced to abandon embodied markers associated with their 'Blackness' in order to gain acceptance in the white-dominated middle class (Rollock, 2014). There is also an emerging

literature examining the specificity and complexity of socially *immobile* middle-class ethnic minority identities in Britain (Wallace, 2017; Meghji, 2017; Maylor and Williams, 2011).

[81] Rivera (2015).

[82] Ashley and Empson (2013); Ashley et al (2015).

[83] It is important to note that there are some exceptions to this from outside the UK, including Sweden (Hällsten, 2013), Norway (Hansen, 2001; Flemmen, 2009) and the US (Torche, 2011). In the US much earlier work also found something similar. For example, Jencks et al (1972, pp 318-50) estimate the direct effect of socio-economic origins on current pay for 30- to 54 year-old men in the US to be about 0.08; additionally Pfeffer's (1977) work showed a class effect on salary, for graduates of the same business school, in the thousands of dollars per year.

[84] In the UK, instead of a grade point average (GPA), students finishing their university education get a 'degree class' – a 'first class' is the best a student can do and can be thought of as having an A average in American terms.

[85] Rivera (2015); Ashley et al (2015); Ashley and Empson (2017).

[86] We include a detailed explanation of our research design in each case study firm in the Methodological appendix.

[87] Details of the degree of inherited economic and cultural capital among each interviewee are included in Tables A.1a-1d in the Methodological appendix.

[88] At the end of all 175 interviews we outlined our headline findings and asked respondents what they thought explained the class pay gap effect we identified.

[89] For example, Battle and Rotter (1963); Judge and Bono (2001).

[90] A striking illustration of this agenda comes from the UK All-Party Parliamentary Group (APPG) on Social Mobility's 7 *Key Truths About Social Mobility* (2012). Here individual character and resilience are presented as 'major factors' in determining social mobility (APPG, 2012, pp 4, 6). For a critique of the 'character' policy agenda more generally, see Allen and Bull (2018) and also Spohrer et al (2018).

Chapter One

[1] The reasons for this popularity are fairly straightforward. As we explained in the Introduction, there is a widespread belief – especially among politicians in the UK and US – that high rates of social mobility can offset the problems of high inequality; first, by breaking the link between a family's resources across generations and then second, by imbuing any inequality that remains with what John Goldthorpe calls 'meritocratic legitimation' (Breen and Goldthorpe, 2003; Goldthorpe and Jackson, 2007). This is the idea that inequality that results from a 'fair fight', in terms of equality of opportunity, absolves governments from their duty to intervene. Mobility, seen through this lens, is therefore the principal indicator of a fair and just society, a society where no individual is prevented from fulfilling his or her potential. However, as Wilkinson and Pickett (2018, p 177) show, global

trends actually show that social mobility tends to be lower in countries where income inequality is higher.

2 Time (2016).

3 Barbière (2016).

4 Taylor (2016).

5 For wide-ranging critiques of this vision of social mobility see, variously, Littler (2017) and Reay (2017).

6 Milburn (2015).

7 The LFS collected data from even more people over this period, but not all of them answered the class origin question.

8 Breen (2005); Bukodi et al (2015).

9 Generally, the US and the UK have among the lowest rates of social mobility (the strongest link between class origins and destinations) among Organisation for Economic Co-operation and Development (OECD) countries, while the Scandinavian countries have among the highest mobility. Countries with higher levels of inequality, and lower investment in their education system, tend to have lower mobility (Blanden, 2013; see also Corak, 2004; Breen and Jonsson, 2005; Beller and Hout, 2006; Chetty et al, 2014a).

10 All of these occupational groupings are part of our set of 'top jobs'; however, not everyone in our set of top jobs is represented among these occupations – there are a few occupations that don't fit with others, but that are too small on their own to be a category here. For example, there are only 75 clergy in our sample, and there are no other occupations among our top jobs that it would really make sense to group them with. There are also around 2,000 people who can be classed as belonging to NS-SEC 1 (the UK's top-class category; see Figure 0.1 in the Introduction), but don't have a specific occupation listed. All these people are included when we depict our top jobs as a whole, but missing when we depict these 19 individual fields. The numbers of respondents from each class–origin group are included in the Methodological appendix, where we also provide detailed specific occupations, see: www.classceiling.org/appendix.

11 Unlike many capitalist nations where a unified service class developed in the 19th century, in Britain only a state-sponsored professional class emerged at this time. When a managerial sector began to appear at the beginning of the 20th century, it assumed a subordinate position within the service class, lacking cultural capital and dependent on capitalist employers. This historical legacy continued to set these two sectors apart throughout the 20th century, with the professions enjoying greater job security and cultural capital (Savage et al, 1992, 2015b).

12 Miles and Savage (2012).

13 This number is different from the 6.5 reported in the Introduction because here we are comparing destinations in top jobs with *any* other destination, whereas in the Introduction the comparison is between professional-managerial destinations and working-class destinations.

14 Weeden and Grusky (2005); Weeden et al (2007).

[15] Weeden and Grusky (2005); Jonsson et al (2009).

[16] Breen and Jonsson (2005); Hout (2012); Reay (2017).

[17] Because of variations in what data is accessible for what quarters of the LFS, analyses up to here are based on 113,234 respondents, 18,647 of them in top jobs, for LFS respondents between July 2014 and July 2016. When discussing type of university attendance, N=73,901, 12,377 of them in top jobs, and we only have respondents from 2014 and 2015.

[18] The Russell Group consists of 24 UK research universities generally considered to be among the highest status and most selective; it is analogous in some ways to the US 'Ivy League'. Members include Oxford, Cambridge, the London School of Economics and the University of Edinburgh.

[19] Stanworth and Giddens (1974); Scott (1991).

[20] People with disabilities here includes anyone coded by the LFS as disabled based on their answers to questions about whether they had any long-term conditions that substantially limit their day-to-day activities or affect the kind or amount of work they might do.

[21] Americans would say 'people of color', but in the UK people most often say Black and minority ethnic groups, or some variation, sometimes abbreviated BME. We will vary the terms we use throughout.

[22] There are nine racial-ethnic categories that the LFS records for the whole UK; because there are so few people from either group in top jobs, and based on a fair degree of similarity in analyses performed with the two groups separately, we combine Pakistani and Bangladeshi into one category here.

[23] In other words, the proportion of people from these groups in top jobs is about 60% of what it would be if they were found in these jobs at the same rate as they are in the whole workforce.

[24] We are not able to address many other important axes of inequality; the LFS data we have includes very limited information on people in same-sex relationships, and no information on whether people identify as gay, lesbian, bisexual or transgender, or on other aspects of sexual orientation or gender identity and expression.

[25] These results echo recent work highlighting the under-representation of BME groups in senior decision-making roles across a range of UK top professions (Li and Heath, 2016; Bhopal, 2018; EHRC, 2016).

[26] We include a more wide-ranging discussion of the importance of intersectionality in Chapter Ten.

[27] As a reminder, about 33% of the UK has working-class origins, 35% are from intermediate class backgrounds and about 31% come from privileged families; this is equally true for adult women and men.

Chapter Two

[1] Grierson (2017).
[2] Female stars call on BBC to sort gender pay gap now, bbc.co.uk, 29 June (bbc.com/news/uk-40696402).
[3] BBC Media Centre (2018).
[4] BBC News (2018).
[5] Goodall (2017).
[6] Again it is worth noting that this question has been interrogated in a handful of other *national* contexts, including the US (see Jencks et al, 1972; Pfeffer, 1977; Torche, 2011), Sweden (Hällsten, 2013) and Norway (Hansen et al, 2001; Flemmen, 2009).
[7] It should be noted that, as this is data from a sample of the UK labour force, these are estimates of the averages. This means that many people in each group will make amounts in a wide range around these estimates. And 'estimates' means that we're not 100% sure these are exactly the right numbers, but we can be 95% sure that the real values in the population are within a certain range; in general in this book we only report pay gaps when the differences between the estimated means are statistically significant at the conventional p<0.05 level.
[8] In earlier work (Laurison and Friedman, 2016) we compared those from working-class backgrounds to those from just the very top of the class distribution – NS-SEC 1, or roughly the same group that is included in our 'top jobs' as destinations, but without the cultural workers.
[9] Falcon (nd); Roberts and Arunachalam (nd).
[10] For the US, see Jencks et al (1972), Pfeffer (1977) and Torche (2011); for Sweden, see Hällsten (2013); for Norway, see Flemmen (2009) and Hansen (2001); for Scandinavia see (Hansen, 2001; Flemmen, 2009; Hällsten, 2013), and France (Falcon, nd).
[11] The scale and patterning of the UK gender pay gap is explored more extensively in Olsen (2010) and Olsen et al (2018), and the UK ethnicity pay gap in Longhi et al (2013) and Longhi and Brynin (2017).
[12] Recall that the gender pay gap in top jobs is on average £10,000 a year and the class pay gap (between those from privileged and working-class origins) is £6,400. Working-class women, however, earn £18,900 less than privileged men.
[13] Woodhams et al (2015).
[14] Skeggs (1997); Hanley (2017); Reay (2017).
[15] This work has emphasised how working-class women are routinely pathologised as bad mothers (Walkerdine, 1990), excessively sexual (Skeggs, 1997; Tyler, 2008) or displaying the wrong amount and type of femininity (Lawler, 2005).
[16] Lawler (1999).
[17] Although less stark, similar patterns emerge when we look at the intersection of disability status, class origin and earnings: those with disabilities earn less in top jobs than those without in each class-origin group, and those from

working–class backgrounds earn less than those from privileged origins, among both those with and those without a disability.

[18] These differences in earnings persist even net of the controls we introduce in Chapter Three; see the Methodological appendix, Figure A.7.

[19] This is surprising in areas thought to be dominated by the privileged, such as journalism, where the SMC recently found that 43% of newspaper columnists were privately educated (Milburn, 2014). But this may be an artefact of a small sample size, or it may be that there is truly no class–origin pay gap.

[20] Friedman et al (2016).

Chapter Three

[1] Belam (2018).

[2] In British sociology Peter Saunders (1995, 2003) has repeatedly argued that social mobility is more strongly associated with educational attainment and IQ than class position. Breen and Goldthorpe (2003), however, discredited these findings.

[3] This was thoroughly debunked by Fischer and Voss (1996).

[4] Johnson (2013).

[5] For thoughtful discussions on this subject, see Plomin and Deary (2015) and Belsky et al (2018). It is also worth highlighting the work of educational psychologist Leon Feinstein (2003) here. Looking at long-term trends in child development, Feinstein showed that while there are important differences in performance on educational tests between children at age 2, these initial differences then shift strongly according to the children's class background as they get older. In other words, no matter their early performance, those from professional parents tended to more readily (than those from poorer backgrounds) increase their test scores in later stages of education. This suggests that even if genetic differences exist between children, they are then heavily magnified by highly classed patterns of socialisation, which are the key means through which children 'develop the ways of thinking rewarded and valued by the education system' (Atkinson, 2015, p 120).

[6] We would follow Flynn (2012), Atkinson (2015) and Wilkinson and Pickett (2018) in arguing that measures of intelligence like IQ are in many ways proxies for social endowments passed on through socialisation rather than through genetics, and therefore cannot be parsed from class origin.

[7] This allows us to check whether differences in these work-related attributes among people from different class origins explain the pay gap we see in top jobs. More specifically, regression models estimate how much a 'dependent variable' (in this case earnings) increases (or decreases) due, separately, to each potential factor included in that model by the researcher. If two variables tend to both be associated with increases in the dependent variable, and are also associated with each other, when we include them both we normally see a smaller independent effect of each one. This is commonly

referred to as 'controlling for' additional variables. See the Methodological appendix, Figure A.1, for a more complete explanation.

[8] Cabinet Office (2009).

[9] The average age of working-class people in top jobs is 47.9; for professional-origin people it is 43.7.

[10] Payne (2017).

[11] Immigrants in top jobs have higher earnings on average than other groups; among those born in the UK, those born in England tend to earn marginally more than the average. What is perhaps most striking, however, is how much larger the class pay gap is among people born in Northern Ireland, who earn close to £16,000 less than privileged-origin people born there with the same ethnicity, gender and age.

[12] See, for example, Budig and England (2001), Blau and Kahn (2007) and England (2010).

[13] See, for example, Jefferson (1817) and Mill (1859).

[14] Hout (1984).

[15] See the Methodological appendix, Figures A.5 and A.6, for details of this effect.

[16] Wakeling and Savage (2015).

[17] This is a group of universities, including Oxford and Cambridge, similar in many ways to the 'Ivy League' in the US.

[18] In somewhat similar results, Britton et al (2016) find that UK graduates from socially disadvantaged backgrounds experience considerably worse employment outcomes than their middle-class peers, including rates of employment and earnings, even after completing the same degrees from the same universities. We don't focus here on graduate degrees, but those who have them do earn more, and Wakeling and Laurison (2017) find increasing class stratification in the attainment of graduate degrees in the UK.

[19] Reeves et al (2017).

[20] See Domhoff (2002) for similar channels in the US.

[21] Crawford et al (2017) find a similar effect earlier in the UK education system. They find that regardless of initial differences in test performance between children from the most and least deprived backgrounds (at age 7), the gap between these two groups widens significantly as they get older.

[22] A list of all the exact control measures used here, and elsewhere in the regression analysis, is included in the Methodological appendix.

[23] Here, and throughout this chapter, when we say that a given set of factors 'explain' some portion of the pay gap, we are drawing on a technique called, opaquely, a Blinder-Oaxaca decomposition. This allows us to say precisely how much bigger or smaller the gap would be if working-class-origin people were similar to privileged-origin people on those measures. Using this approach, we can say that the class-origin pay gap would be 44% bigger if there were no demographic differences between class-origin groups, and 48% smaller if there were no education differences.

[24] Working an additional hour a week translates to an average increase of £964 a year in our top jobs, an extra year of job experience £312 more, and having had training in the last quarter is associated with £2,080 extra; those with significant past health issues earn about £1,720 less per year than those who have been luckier. None of these are necessarily causal, however; it could be (and we'll get to this) that people who have recently had job-related training are mostly doctors and lawyers, who earn more not particularly because of that training, but because of their profession itself.

[25] We present this data in the online appendix at www.classceiling.org/appendix .

[26] Friedman and Macmillan (2017).

[27] Most types of occupations can be found across many different industries. There are nine broad types of industry the UK government classifies: banking and finance; public administration; education and health; transport and communication; energy and water; distribution, hotels and restaurants; agriculture, forestry and fishing; manufacturing; construction; and other services. For all but two of these industries (energy and water and public sector) there is an inverse relationship between the percentage of those in top jobs who are from working-class backgrounds and average earnings: that is, generally industries that have higher concentrations of working-class people also pay less.

[28] This includes very specific occupational codes as well as their job's categorisation in the NS-SEC.

[29] As we explained in footnote 23 above, some variables we measure would make the gap bigger, and others would make it smaller. Therefore, the 'percentages explained' for each model we report above do not add up to the 47% of the gap our full model can explain. For more on the Blinder-Oaxaca decomposition model we used, see the online appendix.

[30] We cannot formally say, based on this analysis, that any of these factors *cause* the class-origin pay gap, as sociologists are very careful to only make causal claims when we can isolate causal processes, which is not generally possible with survey research.

Chapter Four

[1] Legally this is known as the principle of 'equal pay', and in the UK this is enshrined in law under the Equality Act 2010 in terms of gender, ethnicity and other protected characteristics (class background is notably absent).

[2] These are all pseudonyms for real organisations that agreed to allow us access on the condition that we not reveal their organisational identity.

[3] Revealing the precise number of staff would effectively de-anonymise the firm.

[4] However, women make up only 45% of senior staff (compared to 59% in the firm overall) and BME employees only 10% of leaders (compared to 20% in the firm overall).

[5]   To get a broader understanding of the independent television production sector that 6TV works so closely with, we conducted an identical follow-up survey with those working at indies. This was circulated to members of the Producers Alliance for Cinema and Television (PACT), the trade association representing the commercial interests of UK independent television companies. This achieved a response rate of 75% (1,373 responses).

[6]   Some of the staff in some of these departments are in positions that would not be classified as part of our set of 'elite occupations'. We thought it made sense to include the whole firm despite this, as nearly everyone working at 6TV is there because they wanted to, in some way, be part of the creation of television programmes.

[7]   Careful readers will note that an assistant is not an occupation that would belong to the set of 'elite occupations' we analysed in Chapters One to Three. As we shift from the national-level survey data to our case studies, there is also a shift from focusing on occupations as such, to examining whole firms. Assistants at 6TV are often aiming to be part of the higher echelons of the firm, so although they are not already in a 'top job', they are part of the pool from which more prestigious positions might be filled. More detailed discussion of the ways in which the qualitative and quantitative analyses fit together in this book can be found in the Methodological appendix.

[8]   This finding is particularly salient in the context of debates about the production of stigmatising and reductive representations of working-class communities in contemporary British television, particularly via the genre of so-called 'Poverty Porn' and its potential 'epistemological effects' (Jensen, 2014; De Benedictis et al, 2017). A particular concern in this literature is that if the composition of commissioners in this sector is skewed towards the privileged, this may be having an important (and adverse) effect on the type of media being produced – a suspicion substantiated by our findings here.

[9]   We cannot reveal exact numbers as this could reveal the identity of the firm.

[10] We were unable to collect original data on the parental occupations of TC employees. Because the firm were unwilling to collect new data we had to rely on existing data on 'socio-economic background' collected by the firm. In particular we used type of schooling as the best proxy available for class background.

[11] Dearden et al (2011); Green et al (2011, 2016).

[12] KPMG (2016).

[13] For example, a company with a financing problem may source the advice of TC to provide a detailed list of possible solutions, forecasts and outcomes. A one-off fee will be charged for this advice, and the receiving company may choose to follow or discard the advice, and may (or may not) choose to retain the advisory relationship in the medium or long term.

[14] This is particularly the case in audit and tax, where progression is contingent on passing a set of technical exams that have very low pass rates. Advisory, in contrast, does not generally require particular qualifications.

[15] Equally, like 6TV, many partners are recruited laterally from other firms, particularly the 'Big 4'.

[16] This somewhat confounds the qualitative analysis of Spence and Carter (2014) who argue that partners at 'Big 4' accountancy professions are more likely to come from socially mobile backgrounds.

[17] A handful of employees work outside the UK as the practice aims to expand globally.

[18] National comparisons for age, gender and ethnicity are derived from ARB (2017).

[19] This may, in part, be explained by London and large organisation effects, both of which are associated with professionals from more privileged backgrounds.

[20] Data here comes from the GBCS as sample size in the LFS is too small. See the Methodological appendix and Friedman et al (2016) for more details on this data.

[21] It should be noted that these average income figures are substantially higher than other estimates of acting earnings in the UK. This reflects both the more general GBCS sample skew towards the economically successful (Savage et al, 2013, 2015a) and the fact that the survey measured household rather than individual income. For this reason, we must be cautious about using this data to make inferences about actors in the UK population. However, we have no reason to suspect that the people who responded to the survey have different sets of relationships *among* their attributes than non-respondents – that is, it is theoretically possible, but far-fetched, to suggest that our results are driven by a disproportionately large response from working-class actors who are underpaid compared to colleagues from professional or managerial backgrounds.

[22] The class pay gap in British acting is explored in more detail in Friedman et al (2016).

Chapter Five

[1] The UK version of the American Emmy Awards.

[2] Dean (2005); Friedman et al (2016); Beswick (2018).

[3] Littler (2017).

[4] Mijs (2016) has shown powerfully that not only have the traits considered to be 'meritocratic' shifted constantly throughout history but the opportunities to demonstrate merit at any given time tend to be determined by non-meritocratic factors and any definition of merit must favour some groups while putting others at an advantage. In this way, he argues, the meritocratic ideal is an unfulfillable promise.

[5] Becker (1962); Coleman (1988); Groot and Oosterbeek (1994); Piketty (2014).

[6] Littler (2017).

[7] Barristers, for example, not only have to fund an expensive (£12,000-£18,000) postgraduate training course, but then have to undertake a final stage of training at one of the Inns of Court – called a 'pupillage' – where they shadow senior practitioners. During this, they are usually paid a very low salary (approximately £12,000 a year) and often rely on outside financial sources to survive (Freer, 2018).

[8] Of course financial support isn't the only determinant of what kinds of risks people take, or even the only class-linked thing that matters for risk-taking; growing up with a lot of financial security may facilitate a more risk-taking outlook/habitus, even without actual financial resources in the present moment, for example.

[9] Savage et al (2015a); Jarness and Friedman (2017).

[10] Hesmondhalgh and Baker (2011); Allen et al (2013); Banks et al (2013); Banks (2017).

[11] See Oakley and O'Brien (2015) for a summary.

[12] Watson (2017).

[13] Friedman and O'Brien (2017) and Saha (2017a, b) extend this to look at the restricted creative opportunities afforded to BME workers in the UK cultural industries more widely.

[14] Ahmed (2016).

[15] On television production projects runners are entry-level roles with largely basic admin responsibilities.

[16] A term reserved for big-budget light entertainment shows recorded live in expensive studio spaces.

[17] For a detailed discussion of cumulative advantage as a concept, see DiPrete and Eirich (2006).

[18] Although we can't see it directly in our data, the Paired Peers project (Bathmaker et al, 2018) shows this often has a spatial dimension as working-class graduates filter into jobs with less progression opportunities outside London as they can't afford to live in the capital.

[19] Occasionally they also talked about 'luck', but this seemed primarily like a way of deflecting privilege.

[20] As Sayer (2009, p 200) notes, discussions of class in Britain are 'often awkward, defensive and evasive, treating the question as if it were … about whether they deserve their class position or whether they consider themselves inferior or superior to others.'

[21] The contrast here with upwardly mobile actors and 6TV staff was palpable.

[22] Dorling (2014) wrote about this with regard to the bottom of the top 1% feeling 'poor' as they look up towards the top of the 1% (see also Savage et al, 2001; Hecht, 2017).

[23] Sherman (2017).

[24] This is not unusual. In the UK 60% of the population self-identify as working-class, even though only about a third of people work in jobs that sociologists would categorise as working-class. Moreover, 47% of those in professional and managerial jobs self-identify as working-class (Evans and Mellon, 2018). In other countries such as the US this pattern is

reversed – people often self-identify as middle-class even when they work in working-class jobs (Hout, 2008).

[25] Jerolmack and Khan (2014).

[26] This was also connected to the high proportion of overseas architects at Coopers from privileged backgrounds who also spoke about the importance of economic capital in emboldening them to take the risk of moving to London.

[27] This was not necessarily about economic survival as such; most recognised they could, technically, afford to live in London on a trainee salary. However, at the same time many explained that, without access to familial money for a deposit on a flat or house, the prospect of forging a career or bringing up a family in London was simply out of the question.

Chapter Six

[1] Turner (1960).

[2] Significantly, Turner (1960, p 856) did not necessarily advocate contest mobility over more sponsored forms, despite the former's subsequent association with notions of the 'American Dream'. He was notably ambivalent about the virtues of contest mobility, for example: 'the contest norm means that victory by a person of moderate intelligence accomplished through the use of common sense, craft, enterprise, daring, and successful risk-taking is more appreciated than victory by the most intelligent or the best educated' (Turner, 1960, p 856).

[3] Although Whitely et al (1991) later found similar effects in the US.

[4] 'Public' schools in the UK are the most elite and prestigious of private schools; the schools run by the state (what Americans call public schools) are 'state schools'.

[5] Heath (1981); Savage and Williams (2008).

[6] Lin (1999); Burt (2000); Watts (2004).

[7] Granovetter (1973).

[8] Lee (2011).

[9] This finding reflects an emerging sociological literature showing the importance of tastes in shaping networks (Edelman and Vaisey, 2014), particularly strong relationships (Lizardo, 2006) and early relationships (Lewis and Kaufman, 2018).

[10] Sociologists call this dynamic 'homophily' or the tendency of people to like others who are similar, in racial identity, gender and/or class background, to themselves (McPherson, 2001).

[11] While not a formal requirement, the partners we spoke expressed the sense that the success of the firm required, in large part, making shrewd decisions about who to promote to the partnership.

[12] DiMaggio and Mohr (1985); Gigone and Hastie (1993); Mouw (2003); Vaisey and Lizardo (2010); Griffiths and Lambert (2011); Lambert and Griffiths (2018).

[13] Bourdieu (1984); DiMaggio (1987); Bennett et al (2009).

[14] This idea is elaborated in Rivera (2012). See also more generally McPherson et al (2001).

[15] Rivera (2012, p 1018).

[16] In Tables A.1a–1d in the Methodological appendix it is striking that upwardly mobile partners at TC are both older on average and are much less likely to have had 'accelerated' trajectories than their privileged colleagues.

[17] A key issue for socially mobile staff was therefore what many termed 'visibility', the fact that their work was not given the same platform with senior gatekeepers. As one trainee, Jenny (working-class origins), explained: "Senior buy-in is essential. If you get stuck on the same project for a long time, you'll be less visible. You need to be visible across multiple managers. Everyone gets that."

[18] These findings are supported by the research of Casciaro and Lobo (2008) who find that, in understanding the decisions of staff to work with particular colleagues, liking someone is more powerful than thinking that they are competent.

[19] Lee (2011); Grugulis and Stoyanova (2012).

[20] In our follow-up survey of those working in independent television production ('indies'), we find that 28% of executives are from working-class or intermediate origins (versus 10% in commissioning at 6TV).

[21] This issue of uncertainty is the core concern that characterises the production of cultural goods, according to a sociological school of thought known as 'neo-institutional theory', and therefore most action within cultural organisations is devoted to trying to mitigate and address this concern (DiMaggio and Powell, 1983; Bielby and Bielby, 1994; Godard and Mears, 2009).

[22] This is similar to what Pfeffer and Leblebici (1973) found in manufacturing firms.

[23] Stevens (1999).

[24] It is also not uncommon for practising architects to spend some time teaching in architectural school, where they often attempt to cherry-pick the 'best' students to work in their own practices.

[25] The professional title 'architect' is protected. The Architects Registration Board (ARB) maintains a register of people who have successfully completed all three examined parts of an architectural education. In the UK, this usually takes a minimum of seven years – five at university and two in professional practice.

[26] Lareau (2015).

[27] Social mobility was certainly not a phrase that ever passed Gary's lips. Indeed, he felt architecture had come to function effectively as a meritocracy following its reforms in the 1980s. Nonetheless, he was proud of the outreach work carried out in local schools that sits very well in a contemporary social mobility discourse.

[28] De Graft-Johnson et al (2005); Britton et al (2016).

[29] Recent research reveals that such processes are prevalent across many elite labour markets. Here women are found to face a widespread 'commitment

penalty' based on perceptions that they are less committed to full-time, intensive careers (Budig and England, 2001; Correll et al, 2007). Significantly, this commitment penalty often offsets class-based advantages that men from similarly privileged backgrounds experience (Rivera and Tilcsik, 2016).

[30] It is also notable, for example, that there are no women from working–class backgrounds at Coopers, so there may well be a double disadvantage at work here.

Chapter Seven

[1] Future Leaders were very keen to promote social mobility and had therefore collected data on the schooling and parental occupational of all applicants prior to the interview.

[2] Ashcraft (2013).

[3] The classic work of Norbert Elias in *The civilizing process* (2000) is instructive in pointing towards the arbitrary nature of dominant behavioural codes, and how they have shifted constantly over time. As he notes: 'many of the rules of conduct and sentiment implanted in us as an integral part of our conscience, of our super-ego, are remnants of the power and status aspirations of established groups, and have no other function than that of reinforcing their power chances and status superiority' (2000, p 523).

[4] Boltanski and Chiapello (2007); de Keere (2014).

[5] Fleming (2009).

[6] Ingram and Allen (2018). See also Bourdieu (1990b, p 119), and more generally, as Lawler and Payne (2017, p 214) note: 'social magic works to eclipse the social relations that produce it in the first place, casting some persons as naturally bearing the distinctions that give them value'.

[7] See, variously, Ashley (2010); Ashley and Empson (2013, 2016); and Ashley et al (2015).

[8] This is echoed in Spence and Carter's (2014) research on the attributes valued by partners at 'Big 4' accountancy firms.

[9] The term Received Pronunciation (RP) – also known colloquially as the Queen's English or BBC English – refers to the standardised pronunciation and accent of the upper-middle classes in England, especially the South East. See Chapter Eight for more details.

[10] Rivera (2015, p 172).

[11] Lexmond and Reeves (2009, p 54) note, for example that 'character capabilities – application, self-regulation, and empathy – make a vital contribution to life chances'.

[12] Rivera (2015). Rivera, along with others like Ashley et al (Ashley et al, 2015; Ashley and Empson, 2017), draws largely on Bourdieu's concept of embodied cultural capital.

[13] We explore this and other, more emotional, dimensions of the experience of upward mobility in Chapter Nine.

[14] This was also a key theme among trainees from working-class backgrounds. Here there was a particular confusion with polish as a shadowy element of their work that carried significance far beyond the job description. As Yasmine noted: "You can't afford to just get your head down and do the work. I try to get noticed of course ... the social things make a big difference with people inside [TC] and outside. Everyone expects you to act in a certain way ... you can't let your guard down."

[15] For more on this, see Puwar (2004) on the 'somatic norm' in Britain's elite occupations.

[16] See Honey (1977) and Scott (1991). The City of London is an area in the centre of London where financial activities are concentrated, similar to Wall Street in New York.

[17] Mills (1999).

[18] Thrift and Williams (2014).

[19] Kynaston (2012).

[20] McDowell (1997).

[21] Ashley and Empson (2013).

[22] See also Anderson-Gough et al (1998) and Alvesson (2001) on the 'technical-behavioural spectrum'.

[23] Moore et al (2016, p 86).

[24] Pfeffer (1977).

[25] TC – like many firms – publish publicly appropriate 'dress codes' for its staff, and even give guidance on things like dinner etiquette.

[26] This uncertainty about what products will succeed in fields of cultural production is a strong theme in research on the production of culture, particularly among those employing a 'neo-institutional' theoretical approach, such as Escarpit and Pick (1971), Hirsch (1972, 2000), Coser et al (1982), Bielby and Bielby (1994), Faulkner and Anderson (1987), Gitlin (2000) and Peterson and Anand (2004).

[27] Such experiences had also affected the kinds of 'sorting' processes we explored in Chapter Five. For example, many 6TV staff from working-class backgrounds had not only moved into less creative areas for reasons of financial security, but also because the routes, or career tracks, were described as more transparent or less reliant on behavioural codes. Aika (working-class origins), for example, worked in law and compliance at 6TV. She explained that she had chosen to specialise in what she called the "more technical side of broadcasting" because the key competencies were clearer, and it seemed less "schmoozy" and "contacty" than the rest of television, which she said "[is] not something I find that easy."

[28] In other work, Rollock et al (2011), Rollock (2015) and Wallace (2016) have explored how the cultural capital possessed by Black communities in Britain are often misrepresented and invalidated in educational and occupational environments by dominant white gatekeepers based on their stereotyped classed assumptions of Blackness.

[29] This kind of reaction – leaning forward, which could be interpreted as simply listening attentively – when reserved for only certain people or members

of certain groups, can be interpreted as a form of 'microaggression'. This is a kind of interaction that is not on the face of it overtly discriminatory or hostile, but nonetheless lets the recipient know that they are different and don't quite belong (Basford et al, 2014).

[30] The sociologist Maliq Matthew, writing on Twitter, captured this process with the apt quote: 'Well-intentioned people often perpetuate systems of inequality with no malice, yet full effect.'

[31] Paul explained further that he purposefully recruits younger architects from universities that offer more technical degrees that include "learning about the nuts and bolts of construction", rather than more prestigious institutions that focus more on design and theory.

[32] In Chapter Ten we explain in more depth how our conception of technical capital draws and builds on Bourdieu's (2005) conception of the term, and how it helps us understand important variations in the class ceiling across different occupations and firms.

[33] We explore the heritability of technical capital in more depth in Chapter Ten.

[34] See Rivera (2016).

[35] In the UK regional accents are often considered markers of working-class backgrounds and are typically counterposed to a generalised upper-middle-class accent known as RP. We explore the importance of accent in more depth in Chapter Eight.

[36] The exclusionary role of an architectural university education, which lies beyond the scope of this book, is relevant in this respect. Stevens (1999) offers a compelling account of the role of education in perpetuating social advantage, and in particular, how architectural schools misrecognise privilege as talent.

[37] The notion of a 'design-led' practice is important in architecture. Architects we spoke to generally had strong opinions as to whether or not certain practices were 'design-led', although to outsider-researchers, definitional criteria did not always seem entirely clear. Being 'design-led' provides a professional cachet and was most frequently associated with boutique studios and practices whose work is innovative, cutting-edge and less commercially driven.

[38] This was the presumption of a number of Coopers staff who had previously worked at such firms. Even at Coopers, for example, there was a sense that those working on prestigious commercial developments required polished social skills.

[39] Women in architecture experience a gendered pay gap that begins earlier than in many other professions, and is also more profound (Britton et al, 2016).

[40] These include male dominance as studio masters and in architectural juries, restrictive and prejudicial stereotypes of masculine and feminine capabilities, and crass sexism on site and in practice (Graft-Johnson et al, 2005; Fowler and Wilson, 2012).

41 For example, the performance of technical capital at Coopers, as we explore further in Chapter Ten, was gendered in important ways.

42 See Cuff (1992) and Fowler and Wilson (2004).

43 Bourdieu calls these powerful taken-for-granted, unquestioned, rules or codes that operate in particular occupational or organisational domains as forms of 'doxa' (1990b).

Chapter Eight

1 A British slang word for 'house' or 'home'.

2 A common phrase in the UK, meaning a small group of people, normally at the top of organisations, privileged to receive confidential information or make important decisions.

3 The results of the Social Mobility Index 2017 indicated that when it comes to 'senior hires' firms rarely implement the same diversity monitoring as with more junior recruitment, and often outsource to headhunting firms that, even when charged with a brief to recruit diverse talent, investigate the current demographic make-up of a firm and target people who look and sound similar.

4 See Parkin (1979), Weber (1992), Tilly (1999) and Weeden (2002).

5 In turn, gatekeepers recognise these signals and provide individuals with access to top positions that are hoarded from outsiders (Bol and Weeden, 2015).

6 Mills (2000, pp 64-7, 278-83).

7 Mills (2000, p 141).

8 For historical reasons that will be opaque to Americans, the most elite private schools in the UK are called public schools, other private schools are called private schools, and schools that are free for all to attend and funded by the government are called state schools.

9 Stanworth and Giddens (1974); Scott (1991); Maxwell and Aggleton (2015, 2016).

10 Reeves et al (2017).

11 Reeves (2018).

12 Reeves (2018).

13 Lizardo (2006).

14 DiMaggio (1987, p 443), quoted in Lizardo 2006, p 781.

15 Bourdieu (1984). We elaborate further on the significance of the aesthetic disposition in Chapter Ten.

16 Bourdieu (1984).

17 Bourdieu (1977, p 94, 1984, p 437). More generally Bourdieu argues that prolonged immersion in a set of socio-economic conditions in early childhood leaves physical traces in and on the body: in accent, inflection, gesture, posture and so on.

18 This is echoed in the work of Koppman (2016) who similarly identifies a command of the aesthetic disposition as key to the organisational culture of US advertising, particularly the most creative functions.

[19] Coupland and Bishop (2007). See, more generally, http://accentism.org . See also Baratta (2018).

[20] The phrase 'Received Pronunciation' was coined in 1869 by the linguist A.J. Ellis, but it only became a widely used term used to describe the accent of the social elite after the phonetician, Daniel Jones, adopted it for the second edition of the *English pronouncing dictionary* (1924). The definition of 'received' conveys its original meaning of 'accepted' or 'approved' – as in 'received wisdom'. We can trace the origins of RP back to the public schools and universities of 19th-century Britain – indeed, Jones initially used the term 'public school pronunciation' to describe this emerging, socially exclusive accent.

[21] RP probably received its greatest impetus, however, when Lord Reith, the first General Manager of the BBC, adopted it in 1922 as a broadcasting standard – hence the origins of the term 'BBC English'. Reith believed Standard English, spoken with an RP accent, would be the most widely understood variety of English, both in the UK and overseas.

[22] Although RP is often seen as traversing geographical boundaries, it is particularly associated with upper-middle-class groups in the South of England.

[23] It is worth noting that Bourdieu saw this as constituting an important sub-set of cultural capital that he called 'linguistic capital', 'one's ability to demonstrate competence in the use of magisterial, scholarly and bourgeois language' (Bourdieu and Passeron, 1977, pp 108-10).

[24] Puwar (2004).

[25] Reaching partnership is generally considered the pinnacle of achievement in accountancy. Partners in large firms like TC are co-owners of the company and are entitled to a share of profits as 'equity partners'.

[26] Spence and Carter (2014, p 950). See also Anderson-Gough et al (1998) and Robson et al (2007).

[27] See Kornberger et al (2010) and Spence and Carter (2014, p 950).

[28] In her ethnography of Wall Street finance in the US, Ho (2009) finds a similar emphasis on firms privileging those from advantaged social and educational backgrounds, and placing them in client-facing 'front office' roles.

[29] Wajcman (1998).

[30] We would argue that this conception of gravitas, like polish and the other types of behavioural codes explored in Chapter Seven, can be closely traced back to a privileged upbringing.

[31] Ashley and Empson (2013); see also more generally Alvesson (2001).

[32] Brown and Hesketh (2004, p 157).

[33] It is worth noting that this conversion of capital is slightly different to 6TV. TC partners rely less on the aesthetic disposition, or intellectual discussion about culture, in client interactions and more on a sense of the appropriately legitimate cultural topics to discuss or events to entertain at.

[34] See Friedman et al (2015); Laurison and Friedman (2016).

[35] Gary brings to mind Richard Hoggart's autobiographical *The uses of literacy* (2009), the seminal text that charts the possibilities (and pains) of social ascent at a time of expanding opportunities.

[36] He eschewed the contemporary language of social mobility embraced more readily by professional service firms, feeling that architecture was now an established level-playing field.

[37] See Thaler and Sunstein (2009). The Behavioural Insights Team, also known as the Nudge Unit, is an organisation that was set up inside the Cabinet Office to apply nudge theory to UK government policy in many areas, including social mobility.

[38] Erickson's (1996) classic study finds a similar effect in terms of the use of popular culture as a bridging tool that aids cross-class interaction and coordination in workplaces.

Chapter Nine

[1] APPG on Social Mobility (2012).

[2] Sandberg (2015).

[3] Bourdieu (1977, p 495, 1990a).

[4] Bourdieu (1990b, p 65).

[5] Key here is Bourdieu's notion of habitus that we define and explore more fully in Chapter Ten.

[6] Bull and Allen (2018); Allen et al (2013).

[7] Sennett and Cobb (1972); Hanley (2017).

[8] Wilkinson and Pickett (2018) write extensively about this process, whereby those from working-class backgrounds perceive others' judgements of them, in the workplace and other settings, as a highly stressful form of 'social evaluative threat'.

[9] Bourdieu sees such seemingly irrational 'decisions' as entirely logical based on the structuring influence of primary habitus. For example, he notes: 'Through the systematic "choices" it makes, the habitus tends to protect itself from crises by providing itself with a milieu to which it as pre-adapted as possible' (1990b, p 61).

[10] This kind of sentiment was often expressed by those interviewed in Lamont (2000).

[11] This echoes a long sociological literature pointing to the way in which the labour process itself tends to produces meaningful dispositions for individuals (Burawoy, 1982).

[12] This illustrates what Bourdieu (2008, p 510) calls the 'contradictions of succession', where the upwardly mobile experience 'success as failure', as a betrayal of those family and friends who have nurtured and created them.

[13] There is currently a lively academic debate on this topic. While the work of Goldthorpe et al (1980), Marshall and Firth (1999) and more recently Chan (2017, 2017) find that the upwardly mobile often have psychologically smooth transitions, others such as Castagné et al (2016) and Hadjar and Samuel (2015) have deployed different data (qualitative and quantitative)

to counter that the experience can be more difficult, complex and even potentially psychologically destabilising.

[14] In earlier work, Friedman (2016) identifies important 'moments' of upward mobility where there is often an abrupt burst in people's upward trajectories, and that are often experienced as destabilising or emotionally troubling. In Bourdieusian terms, such moments of mobility initiate a 'hysteresis effect' where the habitus suddenly finds itself out of sync with the objective structures of the field it finds itself in. Bourdieu argues that in the 'lag' that follows, as the habitus attempts to adjust to the new field, individuals often have to battle with what Bourdieu and Passeron (1977) call the 'negative sanctions' of those in the field of origin and destination.

[15] Many writers, including Skeggs (1997) and Reed-Danahay (2004), have explored the ways in which upward mobility is often particularly problematic, emotionally, for women. As Lawler (1999) notes, the male upward mobility has long been legitimated through the heroic narratives of the working-class boy done good, and therefore the male habitus may be equipped with a more extensive (and socially acceptable) 'space of probably trajectories'.

[16] Some elements of Natalia's profile have been changed to ensure anonymity.

[17] See Friedman (2014, 2016).

[18] Drawing on the psychoanalytic notion of 'splitting of the self' (Fourny and Emery, 2000; Steinmetz, 2006), Bourdieu argued that such a dislocation of one's habitus (which he himself felt he had experienced) often produced a painfully fragmented self, a habitus clivé: 'The product of such a contradictory injunction is doomed to be ambivalent about himself ... to produce a habitus divided against itself, and doomed to a kind of double perception of self, to successive allegiances and multiple identities' (Bourdieu and Accardo, 1999, p 511).

[19] While we stop short of interpreting this as constituting a 'chameleon habitus' (Abrahams and Ingram, 2013), we do agree with these authors that being 'between two worlds' had endowed many interviewees with a unique capacity for reflexivity and self-analysis (Bourdieu, 2007).

[20] Hey (1997).

Chapter Ten

[1] Bourdieu (1998, p 81) defines habitus as a 'socialised, structured body, that has incorporated the immanent structures of a world or of a particular sector of that world – field – and which structures the perceptions of that world as well as the actions in that world.'

[2] Bourdieu's concept of capital is broader than the monetary notion of capital in economics: capital is a 'generalised' resource that can assume monetary and non-monetary as well as tangible and non-tangible forms (Anheier et al, 1985, p 862).

[3] Bourdieu (1999, p 46) defines field as: 'a socially structured space, a force-field – there are those who dominate and those who are dominated, there

are constant and permanent relations of inequality that operate within this space – that is also a field of struggle to transform or conserve this force-field. Every actor within this universe engages other actors in competition by wielding his relative strength, a strength that defines his position within the field and, consequently, also his strategies.'

[4] Bourdieu's understanding of social practice was famously summarised in the equation (habitus x capital) + field = practice (Bourdieu, 1984).

[5] This difference between these two capitals is best illustrated when Bourdieu notes (1990b, p 73) that 'what is "learned by body" is not something one has, like knowledge that can be brandished, but something that one is.'

[6] See, more generally, the argument in Goldthorpe (2005).

[7] In Goldthorpe's classic 1980 study (Goldthorpe et al, 1980), he looks at mobility in three time points (of father's job when male respondent was 14, of first job on entering the labour market, and of job at time of the survey), and this permitted considerable discussion of 'counter-mobility', the idea that the son of a relatively privileged father initially takes a lower-class job when entering the labour market, but then might have relatively high chances of moving back up to a higher position by the time of 'occupational maturity'. This kind of 'three-point' study has largely died out, however.

[8] This is normally presented as a 7x7 class transition matrix showing the exact percentages of respondents who have a particular origin and destination class. See the Methodological appendix for an example that based on our analysis of the Labour Force Survey (LFS) in this book (Table A.3).

[9] Most notably these tables can be modelled using log-linear modelling. See Erikson and Goldthorpe (1992).

[10] Via the National Statistics Socio-Economic Classification (NS-SEC). For more information on this see www.ons.gov.uk/methodology/ classificationsandstandards/otherclassifications/thenationalstatisticssocio economicclassificationnssecrebasedonsoc2010

[11] See Cabinet Office (2018).

[12] See Reeves et al (2017).

[13] Guttsman (1951); Kelsall (1955); Stanworth and Giddens (1974); Useem (1986); Useem and Karabel (1986); Dahl (1989); Mills (1999); Domhoff (2002).

[14] Of course the social backgrounds of those in elite occupations are not the only grounds on which closure may be enacted in processes of recruitment. However, where the skew in elites' class origins is especially striking, scholars have long considered this highly suggestive of the axes on which closure occurs.

[15] Parkin (1979); Tilly (1999); Weeden (2002).

[16] Scott (2008, p 35); Domhoff (2013); King and Crewe (2013).

[17] It is worth noting, however, that some have been trying to revive this tradition in recent years, including Burrows et al (2017), Korsnes et al (2017) and a recent Special Issue in *Socio-Economic Review* (Cousin et al, 2018).

[18] See Savage and Williams (2008, p 3). However, a number of Scandinavian researchers are an exception (Hjellbrekke et al, 2007; Flemmen, 2009; Ellersgaard et al, 2013; Hansen, 2014; Larsen et al, 2015; Ljunggren, 2017; Strømme and Hansen, 2017; Larsen and Ellersgaard, 2018). See also LeBaron's work on Central Bankers (usually in French, but not Lebaron, 2008).

[19] Rising inequality during the latter part of the 20th century – particularly at the top of the income distribution – has prompted a strong renewal of interest in elites across the social sciences (Savage, 2014). Yet analysis of the social composition of such groups has largely been absent from this new research agenda.

[20] We would reiterate here the point made in the Introduction that we do not regard the elite occupations as a 'governing elite' or 'power elite' in the sense in which Pareto, Mills and other elite theorists have used the term. Instead, following Heath (1981), we would conceptualise elite occupations as constituting a 'reservoir or recruiting market' from which the governing or power elite are drawn.

[21] For much of the 20th century sociologists of stratification and inequality believed class to be the most important division in society, with other axes of inequality 'epiphenomena of little overall significance' (Atkinson, 2015, p 81).

[22] Although we would reiterate our awareness that the 'glass ceiling' has been subject to substantial critique, and that there is a danger that the metaphor wrongly suggests gendered inequalities are apparent only in the upper reaches of women's career progression (Eagly and Carli, 2007).

[23] The possible citations here are numerous, but see Kanter (1993), Hagan and Kay (1995), Hull and Nelson (2000), Bell et al (2003), Gorman and Kmec (2009), Brynin and Güveli, 2012), Modood and Khattab (2015) and Bhopal (2018).

[24] The 'glass' metaphor, although not, of course, without its own limitations, has also been productive in pinpointing more specific dimensions of labour market inequality. For example, we draw extensively on Ashcraft's (2013) 'glass slipper' concept in conceptualising classed notions of 'fit' in Chapter Seven, while Williams' (1992) idea of a 'glass escalator' was useful in thinking through the fast-tracking impact of sponsorship in Chapter Six.

[25] The core insight here, of course, is that major axes of social division such as class, gender and race operate not as discrete and mutually exclusive forces, but build on each other and work together (Collins and Bilge, 2016).

[26] This is illustrated most clearly in heated debates between Goldthorpe, feminists and others in the 1970s and 1980s over the 'unit of analysis' in mobility research (Acker, 1973; Goldthorpe, 1983; Heath and Britten, 1984).

[27] Bourdieu's work has been criticised extensively by feminists (Lovell, 2000; Adkins and Skeggs, 2005) and scholars of race and ethnicity (for a good overview, see Wallace, 2016).

[28] Moore and Jones (2001).

[29] The status attainment tradition in the US used multiple indicators of origin and destination, and Jencks et al's seminal 1972 book showed that class origin was associated with earnings, even after taking into account occupational destination, as did Pfeffer's (1977) work on business school graduates. More recently, Torche (2011) identified a similar effect in the US, and see Hällsten (2013) in Sweden and Flemmen (2009) and Hansen (2001) for Norway.

[30] Thus Goldthorpe et al (1980) note how work–life mobility (intra-generational, that is, mobility within one's own lifetime) can complicate analyses of 'inter-generational mobility', and he repeated this call in his comparative work (Erikson and Goldthorpe, 1992).

[31] Goldthorpe, for example, dealt with this problem pragmatically. He either focused on those who had reached the age of 35, which he saw as the age of 'occupational maturity' (in that he saw it as relatively unusual to change class after this age), or by making sure he was comparing individuals of similar ages (see, for example, Bukodi et al, 2015). Nonetheless, the general point remains that mobility encompasses several dimensions – of individuals and parents – and cannot easily be encapsulated into a standard contingency table.

[32] Blanden et al (2004, 2007).

[33] Bukodi et al (2015).

[34] The micro-class approach calls for a Durkheimian shift away from 'big-class' classifications and towards the analysis of smaller clusters of occupations on the basis of their place within the technical division of labour, since these are seen to be much closer to our everyday experience of cultural identity (Weeden and Grusky, 2005).

[35] Chetty et al (2014b, 2017).

[36] Chetty's Equality of Opportunity project has longitudinal data, but in most publications so far, if this is analysed at all it's usually only to show that a single time-point works reasonably well as a proxy for longer trajectories.

[37] Although see Bourdieu (1987a, 1996) for partial exceptions.

[38] See Goldthorpe (2005).

[39] King (2000); Goldthorpe (2007).

[40] Bourdieu (1984, p 101).

[41] Bourdieu and Wacquant (1992, p 133).

[42] Bourdieu (1984, p 114).

[43] Atkinson (2015, p 105).

[44] Bourdieu (2000, p 161); Wacquant (2016).

[45] Wacquant (2013, p 6).

[46] In other words, primary dispositions are 'long-lasting; they tend to perpetuate, to reproduce themselves, *but they are not eternal*' (Bourdieu, 2005, p 45, emphasis added).

[47] It is also important to recognise that whereas conventional social mobility research focuses on movement within a fixed and stable structure, Bourdieu takes the radical step of recognising that the structure itself is historically dynamic. People are mobile within a social world that is also changing.

Bourdieu is therefore fundamentally a historically oriented sociologist who seeks to broaden our understanding of mobility to look not only at individuals moving within some kind of fixed structure, but who also wants to show how the dynamic historical re-working of structures need to be studied too (Savage and Friedman, 2017). It is also worth noting that while dynamism – in particular in response to the notion of careers – is often advocated in the literature, it is not necessarily applied in empirical research. See, for example, Stewart et al (1980, pp 271-2); Savage et al (1992, p 222); Bertaux and Thompson (1997); Blackburn and Prandy (1997); Savage (1997, 2000); Miles and Savage (2004); Abbott (2001, 2006). Even Erik Wright acknowledges this in multiple places: Wright (1978, 92-3, 1985, 185-6, 1989, 329-31, 2005, 17-18, Wright and Shin, 1988).

[48] We should again note here that differences in earnings by class origin have also been highlighted in a number of other national contexts, including Sweden (Hällsten, 2013), Norway (Hansen, 2001; Flemmen, 2009) and the US (Torche, 2011).

[49] Lareau (2015).

[50] See, famously, Abbott and Hrycak (1990) and Stovel et al (1996).

[51] Halpin and Chan (1998) and Toft (2018) have studied class mobility with sequence analysis.

[52] Notably for this book Bühlmann (2010); Bison (2011); Bukodi et al (2015, 2016).

[53] Moreover, work that has used sequence analysis to illustrate complex patterns of intra-generational mobility has not effectively cross-fertilised with research on inter-generational social mobility. For example, the considerable work of economists (for example, Jenkins, 2011) on income mobility using longitudinal data demonstrates considerable short-range mobility on an annual basis, and the work of geographers (for example, Fielding, 1992, 1995) has long highlighted the role of spatial mobility in understanding processes of intra-generational mobility. However, these advances have largely not been incorporated into the research agendas of sociologists of mobility. It is therefore telling that Abbott's sequencing methods – while widely and often respectfully referred to – have been taken up more commonly in demography in the analysis of family transitions and sequencing rather than in the study of social mobility.

[54] Bourdieu (1984).

[55] In fact, Bourdieu rarely used the term 'class'. Instead he wrote about 'probable' class groups based on clusters of individuals located in neighbouring positions in social space and socialised with similar 'conditions of existence' (meaning stocks of capital and distance from material necessity) (1990b, p 60, 1991, p 237).

[56] For example, while the Great British Class Survey was designed to capture Bourdieusian capitals, it did not ask any questions about a person's aesthetic orientation (Savage et al, 2013, 2015a). For more on this see Friedman et al (2015).

[57] For example, it allows us to establish broad, generalisable and robust patterns about the linger of origin, but at the same time relies on proxies for capital such as occupation or partial indicators such as income.

[58] Following Koppman (2015), we probed interviewees' aesthetic socialisation via three sets of questions: (1) degree of *art ownership* in one's family and degree of participation in *art activities* in childhood; (2) degree of formal *art education* in school or at university; and (3) degree of *art encouragement* and *art exposure*.

[59] For example, actor Faith's father was a priest and her mother a social worker. However, both were immigrants to the UK and she explained in her interview that although her father had done some work at a local church, he had worked in a local supermarket when she was growing up and her mother had looked after her and her siblings. Her parents, she explains, were therefore fairly poor and, with no experience of the UK education system, had fairly low levels of cultural capital. Similarly, Coopers' architectural assistant Amir told us that his father had been unemployed for a long time during his childhood, but before emigrating he had been an engineer in Pakistan, and had arranged for Amir to get work experience on a building development with his brother in Pakistan.

[60] See Silva and Wright (2009).

[61] Bottero (2010, pp 14–15) highlights that individuals' dispositions are always adjusted in relation to 'calls to order' from the group they find themselves in. Here the 'inter-subjective' importance of others is paramount – where we must take into account and act in accord with the expectations of the people (we) encounter in social contexts.

[62] This is Bourdieu's own unique attempt to overcome the familiar social scientific dichotomy between the individual and society, structure and agency. Writing in 1994, in *Practical reason*, he discloses that he sought to create a relational philosophy of science devoted to the objective relations 'which one cannot show, but which must be captured, constructed and validated though scientific work', and a dispositional philosophy of action that notes the relations between 'the potentialities inscribed in the body of agents and in the structure of the situations where they act' (Bourdieu, 1998, p vii).

[63] Bourdieu characterises the field of power as 'a field of power struggles among the holders of different forms of power, a gaming space in which those agents and institutions possessing enough specific capital (economic or cultural capital in particular) to be able to occupy the dominant positions within their respective fields confront each other using strategies aimed at preserving or transforming these relations of power' (Bourdieu, 1996, p 264).

[64] Bourdieu (1984, pp 102–4).

[65] Bourdieu (1993).

[66] The issue of capital conversion has been under-studied in Bourdieusian scholarship. As Bourdieu (1977) noted, those with the same levels of capital do not always derive the same profits. Indeed, he compared this to a card

game whereby a player is dealt a hand but his ability to succeed depends on his gamesmanship or, in economistic terms, his 'investment strategies'.

[67] Bourdieu (1986).

[68] Bourdieu (1986, p 17).

[69] For an excellent Bourdieusian overview of class and embodiment, see Vandebroeck (2014, 2016).

[70] Bourdieu (1986, p 18). This misrecognition is in many ways premised on the basis that the physical body is widely perceived to be the most tangible evidence of a person's 'essence', their innateness, and therefore rooted in 'nature' rather than socially constructed 'nurture'.

[71] Here we would echo Charlesworth's (1999, p 65) proposition that 'class is a phenomenon of the flesh'.

[72] Bourdieu (1977, p 195) elaborated: 'If all societies ... set such store on the seemingly most insignificant details of dress, bearing, physical and verbal manners, the reason is that, treating the body as a memory, they entrust to it in abbreviated and practical, ie, mnemonic, form the fundamental principles of the arbitrary content of culture. The principles embodied in this way are placed beyond the grasp of consciousness, and hence cannot be touched by voluntary, deliberate transformation, cannot even be made explicit; nothing seems more ineffable, more incommunicable, more inimitable, and therefore more precious, than the values given body, made body by the transubstantiation achieved by the hidden persuasion of an implicit pedagogy, capable of instilling a whole cosmology, an ethic, a metaphysic, a political philosophy, through injunctions as insignificant as "stand up straight" or "don't hold your knife in your left hand".'

[73] Bourdieu (1977, p 94, 1984, pp 437, 466-8) and more generally, see Jenkins (2002, pp 74-5).

[74] Atkinson (2015, pp 62, 135).

[75] Kant (1987, p 234).

[76] Bourdieu (1984, p 3).

[77] Bourdieu (1984, p 40) and see more generally, Lizardo and Skiles (2012) on the aesthetic disposition.

[78] Bourdieu (1984, p 291).

[79] Bourdieu referred to this as the way in which forms of capital could be transubstantiated into symbolic capital.

[80] Bourdieu (1984, p 418) sees a key characteristic of the habitus as its ability to transfer dispositions from one domain of practice to another through a general class ethos (see also Crossley, 2001, p 125; Vandebroeck, 2016, p 50).

[81] Bourdieu (1990b, pp 58-9) explains this as the process whereby habitus tends to be 'objectively harmonised' with those from similar backgrounds and 'mutually adjusted without direct interaction or explicit coordination.'

[82] These codes can also be seen in Puwar's (2004) formulation of 'somatic norms'.

[83] Organisations like Turner Clarke are thus effectively recruiting partners on the basis that they believe (at least some) clients will pay a premium for a

particular aesthetic experience (Brown and Hesketh, 2004, p 157; Ashley, 2010, p 723).

[84] As Bourdieu (1984, p 331) notes: 'as self-made men, [the upwardly mobile] cannot have the familiar relation to culture which authorizes the liberties an audacities of those who are linked to it by birth, that is, by nature and essence.'

[85] Bourdieu (1977, pp 93-4). Also relevant more generally is Goffman (1951, p 301) on the limits of 'bluff' among the class parvenu. Also worth reading is Rollock et al (2011) and Wallace (2017) on 'black cultural capital' and, more broadly, work such as Karyn Lacy's (2004, 2007) and Mary Pattillo's (2013) on the experiences of the Black middle class.

[86] See Bennett et al (2009) as an exemplar.

[87] Friedman (2011); Jarness (2015).

[88] This has long been highlighted in the literature. For example, some 30 years ago Lamont and Lareau (1988, p 163) argued that scholars needed to pay greater attention to 'micro-level interactions in which individuals activate their cultural capital to ... attain desired social results. For some rare exceptions see Koppman (2015, 2016); Levy et al (2018); Reeves and de Vries (2018).

[89] Zimdars et al (2009); Sullivan (2001); Hout (2012); Igarashi and Saito (2014); Wakeling and Savage, 2015).

[90] Ashley et al (2015); Rivera (2015); Koppman (2016); Ingram and Allen (2018).

[91] A prominent exception here is the innovative work of Reeves and de Vries (2018) who show that people who consume more culture earn more in professional occupations. However, as outlined, although these authors invoke the concept of embodied cultural capital, they do not have the data to examine the economic returns to either a privileged bodily hexis or the aesthetic disposition.

[92] 'The capital of the DIYer' (Bourdieu, 2005, pp 29, 78-81). We would stress that our focus here is on technical capital amassed in occupational settings and not technical competencies and knowledge amassed through the education system that we would categorise as forms of 'institutionalised cultural capital'. However, it is, of course, hard to fully distinguish in our data between forms of expertise accumulated 'on the job' from that which is amassed via education.

[93] For a rare application, see Emmison and Frow (1998) and Archer et al (2015).

[94] Bourdieu (2005, p 29).

[95] Bourdieu (2005, p 127).

[96] As Vanderbroeck (2016, p 48) argues, the socially mobile are likely to experience the most acute 'lag' where the 'dispositions that organize a given area of practice are 1) linked to the earliest social experiences 2) the product of a largely practical inculcation (rather than explicit theoretical instruction) and 3) evade subsequent restructuration by a systematic, comprehensive pedagogy of the type provided by the education system' or, we might add

in the case of technical capital, an explicit pedagogy provided by technical qualification and/or training.'

[97] Bourdieu (2005, pp 78-81).

[98] Although it is important to remember, as stressed in Chapter Nine, that the ability and desire to engage with the labour market, and therefore amass technical capital, may still be 'classed' in important ways.

[99] See Bourdieu (2005, p 29) and the argument in Savage (2010, pp 67-93).

[100] Following Bennett et al (2009) we would argue that in many ways technical capital is analogous to Becker's notion of human capital, in terms of an emphasis on capacities and skills that can be accumulated over the lifecourse.

[101] Savage (2010).

[102] Edgerton (2005, Figure 4.1, and p 148); see also Harrison (2009).

[103] Savage (2010, p 84).

[104] O'Brien (2016).

[105] Halford and Savage (2010).

[106] Nichols and Savage (2017).

[107] Notably this dichotomy does not match our data perfectly – architecture is particularly closed to the working class in terms of access, for example, while the socially mobile appear to do particularly well in journalism. Yet there is clearly some meaningful patterning to the way class origin plays out across our set of elite occupations.

[108] Of course this is important, but while we see the broad degree or level of technical expertise necessary to do a particular job as discernible, it is very hard for research of this kind to fully untangle to what extent one job truly *requires* more or less technical expertise than another.

[109] Instead we see the emphasis on technical capital as a sensibility that may be found across a wide variety of top occupations and firms, as well as more fine-grained departments or even teams within firms.

[110] Savage (2010).

[111] Bourdieu and Wacquant (1992, pp xiii-xiv).

[112] For more on this, see Prieur and Savage (2014) and Friedman et al (2015).

[113] Of course more work is needed here. In particular we would stress the importance of probing some of the issues we have only suggestively explored, especially the potential convertibility and transmissibility of technical versus embodied cultural capital. For example, to what extent does technical capital really challenge the value of embodied cultural capital in top occupations, and to what extent is it relegated or eclipsed as one moves towards the top of a profession, as demonstrated by Turner Clarke? Similarly, is the acquisition and accumulation of technical capital always more transparent and 'meritocratic', and in what ways can it be passed on inter-generationally? And finally, why is the successful activation of technical capital so contingent on gender?

Chapter Eleven

1 Littler (2017).

2 Weber (1992).

3 Simpson and Kumra (2016).

4 For an overview, see McPherson et al (2001).

5 Lewis and Kaufman (2018) find similar effects in a recent wide-ranging study of tie formation.

6 See, for example, Mills (2000 [1956]) and Rivera (2015).

7 DiMaggio and Mohr (1985); Gigone and Hastie (1993); Mouw (2003); Lambert and Griffiths (2010); Vaisey and Lizardo (2010).

8 DiMaggio and Powell (1983); Bielby and Bielby (1994); Godart and Mears (2009).

9 APPG on Social Mobility (2012).

10 Cohen (2014).

11 We should note that this is intended as a heuristic illustration rather than a causal diagram, and, of course, any number of additional arrows could be drawn between individual mechanisms.

12 See Friedman (2016). This, of course, has implications in terms of the relationship between mobility and inequality, suggesting that high inequality increases the distances one has to travel within social space to be upwardly mobile, and therefore increases the likelihood that a mobility experience will be difficult.

13 Fischer and Voss (1996); Atkinson (2015).

14 Skeggs (1997); Lareau (2011).

15 The highest 'big class' in the UK's official occupational class scheme, and the basis (along with jobs in select cultural and creative industries) of our set of 'elite occupations' analysed throughout the book.

16 In his keynote address to the 2014 Spring RC 28 Meeting in Budapest.

17 Abrahams (2017).

18 Babcock et al (2003); Babcock and Laschever (2009).

19 This is a derogatory term normally aimed at young working-class people.

20 See Jarness and Friedman (2017).

21 For example, we see some evidence of a 'class floor' effect when we compare people with privileged origins to others in class destinations outside our set of elite occupations. We've found that people from *higher* managerial and professional occupations (the upper half of the group we call 'professional-managerial origin' in this book, NS-SEC 1) earn about 16% more in lower managerial and professional occupations (teachers, nurses, etc, NS-SEC 2) than people from working-class backgrounds, and about 4.5% more in intermediate destinations (NS-SEC 3-5) than working-class-origin people (unpublished analyses).

Epilogue

[1] For more information about the Bridge Group, see www.thebridgegroup. org.uk

[2] While the focus here is the UK policy terrain, we believe that many of these recommendations will be relevant in the US and beyond.

[3] Bridge Group et al (2016).

[4] KPMG (2016).

[5] We should note, however, that we are somewhat sceptical of the aims of initiatives like the Employers Index, which turn the goal of improving social mobility into an individualised competition rather than a social problem requiring collective responsibility and collaboration between employers.

[6] Social Mobility Foundation (2018).

[7] See https://ise.org.uk/page/ISESurveys

[8] See www.gov.uk/government/publications/socio-economic-background/ socio-economic-background-seb

[9] Each of these organisations has done so with the specific advice and support from the Bridge Group; see BBC (2017).

[10] See thebridgegroup.co.uk/research-and-Policy/

[11] Television provides some good examples. For example, at the Channel 4 2018 Diversity Conference, leading creative figures at Channel 4, Sky, the BBC and ITV were brought together on a panel to respond to data showing a class ceiling in television, to explain how they planned to tackle it, and particularly the role of behavioural codes in the industry. Similarly, at the 2018 Edinburgh International Television Festival, an event entitled 'Too Posh to Produce' asked an audience of several hundred television professionals to dissect the meaning of 'talent' within the sector.

[12] For example, see an example of a Civil Service blog in the link below, which prefaced a series of events across departments considering issues of diversity and inclusion with respect to socio-economic background: https://civilservice.blog.gov.uk/2016/09/12/defining-our-progress-on-social-mobility

[13] See https://ise.org.uk/page/ISESurveys

[14] This is a levy on UK employers to fund new apprenticeships, introduced in April 2017. It is paid on annual pay bills that exceed £3 million, thus less than 2% of UK employers pay it.

[15] See https://fson.wordpress.com

[16] See https://1forequality.com/take-action

Methodological appendix

[1] Mills (2013, 2015).

[2] We should add that including new questions on a survey the size of the LFS costs millions of pounds and is a long and political process. We therefore want to register our debt to the years of fairly heroic lobbying conducted by both the Social Mobility Commission (SMC) and mobility researchers

like John Goldthorpe, which paved the way for the release of this new data and subsequently, the analysis presented in this book.

[3] The ESRC is the largest funder of research on economic and social issues in the UK.

[4] We used this as the pseudonym for a parallel programme in television.

[5] This is far above the 53% average response rate for organisational case studies found in Baruch (1999).

[6] That Gary did not see progression in architecture as structured by social class is somewhat surprising considering our LFS data suggests few architects come from working-class backgrounds (see Figure 1.3). We offer two further possible explanations for this. First, in contrast with our other professions, there is no conclusive evidence of a class ceiling in terms of pay in architecture. And second, the issue of pay progression is somewhat moot in architecture. It is one of the least well-paid professions, and architects have traditionally been encouraged during their lengthy education to value design quality over personal financial reward, to consider architecture a vocation rather than a profession (Fowler and Wilson, 2004).

[7] Fieldwork was led by Sam who carried out the vast majority of interviews (110 out of 175 interviews). Ian McDonald, our research assistant, did the majority of interviews at Coopers (30 out of 36), Dr Dave O'Brien carried out 20 of the interviews with actors, and Dr Kenton Lewis carried out 12 of the interviews at Turner Clarke.

[8] Our questions here follow the methodological design outlined by Koppman (2015). We explain more about our approach in Chapter Ten.

[9] In Tables A.1a–1d we draw on these narratives to make a subjective judgement about each interviewee's trajectory (accelerated, steady, impeded).

[10] Blanden et al (2004); Bukodi et al (2015).

[11] Cabinet Office, Civil Service and the Rt Hon Ben Gummer (2016).

[12] Due to changes in the way the Office for National Statistics (ONS) made data available to researchers, we were not able to match respondents from 2015 with their responses in 2016. This led to including members of one wave of the survey (those whose first quarter participating was July 2015) twice. The numbers we provide throughout do not count the July 2015 respondents who were surveyed for the final time in July 2016, although we do include these responses in our analyses, to account for this we gave people from this survey cohort a weight that was half what it would otherwise be.

[13] Hout (1984).

[14] See Laurison and Friedman (2016, pp 680-1).

[15] Rose (nd).

[16] In sociology, elites are normally identified in two ways – through position and/or reputation. Mosca (2011 [1939]) famously argued that elites are best understood as 'ruling minorities', empowered through relations of authority and usually occupying formal top positions in organisational hierarchies. This was the theoretical logic informing Mills's understanding of the elite as

those occupying 'pivotal positions ... in command of the major hierarchies and organizations of modern society' (Mills, 2000 [1956], p 4). Others have argued that elites are more usefully identified in reputational terms as those thought to be powerful or important by those 'in the know' (Hunter, 1969) or as individuals occupying some form of centrality in high-status networks (Larsen et al, 2015).

[17] Even more technical details are available in the online appendix at www.classceiling.org/appendix

[18] Goldthorpe et al (1980).

[19] Here we follow the approach taken by Li and Health (2016).

[20] We present full regression tables as well as details about the particular variables we use from the LFS in the online appendix at www.classceiling.org/appendix

[21] Laurison and Friedman (2016).

[22] Friedman and Laurison (2017).

[23] This technique was developed by a woman sociologist, Evelyn Kitagawa, in 1955, but in what looks like a perfect example of the way in which even what ought to be transparent 'merit' sometimes isn't credited when performed by women, the method is named after the two men who published on it 20 years later (Kitagawa, 1955; Blinder, 1973; Jann, 2008).

[24] See Laurison and Friedman (2016).

[25] Accountancy and architecture fall within the top class of the NS-SEC, and acting and television class 2. However, acting, television (and to a lesser extent architecture) arguably carry an additional dimension of glamour, as 'creative' and public-facing professions within the 'cool' culture and creative industries (CCIs).

[26] Plunkett (2014); Denham (2015).

[27] Jencks and et al (1972); Pfeffer (1977).

[28] For example, it may have been more consistent to find people in as many of these 'top jobs' as possible to interview about their career histories. But, following Pfeffer (1977), we hypothesised that a lot of the important dynamics we wanted to see may be happening within firms, and that different fields – as we argue in Chapter Ten – would have different 'doxa' – norms, expectations, etc. So for our case studies we instead looked at people in firms (or the acting field).

[29] However, this does not compromise the fundamental argument we make in Chapter 4, that there is class-origin sorting within the firms, as the majority of people in each of the departments we look at (except, possibly, HR, finance and estates at 6TV, and support at TC) *are* in our top jobs, and the top levels of each firm are composed entirely of people in elite occupations. We also know that many of the people not in top jobs at our firms, especially at 6TV, are working *towards* being in top jobs, or would have liked to have been, and settled for a less-prestigious role in a company working on something they're passionate about.

[30] Jerolmack and Khan (2014).

[31] Jarness and Friedman (2017).

References

Abbott, A. (2001) *Time matters: On theory and method*, Chicago and London: University of Chicago Press.

Abbott, A. (2006) 'Mobility: What? When? How?', in S. Morgan, D. Grusky and G. Fields (eds) *Mobility and inequality: Frontiers of research in sociology and economics,* Stanford, CA: Stanford University Press, 137-61.

Abbott, A. and Hrycak, A. (1990) 'Measuring resemblance in sequence data: An optimal matching analysis of musicians' careers', *American Journal of Sociology*, 96(1), 144–85.

Abrahams, J. (2017) 'Honourable mobility or shameless entitlement? Habitus and graduate employment', *British Journal of Sociology of Education*, 38(5), 625-40 (https://doi.org/10.10 80/01425692.2015.1131145).

Abrahams, J. and Ingram, N. (2013) 'The chameleon habitus: Exploring local students' negotiations of multiple fields', *Sociological Research Online*, 18(4), 1-14 (https://doi. org/10.5153/sro.3189).

Acker, J. (1973) 'Women and social stratification: A case of intellectual sexism', *American Journal of Sociology*, 78(4), 936-45.

Adkins, L. and Skeggs, B. (2005) *Feminism after Bourdieu*, Chichester: Wiley.

Ahmed, R. (2016) 'Typecast as a terrorist', The Long Read, *The Guardian*, 15 September (www.theguardian.com/world/2016/ sep/15/riz-ahmed-typecast-as-a-terrorist).

Allen, K., Quinn, J., Hollingworth, S. and Rose, A. (2013) 'Becoming employable students and "ideal" creative workers: Exclusion and inequality in higher education work placements', *British Journal of Sociology of Education*, 34(3), 431-52 (https:// doi.org/10.1080/01425692.2012.714249).

Alvesson, M. (2001) 'Knowledge work: Ambiguity, image and identity', *Human Relations*, 54(7), 863–86 (https://doi.org/10.1177/0018726701547004).

Anderson-Gough, F., Robson, K. and Grey, C. (eds) (1998) *Making up accountants: The organizational and professional socialization of trainee chartered accountants*, Aldershot and Brookfield, VT: Ashgate Publishing Limited.

Anheier, H.K., Gerhards, J. and Romo, F.P. (1995) 'Forms of capital and social structure in cultural fields: Examining Bourdieu's social topography', *American Journal of Sociology*, 100(4), 859–903.

APPG (All-Party Parliamentary Group) on Social Mobility (2012) *7 Key Truths About Social Mobility*, Interim report, London: APPG on Social Mobility (www.raeng.org.uk/publications/other/7-key-truths-about-social-mobility).

ARB (Architects Registration Board) (2017) *Annual Report 2017*, London: ARB (www.arb.org.uk/publications/publications-list/annual-report).

Archer, L., Dawson, E., DeWitt, J., Seakins, A. and Wong, B. (2015) '"Science capital": A conceptual, methodological, and empirical argument for extending Bourdieusian notions of capital beyond the arts', *Journal of Research in Science Teaching*, 52(7), 922–48 (https://doi.org/10.1002/tea.21227).

Armstrong, E.A. and Hamilton, L.T. (2015) *Paying for the party: How college maintains inequality* (Reissued edn), Cambridge, MA: Harvard University Press.

Ashcraft, K.L. (2013) 'The glass slipper: "Incorporating" occupational identity in management studies', *Academy of Management Review*, 38(1), 6–31 (https://doi.org/10.5465/amr.2010.0219).

Ashley, L. (2010) 'Making a difference? The use (and abuse) of diversity management at the UK's elite law firms', *Work, Employment and Society*, 24(4), 711–27.

Ashley, L. and Empson, L. (2013) 'Differentiation and discrimination: Understanding social class and social exclusion in leading law firms', *Human Relations*, 66(2), 219–44.

Ashley, L. and Empson, L. (2016) 'Understanding social exclusion in elite professional service firms: Field level dynamics and the "professional project"', *Work, Employment & Society*, 950017015621480.

Ashley, L. and Empson, L. (2017) 'Understanding social exclusion in elite professional service firms: Field level dynamics and the "professional Project"', *Work, Employment and Society*, 31(2), 211-29.

Ashley, L., Duberley, J., Sommerlad, H. and Scholarios, D. (2015) 'A qualitative evaluation of non-educational barriers to the elite professions' (http://dera.ioe.ac.uk/23163/1/A_qualitative_evaluation_of_non-educational_barriers_to_the_elite_professions.pdf).

Atkinson, W. (2015) *Class*, Cambridge: Polity Press.

Babcock, L. and Laschever, S. (2009) *Women don't ask: Negotiation and the gender divide*, Princeton, NJ: Princeton University Press.

Babcock, L., Laschever, S., Gelfand, M. and Small, D. (2003) 'Nice girls don't ask', *Harvard Business Review*, 81(10), 14-16.

Banks, M. (2017) *Creative justice: Cultural industries, work and inequality*, Lanham, MD: Rowman & Littlefield International.

Banks, M., Gill, R. and Taylor, S. (eds) (2013) *Theorizing cultural work: Labour, continuity and change in the cultural and creative industries*, London and New York: Routledge.

Baratta, A. (2018) *Accent and teacher identity in Britain: Linguistic favouritism and imposed identities*, London: Bloomsbury Publishing.

Barbière, C. (2016) 'Emmanuel Macron officially enters the French presidential race', EURACTIV, 16 November (www.euractiv.com/section/elections/news/emmanuel-macron-officially-enters-the-french-presidential-race/).

Baruch, Y. (1999) 'Response rate in academic studies – A comparative analysis', *Human Relations*, 52(4), 421-38 (https://doi.org/10.1177/001872679905200401).

Basford, T.E., Offermann, L.R. and, T.S. (2014) 'Do you see what I see? Perceptions of gender microaggressions in the workplace', *Psychology of Women Quarterly*, 38(3), 340-9 (https://doi.org/10.1177/0361684313511420).

Bathmaker, A.-M., Ingram, N., Abrahams, J., Hoare, A., Waller, R. and Bradley, H. (2018) *Higher education, social class and social mobility: The degree generation*, London: Palgrave Macmillan.

Battle, E.S. and Rotter, J.B. (1963) 'Children's feelings of personal control as related to social class and ethnic group', *Journal of Personality*, 31(4), 482-90 (https://doi.org/10.1111/j.1467-6494.1963.tb01314.x).

Bauman, Z. (2000) *The individualized society*, Cambridge and Malden, MA: Polity Press.

BBC (2017) *Equality Information Report 2016/17* (https://www.bbc.co.uk/diversity/newsandevents/equality-information-report-2017).

BBC Media Centre (2018) 'Pay and equality at the BBC', 30 January (www.bbc.co.uk/mediacentre/latestnews/2018/pay-and-equality-at-the-bbc).

BBC News (2018) 'Six male BBC presenters agree to pay cuts', 26 January (www.bbc.co.uk/news/uk-42827333).

Beck, U. (1992) *Risk society: Towards a new modernity*, London and Newbury Park, CA: Sage Publications Ltd.

Beck, U. (1996) *Reinvention of politics: Rethinking modernity in the global social order*, Cambridge and Cambridge, MA: Polity Press.

Beck, U. and Willms, J. (2003) *Conversations with Ulrich Beck*, Cambridge and Malden, MA: Polity Press.

Beck, U., Giddens, A. and Lash, S. (1994) *Reflexive modernization: Politics, tradition and aesthetics in the modern social order*, Stanford, CA: Stanford University Press.

Becker, G.S. (1962) 'Investment in human capital: A theoretical analysis', *Journal of Political Economy*, 70(5), 9-49 (https://doi.org/10.1086/258724).

Belam, M. (2018) 'Toby Young quotes on breasts, eugenics and working-class people', *The Guardian*, 3 January (www.theguardian.com/media/2018/jan/03/toby-young-quotes-on-breasts-eugenics-and-working-class-people).

Bell, E.L., Edmondson, J. and Nkomo, S.M. (2003) *Our separate ways: Black and white women and the struggle for professional identity*, Cambridge, MA: Harvard Business Press.

Beller, E. and Hout, M. (2006) 'Intergenerational social mobility: The United States in comparative perspective', *The Future of Children*, 16(2), 19-36.

Belsky, D.W., Domingue, B.W., Wedow, R., Arseneault, L., Boardman, J.D., Caspi, A., et al (2018) 'Genetic analysis of social-class mobility in five longitudinal studies', *Proceedings of the National Academy of Sciences*, July, 115(3), E7275–E7284 (https://doi.org/10.1073/pnas.1801238115).

Bennett, T., Savage, M., Bortolaia Silva, E., Warde, A., Gayo-Cal, M. and Wright, D. (2009) *Culture, class, distinction*, London: Routledge.

Bertaux, D. and Thompson, P. (1997) *Pathways to social class: A qualitative approach to social mobility*, Oxford: Oxford University Press.

Beswick, K. (2018) 'Playing to type: Industry and invisible training in the National Youth Theatre's "Playing Up 2"', *Theatre, Dance and Performance Training*, 9(1), 4–18 (https://doi.org/10.1080/19443927.2017.1397542).

Bhopal, K. (2018) *White privilege*, Bristol: Policy Press.

Bielby, W.T. and Bielby, D.D. (1994) '"All hits are flukes": Institutionalized decision making and the rhetoric of network prime-time program development', *American Journal of Sociology*, 99(5), 1287–313.

Bison, I. (2011) 'Education, social origins and career (im)mobility in contemporary Italy', *European Societies*, 13(3), 481–503 (https://doi.org/10.1080/14616696.2011.568257).

Blackburn, R. and Prandy, K. (1997) 'The reproduction of social inequality', *Sociology*, 31(3), 491–509 (https://doi.org/10.1177/0038038597031003007).

Blair, T. (1999) 'Tony Blair's speech in full', BBC News, UK Politics, 28 September (http://news.bbc.co.uk/2/hi/uk_news/politics/460009.stm).

Blanden, J. (2013) 'Cross-country rankings in intergenerational mobility: A comparison of approaches from economics and sociology', *Journal of Economic Surveys*, 27(1), 38–73 (https://doi.org/10.1111/j.1467-6419.2011.00690.x).

Blanden, J. and Machin, S. (2017) *Home ownership and social mobility*, CEP Discussion Paper 1466, London: Centre for Economic Progress (CEP), London School of Economics (http://cep.lse.ac.uk).

Blanden, J., Goodman, A., Gregg, P. and Machin, S. (2004) 'Changes in intergenerational mobility in Britain', in M. Corak (ed) *Generational income mobility in North America and Europe*, Cambridge: Cambridge University Press,122-46.

Blanden, J., Gregg, P. and Macmillan, L. (2007) 'Accounting for intergenerational income persistence: Noncognitive skills, ability and education', *The Economic Journal*, 117(519), C43-C60.

Blau, F.D. and Kahn, L.M. (2007) 'The gender pay gap', *The Economists' Voice*, 4(4) (https://doi.org/10.2202/1553-3832.1190).

Blinder, A.S. (1973) 'Wage discrimination: Reduced form and structural estimates', *Journal of Human Resources*, 8(4), 436-55.

Bloodworth, J. (2016) *The myth of meritocracy: Why working-class kids still get working-class jobs*, London: Biteback Publishing.

Bol, T. and Weeden, K.A. (2015) 'Occupational closure and wage inequality in Germany and the United Kingdom', *European Sociological Review*, 31(3), 354-69 (https://doi.org/10.1093/esr/jcu095).

Boltanski, L. and Chiapello, E. (2007) *The new spirit of capitalism*, London: Verso.

Bottero, W. (2010) 'Intersubjectivity and Bourdieusian approaches to "identity"', *Cultural Sociology*, 4(1), 3-22 (https://doi.org/10.1177/1749975509356750).

Bourdieu, P. (1977) *Outline of a theory of practice* (Translated by Richard Nice), Cambridge: Cambridge University Press.

Bourdieu, P. (1984) *Distinction* (Translated by Richard Nice), Cambridge, MA: Harvard University Press.

Bourdieu, P. (1986) 'The forms of capital', in J. Richardson (ed) *Handbook of theory and research for the sociology of education*, New York: Greenwood Press, 241-58 (www.marxists.org/reference/subject/philosophy/works/fr/bourdieu-forms-capital.htm).

Bourdieu, P. (1987a) 'What makes a social class? On the theoretical and practical existence of groups', *Berkeley Journal of Sociology*, 32, 1-17.

Bourdieu, P. (1987b) 'The biographical illusion', *Working Papers and Proceedings of the Centre for Psychosocial Studies,* 14: 1-7.

Bourdieu, P. (1990a) *Reproduction in education, society, and culture*, London and Newbury Park, CA: Sage, in association with Theory, Culture & Society, Department of Administrative and Social Studies, Teesside Polytechnic.

Bourdieu, P. (1990b) *The logic of practice*, Stanford, CA: Stanford University Press.

Bourdieu, P. (1991) *Language and Symbolic Power*, Cambridge, MA: Harvard University Press.

Bourdieu, P. (1993) *The Field of Cultural Production* (Translated by Randal Johnson), New York: Columbia University Press.

Bourdieu, P. (1996) *The state nobility: Elite schools in the field of power*, Oxford: Polity Press.

Bourdieu, P. (1998) *Practical reason: On the theory of action*, Cambridge: Polity Press.

Bourdieu, P. (1999) *On television*, New York: The New Press.

Bourdieu, P. (2000) *Pascalian meditations*, Palo Alto, CA: Stanford University Press.

Bourdieu, P. (2005) 'Habitus', in E. Rooksby and J. Hillier (eds) *Habitus: A sense of place* (2nd edn), Aldershot and Burlington, VT: Ashgate Publishing Company, 43-52.

Bourdieu, P. (2007) *The bachelors' ball* (Translated by Richard Nice), Cambridge: Polity Press.

Bourdieu, P. (2008a) *Sketch for a self-analysis* (Translated by Richard Nice), Cambridge: Polity Press.

Bourdieu, P. (2008b) *The bachelors' ball: The crisis of peasant society in Béarn*, Cambridge: Polity Press.

Bourdieu, P. and Accardo, A. (1999) *The weight of the world*, Stanford, CA: Stanford University Press.

Bourdieu, P. and Passeron, J.-C. (1977) *Reproduction: In education, society and culture*, London: Sage.

Bourdieu, P. and Wacquant, L.J.D. (1992) *An invitation to reflexive sociology*, Chicago, IL: University of Chicago Press.

Breen, R. (2005) 'Foundations of a neo-Weberian class analysis', in E.O. Wright (ed) *Approaches to class analysis*, Cambridge: Cambridge University Press, 31-50.

Breen, R. and Goldthorpe, J.H. (2003) 'Class inequality and meritocracy: A critique of Saunders and an alternative analysis', *The British Journal of Sociology*, 50(1), 1-27 (https://doi.org/10.1111/j.1468-4446.1999.00001.x).

Breen, R. and Jonsson, J.O. (2005) 'Inequality of opportunity in comparative perspective: Recent research on educational attainment and social mobility', *Annual Review of Sociology*, 31(1), 223-43 (https://doi.org/10.1146/annurev. soc.31.041304.122232).

Bridge Group, CEM (Centre for Evaluation & Monitoring) and Cabinet Office (2016) *Socio-economic diversity in the Fast Stream*, London (https://assets.publishing.service.gov.uk/government/ uploads/system/uploads/attachment_data/file/497341/BG_ REPORT_FINAL_PUBLISH_TO_RM__1_.pdf).

Britton, J., Shephard, N., Vignoles, A. and Dearden, L. (2016) *How English domiciled graduate earnings vary with gender, institution attended, subject and socio-economic background*, London: Institute for Fiscal Studies (www.ifs.org.uk/publications/8233).

Brown, P. and Hesketh, A. (2004) *The mismanagement of talent: Employability and jobs in the knowledge economy*, Oxford and New York: Oxford University Press.

Brown, S., Kelan, E. and Humbert, A.L. (2015) 'Women's and men's routes to the boardroom', (https://www. womenonboards.net/womenonboards-AU/media/UK-PDFs- Research-Reports/2015_opening_the_black_box_of_board_ appointments.pdf).

Brynin, M. and Güveli, A. (2012) 'Understanding the ethnic pay gap in Britain', *Work, Employment & Society*, 26(4), 574-87 (https://doi.org/10.1177/0950017012445095).

Budig, M.J. and England, P. (2001) 'The wage penalty for motherhood', *American Sociological Review*, 66(2), 204-25 (https://doi.org/10.2307/2657415).

Bühlmann, F. (2010) 'Routes into the British service class feeder logics according to gender and occupational groups', *Sociology*, 44(2), 195-212 (https://doi.org/10.1177/0038038509357193).

Bukodi, E., Goldthorpe, J.H., Waller, W. and Kuha, J. (2015) 'The mobility problem in Britain: New findings from the analysis of birth cohort data', *The British Journal of Sociology*, 66(1), 93-117 (https://doi.org/10.1111/1468-4446.12096).

Bukodi, E., Goldthorpe, J. H., Halpin, B. and Waller, L. (2016) 'Is education now class destiny? Class histories across three British birth cohorts', *European Sociological Review*, 32(6), 835- 49 (https://doi.org/10.1093/esr/jcw041).

Bull, A. and Allen, K. (2018) 'Introduction: Sociological interrogations of the turn to character', *Sociological Research Online* 23(2), 392-98 (https://doi.org/10.1177/1360780418769672).

Burawoy, M. (1982) *Manufacturing consent: Changes in the labor process under monopoly capitalism*, Chicago, IL: University of Chicago Press.

Burrows, R., Webber, R. and Atkinson, R. (2017) 'Welcome to "Pikettyville"? Mapping London's alpha territories', *The Sociological Review*, 65(2), 184-201 (https://doi.org/10.1111/1467-954X.12375).

Burt, R.S. (2000) 'The network structure of social capital', *Research in Organizational Behavior*, 22(January), 345-42 (https://doi.org/10.1016/S0191-3085(00)22009-1).

Cabinet Office (2009) *Unleashing Aspiration: The Final Report of the Panel on Fair Access to the Professions*, London.

Cabinet Office (2016) 'Civil Service pilots new social mobility measures', 17 August (www.gov.uk/government/news/civil-service-pilots-new-social-mobility-measures).

Cabinet Office (2018) *Measuring socio-economic background in your workforce: Recommended measures for use by employers* (https://assets.publishing.service.gov.uk/government/uploads/system/uploads/attachment_data/file/713738/Measuring_Socio-economic_Background_in_your_Workforce__recommended_measures_for_use_by_employers.pdf).

Campbell, P., O'Brien, D. and Taylor, M. (2018) 'Cultural engagement and the economic performance of the cultural and creative industries: An occupational critique', *Sociology*, May, 38038518772737 (https://doi.org/10.1177/0038038518772737).

Carter, P.L. (2007) *Keepin' it real: School success beyond black and white*, Oxford and New York: Oxford University Press.

Casciaro, T. and Lobo, M.S. (2008) 'When competence is irrelevant: The role of interpersonal affect in task-related ties', *Administrative Science Quarterly*, 53(4), 655-84 (https://doi.org/10.2189/asqu.53.4.655).

Castagné, R., Delpierre, C., Kelly-Irving, M., Campanella, G., Guida, G., Krogh, V., et al (2016) 'A life course approach to explore the biological embedding of socioeconomic position and social mobility through circulating inflammatory markers', *Scientific Reports*, 6(April), 25170 (https://doi.org/10.1038/srep25170).

Chan, T.W. (2017) 'Social mobility and the well-being of individuals', *The British Journal of Sociology*, 69(1), 183-206 (https://doi.org/10.1111/1468-4446.12285).

Charlesworth, S.J. (1999) *A phenomenology of working-class experience*, Cambridge and New York: Cambridge University Press.

Chetty, R., Hendren, N., Kline, P. and Saez, E. (2014a) 'Where is the Land of Opportunity? The geography of intergenerational mobility in the United States', *The Quarterly Journal of Economics*, 129(4), 1553–1623 (https://doi.org/10.1093/qje/qju022).

Chetty, R., Hendren, N., Kline, P., Saez, E. and Turner, N. (2014b) 'Is the United States still a land of opportunity? Recent trends in intergenerational mobility', *The American Economic Review*, 104(5), 141-7 (https://doi.org/10.1257/aer.104.5.141).

Chetty, R., Grusky, D., Hell, M., Hendren, N., Manduca, R. and Narang, J. (2017) 'The fading American Dream: Trends in absolute income mobility since 1940', *Science* (April), eaal4617 (https://doi.org/10.1126/science.aal4617).

Choo, H.Y. and Ferree, M.M. (2010) 'Practicing intersectionality in sociological research: A critical analysis of inclusions, interactions, and institutions in the study of inequalities', *Sociological Theory*, 28(2), 129-49 (https://doi.org/10.1111/j.1467-9558.2010.01370.x).

Cohen, L. (2014) *Imagining women's careers*, Oxford: Oxford University Press.

Coleman, J.S. (1988) 'Social capital in the creation of human capital', *The American Journal of Sociology*, 94, S95-120.

Collins, P.H. (1986) 'Learning from the outsider within: The sociological significance of black feminist thought', *Social Problems*, 33(6), S14-32 (https://doi.org/10.2307/800672).

Collins, S.M. (1993) 'Blacks on the bubble: The vulnerability of black executives in white corporations', *The Sociological Quarterly*, 34(3), 429-47 (https://doi.org/10.1111/j.1533-8525.1993. tb00120.x).

Collins, S.M. (1997) *Black corporate executives: The making and breaking of a black middle class*, Philadelphia, PA: Temple University Press.

Collins, P.H. and Bilge, S. (2016) *Intersectionality*, Hoboken, NJ: John Wiley & Sons.

Corak, M. (2004) *Generational income mobility in North America and Europe*, Cambridge: Cambridge University Press.

Corbyn, J. (2018) 'Labour is back as the political voice of the working class', The Labour Party blog, 3 July (https://labour. org.uk/press/labour-back-political-voice-working-class-corbyn).

Correll, S.J., Benard, S. and Paik, I. (2007) 'Getting a job: Is there a motherhood penalty?', *American Journal of Sociology*, 112(5), 1297-338.

Coser, L.A., Kadushin, C. and Powell, W.W. (1982) *The culture and commerce of publishing*, New York: Basic Books.

Coupland, N. and Bishop, H. (2007) 'Ideologised values for British accents', *Journal of Sociolinguistics*, 11(1), 74-93 (https:// doi.org/10.1111/j.1467-9841.2007.00311.x).

Cousin, B., Khan, S. and Mears, A. (2018) 'Theoretical and methodological pathways for research on elites', *Socio-Economic Review*, 16(2), 225-49 (https://doi.org/10.1093/ser/mwy019).

Crawford, C., Macmillan, L. and Vignoles, A. (2017) 'When and why do initially high-achieving poor children fall behind?', *Oxford Review of Education*, 43(1), 88-108 (https://doi.org/10. 1080/03054985.2016.1240672).

Crenshaw, K. (1988) 'Race, reform, and retrenchment: Transformation and legitimation in antidiscrimination law', *Harvard Law Review*, 101(7), 1331-87 (https://doi.org/10.2307/ 1341398).

Crenshaw, K. (1991) 'Mapping the margins: Intersectionality, identity politics, and violence against women of color', *Stanford Law Review*, 43(6), 1241-99.

Crossley, N. (2001) *The social body: Habit, identity and desire*, London and Newbury Park, CA: Sage Publications Ltd.

Cuff, D. (1992) *Architecture: The story of practice*, Cambridge, MA: MIT Press.

Dahl, R.A. (1989) *Who governs?*, New Haven, CT: Yale University Press.

Davis, A. (2018) *Reckless opportunists: Elites at the end of the Establishment* (Reprint edn), Manchester: Manchester University Press.

Davis, K. and Moore, W.E. (1945) 'Some principles of stratification', *American Sociological Review*, 10(2), 242-49 (https://doi.org/10.2307/2085643).

Dean, D. (2005) 'Recruiting a self: Women performers and aesthetic labour', *Work, Employment and Society*, 19(4), 761-74 (https://doi.org/10.1177/0950017005058061).

Dearden, L., Ryan, C. and Sibieta, L. (2011) 'What determines private school choice? A comparison between the United Kingdom and Australia', *Australian Economic Review*, 44(3), 308-20 (https://doi.org/10.1111/j.1467-8462.2011.00650.x).

De Benedictis, S., Allen, K. and Jensen, T. (2017) 'Portraying poverty: The economics and ethics of factual welfare television', *Cultural Sociology*, 11(3), 337-58 (https://doi.org/10.1177/1749975517712132).

de Graft-Johnson, A., Manley, S. and Greed, C. (2005) 'Diversity or the lack of it in the architectural profession', *Construction Management and Economics*, 23(10), 1035-43 (https://doi.org/10.1080/01446190500394233).

de Keere, K. (2014) 'From a self-made to an already-made man: A historical content analysis of professional advice literature', *Acta Sociologica*, 57(4), 311-24 (https://doi.org/10.1177/0001699314552737).

Denham, J. (2015) 'Christopher Eccleston argues only white, male, middle-class actors get to play Hamlet on the London stage', *The Independent*, 7 September (www.independent.co.uk/arts-entertainment/theatre-dance/news/christopher-eccleston-argues-only-white-male-middle-class-actors-get-to-play-hamlet-on-the-london-10489689.html).

Devine, F. (2004) *Class practices: How parents help their children get good jobs*, Cambridge and New York: Cambridge University Press.

Dews, C.L.B. and Law, C.L. (1995) *This fine place so far from home: Voices of academics from the working class* (New edn), Philadelphia, PA: Temple University Press.

DiMaggio, P.J. (1987) 'Classification in art', *American Sociological Review*, 52(4), 440-55 (https://doi.org/10.2307/2095290).

DiMaggio, P.J. and Mohr, J. (1985) 'Cultural capital, educational attainment, and marital selection', *The American Journal of Sociology*, 90(6), 1231-61.

DiMaggio, P.J. and Powell, W.W. (1983) 'The iron cage revisited: Institutional isomorphism and collective rationality in organizational fields', *American Sociological Review*, 48(2), 147-60 (https://doi.org/10.2307/2095101).

DiPrete, T.A. and Eirich, G.M. (2006) 'Cumulative advantage as a mechanism for inequality: A review of theoretical and empirical developments', *Annual Review of Sociology*, 32(1), 271-97 (https://doi.org/10.1146/annurev.soc.32.061604.123127).

Doherty, C. (2016) 'Theresa May's first speech to the nation as Prime Minister – in full', *The Independent*, 13 July (www.independent.co.uk/news/uk/politics/theresa-mays-first-speech-to-the-nation-as-prime-minister-in-full-a7135301.html).

Domhoff, G.W. (2002) *Who rules America?* New York: McGraw-Hill.

Domhoff, G.W. (2013) *Who rules America? The triumph of the corporate rich* (7th edn), New York: McGraw-Hill Education.

Dorling, D. (2014) *Inequality and the 1%*, London: Verso Books.

Du Bois, W.E.B. (1971) 'That capital "N"', in Lester, J. (ed) *The Seventh Son: The Thought and Writings of W. E. B. Du Bois*, New York: Random House.

Dubrow, J.K. (2015) 'Political inequality is international, interdisciplinary, and intersectional', *Sociology Compass*, 9(6), 477-86 (https://doi.org/10.1111/soc4.12270).

Eagly, A.H. and Carli, L.L. (2007) *Through the labyrinth: The truth about how women become leaders*, Boston, MA: Harvard Business Review Press.

Edelmann, A. and Vaisey, S. (2014) 'Cultural resources and cultural distinction in networks', *Poetics*, 46(Oct), 22-37 (https://doi.org/10.1016/j.poetic.2014.08.001).

Edgerton, D. (2005) *Warfare state: Britain, 1920–1970* (Reprint edn), Cambridge and New York: Cambridge University Press.

EHRC (Equality and Human Rights Commission) (2016) *Race Report: Healing a Divided Britain*, London: EHRC (www.equalityhumanrights.com/en/race-report-healing-divided-britain).

Elias, N. (2000) *The civilizing process: Sociogenetic and psychogenetic investigations* (Revised edn), Oxford and Malden, MA: Blackwell Publishers.

Ellersgaard, C.H., Larsen, A.G. and Munk, M.D. (2013) 'A very economic elite: The case of the Danish top CEOs', *Sociology*, 47(6), 1051-71 (https://doi.org/10.1177/0038038512454349).

Elliott, L. (2017) 'Middle classes in crisis, IMF's Christine Lagarde tells Davos 2017', *The Guardian*, 18 January (www.theguardian.com/business/2017/jan/18/middle-classes-imf-christine-lagarde-davos-2017-joe-biden).

Emmison, M. and Frow, J. (1998) 'Information technology as cultural capital', *Australian Universities Review*, 41(1), 41-45.

England, P. (2010) 'The gender revolution: Uneven and stalled', *Gender & Society*, 24(2), 149-66 (https://doi.org/10.1177/0891243210361475).

Erickson, B.H. (1996) 'Culture, class, and connections', *The American Journal of Sociology*, 102(1), 217-51.

Erikson, R. and Goldthorpe, J.H. (1992) *The constant flux: A study of class mobility in industrial societies*, New York: Oxford University Press.

Erikson, R., Goldthorpe, J. H. and Portocarero, L. (1979) 'Intergenerational class mobility in three Western European societies: England, France and Sweden', *The British Journal of Sociology*, 30(4), 415-41 (https://doi.org/10.2307/589632).

Escarpit, R. and Pick, E. (1971) *Sociology of literature*, London: Cass (www.getcited.org/pub/101373390).

Evans, G. and Mellon, J. (2018) *British Social Attitudes 33*, London: NatCen Social Research (www.bsa.natcen.ac.uk/latest-report/british-social-attitudes-33/social-class.aspx).

Falcon, J. (no date) 'The class pay gap in France.' Unpublished working paper.

Faulkner, R.R. and Anderson, A.B. (1987) 'Short-term projects and emergent careers: Evidence from Hollywood', *American Journal of Sociology*, 92(4), 879–909.

Feinstein, L. (2003) 'Inequality in the early cognitive development of British children in the 1970 cohort', *Economica*, 70(277), 73–97 (https://doi.org/10.1111/1468-0335.t01-1-00272).

Ferree, M.M. (2018) 'Intersectionality as theory and practice', *Contemporary Sociology*, 47(2), 127–32 (https://doi.org/10.1177/0094306118755390).

Fielding, A. J. (1992) 'Migration and social mobility: South East England as an escalator region', *Regional Studies*, 26(1), 1–15 (https://doi.org/10.1080/00343409212331346741).

Fielding, T. (1995) 'Migration and middle-class formation in England and Wales', in T. Butler and M. Savage (eds) *Social change and the middle classes*, London: UCL Press, 169–87.

Fischer, C.S. and Voss, K. (1996) *Inequality by design*, Princeton, NJ: Princeton University Press.

Fleming, P. (2009) *Authenticity and the cultural politics of work: New forms of informal control*, Oxford and New York: Oxford University Press.

Flemmen, M. (2009) 'Social closure of the economic upper class', *Tidsskrift for Samfunnsforskning*, 50(4), 493–522.

Flynn, J.R. (2012) *Are we getting smarter? Rising IQ in the twenty-first century*, Cambridge and New York: Cambridge University Press.

Fourny, J.-F. and Emery, M. (2000) 'Bourdieu's uneasy psychoanalysis', *SubStance*, 29(3), 103–12 (https://doi.org/10.2307/3685564).

Fowler, B. and Wilson, F. (2004) 'Women architects and their discontents', *Sociology*, 38(1), 101–19 (https://doi.org/10.1177/0038038504039363).

Freer, E. (2018) *Social mobility and the legal profession: The case of professional associations and access to the English Bar*, Abingdon: Routledge.

Friedman, S. (2011) 'The cultural currency of a "good" sense of humour: British comedy and new forms of distinction', *The British Journal of Sociology*, 62(2), 347–70 (https://doi.org/10.1111/j.1468-4446.2011.01368.x).

Friedman, S. (2014) 'The price of the ticket: Rethinking the experience of social mobility', *Sociology*, 48(2), 352–368.

Friedman, S. (2014) *Comedy and distinction: The cultural currency of a 'good' sense of humour*, London and New York: Routledge.

Friedman, S. (2016) 'Habitus Clivé and the emotional imprint of social mobility', *The Sociological Review*, 64(1), 129–47 (https://doi.org/10.1111/1467-954X.12280).

Friedman, S. and Laurison, D. (2017) 'Mind the gap: Financial London and the regional class pay gap', *The British Journal of Sociology*, 68(3), 474–511 (https://doi.org/10.1111/1468-4446.12269).

Friedman, S. and Macmillan, L. (2017) 'Is London really the engine-room? Migration, opportunity hoarding and regional social mobility in the UK', *National Institute Economic Review*, 240(1), R58–72 (https://doi.org/10.1177/00279501172400 0114).

Friedman, S. and O'Brien, D. (2017) 'Resistance and resignation: Responses to typecasting in British acting', *Cultural Sociology*, 11(3), 359–76 (https://doi.org/10.1177/1749975517710156).

Friedman, S., Laurison, D. and Miles, A. (2015) 'Breaking the "class" ceiling? Social mobility into Britain's elite occupations', *The Sociological Review*, 63(2), 259–89 (https://doi.org/10.1111/1467-954X.12283).

Friedman, S., O'Brien, D. and Laurison, D. (2016) '"Like skydiving without a parachute": How class origin shapes occupational trajectories in British acting', *Sociology*, February (https://doi.org/10.1177/0038038516629917).

Giddens, A. (1991) *Modernity and self-identity: Self and society in the late modern age*, Stanford, CA: Stanford University Press.

Gigone, D. and Hastie, R. (1993) 'The common knowledge effect: Information sharing and group judgment', *Journal of Personality and Social Psychology*, 65(5), 959–74 (https://doi.org/10.1037/0022-3514.65.5.959).

Gitlin, T. (2000) *Inside prime time*, Los Angeles, CA: University of California Press.

Godart, F.C. and Mears, A. (2009) 'How do cultural producers make creative decisions? Lessons from the catwalk', *Social Forces*, 88(2), 671–92 (https://doi.org/10.1353/sof.0.0266).

Goffman, E. (1951) 'Symbols of class status', *The British Journal of Sociology*, 2(4), 294–304 (https://doi.org/10.2307/588083).

Goldthorpe, J.H. (1983) 'Women and class analysis: In defence of the conventional view', *Sociology*, 17(4), 465–88 (https://doi.org/10.1177/0038038583017004001).

Goldthorpe, J.H. (2005) *On sociology: Numbers, narratives, and the integration of research and theory*, Oxford and New York: Oxford University Press.

Goldthorpe, J.H. (2007) '"Cultural Capital": Some critical observations', *Sociologica*, 2 (https://doi.org/10.2383/24755).

Goldthorpe, J.H. (2016) *Social class mobility in modern Britain*, CSI 21, Oxford: Centre for Social Investigation (CSI), Nuffield College, Oxford (http://csi.nuff.ox.ac.uk/wp-content/uploads/2016/03/CSI-21-Social-class-mobility-in-modern-Britain.pdf).

Goldthorpe, J.H. and Jackson, M. (2007) 'Intergenerational class mobility in contemporary Britain: Political concerns and empirical findings', *The British Journal of Sociology*, 58(4), 525–46 (https://doi.org/10.1111/j.1468-4446.2007.00165.x).

Goldthorpe, J.H., Llewellyn, C. and Payne, P. (1980) *Social mobility and class structure in modern Britain* (http://library.wur.nl/WebQuery/clc/131626).

Goodall, L. (2017) 'The BBC gender pay gap is bad – but its class gap is worse', *Sky News*, 23 July (https://news.sky.com/story/the-bbc-pay-gap-is-bad-its-class-gap-is-worse-10957166).

Gorman, E.H. and Kmec, J.A. (2009) 'Hierarchical rank and women's organizational mobility: Glass ceilings in corporate law firms', *American Journal of Sociology*, 114(5), 1428–74.

Granovetter, M.S. (1973) 'The strength of weak ties', *American Journal of Sociology*, 78(6), 1360 (https://doi.org/10.1086/225469).

Green, F., Machin, S., Murphy, R. and Zhu, Y. (2011) 'The changing economic advantage from private schools', *Economica*, 79(316), 658–79 (https://doi.org/10.1111/j.1468-0335.2011.00908.x).

Green, F., Henseke, G. and Vignoles, A. (2016) 'Private schooling and labour market outcomes', *British Educational Research Journal*, 43(1), 7–28 (https://doi.org/10.1002/berj.3256).

Grierson, J. (2017) 'Lineker £1.79m, Balding £199,999: The list that shows BBC's gender gap', *The Guardian*, 19 July (www.theguardian.com/media/2017/jul/19/lineker-balding-the-list-that-shows-bbc-gender-gap).

Griffiths, D. and Lambert, P. (2011) 'Dimensions and boundaries: Comparative analysis of occupational structures using social network and social interaction distance analysis', *Sociological Research Online*, 17(2), 5.

Groot, W. and Oosterbeek, H. (1994) 'Earnings effects of different components of schooling; Human capital versus screening', *The Review of Economics and Statistics*, 76(2), 317-21.

Grugulis, I. and Stoyanova, D. (2012) 'Social capital and networks in film and TV: Jobs for the boys?', *Organization Studies*, 33(10), 1311-31 (https://doi.org/10.1177/0170840612453525).

Guttsman, W. L. (1951) 'The changing social structure of the British political élite, 1886-1935', *The British Journal of Sociology*, 2(2), 122-34 (https://doi.org/10.2307/587384).

Hadjar, A. and Samuel, R. (2015) 'Does upward social mobility increase life satisfaction? A longitudinal analysis using British and Swiss Panel Data', *Research in Social Stratification and Mobility*, 39(March), 48-58 (https://doi.org/10.1016/j.rssm.2014.12.002).

Hagan, J. and Kay, F. (1995) *Gender in practice: A study of lawyers' lives*, Oxford: Oxford University Press.

Halford, S. and Savage, M. (2010) 'Reconceptualizing digital social inequality', *Information, Communication & Society*, 13(7), 937-55 (https://doi.org/10.1080/1369118X.2010.499956).

Hällsten, M. (2013) 'The class-origin wage gap: Heterogeneity in education and variations across market segments', *The British Journal of Sociology*, 64(4), 662-90 (https://doi.org/10.1111/1468-4446.12040).

Halpin, B. and Chan, T.W. (1998) 'Class careers as sequences: An optimal matching analysis of work–life histories', *European Sociological Review*, 14(2), 111-30 (https://doi.org/10.1093/oxfordjournals.esr.a018230).

Hanley, L. (2017) *Respectable: Crossing the class divide*, London: Penguin.

Hansen, M.N. (2001) 'Closure in an open profession. The impact of social origin on the educational and occupational success of graduates of law in Norway', *Work, Employment & Society*, 15(3), 489-510.

Hansen, M.N. (2014) 'Self-made wealth or family wealth? Changes in intergenerational wealth mobility', *Social Forces*, 93(2), 457-81 (https://doi.org/10.1093/sf/sou078).

Harris, C. I. (1993) 'Whiteness as property', *Harvard Law Review* 106(8), 1707-91 (https://doi.org/10.2307/1341787).

Harrison, B. (2009) *Seeking a role: The United Kingdom 1951– 1970* (1st edn), Oxford and New York: Oxford University Press.

Heath, A.F. (1981) *Social mobility*, London: Fontana Paperbacks.

Heath, A.F. and Britten, N. (1984) 'Women's jobs do make a difference: A reply to Goldthorpe', *Sociology*, 18(4), 475-90.

Hecht, K.M. (2017) 'A sociological analysis of top incomes and wealth: A study of how individuals at the top of the income and wealth distributions perceive economic inequality', PhD, London: London School of Economics and Political Science (http://etheses.lse.ac.uk/3699).

Hesmondhalgh, D. and Baker, S. (2011) *Creative labour: Media work in three cultural industries*, London and New York: Routledge.

Hey, V. (1997) 'Northern accent and southern comfort: Subjectivity and social class', in P. Mahony and C. Zmroczek (eds) *Class matters: Working class women's perspectives on social class* (1st edn), London and Bristol, PA: Taylor & Francis, 143-54.

Hirsch, P.M. (1972) 'Processing fads and fashions: An organization-set analysis of cultural industry systems', *American Journal of Sociology*, 77(4), 639-59.

Hirsch, P.M. (2000) 'Cultural industries revisited', *Organization Science*, 11(3), 356-61 (https://doi.org/10.1287/orsc.11.3.356.12498).

Hjellbrekke, J., Le Roux, B., Korsnes, O., LeBaron, F., Rosenlund, L. and Rouanet, H. (2007) 'The Norwegian field of power anno 2000', *European Societies*, 9(2), 245 (https://doi.org/10.1080/14616690601002749).

Ho, K. (2009) *Liquidated: An ethnography of Wall Street* (Paperback Octavo edn), Durham, NC: Duke University Press.

Hoggart, R. (2009) *Modern classics: The uses of literacy: Aspects of working-class life*, London: Penguin Classic.

Honey, J.R. de S. (1977) *Tom Brown's universe: Public school in the nineteenth century*, London: Millington.

hooks, b. (1993) 'Keeping close to home: Class and education', in M. M. Tokarczyk and E. E. Fay (eds) *Working-class women in the academy: Laborers in the knowledge factory*, Amherst, MA: University of Massachusetts Press, 99-111.

Hout, M. (1984) 'Status, autonomy, and training in occupational mobility', *The American Journal of Sociology*, 89(6), 1379-409.

Hout, M. (2008) 'How class works: Objective and subjective aspects of class since the 1970s', in A. Lareau and D. Conley (eds) *Social class: How does it work*, New York: Russell Sage Foundation, 25-64.

Hout, M. (2012) 'Social and economic returns to college education in the United States', *Annual Review of Sociology*, 38(1), 379-400 (https://doi.org/10.1146/annurev.soc.012809.102503).

Hull, K.E. and Nelson, R.L. (2000) 'Assimilation, choice, or constraint? Testing theories of gender differences in the careers of lawyers', *Social Forces*, 79(1), 229-64 (https://doi.org/10.1093/sf/79.1.229).

Hunter, F. (1969) *Community power structure: A study of decision makers* (1st edn), Chapel Hill: University North Carolina Press.

Igarashi, H. and Saito, H. (2014) 'Cosmopolitanism as cultural capital: Exploring the intersection of globalization, education and stratification', *Cultural Sociology*, 8(3), 222-39 (https://doi.org/10.1177/1749975514523935).

IMF (International Monetary Fund) (2017) *IMF Fiscal Monitor, Tackling Inequality, October 2017* (www.imf.org/en/Publications/FM/Issues/2017/10/05/fiscal-monitor-october-2017).

Ingram, N.A. (2011) 'Within school and beyond the gate: The complexities of being educationally successful and working class', *Sociology*, 45(2), 287-302.

Ingram, N.A. (2018) *Working-class boys and educational success: Teenage identities, masculinities and urban schooling*, New York: Palgrave Macmillan.

Ingram, N.A. and Allen, K. (2018) '"Talent-spotting" or "social magic"? Inequality, cultural sorting and constructions of the ideal graduate in elite professions', *The Sociological Review*, May (http://eprints.lancs.ac.uk/125638).

Jack, A.A. (2014) 'Culture shock revisited: The social and cultural contingencies to class marginality', *Sociological Forum*, 29(2), 453-75 (https://doi.org/10.1111/socf.12092).

Jack, A.A. (2016) '(No) harm in asking: Class, acquired cultural capital, and academic engagement at an elite university', *Sociology of Education*, 89(1), 1-19.

Jann, B. (2008) 'The Blinder–Oaxaca decomposition for linear regression models', *Stata Journal*, 8(4), 453-79.

Jarness, V. (2015) 'Modes of consumption: From "what" to "how" in cultural stratification research', *Poetics*, 53 (December), 65-79 (https://doi.org/10.1016/j.poetic.2015.08.002).

Jarness, V. and Friedman, S. (2017) '"I'm not a snob, but …": Class boundaries and the downplaying of difference', *Poetics*, 61(April), 14-25 (https://doi.org/10.1016/j.poetic.2016.11.001).

Jefferson, T. (1817) *Bill for establishing a system of public education*, Richmond: State of Virginia.

Jencks, C., Smith, M., Acland, H., Bane, M.J., Cohen, D., Gintis, H., Heyns, B. and Michelson, S. (1972) *Inequality: A reassessment of the effect of family and schooling in America*, New York: Basic Books.

Jenkins, R. (2002) *Pierre Bourdieu*, London: Routledge.

Jenkins, S.P. (2011) *Changing fortunes: Income mobility and poverty dynamics in Britain* (1st edn), Oxford and New York: Oxford University Press.

Jensen, T. (2014) 'Welfare commonsense, Poverty porn and doxosophy', *Sociological Research Online*, 19(3), 3.

Jerolmack, C. and Khan, S. (2014) 'Talk is cheap: Ethnography and the attitudinal fallacy', *Sociological Methods & Research*, 43(2), 178-209 (https://doi.org/10.1177/0049124114523396).

Johnson, B. (2013) 'Boris Johnson's speech at the Margaret Thatcher lecture in full', *The Telegraph*, 28 November (www.telegraph.co.uk/news/politics/london-mayor-election/mayor-of-london/10480321/Boris-Johnsons-speech-at-the-Margaret-Thatcher-lecture-in-full.html).

Jones, D. (1924) *An English pronouncing dictionary: (Showing the pronunciation of over 50,000 words in international phonetic transcription)* (Rev. edn, with Supplement), New York: E. P. Dutton & Co.

Jonsson, J.O., Grusky, D.B., Di Carlo, M., Pollak, R. and Brinton, M.C. (2009) 'Microclass mobility: Social reproduction in four countries', *American Journal of Sociology*, 114(4), 977–1036 (https://doi.org/10.1086/592200).

Judge, T.A. and Bono, J.E. (2001) 'Relationship of core self-evaluations traits – self-esteem, generalized self-efficacy, locus of control, and emotional stability – with job satisfaction and job performance: A meta-analysis', *Journal of Applied Psychology*, 86(1), 80–92 (https://doi.org/http://dx.doi.org/10.1037/0021-9010.86.1.80).

Kant, I. ([1790] 1987) *Critique of judgment*, UK: Hackett Publishing Co.

Kanter, R.M. (1993) *Men and women of the corporation* (2nd edn), New York: Basic Books.

Kehal, P.S. (no date) 'Racializing meritocracy: Ideas of excellence and exclusion in faculty diversity', Unpublished PhD disseration, Brown University, RI.

Kelsall, R.K. (1955) *Higher civil servants in Britain, from 1870 to the present day*, London: Routledge.

Khan, S.R. (2010) *Privilege: The making of an adolescent elite at St Paul's School*, Princeton, NJ: Princeton University Press.

King, A. (2000) 'Thinking with Bourdieu against Bourdieu: A "practical" critique of the habitus', *Sociological Theory*, 18(3), 417–33 (https://doi.org/10.1111/0735-2751.00109).

King, A. and Crewe, I. (2013) *The blunders of our governments*, London: Oneworld Publications.

Kitagawa, E.M. (1955) 'Components of a difference between two rates', *Journal of the American Statistical Association*, 50(272), 1168–94 (https://doi.org/10.2307/2281213).

Koppman, S. (2015) 'In the eye of the beholder: The stratification of taste in a cultural industry', *The Sociological Quarterly*, 56(4), 665–94 (https://doi.org/10.1111/tsq.12098).

Koppman, S. (2016) 'Different like me: Why cultural omnivores get creative jobs', *Administrative Science Quarterly*, 61(2), 291–331 (https://doi.org/10.1177/0001839215616840).

Kornberger, M., Carter, C. and Ross-Smith, A. (2010) 'Changing gender domination in a big four accounting firm: Flexibility, performance and client service in practice', *Accounting, Organizations and Society*, 35(8), 775-91 (https://doi.org/10.1016/j.aos.2010.09.005).

Korsnes, O., Heilbron, J., Hjellbrekke, J., Bühlmann, F. and Savage, M. (2017) *New directions in elite studies*, Abingdon: Routledge.

KPMG (2016) 'KPMG reveals employees' parental occupation in a bid to increase social mobility', Press release, 15 December (https://home.kpmg.com/uk/en/home/media/press-releases/2016/12/kpmg-reveals-employees-parental-occupation-in-a-bid-to-increase-.html).

Kuhn, A. (2002) *Family secrets: Acts of memory and imagination* (2nd revised edn), London and New York: Verso.

Kynaston, D. (2012) *City of London: The history*, London: Vintage.

Lacy, K.R. (2004) 'Black spaces, black places: Strategic assimilation and identity construction in middle-class suburbia', *Ethnic and Racial Studies*, 27(6), 908-30 (https://doi.org/10.1080/0141987042000268521).

Lacy, K.R. (2007) *Blue-chip black: Race, class, and status in the new black middle class*, Berkeley, CA: University of California Press.

Lambert, P. and Griffiths, D. (2018) *Social inequalities and occupational stratification: Methods and concepts in the analysis of social distance*, Basingstoke: Palgrave Macmillan.

Lamont, M. (2000) *The dignity of working men: Morality and the boundaries of race, class, and immigration*, New York and Cambridge, MA: Russell Sage Foundation and Harvard University Press (http://site.ebrary.com/id/10314265).

Lamont, M. and Lareau, A. (1988) 'Cultural capital: Allusions, gaps and glissandos in recent theoretical developments', *Sociological Theory*, 6(2), 153-68.

Lancaster University (no date) 'Meet our chancellor' (www.lancaster.ac.uk/about-us/ourpeople/meet-our-chancellor).

Lareau, A. (2011) *Unequal childhoods: Class, race, and family life* (2nd edition with an update a decade later), Berkeley, CA: University of California Press.

Lareau, A. (2015) 'Cultural knowledge and social inequality', *American Sociological Review*, 80(1), 1-27 (https://doi.org/10.1177/0003122414565814).

Larsen, A.G. and Ellersgaard, C.H. (2018) 'The inner circle revisited: The case of an egalitarian society', *Socio-Economic Review*, 16(2), 251-75 (https://doi.org/10.1093/ser/mwx052).

Larsen, A.G., Ellersgaard, C. and Bernsen, M. (2015) *Magteliten: Hvordan 423 danskere styrer landet* [The ruling elite: How 423 Danes rule the country], Politikens Forlag (https://politikensforlag.dk/magteliten/t-1/9788740018004).

Laurison, D. and Friedman, S. (2016) 'The class pay gap in higher professional and managerial occupations', *American Sociological Review*, 81(4), 668-95 (https://doi.org/10.1177/0003122416653602).

Lawler, S. (1999) '"Getting out and getting away": Women's narratives of class mobility', *Feminist Review*, 63(1), 3-24 (https://doi.org/10.1080/014177899339036).

Lawler, S. (2005) 'Disgusted subjects: The making of middle-class identities', *The Sociological Review*, 53(3), 429-46 (https://doi.org/10.1111/j.1467-954X.2005.00560.x).

Lawler, S. and Payne, G. (2017) 'Social mobility talk: Class-making in neo-liberal times', in S. Lawler and G. Payne (eds) *Social mobility for the 21st century: Everyone a winner?*, New York: Routledge, 118-32.

LeBaron, F. (2008) 'Central bankers in the contemporary global field of power: A "social space" approach', *The Sociological Review* (www.u-picardie.fr/~LaboERSI/mardi/fichiers/m64.pdf).

Lee, D. (2011) 'Networks, cultural capital and creative labour in the British independent television industry', *Media, Culture & Society*, 33(4), 549-65 (https://doi.org/10.1177/0163443711398693).

Levy, O. and Reiche, B.S. (2018) 'The politics of cultural capital: Social hierarchy and organizational architecture in the multinational corporation', *Human Relations*, 71(6), 867-94 (https://doi.org/10.1177/0018726717729208).

Lewis, K. and Kaufman, J. (2018) 'The conversion of cultural tastes into social network ties', *American Journal of Sociology*, 123(6), 1684-1742 (https://doi.org/10.1086/697525).

Lexmond, J. and Reeves, R. (2009) *Building character*, London: Demos.

Li, Y. and Heath, A. (2016) 'Class matters: A study of minority and majority social mobility in Britain, 1982–2011', *American Journal of Sociology*, 122(1), 162-200 (https://doi.org/10.1086/686696).

Lin, N. (1999) 'Social networks and status attainment', *Annual Review of Sociology*, 25(1), 467-87 (https://doi.org/10.1146/annurev.soc.25.1.467).

Lindert, P.H. (2004) *Growing public: Volume 1, The story: Social spending and economic growth since the eighteenth century*, Cambridge: Cambridge University Press.

Littler, J. (2017) *Against meritocracy: Culture, power and myths of mobility*, London and New York: Routledge.

Lizardo, O. (2006) 'How cultural tastes shape personal networks', *American Sociological Review*, 71(5), 778-807 (https://doi.org/10.1177/000312240607100504).

Lizardo, O. and Skiles, S. (2012) 'Reconceptualizing and theorizing "omnivorousness": Genetic and relational mechanisms', *Sociological Theory*, 30(4), 263-82 (https://doi.org/10.1177/0735275112466999).

Ljunggren, J. (2017) 'Elitist egalitarianism: Negotiating identity in the Norwegian cultural elite', *Sociology*, 51(3), 559-74 (https://doi.org/10.1177/0038038515590755).

Longhi, S. and Brynin, M. (2017) *The Ethnicity Pay Gap*, Equality and Human Rights Commission Research Report 108, Manchester: Equality and Human Rights Commission (www.equalityhumanrights.com/sites/default/files/research-report-108-the-ethnicity-pay-gap.pdf).

Longhi, S., Nicoletti, C. and Platt, L. (2013) 'Explained and unexplained wage gaps across the main ethno-religious groups in Great Britain', *Oxford Economic Papers*, 65(2), 471-93 (https://doi.org/10.1093/oep/gps025).

Lovell, T. (2000) 'Thinking feminism with and against Bourdieu', *Feminist Theory*, 1(1), 11-32 (https://doi.org/10.1177/14647000022229047).

Major, J. (1990) *Today*, BBC Radio 4, 24 November.

Major, L.E. and Machin, S. (2018) *Social mobility: And its enemies*, London: Penguin.

Marshall, G. and Firth, D. (1999) 'Social mobility and personal satisfaction: Evidence from ten countries', *The British Journal of Sociology*, 50(1), 28-48 (https://doi.org/10.1111/j.1468-4446.1999.00028.x).

Maxwell, C. and Aggleton, P. (2015) *Elite education: International perspectives*, Abingdon: Routledge.

Maxwell, C. and Aggleton, P. (2016) 'Creating cosmopolitan subjects: The role of families and private schools in England', *Sociology*, 50(4), 780-95.

Maylor, U. and Williams, K. (2011) 'Challenges in theorising "black middle-class" women: Education, experience and authenticity', *Gender and Education*, 23(3), 345-56 (https://doi.org/10.1080/09540253.2010.490203).

McCrory Calarco, J. (2018) *Negotiating opportunities: How the middle class secures advantages in school*, New York: Oxford University Press.

McDowell, L. (1997) *Capital culture: Gender at work in the city*, Oxford: John Wiley & Sons.

Mckenzie, L. (2015) *Getting by: Estates, class and culture in austerity Britain*, Bristol: Policy Press.

McMillan Cottom, T. (2016) 'Black cyberfeminism: Intersectionality, institutions, and digital sociology', in J. Daniels, K. Gregory and T. McMillan Cottom (eds) *Digital sociologies* (Reprint edn), Bristol and Chicago, IL: Policy Press, 211-31.

McPherson, M., Smith-Lovin, L. and Cook, J.M. (2001) 'Birds of a feather: Homophily in social networks', *Annual Review of Sociology*, 27(1), 415-44 (https://doi.org/10.1146/annurev.soc.27.1.415).

Meghji, A. (2017) 'Positionings of the black middle-classes: Understanding identity construction beyond strategic assimilation', *Ethnic and Racial Studies*, 40(6), 1007-25 (https://doi.org/10.1080/01419870.2016.1201585).

Mijs. J. (2016) 'The unfulfillable promise of meritocracy: Three lessons and their implications for justice in education', *Social Justice Research*, 29 (1), 14-34.

Milburn, A. (2009) Unleashing Aspiration: The Final Report

of the Panel on Fair Access to the Professions (http://webarchive.
nationalarchives.gov.uk/+/http:/www.cabinetoffice.gov.uk/
media/227102/fair-access.pdf).

Milburn, A. (2014) 'Elitist Britain?' (http://dera.ioe.
ac.uk/20793/1/Elitist_Britain_-_Final.pdf).

Milburn, A. (2015) *Bridging the Social Divide: Making Social
Mobility and Child Poverty Core Business for the Next Parliament*,
London: Social Mobility & Child Poverty Commission
(https://assets.publishing.service.gov.uk/government/uploads/
system/uploads/attachment_data/file/408405/Bridging_the_
Social_Divide_Report.pdf).

Miles, A. and Savage, M. (2004) 'Origins of the modern career',
in D. Mitch, J. Brown and M.H.D. van Leeuwen (eds) *Origins
of the Modern Career*, Burlington: Ashgate, 79-100.

Miles, A. and Savage, M. (2012) 'The strange survival story of
the English gentleman, 1945-2010', *Cultural and Social History*,
9(4), 595-612.

Mill, J.S. (1859) *On Liberty*, London: John W. Parker and Son.

Mills, C.W. (2000 [1856]) *The power elite*, Oxford: Oxford
University Press.

Mills, C. (2013) 'The Great British class fiasco', *Oxford Sociology*,
Blog (http://oxfordsociology.blogspot.co.uk/2013/04/the-
great-british-class-fiasco.html).

Mills, C. (2015) 'The Great British Class Survey: Requiescat
in pace', *The Sociological Review*, 63(2), 393-99 (https://doi.
org/10.1111/1467-954X.12287).

Modood, T. and Khattab, N. (2015) 'Explaining ethnic
differences: Can ethnic minority strategies reduce the effects
of ethnic penalties?', *Sociology*, May, 38038515575858 (https://
doi.org/10.1177/0038038515575858).

Moore, M. and Jones, J. (2001) 'Cracking the concrete ceiling:
Inquiry into the aspirations, values, motives, and actions
of African American female 1890 cooperative extension
administrators', *Journal of Extension*, 39(6).

Moore, J., Higham, L., Mountford-Zimars, A., Ashley, L., Birkett, H., Duberly, J. and Kenny, E. (2016) *Socio-economic diversity in life sciences and investment banking*, London: Social Mobility Commission (www.gov.uk/government/publications/socio-economic-diversity-in-life-sciences-and-investment-banking).

Mosca, G. (2011 [1939]) *The Ruling Class*, Charleston, SC: Nabu Press.

Mouw, T. (2003) 'Social capital and finding a job: Do contacts matter?', *American Sociological Review*, 68(6), 868-98 (https://doi.org/10.2307/1519749).

Nichols, G. and Savage, M. (2017) 'A social analysis of an elite constellation: The case of Formula 1', *Theory, Culture & Society*, 34(5-6), 201-25 (https://doi.org/10.1177/0263276417716519).

Oakley, K. and O'Brien, D. (2015) *Cultural value and inequality: A critical literature review*, Arts and Humanities Research Council.

Oakley, K., Laurison, D., O'Brien, D. and Friedman, S. (2017) 'Cultural capital: Arts graduates, spatial inequality, and London's impact on cultural labour markets', *American Behavioral Scientist*, June (http://eprints.whiterose.ac.uk/117253).

O'Brien, D. (2016) 'What price evidence? The ethics of office and the ethics of social science in British cultural policy', *Journal of Cultural Economy*, 9(2), 127-40 (https://doi.org/10.1080/17530350.2015.1100649).

O'Brien, D., Allen, K., Friedman, S. and Saha, A. (2017) 'Producing and consuming inequality: A cultural sociology of the cultural industries', *Cultural Sociology*, 11(3), 271-82 (https://doi.org/10.1177/1749975517712465).

Olsen, W. (2010) *The gender pay gap in the UK 1995–2007*, London: Government Equalities Office (www.escholar.manchester.ac.uk/uk-ac-man-scw:75226).

Olsen, W., Gash, V., Kim, S. and Zhang, M. (2018) *The gender pay gap in the UK: Evidence from the UKHLS*, London: Government Equalities Office (www.gov.uk/government/publications/the-gender-pay-gap-in-the-uk-evidence-from-the-ukhls).

ONS (Office for National Statistics) (2016) *Quarterly Labour Force Survey, 2013–2016*, UK Data Archive, Social Survey Division, Northern Ireland Statistics and Research Agency, Central Survey Unit (https://discover.ukdataservice.ac.uk/series/?sn=2000026).

Pareto, V., Montesano, A., Zanni, A., Bruni, L., Chipman, J.S. and McLure, M. (2014) *Manual of political economy: A critical and variorum edition*, Oxford: Oxford University Press.

Parkin, F. (1979) *Marxism and class theory: A bourgeois critique*, London: Tavistock Publications.

Pattillo, M. (2013) *Black picket fences, second edition: Privilege and peril among the black middle class* (2nd edn), Chicago and London: University of Chicago Press.

Payne, G. (2017) *The new social mobility*, Bristol: Policy Press.

Peterson, R.A. and Anand, N. (2004) 'The production of culture perspective', *Annual Review of Sociology*, 30(January), 311-34.

Pfeffer, J. (1977) 'Toward an examination of stratification in organizations', *Administrative Science Quarterly*, 22(4), 553-67 (https://doi.org/10.2307/2392400).

Pfeffer, J. and Leblebici, H. (1973) 'Executive recruitment and the development of interfirm organizations', *Administrative Science Quarterly*, 18(4), 449-61 (https://doi.org/10.2307/2392198).

Piketty, T. (2014) *Capital in the twenty-first century*, Cambridge, MA: Harvard University Press.

Plomin, R. and Deary, I.J. (2015) 'Genetics and intelligence differences: Five special findings', *Molecular Psychiatry*, 20(1), 98-108 (https://doi.org/10.1038/mp.2014.105).

Plunkett, J. (2014) 'Working-class talent being priced out of acting, says David Morrissey', *The Guardian*, 15 September (www.theguardian.com/culture/2014/sep/16/david-morrissey-working-class-actors-priced-out).

Prieur, A. and Savage, M. (2014) 'On "knowingness", cosmopolitanism and busyness as emerging forms of cultural capital', in P. Coulangeon and J. Duval (eds) *The Routledge companion to Bourdieu's 'Distinction'*, New York: Routledge.

Puwar, N. (2004) *Space invaders: Race, gender and bodies out of place*, Oxford and New York: Berg Publishers.

Reay, D. (2002) 'Shaun's story: Troubling discourses of white working-class masculinities', *Gender and Education*, 14(3), 221-34.

Reay, D. (2017) *Miseducation: Inequality, education and the working classes* (1st edn), Bristol: Policy Press.

Reay, D., Crozier, G. and Clayton, J. (2009) '"Strangers in paradise"? Working-class students in elite universities', *Sociology*, 43(6), 1103-21 (https://doi.org/10.1177/0038038509345700).

Reed-Danahay, D. (2004) *Locating Bourdieu*, Bloomington, IN: Indiana University Press.

Reeves, R.V. (2018) *Dream hoarders: How the American upper middle class is leaving everyone else in the dust, why that is a problem, and what to do about it*, Washington, DC: Brookings Institution Press.

Reeves, A. and de Vries, R. (2018) 'Can cultural consumption increase future earnings? Exploring the economic returns to cultural capital', *The British Journal of Sociology* (https://doi.org/10.1111/1468-4446.12374).

Reeves, A., Friedman, S., Rahal, C. and Flemmen, M. (2017) 'The decline and persistence of the old boy: Private schools and elite recruitment 1897 to 2016', *American Sociological Review*, 82(6), 1139-66 (https://doi.org/10.1177/0003122417735742).

Rivera, L.A. (2012) 'Hiring as cultural matching: The case of elite professional service firms', *American Sociological Review*, 77(6), 999-1022 (https://doi.org/10.1177/0003122412463213).

Rivera, L.A. (2015) *Pedigree: How elite students get elite jobs*, Princeton, NJ: Princeton University Press.

Rivera, L.A. and Tilcsik, A. (2016) 'Class advantage, commitment penalty: The gendered effect of social class signals in an elite labor market', *American Sociological Review*, 81(6), 1097-131 (https://doi.org/10.1177/0003122416668154).

Roberts, S. and Arunachalam, D. (no date) 'The class pay gap in Australia.'

Robson, K., Humphrey, C., Khalifa, R. and Jones, J. (2007) 'Transforming audit technologies: Business risk audit methodologies and the audit field', *Accounting, Organizations and Society*, 32(4), 409-38 (https://doi.org/10.1016/j.aos.2006.09.002).

Rollock, N. (2014) 'Race, class and "the harmony of dispositions"', *Sociology*, 48(3), 445-51 (https://doi.org/10.1177/0038038514521716).

Rollock, N., Gillborn, D., Vincent, C. and Ball, S. (2011) 'The public identities of the black middle classes: Managing race in public spaces', *Sociology*, 45(6), 1078-93 (https://doi.org/10.1177/0038038511416167).

Ruderman, M.N., Ohlott, P.J. and Kram, K.E. (1996) *Managerial promotion: The dynamics for men and women*, Greensboro, NC: Center for Creative Leadership.

Saha, A. (2017a) 'The politics of race in cultural distribution: Addressing inequalities in British Asian theatre', *Cultural Sociology*, 11(3), 302-17 (https://doi.org/10.1177/1749975517708899).

Saha, A. (2017b) *Race and the cultural industries*, Malden, MA: Polity Press.

Sandberg, S. (2015) *Lean in: Women, work, and the will to lead*, London: W.H. Allen.

Saunders, P. (1995) 'Might Britain be a meritocracy?', *Sociology*, 29(1), 23-41 (https://doi.org/10.1177/0038038595029001003).

Saunders, P. (2003) 'Reflections on the meritocracy debate in Britain: A response to Richard Breen and John Goldthorpe', *The British Journal of Sociology*, 53(4), 559-74 (https://doi.org/10.1080/0007131022000021489).

Savage, M. (1997) 'Social mobility and the survey method: A critical analysis', in D. Bertaux and P. Thompson (eds) *Pathways to social class: Qualitative approaches to social mobility*, Oxford: Clarendon Press, 299-326.

Savage, M. (2000) *Class analysis and social transformation*, Buckingham: Open University Press.

Savage, M. (2010) *Identities and social change in Britain since 1940: The politics of method*, Oxford and New York: Oxford University Press.

Savage, M. (2014) 'Social change in the 21st century: The new sociology of "wealth elites"', *Discover Society*, December (http://discoversociety.org/2014/12/01/focus-social-change-in-the-21st-century-the-new-sociology-of-wealth-elites/).

Savage, M. and Friedman, S. (2017) 'Time, accumulation and trajectory: Bourdieu and social mobility', in S. Lawler and G. Payne (eds) *Social mobility for the 21st century*, Abingdon: Routledge, 81-93.

Savage, M. and Williams, K. (2008) 'Elites: Remembered in capitalism and forgotten by social sciences', *The Sociological Review*, 56(May), 1-24 (https://doi.org/10.1111/j.1467-954X.2008.00759.x).

Savage, M., Barlow, J., Dickens, P. and Fielding, T. (1992) *Property, bureaucracy, and culture: Middle-class formation in contemporary Britain*, London: Routledge.

Savage, M., Bagnall, G. and Longhurst, B. (2001) 'Ordinary, ambivalent and defensive: Class identities in the Northwest of England', *Sociology*, 35(4), 875-92 (https://doi.org/10.1177/0038038501035004005).

Savage, M., Devine, F., Cunningham, N., Taylor, M., Li, Y., Hjellbrekke, J., Le Roux, B., Friedman, S. and Miles, A. (2013) 'A new model of social class? Findings from the BBC's Great British Class Survey Experiment', *Sociology*, 47(2), 219-50 (https://doi.org/10.1177/0038038513481128).

Savage, M., Devine, F., Cunningham, N., Friedman, S., Laurison, D., Miles, A., Snee, H. and Taylor, M. (2015a) 'On social class, anno 2014', *Sociology*, 49(6), 1011-30 (https://doi.org/10.1177/0038038514536635).

Savage, M., Cunningham, N., Devine, F., Friedman, S., Laurison, D., McKenzie, L., Miles, A., Snee, H. and Wakeling, P. (2015b) *Social class in the 21st Century*. Penguin UK.

Sayer, A. (2009) *The moral significance of class*, Cambridge and New York: Cambridge University Press.

Scott, J. (1991) *Who rules Britain?*, Oxford and Cambridge, MA: Polity Press.

Scott, J. (2008) 'Modes of power and the re-conceptualization of elites', *The Sociological Review*, 56(1_suppl), 25-43 (https://doi.org/10.1111/j.1467-954X.2008.00760.x).

Sennett, R. and Cobb, J. (1972) *The hidden injuries of class*, New York: Vintage.

Sherman, R. (2017) *Uneasy street: The anxieties of affluence*, Princeton, NJ: Princeton University Press.

Silva, E.B. and Wright, D. (2009) 'Displaying desire and distinction in housing', *Cultural Sociology*, 3(1), 31-50 (https://doi.org/10.1177/1749975508100670).

Simpson, R. and Kumra, S. (2016) 'The Teflon effect: When the glass slipper meets merit', *Gender in Management: An International Journal*, 31(8), 562-76 (https://doi.org/10.1108/GM-12-2014-0111).

Skeggs, B. (1997) *Formations of class and gender: Becoming respectable*, London: Sage.

Social Mobility Foundation (2018) *Social Mobility Employer Index 2018* (www.socialmobility.org.uk/index).

Spence, C. and Carter, C. (2014) 'An exploration of the professional habitus in the big 4 accounting firms', *Work, Employment and Society*, 28(6), 946-62 (https://doi.org/10.1177/0950017013510762).

Spohrer, K., Stahl, G. and Bowers-Brown, T. (2018) 'Constituting neoliberal subjects? "Aspiration" as technology of government in UK policy discourse', *Journal of Education Policy*, 33(3), 327-42 (https://doi.org/10.1080/02680939.2017.1336573).

Srinivasan, S. (1995) *The South Asian petty bourgeoisie in Britain: An Oxford case study*, Aldershot: Avebury.

Stanworth, P. and Giddens, A. (1974) *Elites and power in British society*, 8, Cambridge University Press Archive (http://books.google.co.uk/books?hl=en&lr=&id=Syg4AAAAIAAJ&oi=fnd&pg=PR7&dq=Stanworth+and+Giddens,+1974%3B&ots=4hIfX8nZvS&sig=2pdEVgm8oGgapvHOczsZoISS_hQ).

Steinbugler, A.C., Press, J.E. and Johnson Dias, J. (2006) 'Gender, race, and affirmative action: Operationalizing intersectionality in survey research', *Gender & Society*, 20(6), 805-25 (https://doi.org/10.1177/0891243206293299).

Steinmetz, G. (2006) 'Bourdieu's disavowal of Lacan: Psychoanalytic theory and the concepts of "habitus" and "symbolic capital"', *Constellations*, 13(4), 445-64 (https://doi.org/10.1111/j.1467-8675.2006.00415.x).

Stevens, G. (1999) *The favored circle: The social foundations of architectural distinction*, Cambridge, MA: MIT Press.

Stewart, A., Kenneth, P. and Blackburn, R.M. (1980) *Social stratification and occupations*, London: Macmillan.

Stovel, K., Savage, M. and Bearman, P. (1996) 'Ascription into achievement: Models of career systems at Lloyds Bank, 1890–1970', *American Journal of Sociology*, 102(2), 358–99 (https://doi.org/10.1086/230950).

Strømme, T.B. and Hansen, M.N. (2017) 'Closure in the elite professions: The field of law and medicine in an egalitarian context', *Journal of Education and Work*, 30(2), 168–85 (https://doi.org/10.1080/13639080.2017.1278906).

Sullivan, A. (2001) 'Cultural capital and educational attainment', *Sociology*, 35(4), 893–912 (https://doi.org/10.1177/0038038501035004006).

Taylor, A. (2016) 'Full transcript: Theresa May's first speech as Britain's prime minister', *The Washington Post*, 13 July (www.washingtonpost.com/news/worldviews/wp/2016/07/13/full-transcript-may-promises-bold-new-positive-role-for-britain-after-brexit/?utm_term=.0067441a8f2a).

Thaler, R.H. and Sunstein, C.R. (2009) *Nudge: Improving decisions about health, wealth, and happiness*, New York: Penguin Books.

Thrift, N. and Williams, P. (2014) *Class and space (RLE social theory): The making of urban society*, London: Routledge.

Tilly, C. (1999) *Durable inequality*, Los Angeles, CA: University of California Press.

Time (2016) 'Here's Donald Trump's presidential announcement speech', 16 June (http://time.com/3923128/donald-trump-announcement-speech/).

Toft, M. (2018) 'Mobility closure in the upper class: Assessing time and forms of capital', *The British Journal of Sociology* (https://doi.org/10.1111/1468-4446.12362).

Tokarczyk, M.M. and Fay, E.E. (eds) (1993) *Working-Class women in the academy: Laborers in the knowledge factory*, Amherst, MA: University of Massachusetts Press.

Torche, F. (2011) 'Is a college degree still the great equalizer? Intergenerational mobility across levels of schooling in the United States', *American Journal of Sociology*, 117(3), 763–807 (https://doi.org/10.1086/661904).

Tumin, M.M. (1953) 'Some principles of stratification: A critical analysis', *American Sociological Review*, 18(4), 387–94 (https://doi.org/10.2307/2087551).

Turner, R.H. (1960) 'Sponsored and contest mobility and the school system', *American Sociological Review*, 25(6), 855-67.

Tyler, I. (2008) '"Chav mum chav scum"', *Feminist Media Studies*, 8(1), 17-34 (https://doi.org/10.1080/14680770701824779).

Useem, M. (1986) *The inner circle: Large corporations and the rise of business political activity in the US and UK*, Oxford: Oxford University Press.

Useem, M. and Karabel, J. (1986) 'Pathways to top corporate management', *American Sociological Review*, 51(2), 184-200 (https://doi.org/10.2307/2095515).

Vaisey, S. and Lizardo, O. (2010) 'Can cultural worldviews influence network composition?', *Social Forces*, 88(4), 1595-618 (https://doi.org/10.1353/sof.2010.0009).

Vandebroeck, D. (2014) 'Classifying bodies, classified bodies, class bodies', in J. Ducal (ed) *The Routledge companion to Bourdieu's 'Distinction'*, London: Routledge.

Vandebroeck, D. (2016) *Distinctions in the flesh: Social class and the embodiment of inequality*, London: Taylor & Francis (https:// books.google.com/books?hl=en&lr=&id=8zMlDwAAQBAJ &oi=fnd&pg=PP1&dq=dieter+vandebroeck&ots=wnaeSFw OF6&sig=wDYsSWSn_iOIGROpyBmLb4xAKFA).

van Galen, J.A. and van Dempsey, O. (eds) (2009) *Trajectories: The social and educational mobility of education scholars from poor and working class backgrounds*, Rotterdam: Sense Publishers.

Vincent, C., Rollock, N., Ball, S. and Gillborn, D. (2012) 'Being strategic, being watchful, being determined: Black middle-class parents and schooling', *British Journal of Sociology of Education*, 33(3), 337-54 (https://doi.org/10.1080/014256 92.2012.668833).

Wacquant, L.J.D. (2013) 'Symbolic power and group-making: On Pierre Bourdieu's reframing of class', *Journal of Classical Sociology*, 13(2), 274-91 (https://doi.org/10.1177/1468795X12468737).

Wacquant, L.J.D. (2016) 'A concise genealogy and anatomy of habitus', *The Sociological Review*, 64(1), 64-72 (https://doi. org/10.1111/1467-954X.12356).

Wajcman, J. (1998) *Managing like a man: Women and men in corporate management*, Cambridge: Polity Press.

Wakeling, P. and Laurison, D. (2017) 'Are postgraduate qualifications the "new frontier of social mobility"?', *The British Journal of Sociology*, 68(3), 533-55 (https://doi.org/10.1111/1468-4446.12277).

Wakeling, P. and Savage, M. (2015) 'Entry to elite positions and the stratification of higher education in Britain', *The Sociological Review*, 63(2), 290-320 (https://doi.org/10.1111/1467-954X.12284).

Walkerdine, V. (1990) *Schoolgirl fictions*, London and New York: Verso Books.

Wallace, D. (2017) 'Reading "race" in Bourdieu? Examining black cultural capital among black Caribbean youth in South London', *Sociology*, 51(5), 907-23 (https://doi.org/10.1177/0038038516643478).

Watson, T. (2017) 'Acting up: Labour's inquiry into access and diversity in the performing arts', The Labour Party (www.tom-watson.com/actingup).

Watts, D.J. (2004) 'The "new" science of networks', *Annual Review of Sociology*, 30(1), 243-70 (https://doi.org/10.1146/annurev.soc.30.020404.104342).

Weber, M. (1992) *Economy and society*, Berkeley, CA: University of California Press.

Weeden, K.A. (2002) 'Why do some occupations pay more than others? Social closure and earnings inequality in the United States', *American Journal of Sociology*, 108(1), 55-101.

Weeden, K.A. and Grusky, D.B. (2005) 'The case for a new class map', *American Journal of Sociology*, 111(1), 141-212.

Weeden, K.A., Kim, Y.-M., Di Carlo, M. and Grusky, D.B. (2007) 'Social class and earnings inequality', *American Behavioral Scientist*, 50(5), 702-36 (https://doi.org/10.1177/0002764206295015).

Weyer, B. (2007) 'Twenty years later: Explaining the persistence of the glass ceiling for women leaders', *Women in Management Review*, 22(6), 482-96 (https://doi.org/10.1108/09649420710778718).

Whitely, W., Dougherty, T.W. and Dreher, G.F. (1991) 'Relationship of career mentoring and socioeconomic origin to managers' and professionals' early career progress', *Academy of Management Journal*, 34(2), 331-50 (https://doi.org/10.5465/256445).

Wilkinson, R. and Pickett, K. (2009) *The spirit level: Why greater equality makes societies stronger*, New York: Bloomsbury Publishing USA.

Wilkinson, R. and Pickett, K. (2018) *The inner level: How more equal societies reduce stress, restore sanity and improve everyone's wellbeing*, London: Penguin UK.

Williams, C.L. (1992) 'The glass escalator: Hidden advantages for men in the "female" professions', *Social Problems*, 39(3), 253-67 (https://doi.org/10.2307/3096961).

Wingfield, A.H. (2009) 'Racializing the glass escalator: Reconsidering men's experiences with women's work', *Gender & Society*, 23(1), 5-26.

Wingfield, A.H. (2010) 'Are some emotions marked "whites only"? Racialized feeling rules in professional workplaces', *Social Problems*, 57(2), 251-68.

Woodhams, C., Lupton, B. and Cowling, M. (2015) 'The snowballing penalty effect: Multiple disadvantage and pay', *British Journal of Management*, 26(1), 63-77 (https://doi.org/10.1111/1467-8551.12032).

Woodson, K. (2015) 'Race and rapport: Homophily and racial disadvantage in large law firms', *Fordham Law Review*, 83(5), 2557.

World Bank, The (2016) *Taking on inequality: Poverty and shared prosperity 2016*, International Bank for Reconstruction and Development, The World Bank (https://openknowledge.worldbank.org/bitstream/handle/10986/25078/9781464809583.pdf).

Wright, E.O. (1978) *Class, crisis and the state*, London: New Left Books.

Wright, E.O. (1985) *Classes*, London: Verso.

Wright, E.O. (1989) 'Rethinking, once again, the concept of class structure', in E.O. Wright (ed) *The Debate on Classes*, London: Verso, 269-348.

Wright, E.O. (2005a) 'Foundations of a neo-Marxist class analysis', in E.O. Wright (ed) *Approaches to Class Analysis*, Cambridge: Cambridge University Press, 4-31.

Wright, E.O. (ed) (2005b) *Approaches to class analysis*, Cambridge and New York: Cambridge University Press.

Wright, E.O. and Shin, K.-Y. (1988) 'Temporality and class analysis: A comparative study of the effects of class trajectory and class structure on class consciousness in Sweden and the United States', *Sociological Theory*, 6(1), 58–84 (https://doi.org/10.2307/201914).

Young, M. (2001) 'Comment: Down with meritocracy', *The Guardian*, 29 June (www.theguardian.com/politics/2001/jun/29/comment).

Zimdars, A., Sullivan, A. and Heath, A. (2009) 'Elite higher education admissions in the arts and sciences: Is cultural capital the key?', *Sociology*, 43(4), 648–666 (https://doi.org/10.1177/0038038509105413).

Index

Page numbers followed by 'fig' refer to figures, by 'n' to notes, and by 't' to tables.

access to 33fig
class pay gap 53fig, 54
family financial support 105–6
female representation 42fig
micro-class reproduction 35fig
progression in 19
racial-ethnic representation
 41fig
see also TC (Turner Clarke)
acting profession
 backgrounds 84–5
 Black ethnic group 97, 98
 Black and Minority Ethnic
  (BME) ethnic groups 99
 class pay gap 85
 cultural insecurity 181–2
 female representation 99
 parental financial support
  87–99, 101, 103, 105, 106
 privileged groups 90, 92, 93
 racial stereotyping 94
 typecasting 89, 93–9
 voice and class 156–8
 working-class 93, 99
advertising 33fig, 35fig, 41fig,
 42fig, 53fig
aesthetic disposition 150–6, 197,
 200–2
All-Party Parliamentary Group
 on Social Mobility, 7 *Key
 Truths About Social Mobility*
 290n90
ambiguity of knowledge 161
ambulance service chiefs 33fig,
 35fig, 40, 41fig, 42fig, 53fig
'anxieties of affluence' 103–5
ARB (Architects Registration
 Board) 301n25
architecture
 access to 32, 33fig, 34, 35fig,
  37, 53fig
 class pay gap 53fig, 72
 family financial support 105–6
 female representation 42fig
 micro-class reproduction 35fig
 progression 54
 racial-ethnic representation
  41fig

see also Coopers
Ashcraft, K. 125, 310n24
Ashley, L. 19, 126–7, 133, 161,
 223
Atkinson, W. 294n5
Australia, class pay gap 47

B

Balding, C. 45
Bangladeshi ethnic group 20,
 40, 41fig, 42–4, 49fig, 51,
 52fig
Banks, M. 288n54
BBC (British Broadcasting
 Corporation)
 class 74, 76
 class inequality 46
 Great British Class Survey
  (GBCS) 54, 239–40, 242
 gender pay gap 45–6
Beck, U. 6, 6n16
Beck, U. et al 6n16
Becker, G.S. 316n100
behavioural codes 122, 124,
 132, 134, 144, 164
Behavioural Insights Team, UK
 government 307n37
Bennett, T. et al 316n100
Black ethnic group 40, 43, 44
Blair, T. 5
BME (Black and Minority
 Ethnic) ethnic groups 40,
 73, 99
Bottero, W. 313n61
Bourdieu, P. 14–15
 and aesthetic disposition
  150–6, 197, 200–2
 on the body 314n72
 on capital 186–7, 288n60,
  309n5, 313n66
 on 'contradictions of
  succession' 307n12
 on culture 315n84
 on 'doxa' 305n43
 on field 308n3
 on field of power 313n63
 on habitus 307n9, 308n1,
  308n18, 314n80, 314n81

female representation 42fig
Labour Force Survey (LFS)
264t
micro-class reproduction 35fig
privilege and 32, 33fig, 205
racial-ethnic representation
41fig
and social mobility 30fig
Just Fair 238

K

Kitagawa, E 320n23
Koppman, S. 305n18, 313n58
KPMG 78, 230
Kuhn, A. 17
Kynaston, D. 132

L

Labour Force Survey see LFS
Lamont, M. and Lareau, A.
315n88
language 15, 128, 137–9, 151,
155–8, 306n23 see also speech
Lareau, A. 15–16, 120
law
class pay gap 53fig
education 37
female representation 42fig
micro-class reproduction 34,
35fig
privilege 32, 33fig, 54, 85
progression in 19
racial-ethnic representation
41fig
unpaid internships 234
Lawler, S. 18, 51, 308n15
Lawler, S. and Payne, G. 302n6
legal protection 237–8
Lexmond, J. and Reeves, R.
302n11
LFS (Labour Force Survey) 10,
30–1, 65, 72, 189–90, 240–3,
263–8, 271
life sciences 33fig, 35fig, 41fig,
42fig, 53fig
linearity of career 196
Lineker, G. 45
'linguistic capital' 306n23

Lizardo, O. 149
'locus of control' 23
London
City of 19, 132, 212
parental financial support 24
privileged employment 22, 66,
69, 80, 106, 212
salary 66–7
senior positions 77

M

Macron, E. 29
management consultancy 33fig,
35fig, 41fig, 42fig, 53fig
Matthew, M. 304n30
May, T. 7, 29
measurement of class
background 230–2
medicine 33fig, 35fig, 41fig,
42fig, 53fig
'merit' measures 67fig, 68fig
meritocracy 232–3
City of London 132, 133
and cultural similarity 111,
168–9
as driver 58, 62, 65
education 21–2, 61–3
and fitting in 144, 212–14,
215–19, 220–2
justification 88
'occupational effects' and
198–9
and popular culture 179
and privilege 102, 103, 226–7
and progression 4–5
and sponsorship 118, 122
and technical capital 204
in UK 5, 7, 38–9
Weber on 4
meritocratic ideal 209, 210,
298n4
meritocratic legitimacy 8, 104
methodology 239–83
6TV 242–4
confidentiality 274
Coopers 246–7
elite occupation definition
265–6

feeding back 219–20, 273
interviews 247, 248t–60t
measurement of social mobility 262–5
Turner Clarke (TC) 244–6
see also LFS (Labour Force Survey)
microaggressions 17, 190, 224–5, 304n29
micro-class reproduction 34–5, 192
middle-class socialisation 126
Mijs, J.J.B. 298n4
Milburn, A. 9, 29–30
Miller, N. 229
Mills, C.W. 132, 148, 319n16
mixed race ethnic group 42, 43fig, 49fig, 51, 52fig
Morrissey, D. 84
Mosca, G. 319n16
multiple race ethnic group 42
Murray, C. 57

N

'neo-institutional theory' 301n21, 303n26
networks
  and highbrow culture 149–50, 168
  and inequality 121–2
  old boys' network 17, 109, 132, 211
  and sponsorship 110, 115, 118
Norway, class pay gap 47
NS-SEC (National Statistics Socio-Economic Classification) 11, 222, 263–5
nudge theory 307n37

O

objectified cultural capital 199
'objective merit' 2, 168, 212, 214, 221
O'Brien, D. 241
'occupational effects' 198–9
'old boys' network' 17, 109, 132, 211

'opportunity cost' 182
'opportunity hoarding' 148, 164
other Asian ethnic group 43fig, 49fig, 52fig
otherness 146
Oxbridge 2, 3, 62, 63, 148, 155

P

PACT (Producers Alliance for Cinema and Television) 243, 297n5
Paired Peers project 299n18
Pakistani ethnic group 40, 41fig, 42fig, 43–4, 49, 51, 52fig
parental financial support 87–107
  for actors 87–105
  at Coopers 105–7
  at Turner Clarke (TC) 105–7
parental occupation 31–2, 231–2, 240, 263
performing arts 33fig, 41fig, 42fig, 53fig
Pfeffer, J. 290n83, 320n28
Piketty, T. 286n25
police service chiefs 33fig, 35fig, 40, 41fig, 42fig, 53fig
Policy Exchange 286n31
polish 19, 127–34, 142, 159, 161, 180
popular culture 149, 202, 219, 307n38
primary socialisation 153–4, 194, 199, 202
private sector pay 68
Producers Alliance for Cinema and Television *see* PACT
professional and managerial sector, increase in 6, 59
professionalism 159
progress in career 19–20, 45–55
  class pay gap 47–55
  cultural barriers 164
  and education 62
  female 143, 167
  fitting in 124–5, 129
  and merit 4, 102–3, 109, 111, 210

365